Publishing Lives

*Interviews with Independent Book Publishers in
the Pacific Northwest and British Columbia*

Books by Jerome Gold

Fiction

The Negligence of Death
Of Great Spaces (with Les Galloway)
The Inquisitor
The Prisoner's Son

Nonfiction

Hurricanes (editor)
Publishing Lives: Interviews with Independent Book Publishers in the Pacific Northwest and British Columbia

Publishing Lives
Interviews with Independent Book Publishers in the Pacific Northwest and British Columbia

Jerome Gold

Black Heron Press
Seattle

Grateful acknowledgment is made to the following for the photographs used in this book: Charlie Cunniff for the photos of Catherine Hillenbrand, Anna Johnson, John Ellison and Lesley Link, Linny and Denny Stovall, margareta waterman, Ruth Gundle, and Lysa and Robert McDowell; Brent Eaton for the photo of Scott Davis; Sandra Hoover for the photo of Thatcher Bailey; Grant M. Haller for the photo of Joe Singer; Peter Vincent for the photo of Harald Wyndham; Andy Mons for the photo of Tim Lander; Horst Siegler for the photo of Karl Siegler; Ed Varney for that of Jerome Gold; Jerome Gold for that of Ed Varney; Timo Pylvanainen Pressfoto for the photo of Barbara Wilson; Natalie Fobes for the photo of Dan Levant; New Star Books for that of Rolf Maurer; Paul Boyer for the photo of Tree Swenson; Tee A. Corinne for the photo of Margarita Donnelly; Strawberry Hill Press for the photo of Jean-Louis Brindamour; Sasquatch Publishing Company for the photo of David Brewster.

Publisher's Cataloging in Publication

(Prepared by Quality Books Inc.)

Gold, Jerome

Publishing lives: interviews with independent book publishers in the Pacific Northwest and British Columbia/ Jerome Gold.—Seattle WA: Black Heron, 1995.

p. cm.

Includes bibliographical references and index.

ISBN 0-930773-40-3 (clothbound)

ISBN 0-930773-41-1 (paperback)

1. Publishers and publishing—Northwest, Pacific—Biography. 2. Publishers and publishing—Northwest, Pacific. I. Title.

Z279.G65 1995   070.5'092

QBI95—20374

FOR LEAH, DAVID, AND JACK

Contents

Introduction

Publishing Lives, as its subtitle indicates, is a collection of interviews with independent book publishers in the Pacific Northwest and British Columbia. The focus of each interview is on what brought the publisher into publishing, this "accidental profession," as it has been called in the United States.

Let me say before I continue that the expressions "independent press" and "small press" are used interchangeably both in this introduction and in the interviews. When the idea of writing about independent presses first struck me, "small press" was, as it remains, the term most commonly used both by people within and without the scene. However, while all of the presses whose publishers I have interviewed are small by the standards of Manhattan or Toronto, there is such variety in the sizes and styles of operation among the presses represented here that I have come to regard "independent" as the more encompassing term.

This book grew out of a notion I had for an article on independent book publishing. A publisher myself, I had become intrigued by the realization that hundreds, perhaps thousands, of us in the northwest corner of North America alone had somehow been drawn into independent publishing, a business that, as far as I could see, offered little reward outside of whatever satisfaction might be had by doing the actual work of publishing. I thought, too, there being so many of us, that we were part of something much larger than any one of us could comprehend. I wanted to know, then, who we all were and how we related to the historic moment, to use an old expression.

My original idea was to interview independent book publishers, try to uncover what personality traits or social background they shared, and write an article on my findings. I thought I should be able to get a statistically significant sample of book publishers in my region. I was not concerned with the person of the individual publisher. I wanted, rather, to identify a type, to manufacture a sort of composite of those people who have become independent publishers. (My academic training, as you might guess, was in one of the social sciences.)

This idea lasted until about halfway through my first interview. I found Paul Doyle, self-publisher of *Nioka: Bride of Bigfoot*, to be so introspective, so forthright, that I was seduced into accompanying him on a compact review of his life. Afterward, I became determined to avoid reducing the experience of life to a list of statistics or to a stereotype composed of parts of persons separated from the context of their lives. I was not willing to give up completely on the idea of commonality, however. (I recognize that the conflict between struggling to apprehend the meaning of a human life and reducing that life to something that has no relation to the experience of the person who lives it is the classic conflict between the humanist and the social scientist or statistician.)

My second interview, with Linny and Denny Stovall, was such a kick, so delightfully silly in parts, that I was forced to ponder how to catch synergy and humor as they are experienced by the actors, and impress them on the page, much less contain them in a series of statistics. (I do not have a good answer.) By the time we had completed the interview and our latest outburst of laughter had abated, I knew that I would be composing a book instead of an article and that the book would emphasize, in the interviews themselves, the publishers as persons rather than as parts of the mass.

Publishing Lives is made up of thirty interviews with the publishers of thirty-one presses. In every case, I attempted to interview a founder of the press if he or she was still actively involved in its operation. Adhering to this standard occasionally necessitated a trade-off. Although Chad Haight is the publisher of Sasquatch Books, and more familiar with that company's daily operation than David Brewster, I interviewed Brewster as the founder of Sasquatch and the president of Sasquatch Publishing, of which Sasquatch Books is a part. I might have interviewed both, but by the time I spoke with Brewster I had realized that I was not going to be able to obtain a significant sample of book publishers in the region, and that this method was probably not the most appropriate for what I was after anyway.

If I had become fascinated with the lives of my peers in publishing,

I was no less intrigued by the diversity of the kinds of publishing they were engaged in. I was becoming hard pressed just to interview publishers whose presses represented the range of book publishing in the region. I determined, then, to interview only one person per press. (There were exceptions, usually among presses founded by or operated by a couple. And there was NewSage Press which, with Print Vision, a print brokerage, formed an interlocking publishing-printing partnership; I interviewed the heads of both companies together.)

When I had conducted enough interviews to begin to compare one publisher's life experiences with those of others, I started to notice the ways in which many of our lives are connected, though often indirectly. Margarita Donnelly's father and Cathy Hillenbrand's father both made their careers with American oil companies in Venezuela, though apparently neither knew the other. The academic crises suffered by Karl Siegler and Margarita Donnelly resonate with memories of my own. David Brewster worked for Thatcher Bailey's father and also for Dan Levant before starting Sasquatch Publishing. Faith Conlon (not interviewed here) of Seal Press also worked for Dan Levant, and both she and Dan had worked for Doubleday before coming to Seattle, though not at the same time. John Ellison studied under Tree Swenson. Ruth Gundle and Barbara Wilson were inspired by Scott Walker (not interviewed here), founder of Graywolf Press. Kent Sturgis has been aided greatly by Dan Levant, I by Anna Johnson.

Because I was interested in independent publishing as a social movement—the larger "something" I mentioned earlier—I was interested in how people came to publishing, whether or not they came from other jobs or careers, and, if they had, what had prompted them to change. I grew to see publishing as an investment of the publisher's life rather than as a career. As Tree Swenson and Sam Hamill, Lesley Link and John Ellison, Karl Siegler and Barbara Wilson have all pointed out, publishing is not something in opposition to, or even separate from, the other parts of their lives. It is not a part of life at all, but pervades all aspects of the ways in which they view the world and live in it.

I have not been concerned with corporate publishing. In this book there are no interviews with the publishers of houses that are owned by larger corporations and there are no interviews with the publishers of university presses.

The publishers and their presses

Although all of the presses whose publishers I interviewed are located in the Pacific Northwest and British Columbia, I have tentatively adopted the view that these publishers represent the small press movement in North America as a whole. The interviews follow one another generally from those with publishers of smaller presses (in terms of gross income and number of employees) to publishers of larger presses, or from younger presses to older. Specific problems are associated with size, and I wanted to highlight these problems and the types of decisions publishers must make to respond to them. In several cases, publishers have opted to remain small rather than change the nature of their operations. In others, publishers have accepted change, welcome or not, as concomitant with growth. The history of Seal Press exemplifies most of the changes an independent press is likely to encounter in terms of growth and organization—from the publisher's infatuation with letterpress printing and a commitment to writing and no budget to speak of, to a company with several full-time employees, grossing $700,000 a year. The example of Seal Press also points out the role of luck in making a success. (Regarding luck, or perhaps something less random than luck, see also the interview with Richard Cohn and Cindy Black.)

But how are we to judge success? In an industry where, according to common lore, most companies fail within two years of start-up, can we say that one that lasts longer than two years is a success? If a company finally breaks even after eight years of operation, is that company successful? If another loses money year after year but consistently publishes work deemed a contribution to literature or to the common good, is that company a success or a failure? If another quits its original mission of publishing work of the highest quality and publishes, instead, work of middling quality, thereby changing itself from a company that is barely surviving to one that grosses over a million a year, by what criteria do we determine the success or failure of that company? Is it the primary responsibility of a company to produce books of the first rank, or to provide career opportunities, health benefits and decent salaries for its employees? The two goals may be in opposition to each other. Every independent book publisher must consider at least some of these questions at some time.

Yet, for all the financial difficulties US publishers have, few apply for grants—only four of the twenty-four I spoke with. (I do not include awards for books already published or contracted for here; a number of presses that do not receive grants enabling them to publish have garnered monetary awards following the publication of particular books. The significant difference here is that a grant permits the publisher to include that money in his or her budget; a later award is a welcome bonus but does not contribute to rational planning.) Those who do not apply offer a variety of reasons to explain why they don't. Maureen Michaelson does not want to turn her press into a nonprofit corporation, making it eligible to receive grants, "[b]ecause then you don't own the company. When you become a nonprofit, your board of directors can kick you out." Harald Wyndham, who publishes his own work, says that writers who apply for grants "become obligated to serve a public that is not necessarily your public.... You become obligated to live within expectations, whatever they might be. And...that...can shape the work you do." Joe Singer suggests that the time it takes to write a grant would be better spent writing poetry.

In Canada grants, mostly from federal and provincial sources, are available to all publishers qualified to receive them, the qualifications being that a press must be publishing "culturally significant" (as determined by funding sources) trade books, it must have published a certain number of titles during its career, and it must have grossed a certain amount of money from them. Although British Columbia publishers received grants totaling only six percent of their revenue in 1991-1992, their profits averaged less than three percent of their gross income (MacSkimming 1993: 3). Of the seven Canadian publishers I interviewed, five received public monies in the form of grants and another hoped to qualify soon. There is no doubt that funding of this type has promoted the publication of Canadian literature and the growth of Canadian publishing.

American grant money, on the other hand, is awarded to the winners of competitions between publishers; the losers get nothing. For the most part, only nonprofit presses are eligible to compete. (There are exceptions to the competition requirement. A few private foundations have been funding certain nonprofit literary presses for several years. These presses were selected by the foundations.)

In almost all cases, a press in its first years is subsidized by personal income. Married couples who have gone into publishing together have generally established the arrangement whereby one spouse works outside in order to support the press (and the household), assisting with the operation of the press in whatever spare time remains, while the other devotes him- or herself full time to the press. Later, if the press grows, the former quits his or her job, also to work full time at the press. Single publishers generally subsidize their presses with income from jobs as well as dedicating most of their remaining time to them.

A couple of Canadian presses established print shops in order to finance their publishing endeavors—one start-up business subsidizing another. Three American publishers have financed their presses with inherited money or the return on investments. (In having this kind of access to money, these publishers have something in common with earlier twentieth-century founders, most of whom came from moneyed families. In other ways the current generation harkens back to the founding publishers of the nineteenth century, as I'll show below.) Subsidy of the press may not end for the life of the press. Another way of putting it would be to say that the press may never grow out of its first years—it may die or it may continue to require outside support in order to live.

Most American publishers emphasize the need to publish for a particular market. This need arises from industry gatekeepers such as reviewers and trade and library book buyers seeming to prefer to classify smaller publishers by niche. Inadvertently or not, as Jean-Louis Brindamour says, "You create an image and if you go out of that image you often ask for the trouble you get."

16

However, Richard Cohn's and Cindy Black's experience, and the experience of the Canadian publishers, is that publishing a diverse list is important to ensure consistent income. Rolf Maurer takes the view that readers of nonfiction are also readers of fiction, and vice versa, and he has no compunction about publishing both. And Michelle Benjamin thinks diversity allows readers to "always find something on our list that's interesting."

Perhaps the difference in perspective is a function of the size of the press (though Brindamour's Strawberry Hill Press has at times been fairly large), so that the larger the press is, the more important it is to diversify. Or the difference may be primarily cultural—Canadian readers may well be more inclusive in their choice of books than American readers. It seems to me, however, that for a very small press, creating a diverse list requires an investment of time and energy, not to say money, that may only distract the publisher from what he or she most wants to publish, while for a larger press employing editors and marketing personnel, diversity may be a necessary survival mechanism.

The publishers themselves

Eight of the thirty-one presses represented here issue, or have issued, works by their publishers, though none do so exclusively. Of these eight, six are literary presses (though eight other literary presses do not issue work by their respective publishers); that is, they publish imaginative literature: fiction, poetry, plays. Two other publishers— one literary, one not—intend to publish their own work through their presses in the future. But few write for publication at all, though several would like to, and others used to write before publishing dominated their creative lives. Their compensation, if that is the word, is their connection with writing by virtue of being publishers.

Most came to independent book publishing with some knowledge of publishing or editing gained by having worked for another, corporate, publisher, or in journalism, or in another aspect of the book industry, such as distribution. A handful had no knowledge of either book production or bookselling. And some had nothing in their backgrounds to indicate they would become publishers except a love for books and a parent or parents who read, though neither trait would serve to suggest anything more than a good possibility that the child would grow into a reader.

A few were drawn into publishing by a fascination with printing. A few others came into it directly from college or not long afterward. One became a publisher through a misunderstanding. Two had been lawyers. Six had, at some time, some experience in a business other than publishing or bookselling. Only four had served in the military; only one had worked at a non-military government job. I interviewed no publisher who was the child of a civil servant. Only two American and three Canadian publishers were younger than forty years old when I interviewed them. Both of the Americans are founders of presses; none of the Canadians are.

There are some things that nearly all of the independent publishers I talked with have in common. One is the close and usually intense identification of each publisher with his or her press. Dan Levant's interchangeable use of the words "Madrona" and "me" is a good illustration of this. I was struck, too, by the extent to which the founder's personality—"obsessions" may be, in some cases, the more accurate term—is interwoven with the direction the press pursues. The nationalistic passion of Karl Siegler, the idealism of Anna Johnson, the outrage of Scott Davis and Margarita Donnelly, the unremitting intellect of margareta waterman—none of these may be separated out from those elements of their personalities that determine which books they see as important, and why, and which books they will publish.

One thing, at least among the Americans, that distinguishes this generation of founding publishers from previous generations is what I have taken to be a sense of disaffection for many of their society's institutions. This, of course, is not universal; you can't get much more into the American mainstream than by making your career with Microsoft, as John Ellison and Lesley Link have done. But, by and large, I think the former statement holds true.

Something else makes this generation different from earlier generations: it is not centered in New York or Toronto. Publishing has decentralized. This trend began even before the advent of desktop methods of preparing a book for printing, and it corresponds to the growth of small presses. John Tebbel points out in his *A History of Book Publishing in the United States* that "[t]he period from 1960 to 1980 proved to be an era of consolidations, mergers and acquisitions [in New York], but it was also a period when small houses proliferated, particularly on the West Coast in the seventies" (Tebbel 1981: 324).

Independent book publishing in the United States has arisen, in part, as a response to corporate publishing's drying up as a market for serious imaginative literature and for books that Manhattan considers too controversial or whose appeal is regarded as limited to special markets. But this has led to the opening of new outlets for traditional kinds of books—Copper Canyon Press for poetry, for example—as well as outlets for books that had only limited access to a large public before— the feminist presses such as Calyx and Seal, as cases in point.

In Canada, literary presses particularly arose not in opposition to the changes in the publishing policies of commercial houses, but as a reaction to the academic conservatism of established literary presses which were seen as "publishing the same kinds of writers and the same kinds of books over and over again," according to Brian Lam. More generally, Canadian presses have grown to challenge the English and American hold on Canadian readers.

If this generation of founders is different in some ways from earlier generations, it also shares certain traits with them. Tebbel's descriptions of Matthew Carey, "the prototype of the early nineteenth-century publisher," as "hardworking, careful, frugal...not given to flamboyance" (Tebbel 1987: 17) and E.P. Dutton, representing a later nineteenth-century cohort of publishers, as "sometimes excessively moralistic and self-righteous" (Tebbel 1987: 44) may be applied as readily to a number of the publishers interviewed in *Publishing Lives*.

It is important to keep in mind that the characteristics of publishers that transcend generations are those that are shared between persons. Nineteenth-century publishers were in publishing because they liked the excitement of helping to create literature and of transmitting ideas into the cultural mainstream. It is the same, I think, with present-day publishers. But the modern corporations that have acquired the New York houses, in Tebbel's words, "recruit more and more...from the ranks of nonbook businesses.... Books are looked upon as simply another kind of article to be marketed. Many publishers today, consequently, are little better than paper salesman" (Tebbel 1987: 464). In a sense, today's independent founders, though several think of themselves as progressive, are perhaps better described as reactionary, throwbacks to the precorporate era in which publishing was fun, literature was considered vital to the culture, and authors were seen as something more than brand names.

While the small press movement has its roots in the late 1960s and early 1970s, as Barbara Wilson points out apropos of her own experience, US publishers did not necessarily consider themselves engaged in any kind of movement. Canadian publishers, on the other hand, were aware of the social and historical dimensions of their endeavors, as they were linked to Canadian nationalism. Today, however, two or three decades after their beginnings, most surviving publishers, American as well as Canadian, have the sense that they have helped to create history, and a history not limited to their particular region.

The interviews

Presses arise and they disappear. Sometimes they arise and disappear and rise again. The directories account for only some—who knows what portion? The thirty-one presses represented in *Publishing Lives*, I estimate, account for not more than ten percent of those that existed during the time I was interviewing, and perhaps much less. I selected publishers to interview out of the *Writer's Northwest Handbook,* 4th Edition. Apart from meeting the criterion of independence, I wanted the presses whose publishers I interviewed to represent the various types of organization that exist among them, from a one-person operation to a company with several divisions. This book, then, taken in its entirety, attempts to describe the general direction of evolution of independent presses in terms of growth and variety.

In all of the interviews published here but one, I was the interviewer.

The single exception was when I myself was interviewed. The interviewer on this occasion was Michelle Willson.

The interviews were conducted over nearly three years, from November 1991 to August 1994. My knowledge about publishing increased as the interviewing progressed, so that information I thought was accurate in one interview may have been shown later to be false. For instance, during my interview with Brian Lam, I believed that there were no presses in the Pacific Northwest other than John Bennett's Vagabond Press that existed prior to 1980. Later interviews proved me wrong. In the interview with Anna Johnson I made much of African American adolescents, but not white adolescents, having a hunger for books. I am now convinced that the desire for reading material, either for pleasure or for clarification of aspects of one's life and its circumstances, knows no ethnic or racial boundaries. The data I drew from originally were valid only for a particular period lasting perhaps five or six months.

In no case do I vouch for the objective truth of information given during these interviews. Sentiment and opinion are interwoven with fact; I leave it to you, the reader, to try to distinguish one from another. All of my conclusions remain tentative, and many of the hypotheses formed early in the course of conducting and comparing interviews have been discarded.

I asked the same basic questions of every publisher (save one) that I interviewed. But I asked additional questions of some as well—for example: "Where do you see your immortality?" "In what part of the country do you sell the most books?" The former question I asked when the publisher's line of thought seemed to lead to it. I asked the latter mostly of publishers of literary presses, because it is so difficult to define the audience for literary works. In those few cases where a publisher chose not to reveal personal information, I did not press him or her.

When, in response to one of my questions, a publisher took off in his or her own direction, I tried to refrain from interrupting except to encourage that publisher to continue. Though occasionally the answers given were off the top of one's head, often what a publisher told me

21

were things he or she obviously had given considerable thought to.

Although a number of topics have been approached from different starting points, none have been covered exhaustively. And sometimes thoughts are not pursued but leave us tantalized, as with margareta waterman's brief description of the conflict between John Dewey and Maria Montessori to determine the nature of public school education in the United States. This is a consequence of my encouraging the publisher to go with the responses to my questions wherever he or she would. So some topics were addressed by some but not by others, some responses perhaps better applied to questions I did not ask, and sometimes we are simply left in mid-air, wanting to know more, but with interviewer and publisher gone home.

The ultimate value of this book may be that it provides a picture of publishing and of non-academic intellectual and literary life in the northwestern part of North America at the end of the twentieth century. Already there have been changes in the fortunes of several of the publishers since they were interviewed. Barbara Wilson (though not Seal Press) moved to the Bay Area. Thatcher Bailey sold Bay Press. (Its new publishers intend to continue publishing cultural criticism.) Tree Swenson left Copper Canyon Press. Talonbooks is now distributed by Inbook, a major US distributor, which arrangement has established Talon as a literary presence in the United States. Black Heron Press's books are now distributed by The Subterranean Company, permitting print runs of two to five thousand instead of five to fifteen hundred. Joe Singer died.

Select Bibliography

Cerf, Bennett. *At Random*. New York: Random House, 1977.

Gold, Jerome. "About Some Area Book Publishers." In *Writer's Northwest Handbook,* 5th Edition, 64-65. Hillsboro, Oregon: Blue Heron Publishing, 1993.

MacSkimming, Roy. *Publishing on the Edge: A Cultural and Economic Study of Book Publishing in British Columbia.* Vancouver: Association of Book Publishers of British Columbia, November 1993.

Stovall, Dennis and Linny Stovall, eds. *Writer's Northwest Handbook,* 4th Edition. Hillsboro, Oregon: Blue Heron Publishing, 1991.

Tebbel, John. *A History of Book Publishing in the United States.* Volumes 1, 3, 4. New York: R.R. Bowker, 1972, 1978, 1981.

———. *Between Covers.* New York: Oxford University Press, 1987.

Les Galloway
1912-1990

Three nights earlier, the phone rang at half past midnight and I thought immediately of Les. Who else would call at this hour? I let the machine take the call. I listened for his voice and when it didn't come I was even more certain that it was he, for he hated talking to my machine. I promised myself that I would call him back but I did not call. I had talked with him a week or two earlier and he had sounded so depressed—he was weak from the dialysis, he said—that I was reluctant to talk with him again so soon. He had asked when I would be coming down to San Francisco. I told him I did not think it would be before August or September and he said he did not think he would be alive then. I had never heard him sound so tired. I did not try to joke with him. We talked a little about books and then we hung up.

On Thursday, May third, a message from his daughter Lisa was on my machine when I came home from work. Les had died—"passed away"—the Sunday before. I called the number she left and got the details. It was a stroke. He had expected to die from an aortic aneurysm he had been nurturing. Instead, it was a blood clot that had traveled to his brain from his foot.

His early life had been an adventuring one. He had sailed to the South Pacific on the last clipper ship to put out of San Francisco. He had fallen in love with a prostitute in New Zealand and jumped ship in Hawaii. Later he was a motorcycle courier for a Bolivian general during a war in that country, and following that he lived in Mexico City for a year. Except for one unpublished novel that took in part of his Pacific voyage, he never wrote about any of this.

Instead, he wrote some exquisite stories about the sea, notably "Where No Flowers Bloom" and "The Albacore Fisherman", and a wonderful short novel, *The Forty Fathom Bank*. Until he became too ill to write, he worked on another novel, a kind of love story. (One must always qualify the genre with Les: *The Forty Fathom Bank* is kind of a sea story, but mostly it's a morality tale of greed and the failure of redemption.) Here is its plot as I remember his telling it.

A young man travels to Utah from California. In Salt Lake City he falls in love with a girl. However, requiring specialized surgery, he must go on to New York. He is in love but also he is looking forward to meeting some of New York's fabled elegant women. In New York, he undergoes surgery and stays on to recuperate. He and his love correspond but then she stops writing. He has not been faithful and wonders what she might know, what she might have gleaned from the subconscious aspect of his letters. Finally, out of guilt and remorse, he writes her a vicious letter, ending their relationship.

Decades later, he returns to Salt Lake City. He searches out the family of the girl he loved and from them he learns that she died in an automobile accident while he was in New York. From the dates on her headstone he understands that she was already dead when he wrote the vilifying letter.

This story is so essentially Les: the flaw in character, the minor decision that takes on tragic significance, the base act that exposes the actor to himself, the ghostly echoes that arise from that act.

I never knew a man who so enjoyed the company of women. It has been said so often that most men do not like women that it sounds true, even if it is a suspect truth. Still, I never met a man who liked women more than Les did. His skin blushed and his eyes positively radiated joy when he was with a woman he was attracted to. But if women were his joy they were also his sadness, for he was haunted by them.

I believe he felt indebted to them. As a small boy, he had required extensive medical care. A relation of his mother's age prostituted herself to obtain treatment for him. He married several times (He once asked me my age and the number of times I had been married. When I told him, he said, "You're still young. You ought to try it two or three more times."), fathered a number of children and raised all but one by himself.

He and I never talked about friendship or love, though we discussed love's delusions and, of course, its betrayal. When the sexual urge finally left him he told me that it was a relief, he didn't miss it a bit.

When he was sixty, he began work on a long novel, *Beyond the Dark Mountain*, finishing it almost ten years later. He met with the usual responses when he sent it out: editors did not read it but pretended they had, or they did not send it back at all. Mostly, they ignored it. Finally an editor from a middle-size house did read it and did like it and offered Les a contract. The week before they were to begin editing, the entire fiction staff, including Les's editor, was fired. The publisher had decided to cease publishing fiction. Three or four years later, Les told me that he had been disappointed and angry, but here, too, he felt a relief: publishing that book, he believed, would have changed his life, and he did not want it to change. He continued sending the manuscript around but nothing happened with it and I think he regarded sending it off as a matter of duty rather than desire.

I knew him only the last ten years of his life. He wrote well until his last year or two when physical pain and medication confounded that special clarity of mind he needed to write. His last decade, it seems to me, was an itemized giving-up of everything that was important to him, including any attempt to resolve the conflicts that had beset him early on. His writing showed no resolution. It showed, instead, wonderment and knowledge. He believed in Nothing as though it were Something. Yet despair was foreign to him. Writing for a few friends, he told me, was enough for him. And he did that as long as he was able.

—Jerome Gold, 1990

Joe Matthew Singer
November 22, 1950-June 25, 1993

Joe Singer, well known to us as the editor and publisher of *The Village Idiot* and *The Printer's Devil*, products of Mother of Ashes Press in Harrison, Idaho, was found dead in his car of a gunshot wound last summer. Joe was born in Powell, Wyoming in 1950 and lived in a variety of places including Kansas City, Los Angeles, San Francisco and Denver as well as Powell before moving in January of 1984 to Harrison on Lake Coeur d'Alene in northern Idaho where he worked as a caretaker and ran his offset press, "Darlene."

Joe was an advocate of free speech, often publishing quotes—infamous remarks in favor of First Amendment rights such as A.J. Liebling's warning: "There is no freedom of the press unless you own the press." His colophons in *The Printer's Devil* were riddled with philosophical remarks and astute comments on American culture, as well as printing and publishing advice. I always read them first, savoring them for quiet time with a cup of coffee.

I got to know Joe when he contacted me several years ago after having come across a copy of *The Redneck Review*. He said he liked the magazine and would welcome the opportunity to print it for me. He printed 3-4 issues of the magazine until I purchased my own printing press and took over the laborious job myself. From what I know now about printing, about the time it takes to run tens of thousands of sheets of paper through even an electric machine, as well as the frustrations of paper jams, ink/water balances, etc., I know he had to have printed *Redneck* at a loss.

I visited with Joe three times in person, once at the ranch in Fairfield when he drove down to deliver the pages of *Redneck* personally. He helped a group of us collate that particular issue. We stacked the pages in rows along the long bar at the Club Cigar in downtown Fairfield, Idaho, where the annually convened "editorial board" for *Redneck* met weekly during the winter months in the early days of publication. I saw Joe again in the spring of 1988 when he delivered a

1902 Chandler & Price letterpress I purchased from a contact of his in Spokane to my "interim" house in Fairfield shortly after I left the ranch. The colorful and amusing story of that printing press' arrival in Fairfield, Idaho has been immortalized in my letters and in a brief essay published in *Boise Magazine*. The last time I saw Joe was at a book fair in Boise. He was angry with me then and wouldn't tell me why.

Joe—in letters and in person—was eccentric, lonely, angry and somewhat confused about life—at least, that's how I read him. He had a drinking problem which led to DUI charges and jail time. When he was drunk, he would call his friends late at night for a dose of human contact of a quality that, unfortunately, remained just out of his reach. It was difficult to be Joe's friend; I believe I tried as well as I could while dealing with my own madness and survival in a puzzling Western American world.

I miss Joe and feel extremely saddened by his death. I am surprised at how often I think of him, how I courted and respected his opinions of *The Redneck Review*. I made the mistake of believing there would always be time to talk, make amends, heal, grow, that Joe would finally get his head together, and I'd return to Idaho and have a "real" house again where he and I and other publishers and poets would sit on the veranda sipping wine in our old age, reminiscing about the good old days of small press adventures in Idaho and the West.

—Penelope Reedy, 1994

Paul Doyle
Daily Planet Press

"If I end up with a lot of misery and I've got another novel... oh, yeah, I'll probably write it, even so. You can't avoid it. I don't see how you can avoid it. It nags at you."

Paul Doyle is a tall man with a seamed face. He moves well and fluidly and I was surprised when he told me he was fifty-three years old. Born in Hoquiam, Washington, he earned a bachelor's degree from Seattle University and a master's degree from the University of Washington, both in English. He has been married one time.

We met when he phoned me in the fall of 1990 to discuss who to go to about getting a manuscript made into a book and what it would cost. Over the next several months we talked often as his story, Nioka: Bride of Bigfoot,*went through editing, then was made camera-ready, then printed and bound. Doyle started Daily Planet Press in 1991 in order to publish* Nioka.

Doyle rents an older two-story house in Wallingford, a Seattle neighborhood about a mile west of the University District. It is a spacious, high-ceilinged house, a little cold because expensive to heat, but solid and lending a sense of security. It is typically Wallingford. The interview took place here on the evening of November 6, 1991.

I basically earn my living by running a movie theater. I own a small theater called the Grand Illusion Cinema here in Seattle. I've been in the movie business probably twenty years, at the Grand Illusion about five years. I started the Grand Illusion twelve or thirteen years go and then I sold it to someone, and so for four or five years I was doing something else. And prior to that I had a theater in Tacoma and ran or rented various movie theaters here in town. Oh, when I was a very young man, yeah, I worked the jobs you work going to school, and then after school I worked as an editor for awhile at a technical writing company. And then I was a technical writer at Boeing for a year. I worked at Weyerhaeuser for a year or so, writing technical stuff, editing technical stuff. And then I did that on a freelance contract basis for a while.

Up until age thirty-one or -two I was doing that on a contract basis. I didn't actually work steady, I just worked project by project, but I usually made enough so that in the interim I could live. And then I began in the movie business and I've basically been in it ever since except for that short four- or five-year gap. After I got out of graduate school I really wanted to go to film school. And I forgot about writing, actually, to go into showing movies. I was, for a time, absolutely fascinated by film.

I should say also, as far as earning my living goes, that I have begun a small hypnotherapy practice. I went through hypnotherapy school. It was a basic course. A hundred and fifty hours of instruction. But there are advanced levels and I certainly need to do more, certainly want to do more.... I've had a few clients. And just about the time I had my first few clients it came time to publish this book. So I put it on a back burner, and now I just had my cards printed up and I'm beginning again.

It would be very difficult for me now to work for anybody else. Besides being basically unemployable, I suppose, by virtue of not having a steady job record, I just.... I used to get headaches every day when I was working for somebody else. You know, when I had to punch a clock. It's hard for me to do.

As a very young man, I had, you know, creative urges to write, and I just couldn't shoehorn myself into a regular profession. And, uh, my father did not hold down a regular job. He was a contractor. I didn't have any role model for going to work on a regular basis. It's possible to make too much of this, of course, but he was very independent himself, and that may have had something to do with it. It must have, because none of my brothers hold down a job. They are all independent.

By the time I got out of technical writing I was supervising publication projects of large technical manuals. That involved, you know, having a deadline, having the writers and the editors and funneling everything into that.... Publications Manager, I think, is the title I had a couple of times. So publishing *Nioka* didn't seem like a big mysterious thing to me. There was nothing that surprised me, really, about publishing. I'd seen it all in one form or another in the course of my work. I was lucky that way.

You said that you gave up writing—
No. Uh uh. Well, you know, what with divorce and the five or six years afterwards it takes to get over divorce, and.... I think basically after my marriage broke up there was probably a gap of ten years, and I thought about writing but I didn't do any. And I think I was probably in some kind of growing-up phase or recovery phase, or whatever, during that entire period. You know, my life plan—getting married, having children, being a writer—it had just simply blown apart and it took a whole long time to reassemble it in some usable form again. And I think it was about ten years before I actually got the idea for *Nioka* and another five years before I did anything about it.

Where did the idea for Nioka *come from?*
All I know is I was driving home from California with a girlfriend. And we were somewhere in Oregon, and I looked up at those Oregon foothills that roll toward the ocean and I thought to myself, "There's a woman out there." It just hit me like that. "There's a woman out there." Then I began thinking about her. I guess during that period, yeah, I had written a bigfoot movie script and tried to find backers for it, to make a bigfoot movie. And I had written a film treatment, with some script, on the Chief Joseph Indian war. Well, nothing came of either one, but the idea of—my first idea for *Nioka* was to let the public see her. Write the whole thing as if you were writing a bigfoot story. There would be sightings and all that, and the footprints, but you never ever encounter her. It's fiction but it reads like nonfiction. That was my original idea. And I toyed with the idea of making something tongue-in-cheek. But after a while *Nioka* got too interesting to do that.
When I couldn't find a publisher, and got tired of the hassle of

trying to find a publisher, or even an agent—at that point I invented Daily Planet Press simply to publish *Nioka*. I never thought of publishing as a career. Now, with the book out, and having gone through the process, it's just sort of wait-and-see. It's opened up a new perspective. If the book—if I manage to sell all the copies, I think I'm far better off having published it myself than if I had gone with somebody else, in a way.

What if you sell half the copies?
Half the copies? Well, then I still would have made about the same amount of money I would have if I'd sold the book to a regular publisher. Maybe even more.

You would have gotten much less per copy but you would have had much wider distribution. I'm assuming that they could sell five thousand to seventy-five hundred copies rather than two thousand. What I'm getting at is weighing the money against recognition.
Well, right. But this is the way I had to go, basically, and after a while I began to look forward to publishing it myself. Despite the advice of people in the business. [Both men laugh.]

I was only trying to warn you. I think, the first conversation we had, you asked me if I thought you were foolish for doing it yourself. And I think I recall saying that anybody is a fool who gets into the business, because he's going to lose money. And it's going to be frustrating. And painful.
Yeah.

Given all that, I'd go ahead. And you did, too.
Yeah, right. There isn't an option that's acceptable. The only option is not having your book published.

Yeah. That's it, right there. It's a matter of getting your book in print and out where it can be sold, or not getting it in print.
Yeah, and I had enough encouraging feedback from editors in

the regular publishing field to know that it was worth publishing. I applied for a publication grant, a King County arts grant, the same one that Ron applied for. [Ron Dakron's novel, *Newt,* won the 1991 King County Arts Commission Publication Award for fiction.] Only Ron won it and I didn't. But I still like him. But that's all right, they were supposed to announce the—the deadline, I think, was February fifteenth—they were supposed to announce the results April fifteenth and they finally announced them, I think, about November first and Ron says he hasn't seen any of the money yet.

As a publisher, do you feel yourself to be in oppositon to anybody or anything?

No. As I said, it was, originally, at least, and still is at this point, a vehicle for getting my book published. I know there are some people that do start publishing with a view to publishing quality literary things, or people who don't get published, or, you know, certain concepts that they want to further, certain lifestyles, but I'm not...no, I don't have a mission. What I'm trying to do is make.... A press should have a marketing director, you know, and a promotion director, and an advertising director and, you know, I have to do all those things, plus sell them, plus run my business, so I'm not really doing a great job of promoting the book, but—

What about your use of time? Do you sometimes feel overwhelmed? That you don't have time to do what needs to be done?

Yes. Yes, exactly. To run a theater, I have to put in twenty to thirty hours a week. Closer to thirty. Just to keep the thing running. I don't go over there at night and run the projectors anymore, although I used to do that, too. You might as well say it's a forty-hour-a-week job just to keep it running. So that leaves me with a hundred things I could do to promote the book. You know, I could go out and hang a banner over a freeway bridge at rush hour, which I thought of doing, but then you weigh that against—

Against the accidents and lawsuits. [They laugh.]

Yeah, I don't know what's the productive thing to do. I've got flyers. I've stuck them out in a few places and people seem to pick them up. Whether that results in a purchase later on, I don't know. I don't know. Well, I do know what will be effective. I think what will be effective is to spend a lot of money. But, you know, I basically don't have anything to spend on promotion, so I have to do the things I can do. I mean I'm actually kind of dismayed at the dollar-fifty or close to two dollars it costs to send out a book to a reviewer. You send out twenty copies, you're into it forty bucks. However, I am optimistic.

Have you anticipated how you'll feel if, six months or a year from now, you're still sitting on fifteen hundred copies?

Well, I don't allow myself to think of that as a possibility. It has crossed my mind a few times—"Oh, God, what will I do?"—but out of the thirty thousand thoughts, at least, that cross your mind every day, that only comes once or twice. But I just don't allow myself... I just... It's not possible. Even though it is possible. But I don't allow myself to think about it at this point. I figure I could always go door to door and look like a beggar and say "Look, you gotta buy this book for five bucks," and probably pay them to get rid of them. It seems unfortunate there isn't a governmental distribution arm like the Canadian Film Board in Canada or something.

Except for the King County award, you haven't applied for grants. Are you going to?

No. I hate paperwork. I hate waiting. I haven't investigated the possibility of grants once you've already published a book. I mean, I've read about them for work in progress and stuff like that, but I run a business. I don't regard myself as a student or a person who's living that lifestyle. I just figure I've got to make good in the marketplace. I mean it seems to me there are people who are literary writers living a literary lifestyle and applying for grants and doing that, and then there are people who are writing and they intend to make some money at it. I don't know where the distinction is, but I belong to the kind that's in hopefully, a commercial venture. Artistic as well. I mean it's something

34

I had to do. But I still want to do it and be successful at it.

Do you have aspirations of being another Hemingway or Conrad or...?

Oh, no. No.

Do you have a literary model?

No.

No hero?

No. For influences on my writing, I suppose I could say Kurt Vonnegut, or a New York writer called Donald Barthelme. And Tom Robbins, by his writing, gave me permission to write any way I want. No, I don't have any aspirations of greatness. I just want to do the things that I want to do. I'd be happy to have a modestly successful—I don't believe in the starving-in-the-garret scenario. I don't believe in victimhood or martyrhood. It just doesn't appeal to me. I used to see friends of mine, you know, killing themselves trying to be filmmakers, and I thought, "God, that's not for me. Either it works or I'm not going to do it." Now with regard to writing, I suppose this is a test case. If I end up with a lot of misery and I've got another novel...oh, yeah, I'll probably write it, even so. You can't avoid it. I don't see how you can avoid it. It nags at you. I've started a second one and I think about getting back to it when this promotion thing is out of the way.

I don't really enjoy this. Publishing it was a snap, as far as I'm concerned. It was easy. But selling it is not easy. In fact, in the Poynter book, *The Self-Publishing Manual*, there's that quote, "It takes brilliance to write a book, but it takes genius to sell one," or something like that. [Both laugh.] I have told a number of people since publishing *Nioka*, Go do it. I mean, do your homework. Figure out if somebody might want this. But publish it in some form or another.

Because, you know, I have a friend who's a literary agent. And she said, "Paul, I like your book. It works on many levels. But I could never sell it to a major publisher." Because they're looking for marketable books. And I didn't know that, you know. And I sent *Nioka* out. Three or four years ago. Total rejection. Although I did get a couple of

35

nice rejections. And I put it in the desk and thought, "That's it, my career is over." And then after recovering, about three years later, I took it out of the desk one day and looked at it and said, "Shit, this isn't bad." So I did rewrite quite a bit of it. And tried to do it again. But I wasted, counting the three years or so of recovery after I sent it out the first time and threw it in a desk drawer—and then I wasted another year and a half, trying to publish it a second time after I rewrote it—you know, I could have been on to something else. I basically wasted five or six years trying to get somebody to publish it.

I think there are many, many very good writers who are doing some very good work and who are never going to be published. And one of the reasons is that they send their manuscripts out to publishing houses who, thirty years ago, would have published them. The stuff they read was published by Random House and Doubleday thirty years ago, but in the past twenty years Random House and Doubleday have become just like Dell and Pocket Books.

That's a good point. Yeah. Right. But I think, for most writers.... You know, I consider myself a good writer, but I'm certainly not in the category of stuff I've read by people who are writing really good stuff. But the difference is, for a lot of those guys, publishing their book is a formidable undertaking. For me, it was kind of easy. Because of my familiarity with the whole field. Apart from technical writing and editing and publication management I'd done, you know, I'd had stuff printed and graphics done on flyers and posters for the theater. You know, it just didn't seem like a big thing to me. But it isn't a big thing.

Scott C. Davis
Cune Press

"Literature provides an opening to the sacred. Readers, like spiritual seekers, have these epiphanies, these looks beyond, little openings into the mind of God. Literature is a point where creation comes forth—without antecedents, without qualifications. It is not entertainment, soma tablets for the educated classes. It is not merely political. It is something clear and pure and new, both primitive and ultimate, a primary phenomenon that organizes lesser opinion, fact, and circumstance."

Scott Davis was born in Seattle on January 28, 1948—three days before the assassination of Gandhi. He grew up in Medina, Washington, graduated from Bellevue High School, across Lake Washington from Seattle, in 1966, and in 1970 from Stanford University with a BA in English and honors in social thought and institutions. In August 1970 he was granted conscientious objector status and in 1971 went to Richmond, Virginia to perform alternative service at the Bethlehem Center. There he got the inspiration and began to gather the material for The World of Patience Gromes: Making and Unmaking a Black Community, *his first book. He spent twelve years writing it, rewriting it, and looking for a publisher for it. In 1988 it was published by University Press of Kentucky and won the State of Washington's Governor's Writers Award the following year.*

When Davis was fourteen he took the Mountaineers Climbing Course. He climbed in the Cascades during high school and began climbing in Yosemite while in college. In the French Alps in 1968, he climbed the Harlin Route on the Aguille de fou and did a speed climb of the Bonatti Pillar on the Dru. In 1969 he made the third ascent of North American Wall on El Capitan which then had the reputation of being the most difficult rock climb in North America. In April 1970, with Chuck

Kroger, he made the first ascent of the Heart Route of El Capitan in a ten-day climb.

In 1993, after a twenty-year hiatus from climbing, Davis began climbing again. In climbing, he says, "I found it easy to identify an objective which seemed impossibly difficult and then to discipline myself. That discipline consisted of a methodical training program, but the larger part of it was spiritual discipline. I found that by examining my thinking and praying to remove materialism, I was able to overcome training injuries and to accomplish climbing goals that had seemed, for me, to be impossible. I have found, strangely enough, that some of the best progress I have made in writing has come after climbing vacations. The mental watching and prayer from one spilled over into the other."

I interviewed Davis at his home in north Seattle on a pleasantly chill night at the end of August 1994. Marilyn Stablein, a mutual friend and also a writer, was present but did not participate in the interview. I began by asking Davis, as a matter of my own curiosity, how he had realized that he was a conscientious objector.

Well, when I was a freshman, all the upper classmen came around and said that I really should be an officer in the army because I was going to get drafted anyway. If you were in the army it would be better to be an officer. So they talked me into enrolling in ROTC. And I had a very difficult time getting a spit polish on my hat brim. I would get the polish beautifully all the way over the edge, and I would just be working that last bit, and then it would start to undo. And I would work harder and harder and harder, and it would just break away, break away, break away, and pretty soon I was starting all over again. And one night I thought: My dad is paying all this tuition for me to go to Stanford and here I am writing this cosmic paper on the origins of scientific thought in Darwin and Galileo and all these people, but I don't quite have time for it because I'm staying up late at night trying to get the polish on the brim of my hat. Finally I thought: This is not the right time for this.

So then I didn't have anything to do with the military until I got my induction notice. And I had a low draft number, and I thought: Well, if I am a conscientious objector, I'd better decide that I am a conscientious objector pretty soon because otherwise I'm going to be carrying a gun. So I gave it some thought. I was religious[1] —I am religious—and I decided I was a conscientious objector. So I wrote a letter to my draft board. And I thought: Well, I'm so nice and religious, they'll approve me. But they turned me down. And so I spent a whole summer being very religious, waiting for the results of my appeal.

And I went back and I was prepared to be the most pacifistic person that ever came into that office. And these guys were sitting there and they just challenged my integrity. They just said, "You're lying." In nicer language. And I said "What! What! You mean you're saying you don't believe me?" And they said, "Yeah. Yeah, that's what we're saying."

And I'd been so strung out for like three months, I'd spent three hours every morning praying, you know, that I wasn't trying to impose my will on the situation, and that I wanted God's will to be done, and just twisting my life all around this thing. And the idea that this guy thought this is just, you know, just "Oh yeah, just lie about this" made me really angry. And I felt like climbing across the table and strangling him. But I restrained myself. Instead, I just shouted at him. I started telling him all these strange things—didn't make any sense—about religious experiences I'd had and how my car had stopped working and I'd prayed and then it started going again, and all these just strange experiences— didn't make any sense—I was just so angry.

And I walked out of there when the interview was done and I said, "Well, I'm going to Viet Nam. But I don't care. I told those guys off. It was worth it. I feel wonderful." So I went home and started packing my stuff. A couple weeks later I got a notice that said "We believe that you are a sincere pacifist."

And I figured out later that that's what they would do, they would just completely challenge you. And if you were nice and pacifistic about it, they wrote that you were a violent-natured person. And if you were just about ready to strangle them, they wrote that you were a sincere pacifist. And I realized that my prayers had been answered, because there was no way in the world that I could have figured out the right way to answer to make them think that I was a pacifist.

So that's how I became a conscientious objector. I'm not sure I technically qualified, because I think you had to say that you were a conscientious objector for all wars and all circumstances at all times. And I was sort of saying, "Well, at this time I'm a conscientious objector. If this was World War II, I probably wouldn't be."

I think they changed that. I don't know when they changed it, but I think they did. Okay. I was just curious. Did you go to graduate—?
No. Mm mm. I never took a writing class either. The thing that helped me improve dramatically was when I realized that any kind of writing you do is difficult, whether it's writing for a newspaper or writing a great novel. And just because you can do one doesn't mean you can do the other. And so I started writing for publication for anybody who would publish me. I wrote for a computer magazine and I wrote for the University of Washington *Daily*. They took my nice, complete sentences and turned them into sentences without verbs, without—they did all kinds of crazy things. And I learned not to care.

The problem is that I would just be writing and I would think these great thoughts and write these words that I thought were wonderful, and then I would read the words again and I would get all those great thoughts. But everybody else would read them and they would just get nothing. Even if you're just writing a letter, it makes a tremendous difference if you're writing and you have someone in mind and you're writing so someone can understand you. You avoid all kinds of really conceited language that doesn't help you say anything.

Are you saying that the U of Dub Daily *improved your writing?*
Well, I knew that however good or bad this was, it was going to get published. So I was exposing myself to an audience. Someone was going to read this. Like I interviewed Earl Emerson and I interviewed a rock-'n-roll group—some friends of mine—and they were going to read it. They were going to use it in their clippings. So it really makes a

difference if you have an audience instead of just writing for yourself. I mean Emily Dickinson could do it, but it just didn't work for me.

You know, when I was in college I wrote academic stuff, and I thought maybe I was a literary writer. So I started doing all these really conceited things that made it difficult for people to understand what I was trying to say. It would have been better if I'd stayed with my ordinary style and just progressed a little bit and heightened it a little. But I remember thinking, Well, it's not significant. In fact, to me, that's the thing: as you become a more experienced writer, you become more confident, so you're willing to trust that your ideas are going to do something for people. And so you don't try so much with your language to make it seem important or significant.

I had a little problem with college because, you know, it's so easy to write a paper at Stanford. The professor is happy if you even turn the doggone thing in. So you're a success right away. Everybody knows who you are, you've talked about the ideas in class, the professor suggested the topic. So all of the most difficult tasks in a piece of writing have already been taken care of before you put pen to paper. You know, like introducing yourself to the reader, where you're coming from, what you're talking about, the approach you're taking, why it's important or significant—all of those things have already been resolved.

And so you go and get good grades in college and you think you know how to write, but you're way behind poor old Ernest Hemingway who didn't get a chance to go to college. Instead, he just had to listen to a few little aphoristic things that Gertrude Stein would tell him, and then write for the newspapers. And I realized later that that guy was way ahead because he was already writing undistinguished stuff for the newspapers but he had an audience. So he was learning how to connect with people, and then he had Gertrude to give him some literary concepts that he probably never would have gotten on his own. It was much better and I was way behind, not having had that apprenticeship.

In college it was ideas, just a feast of ideas, but the technique is left way back in the stone age. Which is bad, but what's worse is not knowing that your technique isn't any good. Because everyone is saying you're wonderful. Then one week after graduation nobody's being paid to read your manuscripts anymore, and now you're just one more barnacle on the bottom of the ocean.

Now you're going to start a press, right?
No, I started one.

What's the name of it?
Cuneiform Press [changed, since this interview, to Cune Press].

When did you start it?
May of 1994.

What does that mean that you started it? You got a letterhead? You opened an account?
I paid five hundred dollars and filed for a trademark.

So your press is going to do...what?
Serious nonfiction books.

Do you have your first title?
Lost Arrow. You read it. You made marks on it.

Yeah. It was very good. I really enjoyed it.
Thanks.

Okay. Lost Arrow, *which is a collection of short nonfiction stories. And you have your book on Syria. That's—*
Yeah. It's scheduled to come out in June '95. What I'd like to do is have it come out in June '95 for mail order, and then have a pub date of September.

Where's your mailing list going to come from? Do you have one? Are you going to buy one?
I'm going to develop one. I'm going to see if I can figure out who

bought my first book. I've got a few lists. And then I want to get some partners for my press. But I don't really want financial partners. I want people who will help to develop a subscriber base. And maybe they're also writers, and they develop a book—we can publish their book. But it wouldn't be a financial partnership. They would raise the capital to cover the cost of their own book. I would provide the imprint. But the most important thing is that the kinds of things that people would be doing would be serious nonfiction that I would be interested in associating myself with. And also that they're the kind of person that knows people and would be willing to work on developing a subscriber base. For example, I'm talking to a woman named Midge Bowman who's offered to help me with the subscriber base part of it, whether or not she does much else with the press, though I think she will.

I come at this a little bit differently than you do, because.... I went back to New York this spring and did a lot of interviews with publishers, just to find out what was going on in publishing. And I ended up coming away from that so furious about the way writers are treated in American publishing that I wrote an article on publishing, and part of my fury was that it's becoming really impossible for writers to have careers if they're depending on New York to publish them. And people in New York don't really care about that.

They don't care about what?

They don't care about writers having, or not having, careers. That's of incidental importance. But, anyway, I wrote my article on publishing. And it was nice because I was going to get this published. And I received, about that point, about sixty-three rejections on my Syria manuscript. And then I couldn't even get my article on publishing published. Not even in the University of Washington *Daily*, because now they're just publishing things written by students.

And I decided that I was really angry. And then I decided that it's not healthy to be really angry, because all the people that got really angry back in the '60s, they just all sort of burned out. It didn't take them anywhere. So I thought, Well, hey, I'm not going to be angry. I'm going to start my own publishing house. I don't need those guys.

43

And in about two hours time I was transformed from total frustration and anger to just utter delight. Because publishing your own stuff is play time. It's the funnest thing you can ever think of to do. The reason that people don't do it is maybe because they're afraid they're going to get laughed at. And I finally got to the point where I realized that I didn't care if people laughed at me; I was going to have fun, and get my stuff published, and get it out there.

So, to go into a little bit more detail about my analysis of the current publishing situation—I found that there were people in New York that are in the business, have been in the business for thirty-five years, who agreed with all my most dire predictions and thoughts about New York corporate publishing.

I'll give you one example. There's a guy named Lawrence Fullerton [fictitious name], and he's head of the society of agents, whatever you call that. Well, I couldn't mention in polite company the names he was calling the corporate editors in New York. He's saying there's anti-trust violations, he's saying that people are coming in from Hollywood that don't know anything about publishing, or from Australia who don't know anything about publishing, and they're giving away huge advances to the writers of thrillers, way more than those books can earn back. And since they don't know very much about publishing, when they go to negotiate an advance, all they can talk is how big the advance is. And since in publishing, as we know, everything is all turned upside down—in any other business, you brag about how cheaply you got something, how little you paid for something; in publishing they brag about how much they paid for something—the prices get really inflated. He thought that a lot of his authors had been slighted—like [a well-known writer] is one of his authors—and he felt that these big publishers were pulling money from good authors and throwing it out the door by giving it to bad authors. And he was extremely disgusted with several agents who, he says, just tear up the contracts. They don't ever look at them, because they know that the books will never earn back the advance. So the advance is all that they care about. They don't need to know the details of the contract. They don't care about rights or whatever comes after.

44

So that's an example where I found that I really wasn't out in left field, that there were an awful lot of strong feelings back there. I spent three or four hours at the PEN Center listening to the tape of the February 28th [1994] protest meeting that PEN held at the McGraw-Hill auditorium in Manhattan.

Did they really refer to it as a protest meeting?
Well, that's what it was. It was like the '60s. They expected a couple hundred people to come. They had four hundred people there—people were out the door—because there was so much anger over the recent firings and consolidations. Which didn't affect that many people but, you know, it's a trend.

I thought the February 28th meeting was about trying to analyze what the future of literary books was going to be. Am I wrong?
There was a little bit about the future, but there was a lot about the current situation. There wasn't much about high technology or the Internet or anything like that.

I thought the driving force for even holding the meeting was because of the concern over what's happening with literary books.
Right. Well, it was the firings in January. And Ticknor & Fields was got rid of, and Atheneum was canceled. But, anyway, it was funny, going back there. I came up with this picture of publishing in which you've got these large corporate houses that are destroying themselves and doing it fairly quickly. They've got these immense, rich backlists, but what they're doing is following General Motors' path to mediocrity. It's really hard to get it back once you've lost your touch. And that's what they're doing. They're losing their touch.

Because they have to have a connection with good literature. In the long run, they can't survive without that, because they need the respect. I mean there are so few dollars that go through publishing, compared to other businesses, that if there wasn't literature, or there wasn't something culturally important involved, no one would pay any attention. So they need the prestige of having serious authors that are addressing serious subjects. But on an individual book basis, they need money. Or they want money. So what they've been doing is cashing in their future prospects and trying to make money in the short term. And they're severely eroding their credibility with the public by not doing nearly what they could for authors now.

It's a combination of things. There's been a recession in the publishing industry, which some people say is the first recession that they've ever really had. Traditionally, the book business has been very steady. Even during the Depression, books sold, sold, sold, sold, sold. And right in the middle of the recession a lot of concern came about high technology, and the corporate reshuffling continued. So you had a situation where midlist writers were getting cut. Every time there was a consolidation they were getting cut, because in the recession publishers were doing fewer books. Like one fellow explained it to me: You have so many seats on the plane and the corporate people are saying, "Let's sell each seat for a larger amount of money." They've succeeded in doing that, but in order to do that, they've had to average the content of the books down.

So you get one book and it doesn't have as much quote specific content unquote as it might have had ten years before. The number of books sold has gone from around four million up to around sixteen million in the last twenty years. But the specificity of the books has suffered. I've gotten rejections on my Syria manuscript where—like at Knopf one editor said, "Well, this is a good book but it's very specific." In other words, it has content. "And we can't sell this book to just anybody. It has to be someone who's interested in what you have to say."

There's a real overconcern with "product," they call it. They want to sell as many units as possible of a given "product." That's the language that book people use now. It's all through *Publishers Weekly*. They're comparing themselves to auto makers. And they say, "In what other business would we sell as few units of a given product?" So I have a problem when literature is analyzed and gauged so much for of its commercial appeal. When the content is watered down to keep from disqualifying itself with a large number of people, I think you end up with pablum.

So this spring I went through the *Publishers Weekly* list of what books had sold in what quantities over the previous year, and I thought, Well, when I get down to around five hundred thousand I'll find books that have some interesting content. But it wasn't until I got to books that sold less than twenty thousand copies that I found that half of the books—whether I liked them or not—that I thought, Well, there's something interesting here. When you get above around twenty thousand copies in sales, most of the books are really vapid.

The idea behind the blockbuster complex, which is what you've been talking about—you bid against other companies for a book on which you know you can't make your money back, but you're gaining prestige by outbidding other companies. Now if that's the way they're gaining prestige, then why would they even care about cultural standards. You say that they have to publish some good books or they lose prestige. I'm saying I don't believe they think that way. Why do they have to do that? If prestige is gained by spending money—it's a kind of potlatch. If it's gained by embarrassing your competition by outspending him, then what's the difference what the product is?

Well, I think the large New York corporate presses are going to be in trouble—I think they're already in trouble—because they're getting a reputation for publishing junk and pushing junk on the public and pandering to the lowest common denominator and not uplifting and leading the readership.[2]

I would say they have a poor reputation among those who are aware that better things exist. But fewer and fewer Americans are even aware that other things exist, because they're not exposed to them. If that trend continues, then within the United States, at least, reputation won't matter because nobody will know enough to know they've been cheated.

Well, I kind of like the analogy of the auto companies. I mean, General Motors just thought it could do whatever the hell it wanted to do. It was producing big cars and made a lot of money on big cars, and it felt like it could just continue putting its effort into big cars and ignore what the marketplace was saying, and it could turn out shoddy stuff and no one would care. It didn't have to have very good service and it didn't have to have this and it didn't have to have that. So it ended up losing customers to Japanese companies that would provide all those things. And it turned out that all these supposedly unsophisticated American buyers who were a quote captive market unquote did care about quality, did care about having a choice between small cars and large cars, and did like to be catered to. And right down the line, all of these things that General Motors ignored kept coming back to haunt them. And I think the same thing is happening with publishing.

Now obviously it's a little bit different, but I think, at a certain point, you're going to find that an awful lot of people are attracted to literary quality. Whether or not they actually want to read the novel, they want to be associated with the person who has thought deep thoughts and has spent years learning how to write and has mastered the craft, and they want to be associated with excellence. I think that's a really wide-spread thing. You know, you buy Michael Jordan basketball shoes, but you don't buy basketball shoes promoted by someone who's some kind of a flunky.

So to me it's extremely short-sighted of them to cut loose as many of their midlist writers as they've done. To me, once you've lost the reputation for fostering literary excellence, it can be hard to get it back. Once Detroit lost its prestige among the American public, it was hard to get it back. So I think these publishers are going to find themselves in a difficult situation in five or ten years.

It's just incredible to me that small presses are being as widely reviewed as they are, and that even self-published books, which is what I'm talking about doing, are as widely reviewed as they are. And you have publications like the *New York Times,* which is supposed to be the voice of the New York literary elite, publishing articles which directly challenge the motives of the large corporate presses. I think it's really strange when you've got commercial institutions like these large houses that are trying to make as much money and have the kind of perks that the other arms of the corporation have, and to do that out of literature. I don't think literature was designed for that.

48

The other thing is that—and this is kind of central to me—I really feel that literature has a spiritual function within a culture. It's essential. A culture dies if it doesn't have literature. And it makes me angry to see that the institutions that are serving the function of bringing literature out, and distributing it, and getting it out where people could have contact with it, don't seem to have the vaguest understanding of this process. To me these are really crucial times, and I accept the idea that there is rapid change going on, and that these are very disorienting times and people are expected to change their careers three times or four times in their life—I mean, this is something that's never been tried before—and I feel that the largest problems facing us as a society and as a people have to do with orientation and understanding and will. If we can understand what's going on and orient ourselves, then we'll have the will to put the money into solving the technical problems, into solving environmental problems. People don't understand what's happening to them. They don't understand where they're going, they don't understand where they came from.

It's a vast simplification, but at one point you had a tribe and the tribe would sit around the fire at night and they would tell stories. And they would say, "Well, this is what so and so did in the past, and this is what so and so should do in the future. And this is where we are now, and this is what's happening to us." And literature would be a way of understanding the world. It would be a way of confronting the world. It would be a way of figuring out how we're going to live through another day. It's essential. It's more important, to my mind, than all of the things that seem so important in the media right now.

I just have a problem with commercial institutions perverting the whole institution of literature, and taking away from the spiritual purpose, and blocking the dissemination of ideas. They say, "Well, we put out too many books." That's not true at all. They put out too many of the same books. They'll do a dozen books on one subject when it becomes hot, or two dozen. And then every publisher has to have a book on another subject when that becomes hot.

But as far as diversity of books, they don't do that well. Now, they may put out too many books relative to their ability to market them, but they don't market very well. They throw things out there, but to actually cultivate and develop readership, you know, from the second grade on up—nobody's doing that. So I think there's a tremendous need for literature, for serious books—books of ideas, books of thought, nonfiction and fiction both.

And I don't buy the idea that people aren't reading as much. Maybe they are and maybe they aren't. But books expand. Someone reads a book, and then they end up writing a play, and someone makes a movie from the play, and this is the way ideas percolate through society. I think we need those ideas, and one book doesn't do it. Things have to be developed, and it takes time, and it takes that kind of circulation. I think it's a real crime that people like Marilyn and you and me, who are, for some reason, devoting our lives to putting words on paper and trying to master the craft, aren't getting the rewards.

You're a rock climber. Do you still climb?
Yeah. I did last year.

Do you see any relationship between rock climbing and any other aspect of your life?
I think rock climbing is a lot more fun than anything else I do.

A while ago you were talking about how much fun it is to publish yourself.
Well, publishing's a lot more fun than rock climbing. Publishing is awfully fun, but with publishing there's a tremendous amount of work. Rock climbing, you've got to work to get in shape, but...I don't know, they're both fun.

But they're not the same, or are they the same?
I don't know. That's an interesting question. To me, alpine climbing, rock climbing, is a lot easier than publishing. You have a physical challenge and you're scared and it focuses your thought. It's easy to keep your mind on what you're doing. It's right there. You can get good results if you focus, if you discipline yourself. You devote

50

yourself to preparing, very carefully, and you can do things that you never thought you could come close to doing.

I think the same thing is probably true in the area of publishing, but it's very difficult for me to keep my mind as focused on what I'm doing and to discipline myself. Because it's vague. It's abstract. And so I have to kind of go in the dark. There is this great precipice out there that I'm trying to get up, and if I really discipline myself I might make it. But you can't see it. You don't know it. I think of rock climbing and alpine climbing all the time in relation to publishing, because I think—I did a new route up Mount Rainier last summer. I didn't think I could ever do that. And I did. And I could probably do more.

Well, how does that apply to publishing? I keep thinking—If I could discipline myself as much, and work as carefully, and keep from wasting my time, do the right things and not waste time on other things, and trust that there's a market out there, and trust that distribution is going to fall into line, then maybe I could do some really wonderful things. But it's really difficult to believe, in publishing. Whereas in rock climbing it's much easier to conceive of the challenge, and so it's easier to discipline yourself.

Notes

1. A couple of weeks after the interview, Davis wrote me: "As a freshman in college I began studying Christian Science. I was attracted by the consistency of the faith and the emphasis it places upon an individual's thought, rather than on ritual or priestly intervention. To me, this teaching was the ultimate for an intellectual— the granting of all power to thought—and crystallized the classic intellectual struggle to submit one's thoughts to a divine Mind in such a way that one's individuality was increased rather than diminished.

"On one side of the divide you have your car wrecks, people like Faust and Prometheus. Entirely unnecessary what those fellows went through, carrying hot coals in hell, having ravens pecking on one's innards. The rest of us hope to solve the puzzle a bit more successfully, to align ourselves with divine intelligence, to discern it rather than trying to barricade ourselves in some limited, selfish, ephemeral position to which, for some reason, we have become attached.

"I found that religion and literature were similar and compatible. At Stanford I grew like a weed, both intellectually and in a religious way. In those days it was still OK to admit that you read the Bible if you read it 'as Literature.' An amazing distortion. Of course the Bible is literature. On the other hand, literature is revelation.

"You could say that some novels are more perfectly revealed than others, some novels may, in fact, be pernicious—may be very imperfectly revealed. But the substance in literature, the creation, the discernment is the same that Bible writers brought forth in overtly religious subjects.

"I went through a four-year-long intellectual rearing at Stanford in the notorious Grove House, the nation's first official coed dormitory. We held seminars in-house, had visiting dignitaries, plays written and performed by house residents. The residents consisted of 49 Marxists and me, the lone Christian. I felt isolated and resented the way the liberal Christian denominations were crawling away from public intellectual engagement.

"It seems very strange to me that the religious right, with its strong, anti-intellectual bias, has come to dominate the scene—fighting it out with the left-wing politicos, the neo-Marxists. Don't we have any choice other than these two tiresome positions?

"As publishers, we are trying to understand what is true and to bring the truth to public notice. This is a religious function. And we would be well advised to rescue the terminology of religion and the sincere spirit of religion from right-wing hate and deceit.

"Literature provides an opening to the sacred. Readers, like spiritual seekers, have these epiphanies, these looks beyond, little openings into the mind of God. Literature is a point where creation comes forth—without antecedents, without qualifications. It is not entertainment, soma tablets for the educated classes. It is not merely political. It is something clear and pure and new, both primitive and ultimate, a primary phenomenon that organizes lesser opinion, fact, and circumstance."

2. Davis, in his letter: "I mentioned that between my two draft board interviews I spent three hours every morning praying. Specifically, I worked with the idea that I did not want my will, or my draft board's will, or any one else's will but God's to be done—my adaptation of Jesus' prayer, "Father, not my will, but thine be done." Jesus spoke these words in Gethsemane when he was struggling with the prospect of crucifixion.

"And my experience with my draft board has carried over to publishing. Are we trying to force our idea of good taste on an unwilling public? If we believe in the material that we are selling, then we should be able to 'place it upon the waters' like Moses' mother did when she set him adrift in his reed basket. We should trust that the inspiration which wrote and published the book will be present in the public to receive it.

"Are our books fluff? Do they try to cash in on human failings, addictions, and weaknesses? Are they exercises in authorial ego? Do they pander to the current literary fashion? Or are they sincere, original work which will delight, instruct, and uplift?

"As publishers, we spend a lot of time in the garden of Gethsemane, sweating blood while our disciples sleep. In the anguish of the soul which accompanies the creation and publication of good literature, are we purifying and improving our offerings? If so, we should expect a positive response from readers."

Joe Singer
Mother of Ashes Press

"Publishing things is my reaction to the fact that I read."

Joe Singer was born and raised in Powell, Wyoming and went to high school and community college there. At the time of this interview, he lived eight miles out of Harrison, Idaho, a town of two hundred seventy, located thirty miles south of Coeur d'Alene. Harrison is a community of retirees and vacationers. When I met him, Singer was a caretaker for one of the houses occupied only part of the year by its owners.

I interviewed Joe Singer on the morning of September 4, 1992 in the Performance Room of the Art Pavilion in Seattle Center. It was the first day of Bumbershoot, Seattle's annual arts festival, and the small press fair where we both would be exhibiting our books was scheduled to begin in less than an hour.

Not quite a year later, Joe Singer committed suicide.

I attended—I have a junior college certificate in English from Northwest Community College in Powell. But I attended four different colleges five different times. I went to MSU in Bozeman. Montana State. That was right out of high school. Nineteen sixty-nine. The fall quarter. And then I went to—now it's Northwest College; it was Northwest Community College then. And then Riverside, to Riverside City College. And then San Francisco State. And then back to Powell and Northwest again. Took some more classes. I had the credits for an associate of arts in English there at Northwest except I wouldn't take PE. So they gave me the junior college certificate which is actually a technical degree. You know, for their technical program. So I figure

I'm an English technician.

Why wouldn't you take PE?

I just didn't, you know, I didn't like PE. And I wasn't too interested in the degree. It didn't make any sense to me, the degree didn't. So. You can't do anything with an English degree anyway.

I think the problem I had with college all along was that when I started, or before I went, I had the idea that colleges were, you know, the university where you go to learn about life and that whole thing. And when I went to 'em—what it strikes me that colleges are, is they're technical schools for professionals. Right? They give you a career, set you on a career path. I guess I just wasn't ever that interested in a career path. So. You know, I just went to college. I went to college to learn things. I didn't really care what they did with—I mean, I was there and I just took a couple of classes.

Do you regard college as having been very important in your life? I'm not sure what I mean by that.

I don't think so. Not really. I mean, I met a lot of nice people there and stuff like that, but I really don't think so. No. Like I was in my twenties most of the time. At least for me it was an age when I didn't know what I was doing anyway, and it was easy to go to college. You know, go and then drop out and go back. Something to do.

Were you in the military?

No. I'm a draft resister. I was drafted and I refused induction.

What happened then? I'm considering publishing a book by someone who deserted, actually.

Nothing. They reclassified me.

This was when you were in Wyoming?

Well, when I was at MSU, that fall was the first lottery. Nineteen sixty-nine. Autumn of '69 was the first, and my number came up nine. But at the time I was in college, so I had a student deferment. But I dropped out—I mean, I just was up there—they have quarters, so I dropped out after the first one. So I was automatically reclassified 1A, and my number was up. But I applied for CO [Conscientious Objector status] and went through all the stages. And they kept rejecting it, and finally they drafted me. And, you know, they just reclassified me.

As what?
Two aitch, I think.

What does that mean? "Draft resister, but let him go"? [Both men laugh.]
Basically. It's like they're sort of gonna ignore this for now, but if the country's invaded they would draft me again. Right? But I was talking with somebody a couple of years ago about this and she was telling me that this was something that they would do. They would, you know, just see how serious you are about this, right? You know, keep saying "No, we're not gonna give you that," and go ahead and draft people and then, you know, and then just, "Well, I guess you are serious." 'Cause I got in where you're actually inducted, and I didn't know until I was in that room, really. You know, like... and I just couldn't do it. Pacifist.

How long have you been publishing?
Um. Twenty-some. I brought out the one magazine, *The Village Idiot*—I brought out the precursor of the magazine in the winter of 1970. And then the first *Village Idiot* came out in the fall of '70.

What was the precursor called?
Grok. From Heinlein's, yeah, *Stranger in a Strange Land.* Someday I'll have to reread that book. But at the time, you know, it was a big influence.

Somebody, some reviewer or some critic, reread it recently and said it was completely different now. It's kind of frightening now.
Yeah. I imagine it would be. That's probably one of the reasons

I haven't reread it, 'cause I know what it can do.

Let's go through your publishing history. You had Grok *for a few months in 1970.*

Yeah. I did two issues of that. I'd type up the stencils and my brother ran 'em off in the high school. 'Cause I was just out of high school. I'd just dropped out of MSU and I was back in Powell. So he ran 'em off on the high school's spirit duplicators and we did a couple of issues that way. And then we got together—there were some people—this was a sort of underground newspaper. This was 1970 and Powell's a little backwoods, so any place else this would be 1964, '65. So it was like an underground newspaper. These other people in town were doing one called *The First Amendment*, and we got together and brought out something called *The Family Paper* which was mimeographed. One of the guys had a mimeograph. That was about the time Charles Manson went to work, right? And so we started thinking it wasn't a good idea to call this *The Family Paper*. And at the same time the guy's mimeograph broke down and his parents wouldn't let him play with us any more. His dad was a Methodist minister and he didn't like his son associating with all these radicals.

I was just out of high school. I think I was the oldest one and the youngest—well, my sister was probably the youngest and she's about four years younger than I am. So, freshman in high school to just out of high school. And we did that through that summer and then we had to reorganize again and that's when I started *The Village Idiot*. It was pretty much the same thing, your standard underground newspaper.

The printer in Powell wouldn't run the job. Gray Bull's about a hundred miles away and we had to drive over there to find a printer. He just ran it off on a little A.B. Dick. Just eight and a half by eleven. Actually, I think the guy was a drunk. He had an office supply store and a little press in the back. We had some friends there who told us about him and he said [mimicking a drunkard's slur], "Yeah, I'll do it." It wasn't bad. It was like twenty-four pages, eight and a half by eleven. I think we got two hundred copies for sixty dollars. So we did a couple of issues that way and then pretty much the magazine folded again because nobody had any money and it wasn't making any money.

And so about five years later I went to work for a web-offset shop in Riverside, California. I'd lived there before for about four years. And then I left and went up to San Francisco and one thing and another and at one point I decided that what I needed was a trade. I found myself, you know, I was in Bath, New York—God—and in the middle of winter. I was there for only three or four months but I couldn't find a job and it was the middle of the winter and it was cold and one thing and another. And I decided what I needed, since I didn't seem that interested in college, what I needed was a trade. And I decided that if I was going to do something like that, what I should do is learn graphic arts or printing. And I'd gone to Riverside City College for a while and knew they had a printing program, a graphic arts program, and it's easy to get jobs in California, or it was at that time. And so I went back there and I was looking for a night job that I could do and then go to school and get the thing in the graphic arts. And I got a job as a flyboy in this printing plant, and so I just forgot the college again.

What's a flyboy?
Basically a printer's devil. Your entry-level position in the shop. You just [mimicking somebody ordering him about] "Fly, boy!" You catch the papers when they come out and you shuffle them together and stack them on the skids and sweep up and, you know, if you stay with it you can learn the press and move up, and that's essentially what I did. I worked up to where at the end I was operating one of their presses.

I guess I'd been there for about a year when I decided—'cause they gave me a discount—so I decided to bring out *The Village Idiot* again, and this time I brought it out as a literary magazine, an annual. I brought out about four issues while I was there. I was there for about three and a half years. And then the last year I was there, 1980, I bought a Kelsey letterpress. A six-by-ten Kelsey. You know, these tabletop letterpresses. And that's when I started the press. 'Cause I finally had a press. And so I named it.

You mean "Mother of Ashes"? Where did that come from?

It started out as a poem but that's all I got written of it, was "Mother of Ashes." And that was about the time I got the press and I started thinking about it, you know, and said, "Well, gee, that'd be a good name for a press." And so there it was. People tend to remember it.

So then you were doing an annual literary magazine called The Village Idiot.

Yeah. And then pretty much—I mean it's been pretty sporadic. That was about, like I say, 1980, and then I guess I've been out here since 1984.

"Out here" meaning Harrison?

Yeah. Harrison since 1984. So in those four years, I don't know, I traveled around a little more and got out about four issues of the magazine. I did the last one the first year I moved to Harrison. And then when I was there I started mimeographing a newsletter for an anti-nuclear group in Coeur d'Alene, "CANWE". It's an acronym. Citizens Against Nuclear Weapons and Extermination. It's a mouthful. I'd gotten a mimeograph—you know, pick up a piece of equipment, take it home—and so I volunteered, "Well, I'll do a newsletter for you," and started mimeographing this thing. Did a couple of issues that way and one of the guys in the group says, "Well, Joe, uh, how'd you like a press?" "Well, what do you mean?" "Well, I got this printing press in my garage and I'm not gonna use it. You want it?" "Oh, yeah."

And the guy gave me, well, sort of gave me—I ended up doing it—this is like a twelve-, sixteen-page newsletter—monthly for two years on my own hook. I mean paying for all the paper, doing all the editing. I paid for that press. Yeah, a little Multi 1261. They're called offset duplicators. What they're built for largely is like quick-print shops and corporate in-house printing, and so like the maximum sheet size is ten by fourteen. And what's mostly run on 'em is business papers, eight and a half by eleven. You know, you go down to a quick-print shop and say, "I want some letterhead." If they run it off on an offset press, it'll either be that or probably an A.B. Dick 360. Or Heidelberg makes one, too. I'd like to get one of those. Heidelberg's supposed to make good presses.

You know, and so this is the first time I've ever stayed in one spot. I mean, I had that job in the printing plant in Riverside for like three and a half years, but even when I was there I was moving every six months. You know, I mean changing addresses. Other than that, I was changing jobs every six months. And so I've been sitting here now for, like I say, the last eight and a half years.

I was in Powell for a year before I got this job. I'm one of the very few people I know who moved to Idaho for a job. Everybody moves to Idaho and then tries to find a job. I was in Powell and my sister still lives there and I stayed with her for awhile. And I couldn't find a job. It ended up that winter I went down and bought a six-dollar scoop shovel. Fortunately, it was snowing like every two or three days. And so I'd just walk out and go door to door and "Uh, shovel your walk?" Actually, I paid the rent that way. And then I got this job in January '84.

It must have been '85. There used to be in Missoula a magazine called *Heartland*. This magazine printed one page from a comic book that this guy had drawn. And the book wasn't published, right? And so I wrote to them and they put me in touch with—his name is Bill Tulp. The comic book is called *El Salvador, a House Divided*. Basically, it's a fictionalized account of life in El Salvador in the latter '70's and early '80's. All the wars and people going—and before that I'd just run a few things off, a couple of broadsides, you know, when I had the letterpress. And I guess I'd done some broadsides on the—you know, "Well, you have the machine. Let's see if it works." I'd run a few things off, but nothing that I really tried to promote. But that did pretty good. I did five hundred. I got two copies left.

Then Eclipse Comics, which is your major independent comics publisher, picked it up and brought out a second edition of about five thousand. That was three or four years ago. I don't know how well it's doing, but I hope Bill got some money out of it. He didn't get any from me. You know, I keep paying people off in copies.

You know, most of what happened is Bill's doing. 'Cause he—you know, you run into writers, some writers don't do anything. "Well, you published my book, man, you go out and get rid of it." And some of 'em actually work at it.

Work at promoting the book, you mean.

Yeah. And those books work a lot better than the ones where—I mean as far as the Eclipse thing, getting them to take it up and then—in fact, a lot of the copies of the edition I brought out and managed to sell went through Bill. He'd take 'em around. In fact, I go into Spokane once in a while and if I see a place that looks like it might be interested in certain things, I'll take something in there and talk to 'em. I went into this like head shop they used to have there. This was just a couple of years ago, right? And I go, "You know, I got this stuff. A comic book, *El Salvador.*" And the clerk looks at me and goes, "You know, there was a guy in here a couple or three years ago with that and we took some then." And they took some more.

Then I did—the next one was *The Blink of an Eye*, which is a novel. Ruth Jespersen. I published her first in *The Village Idiot*. She writes short stories and novels. The first time I published one of her stories I got her name right in the table of contents, but on the story itself I got "-on" instead of "-en" and she let me know about it. But, like I say, I published one or two or her stories in the magazine and I also—

You know, 'cause I have the equipment, sometimes I'll do some printing. Not under the Mother of Ashes imprint, but just job printing. And there's some dispute between Ruth and her husband and me about this, but the way I understood it, she had this novel and she wanted me to print it. She and her husband have published a couple of her books. Short stories. They have an imprint, Biblia Candida. Don't ask me what it means. I thought they wanted me to print this novel for their imprint, right? And I was just going to print it. And then she started talking to me about why don't I print it under my imprint. And I kept saying, "Well, see, I don't do that." I mean, if I bring it out, then I have to have a financial stake in it. And there's no way in the world that I could bring out a novel. The paper was, what? three thousand or thirty-five hundred dollars. Well, it's, you know, it's four hundred and thirty-eight pages plus end sheets, and it's on like a seventy-pound, acid-free text stock, right? It's a nice paper.

It took me three years. 'Cause I'm running it two pages at a time on this little duplicator. Like the sheets are nine and a half by twelve and a half, so I'm printing two pages. But I have to run one side and flip it over and run the second side, right? Plus I did all the typesetting. At that time I had a Compuwriter Junior phototypesetter which is—well, now it's about eighteen, nineteen years old and it's really—you know, I mean the company is abandoned and it's obsolete. And that's eventually why I gave it up, 'cause you can't get parts for it anymore. But just the typesetting—'cause I'm doing this in between other things—well, what happened with the book is they wanted me to bring it out under my imprint and I kept telling 'em that I can't do that without some stake in it. So eventually the deal we reached is that they paid for the paper and they paid for the binding, which was again another like three dollars a copy for a thousand copies. Another three thousand dollars. And then I put up all my time and like incidental expenses and stuff.

So now you have a financial stake in it.
Yeah. The credits page, or whatever...inside the title page it says "Published by Mother of Ashes in conjunction with Biblia Candida," which is how it works out. That took me, off and on—I started the—I do a graphic arts magazine now; I started that somewhere along there—but working in between them and my day job and one thing and another, that took me three years.

What's the graphic arts magazine called?
The Printer's Devil.

Oh, right. I've seen that.
Oh, good.

Yeah, I have seen that. In fact, you may have sent me one once.

62

Probably. It gets around. In fact, I've done a couple mailings around the Northwest. It doesn't appeal to a general audience, but it appeals outside that.

Getting back to Ruth Jespersen's book, who marketed it?

I am. She sends out copies to a few of her friends. Stuff like that. I mean she's, I guess, seventy now. They would disagree. They're under the impression that when they first sent it to me, they submitted it to be published. And so where I think it started out as a printing project, they think it started out as a publishing project. And we had words about that. I guess we're over it. You know, you can't do anything about it at this point.

When did it come out?

That would be '90. The next thing I brought out, I brought out a book of poems by David Coy, called *Rural News*. He teaches creative writing down in Yuma at a community college there. It's a good book. I like it. Obviously. That one I did—I mean I pretty much wrapped up *The Blink of an Eye* as far as anything I could do on it. I sent it to the bindery and stuff. And I'd been talking with David, 'cause I've known David—we went to high school together. At the time I didn't know he wrote. And then, out of high school, somehow—you know, we sort of knew each other in high school, but we didn't—well, there were a hundred and twenty people in the class. Through twelve years of school with them, you sort of know everybody. But I didn't, you know—but somehow after high school, a year or so after high school, I ran into him, and since that time, never real regular, but we always managed somehow to keep in touch.

And he went eventually—it took him seven years to get his bachelor's degree. He went to the University of Arkansas, their creative writing program. I guess it's supposed to be good. I don't know that much about it except that it has a good reputation. He eventually got a master's in creative writing. And we were always keeping in touch, sort of. 'Cause he'd send me some poems sometimes for the magazine. And I said, "Well, some day you ought to let me do a book." You know, *The*

Village Idiot, especially in academic circles, isn't exactly a prestigious magazine. Right? So he's more interested in getting his poetry published in these other magazines that will do him some good in his career.

But he would—you know, I published, off and on, some of his stuff. And then finally we were talking about it and I go, you know, "You put together this book manuscript. Send it up to me." He was always revising it while I was working on it. [Laughs. Then, mimicking David Coy—] "Well, I changed this poem and this poem and this poem." I go, "Oh, David. One more time. Okay." At the same time I was working on Ruth's book, right? And so I'm going, well, you know, um, "Soon as I get this off...," you know. Finally when I got that off, I brought... yeah, *Rural News* came out really shortly—I mean six months or so after the novel.

I keep playing around. I mean, I like printing. Sometimes the rest of the business can just go—I just wanna play with my machines. For offset lithography, traditionally—well, not traditionally, 'cause traditionally you use a stone and you write on it backwards with crayon. But photo-offset lithography uses—you make a negative and image a plate. And now, with the invention of the photocopier, you can make a plate. They make—I have one now—an electrostatic plate maker, which is essentially a photocopier with special chemicals. But they also make what's called a direct-transfer plate that can actually write—it's the old stone surface that's been recreated on a paper plate so it'll fit around your printing cylinder. And you can write rightside-up. You can write forward-facing on it because you're still using the offset process.

So, for *Rural News*, I took these paper masters and I just took 'em down to the copy shop and ran 'em through the photocopier and copied the paste-ups, using just a regular photocopier on these direct-transfer plates. And it works. They're only good for like, well, I did an edition of a thousand from my paste-ups. And I did a first printing of about three hundred and fifty. And that's all those plates are good for. 'Cause the toner cracks off while you're printing, and so the type starts to flake away. But, yeah, for up to about three hundred, three hundred and fifty copies—and all you need is—these plates cost like—you get a box of a hundred for, I think, forty-four dollars, so like forty-five cents apiece and ten cents for running 'em through a photocopier. Right? And you don't need—everything I have is old. My computer is old. My computer is obsolete. To get one new is...I think they're three or four thousand. To get one, a good one, used, they're still a thousand, fifteen hundred dollars. But to do it with direct-transfer plates, somebody has to own a fifteen-thousand-dollar photocopier, but those are all over the place. And a lot of times it's a lot sharper, a lot clearer, than—I can tell. I would say about ninety percent of the time I can. Sometimes it looks better than offset, and that's how I can tell.

Have you done more books since Rural News? *Or are you planning on doing more?*

Well, I just did one. It's a chapbook. It's a story. It's only like thirty pages. Twenty-eight pages. But it's not a centerfold. The outside, the title page, has a third panel that folds in. And it's real small. It's like a three-thousand-word story. "But, Sir! You Can't Pay For Your Obituary Until After You're Dead." A guy named Joseph Glinsky. From Vancouver. The story is about a guy who has AIDS. So he's dying. Joe wants me to believe that it's a true story. But I don't—I mean the story—I'm not willing—'cause writers are such notorious liars. [Laughs.] I'm not willing to say that it's a true story without having researched the thing. I suspect part of it is what they call fictionalized biography. I suspect, like I say, that it's fictionalized a little. I'm not gonna promote it as a real-life account. On the other hand, I think it's true enough.

It's a semi-real-life account.

Yeah. And it's a good enough story. It's an interesting story. And it came along at a good time. I mimeographed it. I've got two mimeograph machines, so I'm set up pretty good for that. I wanted to mimeograph a book. And I'm gonna do a deluxe edition of this. I mean I brought out just a trade edition. I'm doing like three. I'm in a couple of the amateur journalism societies. American Amateur Press Association. The National— And so I did one edition for them, without the cover. I mean I just ran off enough copies of the body of the book so that

I could send it out through their bundle. And then I did a trade edition with a cover. And then I've got some of that paper that I used for Ruth's book left over. So on this acid-free stock I'm gonna mimeograph the body of that, and then I ordered some—there's a woman in Spokane who handmakes paper from plant fibers. And she's making me like thirty sheets of a cattail-fiber paper. And I'm gonna silk-screen the cover onto that. And so I'm bringing out a deluxe edition of a porous-process or stencil-process book, right? For this twenty-eight-page book, right?

How are you going to bind it?

I'll hand-sew it. You know, that loop stitch? Sewn bindings and the acid-free paper and the handmade cover and the whole nine yards. You know, encase each copy. Get these plastic bags they have comic books and stuff in and enclose each copy in one of those and send 'em up to Joseph and get him to sign 'em. Do the whole nine yards. And it's mimeographed. [Laughs.]

And it hit me at a good time, too. I had a lot of people die on me this last year. I mean people I knew were dying. A real good friend I had in Harrison got some kind of leukemia or cancer, they suspect from Agent Orange. You know, after-effect exposure to Agent Orange. And so he's been dying for like the last couple years. He was treated for it for awhile and went into remission, and then it came back. He just died early this summer.

So—and there's a couple other people that—Ruth's husband just came down with bladder cancer. We ended up having to put him in a rest home. And then there was a woman in Coeur d'Alene who I knew from that antinuclear group. Two of 'em. In an auto accident. Somebody swerved out to avoid a truck, right? And slammed head-on into 'em.

So, I was just gonna say, he sent it in to the magazine, right? But it came in at a good or a bad time. It was a story that at that moment really had a lot of appeal to me. He's articulate about what it's like to come to grips with that sort of thing. I mean it's a well-written story and he's articulate about something that was—you know, like I say, it just came in at a good time.

66

I feel a little silly asking anything more about publishing now, but I'm going to.

Good.

Do you apply for grants?

No.

Any particular reason? You just don't do it, or—? Don't want to do the paperwork, or don't want—?

The paperwork's probably the biggest part of it. It gets to the point—people who get grants get to be, I think, better at writing grant applications than they are at writing poetry. It's a skill in its own right. I just don't want to hassle with it.

How does publishing a magazine compare to publishing books? I've never produced a magazine. I have friends who do. Just from watching them, it looks like something I could not handle.

Well, you know, doing a magazine, in some ways it's easier. The only hard part about doing a magazine is trying to stay on schedule. It's just been this last year... well, no. It's been about five years now that I've been doing *The Printer's Devil*. It started out twice a year and now it's coming out three times a year. And now *The Village Idiot* is coming out three times a year. The only hard part is staying on schedule.

On the other hand, you're always going to be doing another one. So it doesn't have to be perfect. What you can't get this time you'll get next time. It takes—'cause like, you do a book, at least it seems to me, there's the book, right? And it's supposed to be a done thing. And that's hard for me. Plus the fact, with a magazine, 'cause it's continuous you can build up a following. You build up an audience. At least for the books I've been bringing out, I have to go out—I mean, because they don't have that much in common with each other I have to go out and do what I can to find an audience. Which is part of the reason why it helps if the writers do it. For one thing, they're a lot better about finding that audience. I mean there aren't—I don't have a big—I've been running ads in the—there's a shopper's newspaper in Harrison that the store puts out. It's just like four or eight pages, you know, eight and a half by eleven. I've been running a series of ads this summer.

Does that help?

I have yet to get an order from it. Part of the reason I did it was just to support—'cause they just started this thing last winter—you know, "Support the local..." sort of thing. And, but, no, I can't get an order from it.

Do you regard your press as having a mission? Or do you have a mission that you're using your press for?

Well, yes and no. I started thinking about this when I started. See, it started for me with *The Village Idiot*, and then—but that's changed a lot, too, from what it first was. Yeah, when I put *The Village Idiot* on this regular schedule—this is like what? one and a half years—the fourth issue where it's been coming out every four months. And I was trying to think about, you know, how to define it, and I started thinking about what got me into this in the first place.

Mostly it's just that I read a lot. Yeah, if there's a mission, that's what it—I can't define it any better than that, but that's what it has to do with, is reading. Yeah. My wanting to publish things gets into a whole— I started out reading, but then you take what you like to do and who you are and— Publishing things is my reaction to the fact that I read. Because I like to run the machines. And I like putting together the magazines—I put up with trying to promote them, the books and stuff.

That sounds similar to what another publisher told me, although she doesn't deal with machines herself: It's a way of being part of a community.

Yeah. Yeah. That's part of it. It's an interactive process. Reading has always seemed that to me. One thing that I—my senior year in high school I took what was called A/V Lab where you were sort of like free labor. And they sent me down one time to record a tape for an English teacher. And it was Robert Frost reading his poetry. So I'm monitoring this, right? I'm just, you know, it's on a record and I'm monitoring it to make sure the tape's all right. It hadn't ever occurred to me before that all of these people that I was reading in English textbooks—you know, in literature classes—were actually real live people. It was like all of this was handed down from on high or something. And all of a sudden I realized no, these were actual people. And there was a communication process going on here. I mean, this didn't all hit me at once. Yeah, communication is two-way.

What I do with the publishing is sort of like—it's action and reaction, question and response. You know, it's just part of the process. Yeah. Community. I would put it more "part of the process" but I can see that other—I think probably it's very close to saying the same thing.

margareta waterman
nine muses books

"Sometimes you have to stretch your mind to see beyond it. It takes an act of imagination, and if there are too many assumptions you don't know that they are assumptions. So you can't overthrow them. And I think that the '60s, the whole psychedelic framework, did a lot of that for me. It enabled me to see through what otherwise looked like opaque walls that I didn't know I could knock down."

margareta waterman was born in Boston and raised in New York. She has been married and divorced twice, has three children and three grandchildren. Other than Massachusetts and New York, she has lived in California, Oregon, the Southwest and Hawaii. She has traveled in Europe, India, Mexico and Central America. These bits of biography tell you little about her. The person who is margareta waterman revealed herself, though not entirely, only as the interview progressed. The course of it is below; I have edited it almost not at all, as the interview itself—at least, for me—was an act of discovery. We talked in my apartment in north Seattle on Thursday, January 21, 1993, the day after a terrific gale took down trees and power lines and gave us a gray light that, this day, the day of the interview, brought the world into clarity, if only for a moment.

Well, how long have you had nine muses?
Nineteen eighty-seven.

Nineteen eighty-seven. Before nine muses, did you earn your living in a different way from the way you do now?
I do not earn my living by way of nine muses in any way, shape or form.

70

Right. But what I'm saying—

It didn't affect my economic—my earning my living at all.

What I was getting at is that it eats up time, nine muses does, and may have affected what you—

No. It didn't. It doesn't affect it. I have to—it's my own time I have to use. Having a computer, though, has improved my earning my living.

Do you do some freelance work?

Yeah. I do freelance work with the computer. My experience of putting books together has improved my computer skills a lot, and I do sell those skills. I do layout for people, and things like that. So I suppose you could say it affects it that way.

I wasn't really getting at anything beyond the question. Now, nine muses publishes books. Before I turned on the recorder didn't we discuss the distinction between chapbooks and books? You said the difference was in length, right?

When I started researching it last year, that's what I came up with. Thirty-five pages or less is considered a chapbook. And I would say three or four of our books are chapbooks. I generally call them little books, but—I would say three or four of our books are small like that.

Do you do poetry exclusively?

Not in principle. But we've only done poetry.

How many books have you done?

Thirteen, maybe, at this point. Fourteen, fifteen, something like that.

Okay, I asked when you started nine muses. Now the question: when did you get involved with publishing

I would say I wasn't involved with publishing before nine muses.

Oh. All right. When you were in college, what did you study?
Philosophy and mathematics.

[Laughing.] Oh, sure. That leads right into publishing.
It leads right into poetry. I don't know about publishing. I do not consider myself primarily a publisher. I consider myself a poet. I don't know where you want to put that, but....

A lot of people I've interviewed—
Feel that way?

Yeah. Harald Wyndham—he has Blue Scarab Press in Pocatello—
That's a nice name—Blue Scarab. Well, you could say that I founded nine muses primarily for the purpose of publishing my own poetry. That was its original purpose.

Okay, so after thirteen or fourteen books you've done, how many are—?
Nine.

Nine were written by you?
Nine. Eleven? Twelve? Nine. Ten?

Most, anyway.
Most, yes. It started out almost entirely my work, and more and more people have become interested in my system. And so I have— that is to say, in 1993 I expect to add four new authors that I haven't done before.

What do you mean by your system? Your system of organization?
Of organization, right. Which is the collective aspect of it, the—I guess you could say artist-controlled books.

72

Okay. Let's get into that. What makes it a collective?

The primary thing is that the book—the physical, the aesthetic, the material aspects of the book are all designed and controlled by the author, and owned by the author. And the investment is made by the author.

When you say owned by the author, you mean the author has the copyright, or—?

The copyright and the books themselves. The physical books are paid for by the author and owned by the author.

Who pays for the printing?

The author.

Up front? Or does the author reimburse you?

Up front. No, no, I don't put any money out for anyone, for any books but my own. That's the system. The author owns—now, sometimes that money has to be borrowed. But the basic ownership—I mean, if the money is borrowed, it's borrowed by the author and owed by the author, so that the author owns the process.

The author does his or her own... well, the computerized version of typesetting? The author makes up the camera-ready copy?

Well, that's done cooperatively, and it varies. Usually, the author does the typeset and together we work on the layout.

The author uses your machine?

No, usually they use a compatible machine. And then when we get to layout, the layout is done on my machine. And we do that together. Where I put the labor in is in the layout. Illustrations and like that are done by conference. I've had help from other people besides the author. The author and I have gotten together with other people for finding illustrations. But the basic idea is that the physical book should be under the author's control in the same sense that the text is. That's the basic idea, that you extend the territory of the author from the text to the whole book.

Do you read everything that's sent you? Or that the author brings in?

No, we don't do it that way at all. If someone offers to send me a manuscript—someone I don't know, someone from somewhere other than Seattle—I send a letter explaining that nine muses is a collective, and how we do it, and suggesting that they go ahead and do it themselves that way.

But supposing it's somebody you do know, even somebody you've worked with in the past. They bring you a manuscript, right?

Well, no. I know the work before there's any question of my doing it. I know the person and the person's work way ahead of the suggestion that they have a nine muses book. And of the people that I work with, that I'm familiar with, whose work I'm familiar with, either I or the person might suggest that it might be time to do that. To get a nine muses book. The choices and the decisions about that are all mine. Those are not collective decisions. Those are my personal decisions. What book will be printed. That's completely and arbitrarily up to me. And I simply do it in terms of what I would like to do, given how much energy and strength I have.

Okay, the things that you control—you control the ISBN numbers, right? Those are yours.

Mm hmm. Those are mine. And which books are printed.

So the imprint itself, nine muses, is yours.

That's right. It's mine and mine only. I have a Washington state business license naming me the sole proprietor of that title.

Supposing you and the author have agreed that this book should be published under the nine muses imprint.

Mm hmm.

And as you're running it out, you see a line or a word that you disagree with for aesthetic reasons, or maybe you say, "This is grammatically incorrect," but you don't have any other grammatical incorrectnesses there, so it doesn't look like a matter of style—do you bring that up to the author?

If I see something in the process of my working with it that gives me any kind of a blip at all, any kind of a question, I'll mention it. I'll say, "What do you mean here?" or "I'm not sure what this means."

I don't look at a text with a critical eye, looking for errors. Usually the author will send a manuscript to another friend to have it gone over for things like that. I don't check for those things, but if I find something or if I'm typing away and I find something I can't type, I'll say so to the author. And usually, if there's anything in it, we'll discuss it. Authors vary a great deal in that. Some are very particular. One of my authors spent a great deal of time adding and subtracting commas. Very much more time than I would have thought appropriate. But in the end all of those added or subtracted commas made the book easy to understand. So usually I feel that the process that made the poems what they are is the same process that's going to make the book what it is.

In other words, there's not a standard that I try to meet. One author will be extremely careful about every detail and one author will not care at all. In an instance like that they will say "Oh, correct it for me." I tend not to do that.

Do you tell the author you're not going to do it?

Oh, yes. Oh, sure. But what I'm saying is, I tend to say no. But if he says "I've made a spelling error. Please correct it for me," then I'll go ahead and do that. Those things that are so much a matter of style— I will tend to be discouraging if an author says, "Do you think we ought to get this up into perfect grammar and put sentences and like that? Do you think it's necessary?" I'm inclined to say no. If the author feels it's necessary, then I can be quite a stickler. I can say "Here's one. Did you mean to leave.that one in or out?" But I tend to think that those things, just as style of dress and all of those other things, are part of the personality of the author, and that one book might be neat and another sloppy and that that would be appropriate.

I don't like to be sloppy in my technical product. I try to be very precise in that. Make sure that the books are trimmed perfectly and bound and that sort of thing, but not on the text.

Thus far, have you had all of your work manufactured here in Seattle?

Yes. That was one of the main reasons for coming to Seattle, because it seems to be so much easier to do that kind of work here than in the other places I've worked. Either larger cities or smaller ones.

When did you come to Seattle?
In 1987.

With the idea of setting up nine muses?
With the idea of publishing and performing my work.

Well, Seattle is known as a performance town. I didn't realize it was known as a—

Well, I knew that I wanted to follow the idea of using the same aesthetic to make the book as I did to make the poem. And the atmosphere of other people who are used to working with a free aesthetic as cooperative colleagues made a very big difference, one, in my ability to set it up in a practical way, and, two, in my having the freedom of imagination to go ahead and do it here the way I felt it should be done.

Did you know people here before you came here?

No. I knew a few people, but not people in the poetry scene. I came to Red Sky as soon as I came to town and my work was immediately appreciated by the people who were there. Of course, I was already in my fifties and had been writing for a long time. And so, when a person comes new to town but not new to poetry, it makes an impression more easily than someone who is new to poetry. You do notice talent even when it's not experienced. Then you have an experienced talent that's already developed quite a bit because I wrote for ten years in seclusion and had no public life.

This was down in Oregon?

Well, I traveled. For the last five years before I came to Seattle I was on the road. I was wintering in Hawaii, and spent spring, summer, and fall in California and Oregon and in the Southwest. Seldom East, but traveling East. But I lived in a nonliterary world. By choice. I had some opportunities, invitations, in the early '70s, but I found the...the book business, the making-poems business, the whole...the commercialism was very depressing and I felt that if I were in that atmosphere—I'm very sensitive to what's around me. I'm influenced by it easily, subliminally influenced. And I felt that if I were in an atmosphere of ambition and position, what I would write wouldn't be as good. That might not be true for someone else. Someone might be less sensitive to that sort of thing than I, so I don't want to imply it about anyone else. But for me, I could see that I wasn't going to be any good at all, that I would become preoccupied with things that were less worthy unless I stayed away from it. So I did, and I traveled and I lived a very private life, and wrote. And my writing was always with me and it was never obtrusive. Many, many people were my close friends and didn't know I wrote. And that was very satisfying until my writings accumulated into too many piles of paper. And then it was as if gestation was over and it was time for birth. So that's when I decided to come to Seattle.

I still travel a lot, but I have a base in Seattle. And I work from here. That was the thing—for writing I could work wherever I was. But when it involves the next step of making books and performing, then you need a base. You need a studio or work place. And I needed a place where I could work, but work as an artist and not as a businesswoman. And at that point it seemed very obvious that the only place in the world where I could get that would be Seattle. It was neither too hyped up on commercial success as the big cities are—the eastern cities and LA and all of those; even San Francisco wasn't fertile for me—it was neither that nor so completely apart from all those things—I mean there's a scene here, there's the company of people who are also actively engaged in things similar to what I'm engaged in, and a very small percentage of people who are actively engaged in making a career for themselves rather than studying an art.

I think that's the distinction I would make. It seems to me that if you're pursuing a career it takes away from pursuing an art.

If you're pursuing a literary career—

Pursuing an art and pursuing a career, whether it's literary or anything else—it's very hard to do them both. They're different pursuits. And if you're doing them both about the same work, well, I think it's very difficult and I won't say no one can do it, but I can't do it. And I wanted my art to improve.

But then after I came here I discovered that there was another art. Namely, the book maker's art that I was studying and learning. And that's the thing that I didn't understand until I came to do it. But that was what I was hoping for on some level, that I would be able to—

Consciously hoping for? Before you came here?

Yes. Hoping that I would be able to do what I wanted to do without turning away from the art orientation. At first I wasn't sure whether I was simply going to seek for a publisher or begin to publish. But then I realized that the time it would take to find the right publisher, the person who really would work for me, might be more time than going and doing it. And further, even if I did, if I found a publisher who wanted to publish my book, it still wouldn't come out looking the way I felt it needed to look. At which point I realized that I had to do it myself if I was going to get it to look the way I wanted it to look.

And this is partly why it ties in with performance. One of my ideas is eventually to have an audiotape version of every book, so that it's available performed as well as written. But it went further than that. It got to the point where I understood—I think maybe even at the beginning I felt this way, because I have a holistic kind of approach to everything—that to look at a poem on a page, the way it's set on the page, what drawings are there or not there, how much blank space

78

there is, the color of the page, the color of the ink, all of those things are a part of the experience that the person who's looking at the page gets, in very much the same way that a performance is an experience to someone in the audience.

That's really what I call the system of nine muses, to make a book from that point of view. Looking to the experience of the person. Reading it, rather than merely putting the information on the page and expecting the imagination of the reader to make the subtle suggestions.

Do you think that the other people published under the nine muses imprint approach it in the same—

Oh, yes. That's exactly why they want nine muses. That's just why they do. In the last year a number of people have decided that they prefer that to the possibly more prestigious form of a very standard, shiny-covered, perfect-bound book which is simply text-filled pages. And there is something prestigious, or at least possibly so, about that. This is a little more innovative, but as it's been around a few years more and more people see the value of it.

Another thing that I think is quite important in relation to poetry—I've talked with you about this before—is the binding. I intentionally make books that are not too thick—they usually run sixty or seventy pages—and they are staple-bound. We put a folded jacket that has a spine on it so that we have shelf recognition. But the book itself is staple-bound because it's sturdier. A novel—you pick up a novel and you read it again the following year. But poetry isn't read that way. Poetry is picked up and put down and thumbed through and looked for and put away. So it gets a rougher treatment. And the staple-bound books hold up under that, and very often perfect-bound books do not. So that's another reason.

And we don't usually have shiny covers. Because, again, we're talking about mood, we're talking about feeling. And this is one reason why I have kept poetry separate from prose in my mind and haven't really considered yet the question of how to do a prose book. I do have a prose book of my own, of stories, that really needs to be in print. And I've put off doing it because I'm just not sure how I would want it to look.

But with poetry, because a single poem is a single experience, if I understand the poem then I understand the impact that I want it to have. And so I'm able to know how I want the pages to look. But it's always done from the content, from the meaning. Looking for what that impact is, rather than to fit a form. And, of course, the number of pages the same way.

Usually when I write it's not so much a period of time—whether it's a year or three years wouldn't be a distinction, but there is some intrinsic content. A book will start and I'll be writing along and not thinking of anything but the immediate poem that I'm moved by at the time. But as I read an accumulation, there's...implicit like the statue in the marble, there's a book in there and you read them, read the poems over and over, and you look at them and you see the book. You begin to see the book. My other authors have found the same, and some of the reviewers or friends who've looked at them, they may be familiar with all the poems but when they see them together in a book, when they see that structure—and we work hard to detect it, because we do think it's intrinsic—and they see that, the poems laid out that way, they see a meaning that they didn't see before, even though they may be the person who wrote them. And that happens to me, too. But that seems—we find that every time. We go about it this way since we don't have a form. We go looking for the form and we discover a lot about the content that we didn't know. It makes it easier for people to read. So the books have an integrity also.

Let's back up again.
Okay.

You had an idea of self-publishing before you came to Seattle.
I was considering it as a possibility. I wasn't completely sure, at that point, whether I would try to send them out. But pretty quickly I realized that it wasn't going to make sense. I wasn't going to get the illustrations I wanted, and those things. I already had some of the illustrations together for some of the books.

80

Did you know, before coming to Seattle, other people who were self-publishing or who were involved with the small press scene?

Well, yes. Among my friends were a number of people who were poets, some of them quite well-known, who were involved in starting—Kitchen Table: Women of Color Press was started by Audre Lorde, who was a school friend of mine. They didn't publish her books. She was terribly well-known and Norton was her publisher for many years, but one of the things she did in the course of her life as a poet was to create publishing organizations. In the '70s a number of feminist presses were started by people I was acquainted with. And I guess the idea that you could do that yourself goes back farther than that. In the '50s and '60s in New York there were also people who were doing that. Even before there were computers there were people who—Diane di Prima did Poets' Press in the early '60s. And I was involved, not involved in the sense of doing any work, but involved in a personal way with those people. So I knew it could be done. But I didn't plan to write, and I didn't plan to publish.

"Planning is what you do while you're waiting for life to happen." John Lennon.

Well, I wasn't thinking that. I was thinking that the things you really have in you, you can't decide about. And I couldn't imagine choosing—but that also has to do with my personality which, as I said, is extremely sensitive to influence.

How did you get from mathematics and philosophy, which— okay, certainly they are related to poetry—

Well, the step is metaphysics.

I'm not talking about the subject matter. I'm talking about the life of studying mathematics and philosophy, apparently in a university environment—

Well, when you grow up you leave school. [Both laugh.] Well, let's say this. Let's say LSD.

Okay.

I think I was brought up to be an intellectual. I would distinguish between an intellectual and an artist in this context. Intellectuals live middle-class lives. Middle-class life was extremely uncomfortable to me all my life. It was the demon that was going to get me if I didn't escape. Since I am a writer and not a painter or a dancer or any of those other things, and intellectuals also use words, I didn't believe in my talent to the extent that I could say to myself, "I am an artist." I believed in my intelligence. I had no doubt about my ability to think. But what was buried inside me was hidden from me and I had no expectation that I would be able to access it. I didn't really know that it was there to access. I felt that I wished that I had a talent, not knowing at all that the hatred for middle-class life was really where my talent was hidden. Underneath. Because those things do get mixed up.

I would have said that I didn't write, though, in fact, many, many words poured from my pen in letters and in notebooks. I don't know that I would want to read those words now, and I'm sure no one else would. But it gave me the outlet that my self, that me that no one around me had any use for, my real self—I had children, I had a family and a family life, and everyone was very fond of me. But that was what they wanted. And the rest that was in me had to come out, and so it came out writing. But that that would turn into art was something I didn't really believe.

In the late '60s my children were half grown and my family and I came and lived on a commune in Oregon. And that took some of those burdens away from me. I was already writing but I hadn't—some of what I was writing was beginning to form itself into poems. Then I had a little more space to myself and that process continued. And the more I was free to discover myself, the more I discovered until—now, that was twenty-five years ago. So there's been time for me to allow it to be what it is, what it wants to be, and to try to get my skills to support it. I'm not sure what the thread was. What question were we answering?

I was curious as to how you went from philosophy and math, not the subject matter so much as the life style that would have surrounded that—

Well, I think that covers it then. I think I did cover it. Because, of course, it was the subject matter, not the life style, that was interesting to me.

But you deal with that in a very structured environment, which was anathema to you apparently.

No. It's not the intellectual structure that's anathema. It's the emotional structure of middle-class life. They don't really belong together. In my mind, it's the vitiation of the intelligentsia to live in a middle-class world. Because you organize things inside a box, you don't know anything. All you've done is organize things inside a box. And if you live that way, if your emotional investment is that, then you're not going to be able to be open-minded. And if you're not open-minded, then you're betraying your intellectual talent. That was my approach to it.

In college I was very well thought of by my teachers because I did have an original mind. But I could never get anyone to understand that an original mind comes from not putting those three-dimensional restrictions on it.

Like Anais Nin attracting the attention of Edmund Wilson who then wanted her to write like someone else.

Yes! Right! Right! Right! And because I was intelligent I had a good time in school and it would have been too easy to have stayed there. I feel very fortunate that that didn't happen, because...it's the ceiling. And a creative life can't tolerate those emotional ceilings.

Where did you go to school? What college did you go to?

I went to Williams College which at that time had only three women there. I was one of them. Before that I'd been to Hunter College and Connecticut College, and then was married. And so I went on and finished my work at Williams College, but they didn't matriculate me because I was a woman. At this present time they do matriculate women, but at that time they didn't have the charter for it.

But it did put me in an environment that was physically oriented to an intellectual approach. Not the people, I think. I was very naive about the real world in those days. I saw things a certain way. I saw the intellectual content. I saw the life of the mind. I assumed that those were everyone's motives. I really didn't understand how much venality there is in most people's motives and standards. I just took it for granted that these great ideas which were so exciting to me for their own sake would be exciting to anyone for their own sake. I didn't know the world was full of people who only look at things in terms of what can be gotten from them. What advantage. I just didn't really understand that. So, to me, philosophy and mathematics and metaphysics and poetry are in no way different.

Variations on a form.

Well, no. It's the content. No, what I'm saying is the content is what meant something to me. And I didn't realize that that wasn't true for everyone. So I wouldn't find, at any point, that mathematics and philosophy and poetry would seem different. Because the content is what I notice. And, as I say, I think it's the other way around. I think the restrictive life style limits the content you're willing to accept. You see that very often when people speak of poems. They will review back what they think the poem means, and it's always somehow tamed. You say to the world, "Open!" And it says, "In this tiny little box only, please."

Years ago I went to see the movie The Deer Hunter. *Parts of it had quite an emotional impact. I was a graduate student at the time and I went to see it with a friend who was on the faculty. During this very emotional part of the film I heard this...sound...near me. At first I couldn't figure out what that sound was. Then I saw that he was crying. The sound was these deep sobs that were coming from him. So after awhile the movie ended and we left and I asked him if he wanted to talk about the movie, get some coffee or something. He said he was in no condition to talk about it but he'd like to another time. So about a week later I looked him up and asked if he wanted to talk about the movie now.*

And he said in a very offhand way, "Oh, okay." And he started going into the movie's symbolism in this very detached, abstract—I felt as though I had been cheated.

Yes. Yes. Yes. Yes. This is what Sartre calls "bad faith." In my education this was one of the main things—this is the sin of the middle class, to...to...to do exactly that. To deny the personal and speak not what you mean but what you choose to hold as an opinion.

What you choose to hold as an opinion.

Well, those aren't the best words, but it's like somehow we believe, Europeans and Americans, that what we feel is irrelevant. And I think this is false and vicious.

Well, not "somehow." We're trained that way. That's how schools train us to be.

Ah, now we're getting to politics. The old system of seeing who benefits. And, you know, you go back to John Dewey and Maria Montessori and the battle to determine who was going to dictate the system for how schools would be organized. And Maria Montessori lived with a man that she wasn't married to, and so John Dewey managed to discredit her. But underneath the benefit of routine to rote-minded citizens taught that reality consists of a subject, a verb and an object, that *reality* consists of this, there's an advantage to this, a political advantage to people who care about population control. There is that.

But that runs pretty far afield from how you become a publisher. Maybe not from why. When I was living in the commune, when I first lived alone after my children were old enough to live a little apart from me, I had my own little house and I spent a great deal of time teaching myself to write, in the sense of improving my ability to use words to serve what I felt. And one of the first things I discovered was that I had been very badly conditioned into thinking in terms of a subject, a verb and an object. And that reality wasn't like that at all, but it was how I was taught to use sentences, and that sentences didn't have to be that way at all. I spent a couple of years doing that, going through everything that was in my mind.

I think, from a writer's point of view, it has to do with slowing down between words. Because we hold not words but phrases in our minds and they always go together. And when you're writing along and you slow down between them and stop, and you realize that it's a cliché in your mind, and you break it and think more carefully and find exactly what you mean instead of the convenient cliché that's almost what you mean, and if you do that long enough, then you become an original thinker instead of a cliché-thinker. And I think that's really what the commune did for me. It clarified my language habits for me and showed me how to look further and find more exactly what I meant.

Was this something that people in the commune helped you to do, or—?

No. No. In no way. I was able. I mean I no longer had so many other duties that I had no time. And I could live to myself. So that was really my first—I mean, even though I was nearly forty, it was really like getting out of high school and living by yourself and being free to have your own thoughts for the first time.

Did you regard going to the commune with your children as a courageous act? Have you thought in terms of courage?

No. No. I didn't think in terms of courage. I think, looking at it now, you can say that I'm a person with a lot of courage of that kind. But I think that kind of courage, if you have it, you don't think of it as courage. And also, I mean, you don't have any choice. Because you're driven. You need something. Something is uncomfortable to you. For me, it would have taken a great deal more courage to be a schoolteacher. You know what I'm saying?

Yes, I do. I knew a woman quite a few years ago who had to make the decision whether to leave her husband or not. And did. But then went back to him. I don't know what would have been the more courageous thing, but certainly she was suffering. She was just in a situation where she was going to suffer no matter what she did. Just a different type of suffering.

Oh, yeah. I understand that. Well, I would say that certainly does take courage, to do that. But I didn't leave my husband at that time. I took him with me. I mean he, possibly, would not have had the imagination or the courage to think of leaving the protection of the life we were in. But he was very happy to come along. We all came together, all five of us. Three children. It's not that I left the family. That, I think, would have taken more courage than I would have had.

I wasn't using her example as a parallel to your—

No, no. I understand. But later on I understand that, because it does take—to be alone, after being with a family, does take a lot of courage. But what I was saying is, I don't think you necessarily think of it as courage at the time, if you have it. If you don't, then sometimes you see that that's what it is. And I had it at that point because I was driven. Because I had a need leading me forward.

This discomfort you felt, if that's the right word, with middle-class life—did you say earlier that you'd always had that discomfort?

Yes.

As far back as you can remember.

Yes. And I didn't live on a street in a house in the suburbs or anything like that. I stayed in New York City and.... So it wasn't so terribly middle-class. I mean, as I said, it wasn't a suburb and it wasn't a very small, narrow-minded neighborhood. But it still was a little more constricted than I wanted to be. I was always reaching, stretching, trying to get out of it. And then, of course, in the '60s when marijuana and LSD—they had a lot to do with freeing my mind from...the expectations.... I think, what I was saying before about a sentence being a subject, a verb and an object, and this being our notion of what reality is—a lot of time people.... If you have a limited framework, it's hard to think your way out of it. Sometimes you have to stretch your mind to see beyond it. It takes an act of imagination, and if there are too many assumptions you don't know that they are assumptions. So you can't overthrow them. And I think that the '60s, the whole psychedelic framework, did a lot of that for me. It enabled me to see through what otherwise looked like opaque walls that I didn't know I could knock down. But I did feel very constricted.

When I came West, that made a big difference. Last summer at Bumbershoot June Jordan was talking about moving from New York to Berkeley. It was the same thing. She said, "Before, I was assuming that everything would always fail, that I had to go on anyway. Now I realize that everything is open." She was describing that as a difference between East and West Coast.

Do you think that's true?
I think it's true that there is that difference. The closed situation is assumed in the East because it is so much more crowded, so much fuller. You really have to push a lot to find a place in a room that's so full of structure already. Out here there's more space. And I think there's more of an assumption that things are open and things can change and things are different. There's always a new way and you can always tear away an old form and put up a new one. I think that is a West Coast, more than an East Coast, thing.

I had to leave the country. I had to get out of the country.
I can understand that. I did that too, in 1966. Where did you go?

Samoa.
For long?

A year.
Yeah. Then you know what I'm talking about.

Yeah. Even now, little trips, just to Canada, are a big help. But I could not have got into publishing, small press publishing, had I not gone to Samoa. It would never have occurred to me.
What would you have done, do you think?

88

I don't know. I was studying for an academic career. In retrospect, I don't think I would have had an academic career. I finished my degree, but I never applied for an academic job. But I don't think I ever would have been hired, had I applied.

You were an anthropologist.

Yeah. I did my field research in Samoa. And while I was there other things happened.

Okay. I understand. Yes. Yes. Salvation. Right. You were saved from an intellectual's life.

Yeah. Not from intellect, but from an intellectual's life. What did your parents do? What was their life style?

My father worked for a newspaper and my mother was a schoolteacher. They were both involved in their separate fields, of unionizing their separate fields on the principle of—there was a great, strong movement in those days to operate, to manipulate by snobbery, with the implication that professionals and intellectual workers were not workers. Though they were badly paid, they weren't to be unionized. My father was very instrumental in forming the Newspaper Guild in New York. That was in the '30s. And my mother, twenty years later, in the '50s, the New York Teachers Federation.

Was your father a reporter or an editor or—?

He was a sports reporter. So there is that literary quality. My intellectual style is my father's. He was not very much educated. But he was intrinsically an intellectual. If his circumstances had allowed, he probably would have been something like a history teacher. But his circumstances didn't allow for that, and he was a sports reporter. Later, at the very end, he wrote a column very much like Herb Caen's column, but for the Bronx.

What did your mother teach?

French. And later music. Music was the most important influence in her life.

If we human beings are made up of environmental and genetic influences, and if you always felt uncomfortable with a middle-class life style, do you feel comfortable in saying that you are genetically predisposed to dump a middle-class life style? [Both laugh.]

No. I consider that totally moot. No, that's a made-up question. No, that's not real.

What would be a real question?

I'm really not sure what it was you wanted to know there.

Okay. As far back as you can recall you felt uncomfortable— where does this discomfort come from? You're not the only person to feel this discomfort.

Well, I think the discomfort is there because the thing is uncomfortable. I think it's anti-ecological, the society we have.

But not everybody feels that discomfort. Some people, whether they're trained to it or not—

Right. No, that's the thing. We're all different. I think, though, that drinking bad water is bad for everyone. But not everyone notices it. I think that many people don't notice what they eat, but it affects them. But they don't care. People—what matters is what they care about. And why I care? I don't know. You have to get into individual psychology, too, but I'm not sure that defines it all.

One of my sisters takes a great deal of refuge in middle-class life. It's very important to her. And the other one is perfectly comfortable in it. But she is not...prevented. She doesn't take repression. It doesn't work on her. So it doesn't affect her the same way it affects me. So she doesn't have to overthrow it, because it doesn't hurt her. Now my other sister brings those walls in around her because she needs them.

So I don't know about that. I think there are metaphysical things which are sort of genetic. But I don't know about—

But your metaphor about bad water is bad for everybody but some people can tolerate it, some people don't know that it's bad for them—

Right. But I don't know that middle-class life is bad for everybody. It may be bad for the world, but it may not be bad for everyone in it. There are complacencies, and there are so many different values and needs people have. I don't think that my make-up leads me to be in the center of the bell-shaped curve. I don't think I'm average. I used to think that. I used to think, Well, isn't everybody this way? But I think I'm a little unusual, the way I'm affected by things.

Do you think this self-knowledge, or whatever it took to see through boundaries, is owing to your experience with LSD? Or did I misinterpret what you said?

No, I think that's right. The ability to break through the boundaries was very much helped by LSD and marijuana. The need to break through was probably intrinsic to me.

What are your hopes for nine muses? It's apparently changed from what you originally—you started out by using it to publish your own work, and now you're publishing other people's work. Do you see any changes for the future?

Well, no. There was always the possibility of other people doing the same as what I was doing. And it seems as if more and more people are finding that attractive. I think there's a limit to how many people I can work with directly. But, as I told you before, when people I don't know approach me, I suggest that they consider starting such a collective. I will say that having a collective to do it, rather than being simply self-published, takes care of a lot of little difficulties that people have. Because we live in a society where results, money, acknowledgment, recognition, are important things. And artists don't get acknowledgment, recognition, because they are, in a sense, outside of the structure that it happens in. And so the idea of self-publishing is all too mixed up, for many people, with the idea of vanity publishing where the implication is that the thing has no value and that nobody but the person who created it would want to see it in print. And nine muses takes care of some of that.

People want to be published for these reasons, recognition and so on, and in order to be published they will do whatever it takes, and then their books are not their own. This way your books can be your own. And yet these are serious artists. We don't do anything remotely like vanity publishing. Of course, I'm not making any profit either, so I'm not in the business of selling ego to people. Which is what vanity publishing can be. I mean a person makes money by putting out a book, whether it's a printer or a so-called publisher or whatever it is. This isn't working like that. But for the people involved, there isn't so much of a stigma working with a collective. That is something people understand.

So that's what I try to do, is to suggest that someone who is interested should try having a collective of their own. You can collectively own equipment that you maybe can't individually afford, and things like that. And I think that might happen. But I have nothing to gain or lose either in my mind or in reality by that happening.

I think nine muses will be more known than it is. Many of the previous generations' innovations are now standard. People want to go to City Lights, but when they started City Lights they didn't go to City Lights; they just created it. If I want to see anything in the world, it's more people creating what they need rather than imitating what I've created. What I hope to do is to put out audiotapes to go along with the books. That would be my mission, is to be able to have one's tapes available and not just books. That was my vision at the beginning. To see a bunch of books and tapes side by side. You could buy this book, you could buy the performance of this book.

I've asked all the questions I have. Is there anything you want to—?

Okay.

Tim Lander
Nanaimo Publishers Cooperative

"I sell hundreds. I get rid of hundreds. I give a lot away too. But I publish as cheaply as I can. I'm not in the business of making books, I'm in the business of publishing poetry."

In the 1930s Tim Lander's father was a tea planter in Ceylon when the company that employed him went bankrupt. Returning to England on ship, he met the woman he would marry. She was returning from Australia where she had escorted a group of children from the London slums who were slated to work on Australian farms. In England, her father offered him a job, which he accepted, and he worked for his father-in-law until the Second World War. He died in the war.

Raised in London, the middle one of three children, Tim Lander went into the army after his schooling.

I spent eighteen months in Malaya. I was in the engineers. It was at the end of the Emergency. I was there when Malaya got its independence. The British troops stayed on there. They had to. There was the war with Indonesia after that. After I left. After the Independence, Malaya became the Federated States of Malaysia. At first Singapore and Borneo, the British colony of Borneo, federated with Malaya. And Indonesia rules most of the island of Borneo and it wanted the Malaysians out. They wanted the whole island. It went on until Sukarno fell. This happened in the '60s. It was after I left. When I was there, it was pretty peaceful.

I had an interesting job digging up bombs from the Japanese period. It was more like archeology than bomb disposal. It was quite interesting. These bombs were stored in caves, and the roofs of the caves had fallen in so we had to dig down through the top and then haul the bombs out, take them into the jungle and blow them up.

Following military service, Lander attended a year of teachers college, taking courses in geology, biology and chemistry, and worked as a lab technician at the London Zoo. In 1964 he took a boat to Montreal from England, went to California—"I just got claustrophobia in London. Got fed up with it. Traveling across London to work. And there was this girl that I met who lived in California. I went down to visit her but nothing came of it"—and then went up to British Columbia which he had heard about from a friend who had worked in the mines in Cassiar. Lander currently lives in Nanaimo, "halfway up Vancouver Island. You take a ferry from Horseshoe Bay."

We originally met at a book fair in Vancouver in the spring of 1991. I was displaying a novel, The Confession of Jack Straw *by Simone Zelitch, that he was taken with. He would walk around to the other tables but he kept coming back to that book. At last I offered an exchange: a copy of* Jack Straw *for some of his poetry. And so we met. He is tall and stands very straight with hardly any curve to his back. His hair is thick and gray and he usually ties it back behind his head. He sports a gray beard and metal-framed glasses.*

The interview was conducted on September 4, 1993, beginning a little before ten in the morning at Bumbershoot on a gray, overcast day. We were out of doors, sitting near one of the gates because he did not have the money to buy an entry ticket and I did not have the money to buy one for him. The morning air had that feathery heaviness that portended later warmth. In the background a bus made a terrible roaring noise that would subside briefly, then start up again.

So from 1964, when you came to Canada.... For the last twenty-nine years, what have you been doing?

Oh, I've done a few different jobs and written a lot of poetry. I lived for twenty years with a woman who had schizophrenia. We had

94

a couple of kids.

She had schizophrenia?
Yeah. It ended up, I was sort of the adult of the family. And so we ended up on welfare. And I was the responsible adult. In the end that just got to be too much for me.

When did the end of that come?
About a year ago.

Oh, that recently?
Yeah. Or two years ago.

So you've been on welfare for the last twenty years?
Well, I drove a bus for the hospital for a while. In Nanaimo. I did a few odd jobs. And then we ended up on welfare because of the family situation.

That absorbed all your time?
Well, yeah. It certainly absorbed all my energy.

What became of her, do you know?
She's actually living in the house that we bought. I have two kids. My youngest kid's going to college in September. My oldest.... I think I made the right choice, because if I hadn't the kids would have gone—I don't know what would have happened. The family would have broken up.

Are you still on welfare since you split up with your wife? Were you married?
No, we weren't married.

Well, since you split up—
Yeah, I am actually still on welfare. That shouldn't appear in the book though. Preferably. I want to get off. [Lander later changed

his mind, and asked that these lines not be expunged from the interview.]

Okay.
But it's a real trap.

How so?
Well, they're pretty good in Canada. They give you lots of money. But it ends up that most of the money goes into the pocket of the landlord.

Because of high rents?
High rents. And they know that they can keep the rents up because the welfare pays it. The rents are really high. Yeah, I've got a lot of feelings and thoughts about welfare.

Go ahead and say it. If you want to.
No, I'd have to write it down. Work it out.

Do you regard yourself as idealistic?
Well, I have a certain... I have an idealistic streak. But I'm also lazy and greedy and all the other things.

Do you regard yourself as spiritual?
Not in the way that spiritual people regard themselves as spiritual. No, I don't, actually.

You write a lot about love. But you're not sentimental about it. You write about things that transcend.
Yeah.

That's what I mean by spiritual.
Yeah. But I'm also sort of matter-of-fact, and I don't enter deeply into my own spirituality in my writing. I'm not good at that. I don't think I'm any more spiritual than anybody else. There are two

96

ways of looking at poetry. One of them is to look at the poet as a shaman. And the other is to look at him in the medieval way as Everyman, or Everyperson. And I see the poet as Everyman. I see the poet as the representative of the human condition, no better, no worse, and very often no more perceptive.

Then why is that person a poet?
Because he writes. Because he puts into language what is ineffable. That's a lovely word. That means that you can't find words for it. I looked that word up in the dictionary and I found ineffable means you can't find words for it. And it's a beautiful word, you know? You've had this ineffable experience; it means you can't find words for it. But it's a poet's job to look for words, to push back the frontiers of the inarticulate. Raid constant raids on the inarticulate with shoddy equipment always deteriorating. That's what Eliot said in the *Four Quartets*. I love that symbol because he wrote that at the beginning of the war and he was taking the image from the lot of the British army which was poorly equipped at the time.

I guess we can say you self-publish. You make up these small books of your own poetry.
Yeah.

How do you sell those?
I sell them on the street. People I meet.

Literally on the street? You just walk up to people on the street?
Yeah.

In downtown Vancouver?
Vancouver and Victoria. Yeah. I've been doing a lot this year. I kind of got burned out by it. Just recently I got fed up with being on the street the whole time.

Do you go from door to door in the residential areas, or just

downtown areas?
Yeah, downtown areas.

How many do you sell that way? Of a particular title, how many do you sell?
I sell hundreds. I get rid of hundreds. I give a lot away too. But I publish as cheaply as I can. I'm not in the business of making books, I'm in the business of publishing poetry.

We probably ought to describe one of your books. It's bound by thread. Hand-sewn.
It's a sheet of eight-and-a-half-by-fourteen, folded twice. Well, there's usually three sheets, or maybe four sheets of eight-and-a-half-by-fourteen, folded twice and then hand-sewn, saddle-stitch.

The paper itself: is that copy paper or bond paper?
Yeah. Cheap. Cheap paper.

It's hand-written, right? It's done in ink.
Yeah. Usually.

Have you ever gone, or tried to go, a more traditional route in publishing?
I did one book, that I edited, of poems by people up and down the coast. And I hand-sewed that in signatures. Six signatures. About an eighty-page book.

Were you the publisher of that one?
Yeah, I was the publisher of that. It was done on a computer. Typeset on a computer. But I didn't do that. I don't have a computer and I don't have skills to do that. It looks like a pretty normal book.

What imprint did it come out under?
The Nanaimo Publishers Cooperative.

Is that you?
Yeah. And a few friends.

How did you sell that one? The same way?
I sold a few to bookstores. But not very many. Yeah, mainly to people I met. And through the contributors.

Was it your idea to do it that way?
Yeah. It works out very cheaply. It's the only way that someone like me can afford to publish a book. The economics work out very well because I get them printed in batches of a hundred. It comes to about a thousand sheets of paper that I fold by hand, maybe ten at a time, and then sew maybe ten at a time.

Has anybody that you sold one to on the street, or gave one away to on the street, ever got in touch with you later, for any reason?
Yeah. Yeah, I had a post card from Kenya, actually. A guy I sold one to—he gave me a ride from the ferry into Vancouver. He was going as a missionary to Kenya. And he sent me a post card.

Is there any reason other than economics that you prefer to publish this way?
Well, then you have complete control over what you do. I don't think that poetry should—like when you look at the cost of a book, you're looking at the cost of the printing, not of the poetry. It makes it very hard for poets. It's made a book of poetry into an expensive item. I wouldn't go out and buy a book of poems. Not very often. And I don't like that. I'm really enthusiastic about poetry and about publishing it. I'm very enthusiastic about self-publishing.

When did you start self-publishing?
About twenty years ago. I was in Edmonton then. Actually it was longer than that. It was about twenty-two years ago.

What were you doing in Edmonton?

Well, when I was in Edmonton I'd just been tree planting. I'd made some money tree planting. I was staying with friends up there. I had worked at the university library there before, and I'd worked as a baker. I went to college in Edmonton. I took a bunch of Oriental studies and English and German. I was very interested in Middle English literature. In Chaucer and William Langland, particularly. He was a hippie poet who lived at the same time as Chaucer. He wrote a book called *Piers Plowman*. Yeah. He was a typical hippie. He wrote this one poem and he spent the rest of his life improving it. He was a great big, tall guy. They called him Long Will of Ludgate Hill. I think I sort of empathize with him because he was a big, tall guy. And he talks about that in his poem. Talks about his tallness, this long, thin guy.

I worked for a year at the university library there. Then I went down to Nelson, in the Kootenays. That's sort of southeast British Columbia. It's sort of an interlinked bunch of lakes, long, narrow lakes and mountains. It's very pretty country. It's very similar to the country where I was brought up in England. During the war we went up to the northwest of England, to the Lake District.

To get out of the city?
Yeah. Out of London. There were the same long, glaciated valleys.

Do you miss it?
Well, I don't miss London, you know.

Do you publish, or have you published, anything other than poetry?
There's a journal entry that I've just published called *A Day in the Life of a Street Poet*. I started off writing a story halfway through the day. They tried to throw me off this place where I was going to sell my poems and I had a bit of a confrontation with the law. So I went to McDonnell's and wrote it down. Just in my journal, for my own purpose. And I went out of McDonnell's and about half an hour later this other incredible experience happened on the street. Well, I went

up to a crowd of teenagers and tried to sell them a poem. You know, "Want to buy a poem for a penny?" And this beautiful girl screamed at me, "Fuck off! Get the fuck out of here!" So I went off, pretty shaken. And then I was standing on the street, playing my flute, and along come all these teenagers and she bends down and picks up my hat.

The same girl?

Yeah. And she walks off down the street. There's a few pennies in it. I hadn't made any money since McDonnell's and I was just thinking, What's going to happen? I was just standing there, playing my flute. I didn't know what else to do. She got about fifty yards down the street and she turned around and said, "You want it? Come and get it." So I carry my flute down and just get to her, I don't know what's going to happen, and she lifts up the hat, like in ritual benediction, and says, "God be with you."

She said that?

Yeah. And I bowed and I said, "With you, too." And took the hat. It blew my mind. So I wrote it down and I published it.

When did this happen?
Oh, a couple of months ago.

You're also a street musician then?

Yeah, I got fed up with selling poems and people saying "No, no" every different way they say no. I play the flute a bit. I found it easier on my head to play the flute. I kind of got burned out with selling poems. I was doing it every weekend this year.

What were you doing during the week?
I'd go home and look after my kid.

Is that the same house where their mother is?

Well, my kid and I live in an apartment together. He's eighteen. He's going to college this year. But he still likes having me around.

101

Are you eligible to apply for grants for your writing or your publishing?

Well, the Canada Council doesn't like self-publishers. They don't recognize that as publishing. I have a couple of books that I did with—Ed Varney did one back in the early '70s. The book was called *Meditations of Caliban*. So that's enough to get me in. I am recognized by the Canada Council, but barely.

Because you published somewhere else.
Yeah.

You said you published two books with somebody else?

I published that one and before that I published some chapbooks with Tree Frog of Edmonton.

So the Canada Council, you say, barely recognizes you. Do you get any benefit by their recognizing you at all?

Sometimes—about once a year or so—I get a reading. I get two hundred dollars for it. And then they used to have a National Book Week, which they canceled. I used to—

They canceled that? When did they cancel it?
This year was the last year.

Why did they cancel it, do you know?

I don't know. It seemed to be the best thing they were doing for the publishers and writers. But now it's all just big star—it's going to be a big-star deal and a star thing. Which I think is just disgusting. I basically take a very democratic view of poetry. I think that poetry really belongs to the people. Everybody writes poetry. Part of what we do as a verbal species is make poetry.

You mentioned Eliot and Pound and alluded to some of the more classical writers and poets. They were not populists. Eliot and Pound were definitely not—well, Pound wrote as though he was, but he wasn't.

102

I think Eliot was more populist than Pound.

Eliot was very aristocratic, or liked to think of himself that way.
Yeah, but I was living in London when I read *The Wasteland*, and *The Wasteland* is the most incredible poem about London! He's got that place down to a tee! It's a fantastic—and all the smells and the feel of the place!

But that doesn't make him a people's poet.
Well, Eliot was a very strange person, because he had a lousy life. Eliot had the same problem as I did. Or I had the same problem as Eliot did. He lived for a long time with a woman who was crazy. And this really influenced his life. It affected his life. I think to be a populist poet—like people say "I'm going to be a populist poet," but that doesn't make them a populist poet. I think Eliot's a populist poet because you can understand him. He gives you things that you can hang onto and you can understand.

Not only through his meter and his choice of words, but because of his metaphors. They're metaphors that are recognizable—
Yeah, yeah, yeah. Though a lot of them are somewhat dated now. You know, when he says in one of the *Four Quartets*—like he meets his double "in a dead patrol between three districts where the smoke arose." A "dead patrol" is a patrol during an air raid. And he's talking about the air raid. He used to work as an air raid warden in the war and he's talking about that experience. You know, it completely goes over your head.

Actually, I knew that when you mentioned it because I'd read Graham Greene who was also an air raid warden for a time.
But would you say he was a populist? He was an incredibly popular writer. Like who would be a populist poet? Auden? Auden has aged worse than Eliot.

I can't think of any.

Dylan Thomas maybe. But he would be populist because he worked in a populist medium—radio.

In the United States we have cowboy poets. By definition they're populist. I guess I'd say they're more folk than populist. But I think that's what populism is—it's something that appeals to the folk aspect of society. Who would be the poet of the folk element of English society? Is there one?
Well, there'd be Robbie Burns.

That was a long time ago though.
But the folk element is a rural element. Very much a country element.

Right. Or the working class in the cities.
Yeah, but that's a very different voice.

Right. Yeah, you wouldn't have the same voice for both. Do you read contemporary poetry? Do you read anything but poetry? Well, you read Jack Straw.
Yeah. I like reading history. I read a certain amount of contemporary poetry. I don't read as much as I should, I don't think. I go to quite a few poetry readings. Most of my contemporary poetry I get through listening to it rather than reading it.

You don't draw on contemporary poets for inspiration though, or do you?
Well, I think a lot of what they say winds its way into my poetry. Yeah, I think I do draw on it for inspiration. I really like open mikes. I tell you this: I really like open mikes and I really don't like poetry slams.

You know, I've never been to a poetry slam. I don't really know what that is.
Well, the first thing is they set up this atmosphere of competi-

tion, and they've got very brash. Like in an open mike there's a feeling of respect, like everybody respects everybody else's work. But in a poetry slam that doesn't exist. You get a completely different atmosphere.

Are there judges for a poetry slam, or does the audience judge?
Well, there're judges or the audience judges. And it is a competition.

There's something to be won?
Yeah, sometimes there's something to be won, and always there's prestige to be won. That's always very dangerous.

Dangerous? In what way?
Well, this whole prestige thing in poetry is dangerous. And the poems that win are always the poems that can get a quick laugh.

I see. Appealing to the common denominator.
Yeah. And to the quick reaction of the common denominator. They're not the kind of poems that you go away and then you realize afterwards that you've heard something really good. It's not so much the common denominator, it's the quick reaction.

Have you always been so democratic or egalitarian in your view of poetry?
Yeah, I think so.

Did you read poetry as a child?
I think my father used to read it to us. Like when we were very young. I think he used to do a lot of that. And then when I was a kid at school we used to read it. I've always enjoyed reading aloud. It's always been very important to me, reading aloud. I think poetry really exists when it is read aloud. And that's why I'm so down on poetry slams. 'Cause they're really attacking it at the root.

105

Do you still read Chaucer and Shakespeare?

Yeah. Right now in my bag I've got, not Chaucer, but....Chaucer lived in a very interesting time. There was a real golden age in English literature. These are contemporaries of Chaucer. Sir Gowan and the Green Knight and.... If you read them in academic books, they seem to have been written by one poet. But if you read them with any poetic sensibility, you realize that they're written by four different people. You know, they've got a completely different way of looking at language and at life. I kind of like the texture of the language of Middle English. Once you get the hang of how to read it, it's not really difficult. In some ways it's easier than Shakespeare, because Shakespeare has such a wide vocabulary. There's a lot of wit in Shakespeare that's very hard to catch.

Do you have any expectations about what you'll be doing or where you'll be ten years from now?

No.

Five years from now?

I'll probably be hanging around the coast here, doing the same thing. I don't think I'll have made it in the big time.

Did you ever have the hope of making it in the big time? Did you ever want to?

Yeah, but then I wonder what the big time is.

What would it have been? When you fantasized about the big time, what would it have been for you then?

I would be able to travel to readings in Toronto or New York or, you know, people sending me air tickets. I'd rather have a life.

Ruth Gundle
The Eighth Mountain Press

"I either had to publish some kind of nonfiction book that I could sell to a broad audience or I had to go nonprofit and apply for grants. And I didn't want to become a nonprofit. I didn't want to be in a position of charming and beseeching people for money. And my press is a feminist press. Many of the books are lesbian in content or by lesbian authors. And, you know, political tides come and go as to what's considered acceptable or within the bounds of literary whatever, and I just didn't want to get involved in that."

I interviewed Ruth Gundle, owner and publisher of The Eighth Mountain Press, in her office in the upper story of her house in southeast Portland at a little after one in the afternoon on April 1, 1993. She was still decompressing after an unexpectedly busy morning. A few hours earlier a freight company had delivered a shipment of books only minutes after its representative had told her the books would not arrive until the following day. She had been on her way out to talk with the people who do her color work when she saw the truck, so she had had to postpone the meeting until the next day. It was raining when the books arrived, packed in cardboard cartons, and she was alone, so she went down to the corner where there is a home for retarded people and got several of the residents to help her with the books. They worked very slowly but they were fast enough to keep the books from being destroyed.

I was born in Augusta, Georgia. My father was at Camp Gordon right after the war. He was a medical doctor. He was in charge of the German prisoners of war. He was a German Jewish refugee and got drafted. And that's what they had him do because they didn't want to send him overseas. They put him where they could use his language, and my dad was a doctor, so they had him taking care of the German soldiers. We left shortly after I was born. I wasn't raised there.

Where were you raised then?
In Kansas.

How did you get out here?
My sister came out here to go to Reed in, I guess about 1968, and stayed. It was probably related to the fact that she was here that I ended up here. I came out to visit her several times. And then my brother moved to Seattle. He's a psychoanalyst.

I've lived here since the mid-'70s. I went to law school, actually, in the East. I came out here and started practicing law and then decided I wanted to do something else. I kind of fell into publishing. I also started doing letterpress work and did a broadside. And I had decided to do a letterpress poetry chapbook and then at the last minute decided to do it as a trade paperback. And from then on one thing led to another.

How did you "kind of fall into publishing"?
Oh, that's just, you know, one of those things that you can't explain. I don't know. Why did I go to law school? Those sorts of questions.... I was planning to leave my job. I was the litigation director for the Oregon Legal Services Corporation. That's the poverty law program. I planned to leave well ahead of the time that I actually left. I couldn't just leave overnight, obviously. So there was a period of time when I knew that I was leaving and was thinking about what I was going to do next, and I thought that I would take a year off and see what else life had to offer. And I've just always been interested in books. And I decided to take a course on letterpress printing, which I knew nothing about, at the Oregon School of Arts and Crafts. I was doing it really just for my own amusement. One evening a week, I think it met.

I started doing that, actually, while I was still working. And I really loved it and took another course and then rented this studio space and did some of my own work and...I don't know...I think of it as wanting to get back to my art past—I majored in art in college and then went to law school. You know, by law school and working as a lawyer for ten years, I was a good fifteen years out of college and hadn't done anything that was even dimly related to my art past, if you want to call it that. And it was something new, it was something I was just interested in and didn't seem...I don't know, I didn't think of it as leading to anything. It was really just that I was interested. I did some engravings and little woodcuts and things. I actually did some really nice broadsides and would love to be doing them again if I had the time or if I had a letterpress.

But, I mean, it's hopeless. I work here every day, all day. Evenings, if I'm not exhausted.

Was that first broadside one of your own? Something you had written?

No, I'm not a writer. But the first book I did was my partner's book. Judith Barrington. It would have been a chapbook, a letterpress-printed book. And then I decided to do it as a trade paperback [titled *Trying To Be an Honest Woman*].

Why did you make that decision?

Well, at the time I didn't really necessarily commit myself to being a publisher. I was just doing that one book. You know, I was in an interim stage. I had left my job and I was taking some time off. I had time to do it. I knew quite a bit about publishing from friends who were publishers. I had, coincidentally, three friends who were publishers— Barbara Wilson at Seal, Judith McDaniel who used to own Spinster's Ink, and Lillian Mohin who was the publisher, and still is, of Onlywomen, in London. So through knowing the three of them, I knew a little bit about publishing. And just thought I would give it a try. Just doing that one book though. And once I did that book I got pulled into things. And then the next book I did was a book of Barbara Wilson's called *Cows and Horses*. And that book was very, very successful. Judith's book was very successful for a poetry book, but, you know, in small numbers. *Cows and Horses* sold really, really well. It's sold over ten thousand so far.

The first book was published in the fall of 1985. *Cows and Horses* was published in 1988. So I didn't do anything in between, but thought about it and piddled around. And I helped out at Seal during a time when Barbara was in England and Faith [Faith Conlon, copublisher with Barbara Wilson of Seal Press] was sick. It was about six months in the fall of '87. Maybe it was the fall of '86. To tell you the truth, I'm not sure now. Right around then.

Shortly after that, I did *Cows and Horses*. And once *Cows and Horses* started really selling I got hooked and started thinking of myself as a publisher and started looking around for books. So the next book I did was a second book of Judith's, *History and Geography*. And then the next book I did was the first book of The Eighth Mountain Poetry Prize which was launched in '88.

An anonymous donor puts up five thousand dollars a year and we do a nationwide announcement. We get about five hundred manuscripts and hire a judge of national reputation to judge it. The author of the winning manuscript gets a thousand dollars advance against royalties. We're now on our fourth one. I was trying to get my cover to the lab when Consolidated Freightways arrived.

This is an annual prize?

It's been annual thus far. It has become clear to me that it's way too much work to do annually. And so now it's biennial. So now we're just doing it in even years. We'll read manuscripts one year and publish the book the following year. Even with the donation of five thousand dollars, you know, it's a labor of love. The prize is pretty well known now. We've gotten excellent reviews for the first four, and a very nice write-up of the prize series itself in *The Nation* which was very enthusiastic about it. It's one of only two poetry prizes in this country that are for women only. The other one is the Barnard New Women Poets series.

So we started with *Trying To Be an Honest Woman*, then *Cows*

110

and Horses, then History and Geography, which was Judith's second book, then the first of the poetry prize series which was *The Eating Hill* by Karen Mitchell, which Audre Lorde picked. And then I published two books of fiction by Anna Livia who was a British author but was now living in the States. And then somewhere in there I published an anthology that Judith edited, called *An Intimate Wilderness: Lesbian Writers on Sexuality*. And every year I publish the winner of the poetry prize. When the one that's at the printer now comes, there'll be four out. And the latest book is *A Journey of One's Own: Uncommon Advice for the Independent Woman Traveler*, which is our first really big seller. This book came out in the beginning of January and we're already on our second printing. We've got twenty thousand in print. We sold ten thousand in three months.

Through Consortium [a master book distributor]*? Are you with Consortium?*

Well, through Consortium and through catalogues. I deal, actually, with the catalogues myself; they're exempt from the Consortium contract. It's been in the Daedalus catalogue since the fall. It's now in its third Daedalus catalogue and they sold a thousand. They just ordered another eight hundred, nonreturnable. They expect to sell about two thousand the first year. And it's in a number of other catalogues, travel book catalogues, and a travel catalogue called Norm Thompson. They're actually in Portland but they distribute nationally. It's a catalogue of sort of very fine goods. Not books; this is the only book that's in it. So it's selling, you know, to libraries, it's selling to bookstores, it's selling in catalogues. It's our first really big seller and I think it will probably sell twenty-five thousand the first year.

In February, I guess, she [the author] did some readings up in your neck of the woods. She did a reading at one of the U's and she had a reading at Elliott Bay. Her readings have just been phenomenal. Standing room only, bookstores selling every book they have in the store. It's just—for us, it's kind of amazing because all the books we've done up until now have been literary books. This is the first popular nonfiction book we've done, and the possibilities are just so different in terms of promoting it.

We just got a little review in *USNews and World Report* and we sold reprint rights to *Glamour*. We have reviews coming out in *Parade Magazine* and, you know, the glossy travel magazines, things like that. It's just a whole different ball game. It's...it's...it's interesting. I mean it's interesting to me as someone who's been doing this—I've been doing this, I'd say, fairly seriously since '88, since *Cows and Horses* came out. That was really when I started. Since '88 I've done either two or three books a year pretty steadily, and a lot of them actually have sold very well. But they sold kind of slow and steady, you know, over time.

I've never had a book that sold that quickly. And I've never had a book where the publicity possibilities were so broad. This was a book that was aimed at a very, very broad audience and so we're publicizing it all over the place. All the other books have been publicized in the literary media and the feminist media, and in the mainstream only, you know, in the town where the author lived or where there were other opportunities that were sort of specific. But with this book we're getting ready to send out review copies to every newspaper in the country, with a good chance of getting author interviews. I could do that with any book, but the chances of getting them reviewed are virtually nonexistent. So it's exciting. It was not entirely unplanned. I realized at some point that I couldn't make it as a literary press. It's not a nonprofit press.

When you say "we"—sometimes you say "we" did this or "we" do that—

Yeah. There's a group of women who volunteer, a group—two women who I work very closely with and have from the beginning, who work on a freelance basis. One woman is the book designer—Marcia Barrentine. And then, to a lesser degree, various people who've done proofing and copy editing and things like that for me, but who have done it on a sort of steady basis. They read manuscripts, staff tables at book fairs...but Marcia particularly, and then I'd say about four volunteers, including the donor of the Poetry Prize.... I don't make decisions on my own, and I don't feel like I take total, a hundred percent credit, for

112

everything either. I make decisions almost always with at least one other person. With the donor of the prize about choosing a judge and various other things. With Marcia about book covers.

What about accepting a manuscript? Do you do that by yourself?

No. I always get feedback from lots of other people and consult with this small group of people that I described. And I almost always have an intern or two or three sometimes, and other volunteers who are here at the time. And they will also read the manuscript and give feedback. So although I'm the only full-time person, I don't consider it to be a kind of solitary thing. I do feel like there are other people involved.

Have you been subsidizing Eighth Mountain with your own money?

Well, I suppose you'd say I have, because I haven't paid myself much. I mean I didn't pay myself anything for quite a long time. I haven't actually lost money, but I've been subsidizing it with free labor. And I'm forty-six and I could see I wasn't going to be able to do that forever. And I needed to earn a living as well.

How have you been earning a living?

Well, until this year I'd been earning a living doing other things. I taught part time at the law school here and did editing jobs, you know, just sort of a variety of things to make ends meet. This year I'm beginning to pay myself out of the press. With this book, yeah.

But I saw that I had two choices. One was to go nonprofit. You know, try to be a Graywolf-type press. Probably not as successful as they are because there's very little public money in Oregon for the arts. But, you know, sort of model myself after what they did. Or, model myself after what Seal did, which is to have a best-seller. Have a book that really sells. Their book was *Getting Free* by Ginny NiCarthy. They didn't know it was going to be a best-seller. But it was. It's been a huge source of income for them and made possible, really, the expansion of the press and their whole operation.

So I saw those as my two choices. I either had to publish some kind of nonfiction book that I could sell to a broad audience or I had to go nonprofit and apply for grants. And I didn't want to become a nonprofit. I didn't want to be in a position of charming and beseeching people for money. And my press is a feminist press. Many of the books are lesbian in content or by lesbian authors. And, you know, political tides come and go as to what's considered acceptable or within the bounds of literary whatever, and I just didn't want to get involved in that. I didn't want to stake my life on needing support outside of my own business.

So I decided I would try to find a book that fit in with what I was doing and that I really liked, but that was a popular book that I could sell in large numbers. And right around the time that I was looking for a book—I didn't necessarily think about it being a travel book; I didn't know what it would be. I was just sort of thinking about a book like that—through an odd set of coincidences that are very kind of classic Portland—I've lived here for eighteen years and I've done lots of things. I've been involved in all kinds of organizations and political movements and various things here. I know like half the town maybe. So I'm constantly running up against people who know people—a book came to me that I was interested in, but I was uncomfortable with certain aspects of it. It was a book that would have fit the scenario perfectly, but I didn't like it enough.

The "scenario" of—?

Of a popular book that would be a book for women but that would be a big seller. And I contacted the author of this book, Thalia Zepatos, to see if she would be interested in working with the author of this other book and bringing it up to speed. And she wasn't at all. But then she told me she had this other book that she was working on, which I had no idea about. And she's someone that I had known for a long time.

Oh, you didn't know that she had A Journey of One's Own?

114

I didn't even know that she was writing. I knew her through other contexts. She had an agent in New York who was trying to sell this book, who had two presses interested. But one of them didn't want it to be for women only. They wanted it to be just a travel book directed at anyone. And the other one wanted her to take out the travel stories that are in it. And she wasn't at all keen to do either of those things. And then she and I had this connection. I said to her, you know, as soon as you're done with your agent I'm really interested in talking to you about that book.

You didn't want to deal with the agent?

Oh, I would have been happy to deal with the agent. I think that—Thalia and the agent had an agreement that if Thalia found a publisher for the book, that would be Thalia's arrangement. She found two publishers for Thalia, but neither really wanted the book as it was written. And Thalia wasn't willing to make either of those changes.

Right.

She said "Thanks, anyway," and then she and I started talking. But it was just a fortuitous sort of timing. I actually had contacted her but about something else, and found out by chance that she had this book which I would never have known about.

Isn't that amazing, how that works?

I know. I think, in a town—probably Seattle is like this too, but in Portland, if you live here long enough and you know enough people, it's astonishing how you can find the people you need just when you need them. It never ceases to amaze me.

And not being able to predict that something would happen, and yet it did. Seal Press was very lucky, aside from their book. Being able to establish offices so they could bring in more people—all of that was for free because the city had kicked them out of their previous place.

Right. Right. I know. Yeah. Although their big source of

115

income, as far as I understand it, was the *Getting Free*. I mean that's a steady stream of money that they could count on. And that was really what inspired me to think that I could continue in the way that I have rather than become a nonprofit press.

Is this going to change the direction of your press?
No. What I plan to do is to continue doing exactly what I was doing before, and have some kind of a line of nonfiction books which it now looks like will be travel books for women. I'm thinking now that I'll use this as the first of a line of travel books for women which will have the same book design, and I'll use the same illustrator, and have them be recognizably Eighth Mountain travel books for women. Books that are, well, this one is a combination of a how-to and information and advice as well as stories. It has a little bit of travel writing in it, but it's a kind of a regular nonfiction rather than either creative or literary nonfiction. And that's what I'm looking for.

When you started publishing, did you have a purpose? When you did Judith's book, I assume that was, well, not a favor, but you weren't thinking of that professionally anyway. Or were you?
I was thinking of it somewhat professionally. But I wasn't committing myself to it. I was really just trying it out. She considered it a favor on her part to give me the book to do. I suppose you can look at it either way. I certainly wouldn't have had access to any other book to do as a first book. So that's how she thinks of it.

You wanted to do a book and she offered you her book?
Yeah. Well, it's hard to say. I suppose the idea of doing the book perhaps wouldn't even have occurred to me except that I was very close to Judith and her book. But I was involved in the feminist literary and writing community and doing letterpress broadsides which.... So when I decided I didn't want to be a lawyer anymore, I went back to some of my art interests and doing letterpress printing came out of that. So I was printing poems of writers who were friends and writers who weren't friends, and then got this idea of doing Judith's book. But I wouldn't

116

say I hadn't thought of it becoming a publishing house. I did certainly think about it because, as I said, I knew several publishers. I knew quite a bit about publishing just through that. But I wasn't sure I wanted to do it. And I wasn't actually—I don't know if there was ever a moment when I really said Yes, I am going to do this. It was really kind of just one thing led to another, and then at some point I looked back and I could see that I was doing it and that I was pretty deep into it. And decided that was fine, that was what I was going to do. From then on, I was pretty steadily charging ahead.

Some publishers I've talked with—Dan Levant from Madrona Publishers, for example—his intent originally was to build a publishing company. He wasn't so much concerned with individual books as with a publishing company. Others, like Barbara Wilson, love the books, but now Seal Press's circumstances are such that she has to think of the company because she has employees and she has to take care of those employees. So she's got an organization too. Others are focused on the books or the authors. Thatcher Bailey likes the company of intellectuals who write. Is there a mission or a purpose that you have for your press now?

Yeah. I think that it has always been very much a part of the feminist print movement and will remain so. I see its purpose as publishing books that are important to women and to the world at large, that come out of a feminist sensibility, whether it's literature or nonfiction.

New York houses and other small presses do publish important books by women and even some very feminist books that are important to all of us. But I think that the feminist presses have been crucial in providing the full range of books that are needed. And also the existence of feminist presses and the books that feminist presses have published are very much responsible for the fact that other presses publish those books too. The demonstrated success of these books by feminist presses shows New York that there's a market for them, and they'll pick up some of them. They won't pick up very many. They won't pick up the most radical. They won't pick up many that are lesbian in content,

117

for example, or any ideas that haven't yet become solidly acceptable to the mainstream. That's always been true. The feminist movement has actually been sort of fueled and inspired and pushed along by the feminist print movement, which includes the publishers, magazines—what?

Are you going back prior to the '60s when you say that?

No. Beginning in the late '60s. I mean from the very beginning there were some feminist presses that published some amazingly wonderful and important books. Some of them were just mimeographed in someone's basement, and none of those presses are around anymore. It's sort of like a first generation. But the second generation of presses, many of those are still around. Seal Press is one of those.

But there's a sense that the feminist magazines and journals and newspapers, and the feminist book publishers and the feminist bookstores and feminist writers and feminist writing workshops—there's a whole world of organizations that are dedicated to bringing women's words and women's issues into print. Again we see Eighth Mountain as part of that. Even though much of what I've published has been literary.

I haven't published much theory, although I have published some. Irena Klepfisz's essays fall in that category. And there's quite a bit of that in the anthology that Judith edited, *An Intimate Wilderness*. But I've been primarily interested, until recently, in literary work which I do see as central to what I was just talking about. Particularly the poetry, yeah. Feminist poets have been the visionaries, really, of the feminist movement, and its most important theorists as well. Adrienne Rich and Audre Lorde. Judy Grahn.

Do you love poetry?

I do. Yeah. Most—well, I don't know if it's most—one, two, three, four, five of the books I've published are poetry. And I would publish more if I could afford to. I mean my original idea was just to publish literature, and I thought much of that would be poetry. And everyone said, Oh, you'll never make it, and it's impossible economically. And I thought, Oh, you know, I'll find a way. But it is impossible.

118

The economics of the book industry are just—you have to sell more than you can sell of poetry to make it. Unless you're subsidized. So I've had to cut back. But I see The Eighth Mountain Poetry Prize as a sort of steady, long-term commitment to publishing feminist poetry.

Very few feminist presses publish poetry. In fact, there are only two of the larger feminist presses that publish poetry. Firebrand publishes some. And Eighth Mountain. Seal's published, I think, two books of poetry in the last couple of years. But they're not really involved in publishing poetry.

I consider that the press lives in sort of two worlds. I talked a bit about the feminist print movement which is really still alive. You know, every year at the ABA [American Booksellers Association conference] the feminist publishers meet for an entire day, the feminist bookstores meet for an entire day, and until recently there were fairly regular Women In Print conferences where everybody came together. There are still international feminist book conferences that take place every two years. But I also see that the press belongs to the world of literary small press publishing as well. I feel very akin to other literary book publishers too. Some of my books are more closely aligned to that world than they are to the feminist publishing world. So I guess I feel like I belong in both.

But my motivation for becoming a publisher probably was more related to the feminist purpose, and then maybe secondarily to my interest in books.

Will Peterson
Walrus and Carpenter Books

Harald Wyndham
Blue Scarab Press

"...there's another world that would not exist if there weren't small presses."

"The small press has one function. It gives writers hope."

Will Peterson is the publisher of Walrus and Carpenter Books. An Idaho native, he was born in Gooding, raised in Twin Falls, and now resides in Pocatello. He took a degree in English at the University of Utah and traveled in Europe—a year in Vienna as a student, another in France "to become a great writer." From 1978 to 1988 he was a golf pro in Twin Falls. "I ended up in the golf business because I was a golfer as a child, and as a young man I won a couple of golf tournaments. The worst thing you can do is win a golf tournament. You suddenly think you can become a golf pro. So that's what happened." Since giving up professional golf he has earned his living from his bookstore, The Walrus and The Carpenter.

Harald Wyndham is the publisher of Blue Scarab Press, publishing primarily his own work, in Pocatello. He was born on Richard Wagner Strasse in Munich of German parents a year after the end of the Second World War. His parents divorced, his mother married an American serviceman who adopted Harald, and the new family came to the United States.

"I was raised in Ohio as an American. My stepfather was a public accountant. My mother was a housewife. That's a vanishing profession. My mother was also a semester away from having a master's in chemistry at the German Technical University in Munich

120

when they bombed the university. So she didn't get her master's. My American father, God bless him, read books to us on his lap when we were children. I remember sitting there in my little footed pajamas, listening to "The Wreck of the Hesperus" and Paul Revere's ride and all the Dr. Doolittle books. We would sit on his knee every night and he would read. Mother would read to us, too. We had a lot of reading at home and I did that with my children as well. So he, my American dad with his own New England and Ohio traditions brought that sort of Yankee quality into the family while Mother brought the Bavarian quality in. It was not a literary house, certainly, but a house of interesting melodies. Mother with her German singing and accents and Father with his more conservative, staid, Republican, New England, do-your-homework-and-mow-the-lawn kind of philosophy. And me sort of manipulating my way through all of that as the oldest kid."

After five years he was naturalized. He went through school in Ohio, earned his bachelor's degree in English and philosophy, an MA in American literature (thesis on Henry Miller's Tropic of Capricorn*) and his MFA all from Bowling Green. "I was on an NEA fellowship for the Ph.D., which I resigned, and took the MFA instead. My professors told me it was the biggest mistake of my life—I would never work professionally. They were basically right, but I don't regret it. I had a free ride for the Ph.D. I had an NEA fellowship and I gave it up. At that time, 1969, I looked at the English faculties and I thought, Man, this is like a sidewalk laid out for the next fifty years of my life."*

He did get a job at Idaho State University. "It could have been Missouri, it could have been Iowa, it could have been Illinois—I would have gone anywhere. At any rate, we came out in '71, I taught two years, my contract wasn't renewed and I decided to stay in town." Eventually he found work with a semiconductor company as a technical writer. He stayed with the company and is currently its European program manager.

I talked with Will Peterson and Harald Wyndham on the evening of July 29, 1992. I arrived at Harald's house near the university campus before Will. Harald's wife was out of town and he decided to cook for the three of us. We drank white wine in his kitchen

121

and ate cheese and rye crackers and talked. Then we went out into the backyard where he heated the charcoal for steaks. Will arrived soon afterward, saying he couldn't stay late because he had to do his laundry. With the sirloin we had three kinds of salad, two containing pasta, and a burgundy, French.

The interview began outside after dinner and went until the night grew cool. We continued talking inside over coffee and, later, Dreyer's vanilla ice cream.

Walrus and Carpenter Books. You publish Chapbooks. I saw some of your poetry chapbooks in your store. Do you publish perfect-bound books as well?

Will Peterson: Not yet. The next project will probably be that. I want to get more into fiction.

Do you self-publish?

WP: Most of my work has been by other people. *An American Solace* is by John Wolf. It's an extended poem, kind of an American zeitgeist poem. Harald reviewed that in *Rollingstock*, Ed Dorn's now defunct literary magazine out of Boulder. The second one was *Another Tough Hop* by Ford Swetnam, an excellent book. Then we did an anthology of Idaho poets that we called *Mountain Standard Time*. We're going to have to put one out this year so we can say we do one every two years.

Who's the editor of that?

WP: I found a young woman, Ana Peña, with Chicano and feminist leanings to do it. Give it a little different slant.

When did you get involved with publishing?

WP: When we came to Pocatello I was going to go back to get a [graduate] degree in English. I came to Pocatello in 1988. And there was a very depressed economy and we had a little money so I opened the bookstore on a shoe string. Until then I wasn't aware of the writers' community that's here. The first reading we had, we had, I think, twelve or thirteen really first-rate writers and readers. Harald and some other people started a poetry-reading tradition here in about 1970, probably a little earlier than that, with Ed Dorn and Charlie Potts. This reading tradition over the years gathered an audience.

They read first at a place called The Dead Horse Saloon [originally called The Bistro; now out of business]. But it's one of those things where—anecdotally, the first poetry reading we had in the shop, we had a hundred people there. Every reader was just fantastic. And it's the oral, live-performance complement of poetry that is so fantastic here. All the poets here are performers. I'd never—if you've ever heard Harald read, it's just the experience of the live voice that gets you all excited. You know, it's like you wrote a poem about the original church. I don't think Harald would have written that poem if he hadn't been in a community where the living word is so vital. [Harald had been cleaning up after dinner while Will and I talked. Now he joined us.] I was telling Jerry that the tradition of performance poetry in Pocatello was twenty years old before I came here, and I was just astounded at the quality and the excitement of it. We had a hundred people here. We'll have readings where we'll have a hundred people.

Who are some of the writers?
WP: Harald Wyndham. Steve Puglisi. Leslie Leek. John Wolf. Janne Goldbeck. Margaret Aho. Who else?
Harald Wyndham: Scott Preston.
WP: Yeah, Scott Preston. A great performance artist and an abrasive literary critic. He's an excellent reviewer because he has a very volatile, abrasive, obnoxious style—
HW: Confrontive style.
WP: Confrontive style.
HW: Some people find it obnoxious, others find it confrontive. But he doesn't pull punches.
WP: No. He makes criticism kind of alive.
HW: He is also, I think, on the mark on a lot of things. Not

everything.

WP: Absolutely.

HW: But he goes for the jugular. He's also a very good performance poet, with musical accompaniment. He accompanies himself on a variety of musical instruments. He's also a champion of cowboy poetry. He's been going to Elko lately. The thing about Scott is that he's bringing back recitative poetry. And not just cowboy poetry, but all sorts of poetry. You know, the performance poetry which is happening all around the country. He's getting into that and he's quite good at it.

We were in the Cactus Bar in Boise with Bill Studebaker, another fine Idaho poet that's read at Will's shop, and Penny [Penelope Reedy] of *Redneck Review*, and Rick [Rick Ardinger of Limberlost Press] and the whole crowd, the old Idaho crowd, and Scott and I did Dylan Thomas's "Refusal to Mourn the Death by Fire of a Child in London". Reciting. Just did it, you know? And the bar was full of college kids and the television was playing, everybody was shouting and drinking. When we got done the place was still, man. The only thing left was the TV. They were all glued to that poem. And then they applauded. It was incredible. We shut that place down. That was a night to remember. What a kick. What a kick.

WP: That's the power of it.

HW: That's when a living poem just takes presence, man. It was just there, and people were in it.

WP: It actually has more power than music. Anyway, this was my introduction to it and I was so astounded that I said, "Well, we've gotta have an outlet." So I published the first *Mountain Standard Time* with pretty much those poets. The upstairs of the bookstore—I've got auditorium seats in there and it's gradually evolved into a perfect place to listen to poetry. But the thing is the quality. There're just so many good writers. Pocatello has such a powerful tradition of political, iconoclastic poets, from Charlie Potts to Ed Dorn. It's not boring, pastoral, bucolic poetry. And that's what got me into publishing.

Having the bookstore, it's kind of a nice center. It's got an address, you know? It's like—it's excellent advertising. I'm still

124

behind on what I publish, but it's wonderful advertising and if somebody sees a book and says "Oh", you know, it's got a place. You know, like City Lights.

But mainly this is a great scene for readers and writers. If we have a poetry reading, we're gonna have sixty, seventy people there. It's just guaranteed to do that.

Do they come mostly from the university, or—?

WP: It's all over. It's a tradition. People know they're gonna have a lot of fun and they're gonna run into something that's extraordinary. It's a tradition. It arose, like I was saying, from '65, Ed Dorn and Charlie Potts. Potts and Dorn and all these guys left, but Harald stayed, along with Leslie Leek and Margaret Aho.

HW: There was a period though—Duane Ackerson, you never knew. He was here when I arrived in '71 and he left, I think, in '73. He went back to Oregon. But he had been in the creative writing program and sort of carried the torch. I mean he was "the writer."

WP: I never heard his name.

HW: Yeah, *Dragonfly* was the magazine he put out.

WP: I'll be darned.

HW: And he did a magazine of one-line poems. So Duane was the writer around. And things were really beginning to pop for writing in town. Then the chairman of the Department of English changed and Duane and I looked at each other and we knew we were doomed. The next spring we were gone.

Both of you went at the same time?

HW: Well, he quit. He resigned and went to Oregon and I was let go. They've hired other writers. I mean there've been writers on campus. It hasn't died.

WP: But they have never supported them. They've never published them. They've never given them a venue for reading.

HW: Who-o-a—

Who is "they"?

WP: The university.

HW: No, the university press did publish the fiction anthology. ISU Press did put out Ford's and Rick's Idaho fiction anthology.

WP: That's right.

HW: And they have a magazine called *Rendezvous* that has published poetry, and *Ethos* has published—

So there's still a literary life on campus.

WP: Yeah, but, no, I disagree—

HW: But the real literary life in town has always been off campus.

WP: Yeah. There's no doubt about that. Since I've been here they've had a couple of poets in, but it's pretty much—it's a very conservative university.

HW: Wha-a-a?

WP: See, that's the paradox of Pocatello.

HW: They brought Wendell Berry in. I went and heard him.

WP: Oh, yeah.

HW: They've had some good poets come and read. But when you have a poetry reading at The Walrus and Carpenter, the English faculty typically, with one or two exceptions, isn't in attendance. So it's not like the faculty's really turned on for literature and supporting it.

WP: It's kind of like the Francois Villon stigma of poetry, you know? That's the paradox. There's really very little support, but a good tradition of writers.

Has there been a succession of editors at the university who simply don't want to publish local people?

WP: No, they just have never published.... They've had several good poets hired by the university and they're pretty much.... It's a political liability to have poets because, see, poets will say things that might be inflammatory, and you can't have that.

Ah. I see.

WP: That's the other paradox. You'd think the major funding or support for publishing all these good writers would come from the university, but they haven't done anything.

Does Walrus and Carpenter Books have a mission?

WP: I think we've published, the little we've done, we've published really good stuff that I enjoy reading. I haven't actively solicited writers, but now it's kind of in another phase. And now that I have somebody to edit it.... I just look at it as there being more good writing than is being published. We just have to—somehow we've just gotta publish all this good writing.

HW: You've created a vortex, though, which has drawn more writers to the surface than before. Because of The Walrus and Carpenter, writers have appeared that none of us knew about. Okay? One of them being your friend Doug Bob [Doug Airmet]. He lives up in Blackfoot, he's a Ph.D. in physics, writes incredible, weird poetry. Real unique stuff. He's got a whole series of poems on writing poetry called The Doug Bob Series, about a character he's invented—Doug Bob.

WP: That's his own persona.

HW: But it's great stuff and there's a vortex created that Pound talked about that draws—

WP: Absolutely.

HW: —writers in and that brings them to the surface so they can be seen.

I think that's right. I think you're right.

HW: And that's what Will has been doing. That's why when he publishes *Mountain Standard Time....* We put out a book some years ago called *Famous Potatoes* that culled from every writer we knew about in southeast Idaho. After it was published there were five or six others who showed up who we didn't know about. Including Margaret Aho, a very gifted writer. She's an excellent writer. But at the time of *Famous Potatoes*—in fact, her son went to school with my son. I knew her personally. [But] I didn't know her as a writer. I didn't know she did poetry. And then Doug Airmet, who I didn't know until Will had his

127

store and we began to run into him.

And there're just scads of others that have come to the surface at all different levels of ability, that are kind of drawn into the vortex of this community where they feel they can express themselves and be writers without being embarrassed or without being [considered] weird or odd. And I think that's what the bookstore and what the non-university, non-funded, free center that the bookstore is, creates. It creates a place where people who are writing feel comfortable coming together and expressing themselves—"coming out," as it were, as writers. [To Will Peterson] Because they feel safe around you, they're coming out around you, they're beginning to publish and express themselves. That's all because of what the bookstore creates.

You mentioned doing your anthology at least every two years.
WP: Yeah. We've gotta put one out this year so we can call it a biannual.

Do you have any other plans for the press beyond—
HW: —your pocket book?
WP [laughs]**:** Yeah. Well, the nice thing about publishing is that it's good advertising for the bookstore. The only reason I don't do more of it is that, unfortunately, people demand that my bookstore have more books in it every year. So there's kind of a pull with me. But, like I say, there are so many good writers. In the Idaho vernacular, Idaho is a very strange state.

HW: Idaho is a state of expatriates. Except for you, born in Gooding, and Bill Studebaker, born in Yellow Jacket, and Leslie Leek, most of us have come here from other states. We've stayed because we like what we find, which is, basically, no civilization.

WP: Yeah. No civilization.

HW: When I came out here in '71 I felt like I was in Siberia.

WP: Yeah.

HW: Like it mattered not that I was a writer. If I was a bull rider, it might matter. If I was a potato farmer, it might matter. But that I was a writer—and that freed me to do whatever I wanted to do. In

Ohio there's a strong writing community. At the university there was a strong writing community. We all wrote for each other. But out here, if you want to write, man, you're writing for yourself and whatever market you can find.

And you prefer that?

HW: I do, yeah. I've found it really enjoyable to be in a small pond. When I came out here there were only two writers listed in *Poets and Writers* in Idaho, myself and Charles David Wright in Boise. And now there's only seven or eight.

Charles David Wright?

HW: He came out from North Carolina, he was a Boise writer, he died in '74, '75. He has a certain repute. He was published in *Eight Idaho Poets* and is still published in Idaho anthologies. But, basically, this was not a state that was visible. Although it's full of writers. Not just writers, but musicians and artists. A lot of people here are very talented and live here because it's isolated, because it's non-urban, because they can be alone. The community is not uncultured. But it's not commercially cultured the way a large city is. [To me] Would it be easier for you if we went into the house? Or is this good?

I think it would be, yeah. If you don't mind. Because I can hardly read my writing here.

HW: Why don't we go in the living room.

[At this point we moved indoors. When the recorder was turned on again Will Peterson was speaking, referring to a book on the coffee table.]

WP: You ought to get one of those. You will be amazed at the diversity and quality—

The Idaho Centennial Anthology—

WP: —of the short story writers. It's just—

—that the university published?
WP: Yeah. They pretty much had to. As an agreement for the centennial, the University of Idaho did the poetry and Idaho State was obliged to do the short story. But, God, the quality of the writing!

Do you apply for grants, or do you intend to?
WP: No, I'm just too lazy.

So it's not on principle. You just don't want to do it.
WP: No, I'm sure if I could, I would. But I work six days a week keeping the shop open and just don't have the time to get organized. 'Course I want to start getting to my own writing, so—but, you know, it's just a little thing of independence. It's nice just to do something and if you break even on it....

For some people a grant confers legitimacy.
WP: Yeah, the whole thing about being self-published, the stigma of being self-published. Well, I just don't think it's valid. The writing is the important thing. It's important to get the writing out and, again, that's kind of my theme, is the more good writing you get out, the more you create a regional identity and literature for the next generation. "I'm not here alone," you know? "Even though I'm in Idaho." At one time Mississippi was far out. I mean, every culture begins out of nothingness, especially in the regional sense. And that's what gives it its universality, is the fact it's from Mississippi or Kansas or Idaho.

When you talk about regional writing, are you talking about anything that's done by somebody who has lived here for a certain number of years, or who was born here, or does the writing itself have to be about the region?
WP: I go with Maupassant. Wherever you are is what your literature is going to be. That's its value, you know? His *Provincial Sketches* are so true to tone, or seem to be, anyway. Or Steinbeck. It just seems true to tone. *Cannery Row* or *Sweet Thursday*. You believe in it and it gives you a vision. There's a lot of literature that just has no color

to it, no warmth. It's written in a New York apartment for a market and there's nothing there, you know? Not that regional literature can't be written from New York. It's just that most of the stuff that you read doesn't have it. But that's why I think it's important to the small presses. The small presses are going to create the medium for the good writers to come through.

I think I would maintain that all writing is regional. New York writing is regional also. But New York has so much wealth. And the mechanisms for distribution are located in New York more than anywhere else. And so that region tends to dominate. Not as much as it did forty or fifty years ago, but it still tends to dominate.

HW: Do you tend to follow William Carlos Williams' idea of "the local"?

I haven't read that.

HW: All writing is local, basically. The idiom, the way of speaking, the local environment influences the writing.

Well, in a sense I do. But I can think of writing in which—well, all right, I think all writing is local or regional, however we want to term it, in that the writer is influenced by his environment. But I can think of writing by Stanislaw Lem, the Polish science fiction writer, and Solzhenitsyn—that play he did, Candle in the Wind. *It dealt with academics but you couldn't tell—he intentionally wrote it so you couldn't tell what country they were in. You had the sense that it was an East European country, but you didn't know. It wasn't Russia. And that was his point. It could be anywhere.*

WP: Well, then there's Borges. I mean Borges writes fables, but they still have this intensity of the Buenos Aires intelligentsia. I don't want to be dogmatic. I just think that's why small presses have to keep putting stuff out. Because there's another world that would not exist if there weren't small presses.

HW: The small press has one function. It gives writers hope. That's what it's for. It may get lucky and publish something wonderful,

131

and once in a while that happens. But most of the time it's a forum for people who aren't yet known. It's an environment. It's a local bookstore. It's a local tavern. It's a local place where you can be accepted. I mean, that first time you have a poem accepted by anybody, you're on top of the world. I remember the first poem I had published, in 19— Christ—68. By *Zeitgeist*. In Michigan. The fact that the magazine took a piece of my work and published it—I mean, it was wonderful! There were months of rejection slips after that, but the fact that one person did it gave you hope that you were worth something.

And I think that's what the small press does. It validates the worth of writers who are not known, who have no reputation, who have no other validation except this publication and this press. This editor liked my poem. This editor published my work.

For the past two or three years I've been getting letters of inquiry from writers who are commercially successful. They've published mass market stuff, but they can't get their literary stuff published. So it isn't only the writer who has gone unpublished who needs hope. It's also writers who are established but who can't get the stuff that means something to them out.

HW: That's where I think, oddly enough, self-publishing is such a valid pathway. I mean we would all love for somebody to say to us, "My God, you are so wonderful, your writing is so wonderful, that we will publish you." Right? We would love that. We would love to have someone say "I will pay the freight. I will pay your bills. I will publish your book. I will distribute, I will advertise—"

"—and I won't edit your material."

HW: "I won't edit your material. You are wonderful. You're a walking god. I think you're the greatest thing since God knows who. Here you are." But when that doesn't happen, what confronts a writer is the need to go on to the next piece of work. You need to get this work done, you need to get it in print somehow, and you need to grow beyond it. You cannot wait twenty years, or fifteen years, working it over and sending it out eighty-five times. You can, and people do, I'm not saying you can't. But one reason to self-publish is to get the work in print. Maybe it isn't in its final form. Maybe it isn't as good as it can be. But if you're done with it, you need to get it into print.

And sometimes that's the best way to do it, especially if you know that it's the kind of work that very few people would risk their money on. That's the problem. You gotta find a publisher who's willing to risk thousands of dollars publishing five hundred to a thousand or more copies of a piece, and the only reason he's willing to do it is that he knows that he'll get return on his investment. That's where I think self-publishing has validity. Call it vanity if you will, but I think it's different, in many cases, from what we call "vanity publishing." It's valid for the writer who has an important piece of work that no one else will risk money on.

Both of you sound very idealistic about the small press.

HW: You have to be. How [else] could you do it? We're idealistic about ourselves too, I think. I mean that's part of it. You have to believe in yourself, and believe in other people, and believe in their work, to do small press. You cannot, you *cannot*, go at it as a business-man from a businessman's point of view. It makes no sense, economically. Unless you're very shrewd and work an angle. But most small press people are not business people. They are not gonna make money. They are not in it for money. They're in it for love. They're in it for the First Amendment.

And you would love it if every edition sold out. I mean, that would be amazing. But you don't ever expect that. You often, at least myself, I'm often optimistic as hell. I mean I believe in the book. I bring it out, I'm excited, we have a reading, we have a party, I think, "My God, I always bring too many books. I always bring five times as many books as I'll ever sell. When will I learn?" But every now and then I've come with just enough books and I've hit that crowd that bought me out. But that's very rare. But without that idealism, without that excitement, you wouldn't do it. It's not a cold-hearted, let's-make-money-on-this venture.

Now you started by self-publishing.

HW: Yeah. I started at Bowling Green. I put out a letterpress book and an offset book in 1970-'71.

Of your own stuff?

HW: Right. Those are the first two books I published. Both self-published. And then came out here and began to self-publish. I just began to have a lot of fun doing literary things. We had a radio program on public radio. We did twenty-five half-hour radio programs of poetry readings in '72 and '73 which were heard once. Except for my cassettes of them, there are no extant recordings, I think. We did "Howl", we did "Asphodel", we did "The Wasteland", we did everything. Most of the readers came from the theater department or were friends, English department friends and theater friends. They were great readers. We'd come in with no rehearsal, read live on the air...well, actually, taped, but no rehearsal, no retakes. This was through the public radio station at ISU. KISU, it was called. Since then we've done, over the years, various publications. The *Famous Potatoes* anthology, the *Things to Do in Idaho* anthology, and then publications of mine and publications of several other Idaho writers as part of what became eventually Blue Scarab Press.

Initially I just published my own books with no press name. But then in 1984 I began to use Blue Scarab. It's an odd name. I had a little scarab paperweight on my desk since I was a boy. My father's aunt Jessie was a world traveler and one of the many relics she brought back, including dried sponges and Arab swords and God knows what other paraphernalia, was this little plaster scarab from Egypt. And I appropriated it. It's always been on my desk. So when I needed a logo it was just natural. The scarab is a dung beetle, but it's a symbol of resurrection to the Egyptians. It comes out of nothing, basically. Spontaneous generation, which to me is the small press in essence. It always just arises, you know, out of nothing, and then disappears often after two or three editions.

Will, you did not start by self-publishing. Your idealism seems to be separate from yourself.

WP: As I said, I was so impressed by the oral performance tradition at Pocatello that I just wanted to document it. I guess I see my role as just documenting the artistic progress of this little neck of the woods. I don't really...but it's more important to—if I were writing really good stuff, I guarantee I would be self-publishing.

HW: Will, goddamnit, I have to tell you. You are modest to the extreme. That's a fault. What Will has done—and maybe his calling isn't to be a writer. Maybe his calling is to be a publisher and a bookstore owner. I don't know. But what he seems to get most of his joy out of is being in the company of writers and providing a place where literary and intellectual people gather. Any time you go in his store, you'll find two or three people drinking coffee, having a discussion about Nietzsche or God knows who. There's nowhere else—*nowhere else*, I'll guarantee you—in this town that that's going on. Only in his bookstore. You've got the *New York Review of Books*, the *New York Times Book Review*, you've got all the stuff that says "Be a writer here."

And if on top of that he's got a talent of his own that can come out, and that's what he wants, it'll come out. But I think his gift is the gift of an impresario. He is able to bring people together and make them feel welcome. I don't know about his literary gift, except the things I've seen I think are capable and promising. But if he's got enough guts to be a writer, that's his. If he has the demon, put it that way. If he can't avoid being a writer. Most of the people he's talking about can't do what he does. They can't run a bookstore. They can't bring people in. He has the ability to do that. We don't have the talent that he does.

WP: Ten years of being a golf pro.

HW: It's a kind of literary golf pro then. You're helping us out.

WP: But I'm learning a lot from the poetry readings. All the good poets in this area have a totally honest and dramatic way of presenting their work. I've gotta start writing so I can read so I feel good in front of an audience. That's how powerful the oral tradition is here in Pocatello. You don't want to write something you can't read to people. It's not a literary, bookish style of writing in this neck of the woods. It's purely performance stuff and it's so good that I think when I get to writing where I can really connect with people—

It's kind of folk. Cowboy stuff is really folk. It's a folk performance.

HW: No. Cowboy stuff is artificial as hell. It is a genre that's like...like...it's like Longfellow. It pretends to be folkish, but it is not. It is a Robert W. Service and American-patriotic and Western, Remington type of mythos. The big thing, I think, that cowboy has done and is doing for American poetics is revitalizing memorization and delivery. It's the ethos of the cowboy poet to stand up without your papers, without your book—do not read it, but deliver it. If you can't deliver it, don't even get up. Don't even stand up. If you don't have it by heart, then don't even get on the stage. That's the thing. They say, "Don't bring your papers up here, boy. Come up here as a man, without your papers, and do the poem." Well, why can't we do Robert Frost and Yeats and Eliot and whoever-the-hell—and our own stuff—that way? Why don't we do it? The cowboy poets do it.

They've shamed other poets into wanting to come back up and be able to do—I mean, hell, I love oral poetry. And I love trying to learn it and perform it. But I don't want to do Robert W. Service for the rest of my life. I mean I could do a nice parody of a cowboy poet once in a while, and it would be fun. But the point of it is to love the words enough to memorize them and stand up and do them. And that I'll give the cowboy poets. That they have done.

Can you name some of the titles you've published?

HW: Well, I started the press with two pieces of my own, one called *Homeland* in 1984, and *Ohio Gothic* in 1985.

But didn't you do something earlier, before it was called—

HW: Oh, I did a lot of books before Blue Scarab—books like *Cheap Mysteries, Exile in a Cold Country, Exile's Pilgrim into Christmastide—*

Cheap mysteries?

HW: *Cheap Mysteries.* It's a dime-store collection of poems. It was the first ten-year collection of—

Oh, I thought you were describing them.
HW: No. The title of the book is *Cheap Mysteries.* It's a collection my wife likes. My children like it. It's just sold out this year.

What was your run on that?
HW: Five hundred. Published in '81. Took ten years to sell out.

Freud's Interpretation of Dreams, *which he self-published, by the way—*
HW: Good for him.

Well, his first book was, I think, a neurology text. But his second book, which is certainly one of his most important, was The Interpretation of Dreams. *He self-published that. It took ten years to sell six hundred copies.*
WP: Yeah.
HW: Well, actually, *Cheap Mysteries* is probably the most popular thing I've ever published. It's the one book of mine that almost everybody finds something in that they like. But I do a lot of weird things. *Ohio Gothic* and *Homeland* were two books that sort of said goodby to Ohio. Prior to that, *Exile in a Cold Country*, a very important book for me, was the settling-in-in-Idaho books.

Those are nice titles.
HW: Thanks. There was a little book published by Confluence Press, the only book I didn't self-publish, called *Pebble Creek.* Strictly outdoor poems about southeast Idaho. About hunting and fishing. Several of them have been anthologized. One called "Entering the Water" has been in two or three anthologies. People were saying, "Why don't you just do more of those, man?" I had another agenda. Then I've done the *Famous Potatoes* anthology, a collection of southeast Idaho writers. I did an Edson Fichter book and a book by Leslie Leek called

Heart of a Western Woman. Short stories. Edson's book and her book have sold out.

On my own, I put out a trilogy—a triptych, basically—of three books, very ambitious pieces of work called *Mount Moriah Studies*, *Cathedral* and *Prodigal Psalms*. The cemetery in town is named the Mount Moriah Cemetery. The book was started in the early '70s. I lived across the street from the cemetery and walked there all the time. Anyway, there's a triptych and that's the last piece of work that's come out of Blue Scarab.

I've always got projects cooking. Most of my books are ten years in the making. I mean they're written, they're in manuscript, they're thought about, they're worked up and they're—

Most of the books that you write, you mean.

HW: That's right. Very few of them are just done and out the door. They're all many, many years—I do all my writing in longhand in notebooks, and let them sit, and kind of stew over them, and then I come back later and just totally change them and rewrite them two or three times and finally put them to press. Blue Scarab grew out of my own self-publishing. I don't take unsolicited writers. Period. But I do solicit manuscripts from writers I'm interested in.

I also write songs. Under a pseudonym. I write songs under the pseudonym of Chalmers Ferguson. I've got two song books out that I've self-published. Fifty songs.

WP: The truth comes out. I've had Chalmers Ferguson in my store for four years.

HW: And you didn't know who that was? That's me! Those are my songs, man! "Strong in the Spirit" and— [There is uproarious laughter from all three men.]

Well, how'd they get in the store?

HW: 'Cause I brought 'em in, for Christ's sake! [The laughter continues.]

I love this!

138

WP: Who is Chalmers Ferguson? Isn't that a great name for an Idaho cowboy?

It sounds like a Harvard scholar.

HW: I wanted to have a band called "Massey and Ferguson", after the tractor. And I thought I would be Chalmers Ferguson and the other guy would be Alice Massey and we'd have a drummer named John Deere. It was just kind of a fun little idea, but I never did find the combo so I just took the name. I'll tell you, I was so afraid—now, this is the truth—that the songs, and they were wonderful songs, were so wonderful that they would become famous, world-wide, immediately, and that I'd better guard myself by publishing them under another name. 'Cause I didn't want my personal life to be destroyed. And it worked. My personal life has not been destroyed. [Laughter again] In fact, nothing has happened.

WP: Right, right. Well, now I'm gonna have to read those.

Have you sold any of them?
WP: I don't think I have. Well, now I gotta read 'em.

You don't have to read 'em. You can just tell him you read 'em.
WP: I figured it was by some yoyo named Chalmers Ferguson. I wondered who the hell was that. I had no interest in him at all.

HW: It's *moi*, baby! It's *moi*!

WP: We're gonna have to have a party and sing Chalmers Ferguson.

HW: There're some good songs in there. Not all. But some of them are okay. Some of them are as good as anything around.

WP: Yeah. Uh huh.

Here's a question that I haven't asked anyone else I've interviewed. But it's something I've thought about because you both talk so much about performance. Performance is transient—

HW: That's the beauty of it. It's like poetry. It's like sand castles. The doing of the act of poetry is so unique—it never happens

139

again—that even a recording of it isn't faithful. It's like taking a camera to Europe. I've quit taking my camera when I travel because you cannot record what things smell like and feel like and are at that moment. You cannot do it. You can do a facsimile, a poor imitation, with a photograph or a tape recorder, but you cannot be there, and the act of being there is what's real. And so you do a sand castle—an incredible, elaborate, wonderful piece of work, and the ocean comes in the next morning and wipes it out.

Then why publish your own writing?

HW: Because there's joy in it. Because the gratuitous act is a wonderful thing to do. It is reality. It is life. It is art. I'm not talking about things that hang in museums. I'm talking about Vincent painting the painting out in the field in Provence one afternoon and one evening with candles in his hat. It's more important than the painting that hangs in the Musée d'Orsay that you can go in and look at. The experience that Vincent had is art. The rest is secondary.

Vincent painting the field is equivalent to performing poetry?
HW: Yes.

Then why not simply perform your poetry? Why publish it?
HW: Ah. That's a good question. I don't have a good answer.

Oh. Okay. [All three laugh.] *That's fine.*

HW: I think, as a matter of record, when something is finished, the publishing is different from the performing. The publishing is a matter of history. There's a saying: "How do I know what I think until I see what I say?" There is the writing down of your growth as a human being and your discoveries and your explorations, like diaries of travelers who go up in the Arctic. That is something that you can pass along, that can be shared.

It outlives you. Is that what you mean?
HW: Yeah. For instance, I'm not writing—I know I'm not

140

writing for my contemporaries. If I'm writing for anybody, it's for [people] two generations from now. For my grandson, for his generation. If my work has any value at all, it's for them. It's not for my contemporaries who have their own traditions, who were schooled on the writing of their grandparents, people who are now dead. Those are the people we've all learned from, and that we've admired. We have guarded esteem for our contemporaries. We cannot esteem them fully because we have our own lives to live. But we're writing for the people who haven't been born yet. And that, I think, has some value to it beyond the sand castle value of the performance.

But, like theater—I mean you go to the theater and, even if you videotape the theater, it isn't theater. When you're watching the play, something happens that happens only once, that night, with you present. You're a witness and you take part in it. And what you take away from the theater is different from what you take away from television or anything else.

I think performance poetry, if it's lucky, has that ability. Like that night I told you about in the Cactus Bar when we shut the place down with Dylan Thomas. That could not have been staged. You couldn't have invited people to come. You couldn't have given them a ticket. They just had to be there. And it happened. And it couldn't be reproduced. For me, at least, it was indelible.

The other part of publishing is finding people that are really genuine and saying, "Wow. This is fun. These are people that deserve to be known, to be published, and I get the opportunity, yeah, I have an obligation even to publish these people, and to publish their risky work. I mean Bruce Embree's work is real risky stuff. He's got things fairly offensive in all sorts of categories, to all sorts of people. But, my God, when he's on, when he hits the mark, he hits it.

WP: Yeah, the diversity of the readings is really extraordinary. There really aren't two poets in Pocatello that write the same. Bruce has a poem that he read—we televised the poetry festival. I've had two years at the Idaho Poetry Festival. Anyway, I told Bruce not to use obscenities and religious denominations contiguously. And he didn't speak to me for a year.

141

HW: Yeah.

WP: So the next time he reads something that's televised, he reads this poem that's called "All Mine".

HW: Oh, "All Mine". God, he—

WP: He catalogues all his old Jimmy Reed tapes and his dog food and—

HW: And the dog shit on the floor.

WP: —and old cars and all this stuff and then he gets to the end and he says, "This is all I have. All I can give of this is atop Red Hill [in a note] enclosed in a canister, which comes from the ancient such-and-such and which can be translated as follows: 'Dear Lord, this is a tough life. Give us everything we ask for. Or go fuck yourself.'" [All three laugh.]

HW: But this is after twenty minutes of "All Mine". I mean, "I've got fluff under the carpet and it's all mine. I've got these books, they're all mine."

WP: I was sitting on a stool by the front door, you know, trying to—and I'm just laughing and hanging on every word, and he sets you up with—what that punch line is is basically a right cross coming like that—

HW: Yeah. Yeah.

WP: —and I hit the floor. It was just like—it was wonderful.

I have one more question. Do you apply for grants?

HW: No. I have a personal philosophy about that. I don't believe in state-supported poetry. Or literature. I do believe in state-supported symphonies and ballet and very high-cost things. I think that's important. I'm not against the NEA or the foundations for the arts. But I think that when writers begin to apply for grants and fellowships they are taking great risks. Now I say that. I did in the past apply for a writer-in-residence position. Well, when it became obvious that it had nothing to do with the Idaho writing tradition, I ceased applying for it.

What are the risks that writers take?

HW: You become obligated. You become obligated to serve a

142

public that is not necessarily your public, whatever your public is. You become obligated to live within expectations, whatever they might be. And I think that shapes, or can shape, the work you do. Now the other reason I don't apply for grants is that I'm fortunate enough to have a good job and I don't need to. So maybe that's a cop-out. But, basically, it cuts into your freedom, it puts an obligation on you.

If you're a real self-publisher and a real independent press, you don't take grants. You live or die on your ability to put out your work. Now I, when I was poor, I put out work real cheaply. I put out editions where I saddle-stitched 'em, I collated 'em myself, I used cheap paper. In fact, my wife and I put out at Bowling Green a couple of literary magazines that were mimeographed. We had no money. We still published.

Why did you start publishing then?

HW: For the same reason I do now. Because there was no outlet for the writers. Because it was fun. Because it looked like an exciting thing to do. Because I had ink under my skin and wanted to do it. So we started doing it.

WP: I gotta go and do laundry. Jerry, thank you and next time you're coming through, you've always got a place to stay. Harald, thank you.

Jerome Gold

Black Heron Press

"...I take fiction very, very seriously. More seriously than nonfiction. It's a much more comprehensive form, a much more inclusive form."

Jerome Gold founded Black Heron Press with Les Galloway in 1984. Since Galloway's death in 1990 Gold has been the press's sole publisher. Black Heron publishes mainly fiction, occasionally personal essays or other nonfiction. One literary agent characterized Black Heron's list as one that "pushes the edge of acceptability." Roy Overstreet of Elliott Bay Book Company in Seattle commented that the characters in the Black Heron novels he had read—infra, The Inquisitor, The War Against Gravity—*were without moral compass. Gold takes pride in both of these comments, though he says he would have added to the latter that the characters are also trying to invent a moral code by which they can live, those that are established being ineffectual.*

Gold has been married twice, has three children, fought in Viet Nam, was a local-level organizer in the War Against Poverty, earned a doctorate in anthropology and is now a counselor in a prison for juvenile felons. He has lived in Chicago, Georgia, Indiana, California, Montana and Washington. He has traveled for lengthy periods in Central America, Southeast Asia, and the South Pacific. He is the author of three novels, The Negligence of Death, The Inquisitor *and* The Prisoner's Son, *and, with Les Galloway, a collection of stories,* Of Great Spaces. *He also edited the collection of writings on hurricanes entitled, appropriately,* Hurricanes.

The interview was conducted by Michelle Willson at her home in Auburn, Washington, about thirty-five miles south of Seattle, on a

144

chilly afternoon in the last week in December 1992 when the fog was settled like industrial particulate on the Kent Valley.

I learned to write through the distractions. I remember one occasion—we had two kids at that time, and a dog and a cat, and all four of those little things were chasing each other around the chair I was sitting in. And I was just writing through it. This friend of ours came over and he couldn't believe I was writing. I was able to do it.

I think certain passages are easier to write than others. If it was something that required thought, required analysis, I couldn't do that. But if it was dialogue, which happens in my mind very fast and it's a matter of simply getting it down, I could do that. But if it was going to be a narrative and I had to pay very close attention to the logic of it, or had to remind myself of what had gone before, I wouldn't be able to do that.

Let's see. I have a bachelor's degree from the University of Montana. In history. A master's degree from the University of Montana, in anthropology. And a Ph.D. in anthropology from the University of Washington.

From the time I was very young I knew that I wanted to be a writer. I wrote my first story when I was nine, and it, writing it, felt so good. There was something that in some way made me feel that I wanted to have more of that. By the time I was thirteen I could say to my English teacher, "I want to be a writer." But in college I took only those English classes that I had to take in order to graduate.

I did not study English in college because I loved reading and I didn't want it ruined. Exactly. Exactly. One of the books we read in Freshman English was *Catch 22*. I had read that thing about three times already, and to see what was being done to it in class—it pretty much destroyed that book for me. I was able to read it one more time. What they do with books in classes is very naive, I think.

Where they dissect it, that kind of thing?
Yeah. Professors do that for their own purposes, but it really

doesn't have much to do with the book itself. At least that was my experience. But I knew after that that there was no way I was going to have reading destroyed for me. It was too important to my life.

I did take a creative writing class when I was in high school. It was actually put on by a community college. We called them junior colleges in California. It was pretty good. But on an intuitive level, I felt that if I was going to learn something well, if I was going to really be creative, if I was going to make a difference in the world of writing, then I should not take those classes. Because there was a certain—they standardized writing. This was strictly intuitive. Later I became even more convinced of that. Somebody said about Faulkner that his strength was that he hadn't learned to write in college. Although he did take some classes at—

In college writing classes there seems to be this emphasis where everything is focused on particular writing exercises that everyone does. What do you think about that in terms of developing or stunting writing?

Well, it's one way in which standardization is accomplished. The goal is to achieve a norm. You do something well. And somebody decides whether you've done it well or not. And you internalize that. If the universities teach to a uniform standard, and they appear to, then their success is rated according to the uniformity of the writing of their graduates.

Judging from the books you've published that I've read, you're usually looking for an idiosyncratic sort of—

I would say "innovative." [Both laugh.] Although one agent back East says "weird." He said he was glad I'm doing what I'm doing, but he'd never be able to sell my stuff.

What's your response when somebody says something like that? I can see pride, but on the other hand, isn't there a little bit of irritation at that point of view?

If I still had any hope of making a commercial breakthrough,

146

yeah, I think I'd be upset. But that's gone by the way. Now I'm just contemptuous of—not of him, but of the system that he's part of. The book we were talking about I regard as a very nice, certainly not a weird, book. The title is *When Bobby Kennedy Was a Moving Man*, written by Robert Gordon.

Is he somebody you've published before?
No.

Then how did you get—?
Almost the same way I got David's [David Willson, Michelle's husband] first manuscript. I was getting ready to put Judith Roche's book, *Myrrh,* into production. She had a friend. She asked me if I would look at his manuscript. I said yes. And I liked it. It was as simple as that.

It's a very skilled novel. He's a graduate of a writing school, I don't remember which one. It isn't that he's doing anything innovative with the language, but his idea for the book is nice. It's a moving book. No pun intended. Honest.

You prefer publishing fiction.
Yeah.

Why is that?
Because that's what I write. I feel most comfortable with fiction.

How do you view your relationship with a writer? Once you've decided to publish something, do you view yourself as an enabler, or do you see yourself as a colleague, or is it different, depending on the personalities?
If I can see that there's something in the manuscript, and the author's having problems with it, or at least I believe that the author's having problems with it, it's more of an enabling relationship. As much as I can, I like to involve the writer with the production of the book. I'm not talking about his actually doing anything. I just like to keep the author informed so he knows how it's done. In some cases it's definitely

been a mistake to do that. Because the writer then thinks he knows more than he really does, and he wants things done in certain ways, and then it takes time to explain to him that something will cost a thousand dollars more and I can't afford to do it.

Some writers believe that they and their publishers are supposed to be antagonists. I began to suspect this about one writer because she was making it so difficult to get her manuscript into a book. So I asked her about it. And she said that's the way it's supposed to be.

It took almost a year longer than it should have taken to publish that thing, because of these games she was playing. And I think there are other writers who believe they have to treat their publishers as antagonists. If I see that, I'll do what I can for the book, but I'll be reluctant to publish a second book by that writer. I guess that sounds kind of authoritarian, and maybe it is.

I was just going to say that there is a power imbalance there, because the publisher is the person who has his hand on the switches.

Yeah. So. There are a couple of people...offhand, I can think of three people I've published who, if they submit something to me, I'm going to publish it. I have that much confidence in them. And we've worked well together. And I find their suggestions helpful. And they're realistic in their expectations. David [Willson] is one. Ron Dakron and Marilyn Stablein are the others I have in mind. There may be others as well who are just not in the fore of my mind right now. I may have to work with something a little bit to polish it, or get them to polish it, but I have enough confidence in them.... Simone Zelitch is another. I loved working with her.

Marilyn's style, the way she constructs her sentences and paragraphs—the separate thoughts that are implied by separate sentences create something else, something apart from what you see on the page. And very often I think it's really funny. She has such a dry sense of humor. Although in her latest writing—it hasn't been published yet—there's an element of anger.

Do you consciously go for any balance in terms of male to

female writers?

No. I was asked that once before. It really surprised me. No, I don't think about that at all.

It's a politically correct question these days.
Yeah.

Do you get more manuscripts from—?
I don't know.

You just don't pay attention?

No. Of the writers I've published, I couldn't tell you without looking at my catalogue how many are women and how many men.

Well, how do you decide? Because Tracey—*that seems so different from the other books you've published, that I wonder where did that come from?*

I thought what it's about was an important issue. Even though Black Heron is a literary press, certain social issues which are presented in a certain way, in a way that is not abstract, in such a way that I can see human beings playing out their lives around these issues, appeal to me.

Do you give special attention to manuscripts that come in that are Viet Nam-related, or war-related?

Well, I get a lot of them because the press has become known for its Viet Nam books. Yeah, I probably do give special attention to them. But I turn most down. The same rules apply. It has to be very, very good and it has to be a little different. Most of the manuscripts I get, whether Viet Nam-related or not, are competently written. But they're not what I'm interested in, either in substance or in style.

When you send things back, do you give suggestions to writers on other places to go or things to try, or—?

Sometimes. If I know of a place where I think it might fit, I'll suggest it. Often I don't know of a place. Often it should be out there in the mainstream. It shouldn't be with a literary press. It's not good enough to be with a literary press.

How do you distinguish? Give me the definition of a literary press as opposed to a mainstream press.

Well, for me, a literary press is.... Well, there's what I do. I try to find very talented, unrecognized writers, or unpublished writers. And, as I'm able, publish them. That's probably why people say I'm avant garde, or why New York says I'm avant garde, those in New York who are aware of the press. I don't think I'm avant garde, but....

That was my next question. Where does avant garde come in? Because New York doesn't do it, it's avant garde?

Well, not only do they not do what I do, but most of what I do is a little different. New York won't do it, and it's good: that's not my definition but I think it's what's implied in what New York editors say.

What would you call an avant garde press?

An example of one? I don't know of any.

What would one have to do for you to consider it avant garde?

Publish books that are more different than those I publish. Be extreme. I consider myself very cautious.

The internal logic of the manuscript has to be rigorous. And I look at it carefully. If there's a line of thought that the writer's developing and he hasn't taken into account something that may contradict him, then he has a problem. And I start wondering, can the writer do this? Is he able to take into account this other thing? Or should he? Maybe he's doing the right thing. So I consider myself pretty cautious in thinking through a manuscript. Because I take fiction very, very seriously. More seriously than nonfiction. It's a much more comprehensive form, a much more inclusive form.

Do you think, when you're deciding what to publish, about

150

marketability? Whether anybody's going to buy it? You have to think about it somewhat, I imagine.

Yeah. That does play into it to some degree. I assume I'm not going to get my money back. But I want to be able to get a good portion of it back. If I print a thousand copies of a book and I sell only two hundred, that isn't enough. I have to sell more than that. And it isn't just to get the money back. A lot of effort and time goes into making a book. On the other hand, I might feel that I could sell two hundred or four hundred copies now and then, over time, I would have it on my backlist and I might make it up later.

I got a manuscript once that was seven hundred and some pages, single-spaced. I didn't read it all, but what I read I liked. But there's no way I could publish it. There's no way I could publish a fourteen-hundred-page book. And there's no way I wanted to take the time to edit it down. So there was an obvious limitation in that case. It would be too time-consuming and much too expensive. So at one or another level of consciousness I do take all that into account. Or it might be a very good book, but if it's written in such a way.... And maybe I know the author will not do readings to promote his book—I don't demand that an author do that, but it sure is a help—and so I figure that I can sell only fifty or a hundred copies—I probably wouldn't do it. So those things you mentioned, sales and marketing, trying to anticipate a market—I do have to take all that into account. I'm not a purist. I probably wouldn't want to be a purist.

To change the subject entirely, there's something I'm curious about. What was your role in the military? What's your military background? How did you initially become involved?

Well, I was nineteen years old. I was living in California and I wanted to leave. I was unhappy because my marriage, my first marriage, was over. I just wanted to get away. I wanted an adventure away. So I enlisted. This was 1963. There had been a *Time* story on Special Forces. They had done some sort of PR thing, rappelling out of a building in Manhattan. And *Time* had covered that. And I wanted to do things like that. I wanted that adventure.

You wanted to be in Special Forces.

Yeah. Because that would have been the most adventurous thing I could do at the time. At least the most adventurous thing that I was aware of.

Did you have any friends or relatives who were in the military at the time, or had been in?

I have an uncle who was in the infantry in Korea during that war, and I have an uncle who was in the navy in World War II. He was on a destroyer in the Battle of the Coral Sea. The first uncle was at Pork Chop Hill.

And your father?

No. My father was on the Manhattan Project. At the University of Chicago. The navy wanted him but the Atomic Energy Commission, or whatever it was called in those days, would not let him go. My father was at the University of Chicago during the war and afterward. He continued to work for them through the late '40's.

Now how long were you in Special Forces?

Well, once I got out of basic training and AIT, advanced individual training, and then jump school, I went right into Special Forces. As it turned out, the guy who recruited me into it was one of the guys who had rappelled out of the building in Manhattan, Don Duncan, who later became the military editor for *Ramparts Magazine*. That was a radical magazine that existed because the war existed.

And you did how many tours in Viet Nam?

Me? I did only one.

You did only one. Okay, and then you came back. How long after you got back did you get married again?

I got married before I went to Viet Nam.

152

Oh, before you left.

I got married five days before I left for Viet Nam. I don't recommend that. It made for two very unhappy people. You should have at least six days.

I got back in '66. Within a few months I was in college, in California again, and my wife was pregnant. I transferred to the University of Montana after two years.

What was your goal when you were in school? When you were at the University of Montana?

Well, I wanted to get the bachelor's degree and then go to law school. And actually I did start law school at the University of Montana. It lasted for one semester. They did not like me. I did not like them. I got close to failing grades at the end of the first semester and asked to see my tests that they had graded. There was nothing written on the tests. They had done their critiques on different sheets of paper, they said. They wouldn't show me those. I went to the dean about it. Essentially I was saying there's something suspicious here. And all he told me—the only sentence he ever spoke to me—was, "I saw you sitting in John Bull's [fictitious name] seat." John Bull was a student there. A Crow Indian. And that was all the dean said to me.

And then I found out that not only was I being failed out but so were all the Indians except for John Bull. And then the following semester—John and I were friends—the following semester, John told me that they had tried to persuade him to leave. To quit. The line of reasoning they were using was if he quit now, after one year, he could do a lot for his people. But if he stayed and became a lawyer, then he'd be just another middle-class lawyer. [Laughs.] Great legal minds.

They had let a lot of Indians into the law school that year, and they had let me in, and I think they associated me with them. We weren't radicals, by any means. I don't know. I don't know what they saw or thought they saw. But they dumped me and them, all but one.

At that time there had been only one Native American student who had graduated from there and, according to him, they did not know he was a Native American until his senior year. And suddenly, although he had gotten consistently high grades, he flunked a class. As it happened, it was a class he needed in order to graduate. So they were trying to get him out of the law school. But he went down to New Mexico and took the same class there during the summer. Sam Deloria, Vine Deloria's brother, was the dean of the school, I think. And Gary took that class there and was able to graduate.

I really despised my experience in law school, though leaving it was traumatic. I was pretty idealistic. I would say things like "There's such a discrepancy between the law and justice." And they didn't want to respond to that at all. Finally, one of them said that justice is an abstract concept; it has nothing to do with law. This was the law school liberal who said that. It was a terrible experience.

Then how come you went ahead and got a master's degree? Because that was a different group of people with a different attitude from the people at the law school?

Right. And, actually, I consider myself fortunate to have studied anthropology there, under those particular people.

How did you make that switch? Law school didn't pan out and so you immediately switched to anthropology?

Yeah. I decided in February that I would not return to law school. I started graduate work in anthropology in March of '72.

Were you writing at that time?
Yeah. I was always writing.

Were you thinking then about trying to get published?

I sent a short novel to [a Manhattan publisher]. It was a war novel. It came back and every second page had been stamped with the peace symbol. About a dime-sized symbol. Essentially someone had mutilated the manuscript and sent it back to me. Somebody had gone to some work to do that. So I figured, Well—

Wow.

154

Yeah.

Did that story become part of any future writings, or what—?
Yeah. That was the first version of what became *The Negligence of Death*. I probably still have it. I don't know how much it resembles the final book.

Living in Montana, you had access to news—well, not a very good newspaper, but you had news magazines and television. But, still, they didn't clue you in to attitudes in other parts of the country. We know now, of course—it's been written about now—that editors in those days actually did prevent Viet Nam manuscripts from getting published. It's in Lomperis's book [Timothy Lomperis, *Reading the Wind*]. But in those days, in the '70s, that didn't fit with my idea, and probably many people's idea, of what the United States was about. It took a long time for me to get used to the idea that you could have a good manuscript and have it rejected because of something that one of the characters says, or because of the subject matter, or because of any one of a lot of reasons. And it took even longer to accept the idea that there was active...what? Collusion is probably too strong a word....

You're a publisher now. If you received a manuscript that espoused a viewpoint that you found abhorrent, but you felt the writing was good—
Would I publish it? Or would I be tempted to publish it? There are manuscripts I wouldn't publish, no matter how good they are.

Mm hmm.
There's no way I would publish a book espousing Holocaust revisionism.

Uh huh.
There's no way I would publish anything that advocates, not satirizes but advocates, harm to a category of person. The writing could be very good. You don't have to be a nice person to be a great writer. Yeah, so there are things I wouldn't publish. There are things I would

155

probably look down on another publisher for publishing.

Okay. I want to go back now to when you were at the University of Montana. After you earned your master's, then what? How did you end up in this area [Seattle]?
My wife had applied to school here and was accepted by the University of Washington. So we came out here.

What did you do while she was going to school? Did you work?
We only lived together for another year. For most of that year I was Chief of Security for [a hospital in Seattle].

Oh, I can see now where a piece of your writing came from.
In that part of *The Inquisitor* there's not a lot of fiction. Some of it is exaggerated, but—

It felt very real.
Even the part about the guy being held against his will in the psych ward, that's true. That's right from life.

So you did that for a year, and then you got divorced?
Yeah. I had also applied for graduate school but was turned down. This is another nasty story.

Why?
The Department of Anthropology did not take white males that year.

Did they tell you that?
They told me later. After I was accepted.

They took no white males?
They took no white males that year. Academic year '76-'77. I reapplied for '77-'78 and was accepted. They took white males that year. I didn't know all this at the time.

156

What did they give as their reason? Did they give a reason?

They were under government pressure to achieve racial and gender balance among the students, at least the graduate students, in the department. They were threatened with loss of federal grants. This is what I was told. So they solved the problem by not admitting white males for one year. Of course, they didn't tell the white males who were applying. I only found out later. Anyway, I started graduate school in '77.

You were in the doctoral program from '77—

To '88. I graduated in '88. For two of those years I was in the Bay Area, working.

Is that where you met Les Galloway?

In San Francisco, yeah. The first time I saw him was at an International House of Pancakes, an IHOP, on Lombard. It's still there. I heard him talking with one of the waitresses about writing and he seemed to know what he was talking about. And he seemed to have a lot more experience than I had. So I kind of eavesdropped for awhile, and then I saw him again maybe two weeks later at the cafeteria at Presidio. The cafeteria was open to civilians. Presidio was an open post, anybody could go on. You didn't have to be a soldier to use the cafeteria. So Les would go there.

He was a little man with thin white hair and one leg shorter than the other. He used a cane. He would carry this shopping bag into the restaurant and he would order tea and maybe a muffin. Then he'd take a papaya out of his shopping bag. And a lime. And that would be his lunch. The papaya and the lime and maybe a muffin. And he would have some tea. Tea or coffee. He just carried his food with him, and his manuscripts, all in the same bag. And he'd sit there and he'd write. I don't think he read much in restaurants. He'd read the paper.

Don't you do something like that now?
Yeah.

Mm hmm.

Yeah. I don't carry papayas with me. Well, so when I saw him at Presidio I went over and introduced myself. Told him I had seen him before and I sat down and we talked for awhile and agreed to exchange manuscripts. He had a book-length manuscript that he had completed. I had one too. *Negligence.* And we liked each other's work. That meant a tremendous lot to me, to have my work appreciated by another writer. And after having read Les's manuscript, I really respected him as a writer. This was *The Forty Fathom Bank.* So it was a good ego boost. And we started running into each other and, quite honestly, going out of our way to see each other. We would have dinner together. He was already seventy then, I think.

Did getting involved with publishing come as an outgrowth of that relationship?

Indirectly. I did my anthropological fieldwork in Samoa in 1982-'83. While I was there I met an American who was an editor for a small press located, I think, in Milwaukee. Milwaukee and Pago Pago. Which means that the other editor was living in Milwaukee. I showed John—this is the guy in Samoa—Les's manuscript of *The Forty Fathom Bank.* I wrote to Les and had him send it to me. John liked it, a lot. Didn't like my stuff, but he liked Les's stuff. They had published one book, which was a book written by the guy in Milwaukee, and they were looking for other manuscripts. As far as John was concerned, they were looking for other manuscripts.

So John sent it to the other guy. The other guy turned it down. It was just a very perfunctory rejection letter. It didn't really say anything. What he said to John was that if Les were a younger man, then he might want to publish it, but—

What did that have to do with it?

Good question. John had trouble with that, too. But the arrangement was that they both had to agree on the manuscript in order to publish it. I thought then that the guy was threatened by Les's manu-

158

script, that he was afraid it was better than his own book. And I saw John again. I went back to Samoa in '89 and I asked him about that. And he said that eventually he came to the same conclusion. The press finally died because the other guy would not agree to publishing another book.

But in the meantime I had been getting information from John about publishing. This is still in '82 or '83, on my original trip. John had been an editor at the University of California Press at Berkeley. And he was a poet himself, and wrote literary criticism. He knew some aspects of publishing. He certainly knew more than I did. I wasn't aware of small presses at all. I just assumed they were vanity presses.

So I came back from fieldwork. And I stopped in San Francisco to spend some time with Les. And I said, Let's publish your book. My thinking was, if we don't do it, how are we going to feel in five years? So we decided to publish his book. And shortly after that I thought the same thing about my book: How am I going to feel in five years if it doesn't get published? And I knew it was good. So we decided to do both books. Each of us found financing. I don't think he needed financing for his book. Les was well-off. So we decided to do both books. I found financing for mine. I sold shares in a limited partnership. And we formed Black Heron Press.

How did you find a printer and learn how to get the typesetting done and laying out the book and all those logistics?

Yeah. I was talking about my book with a friend and he put me in contact with a guy who was a typesetter. Everett Greiman at Dataprose. And Everett talked me through his part of it, getting it onto the page in camera-ready copy, so I understood it. He and Kate Robinson, who was working for him at that time. Kate connected me with a local artist. There was a local printer they knew of who I used for that book. As you do things and talk to other people, you become aware that there are always more options. There is always a different way of doing something. I learned by doing that one book.

So when you started the press, it was just to—

Just to do the two books. My intent was to get the books out and close up the press. That was probably Les's intent too. We never discussed it, actually.

Why did you decide to do it yourself, as opposed to going to another small press?

I had sent it to some small presses, once I knew there was such a thing. One wanted it, so I asked to see something they'd published. So they sent a sample, and it was a botch. The quality of production was terrible. It was just horrible. I never communicated with them again. I did not want them touching my manuscript.

So after you published Negligence of Death *what happened?*

Well, for one thing, I thought I wasn't going to be able to sell it. I printed a thousand copies and sold a hundred right off the bat to people I knew. And at Bumbershoot [i.e., the small press fair at Bumbershoot, Seattle's annual arts festival]. I think I sold eleven copies there, which is pretty good for Bumbershoot.

Trudy Mercer, from Red Sky [i.e., Red Sky Poetry Theater], saw it as it was being printed and read part of it. So she started talking it up, and I got invitations to read then. I was unaware that this was important. People were stepping in and guiding me. That's probably not the way they were thinking, but I used them as guides, to find out what I needed to do. Because I didn't know anything that needed to be done. I was so ignorant.

But I had sent it to *Library Journal* for review, not knowing that *Library Journal* wants galley copies. They want to see the book before it's published. But they reviewed it anyway. They reviewed it five months after it was published. And they highly recommended it. "Highly recommended" in quotes. And, based on that one review, I sold the entire print run and went into a second printing.

After you published Negligence of Death, *what was the next—?*

A poet named Ralph LaCharity had an idea for a book of his poetry. He wanted to use the Black Heron imprint. He would put up all the money. I wouldn't get anything out of it, but he would use the imprint. I don't do that anymore.

He was a friend of yours?

He wasn't. But he knew Les. I was giving a reading at Red Sky and I started talking about Les's book after the reading. And Ralph was there and he says, "Does Les still hang out at the Presidio cafeteria?" I had never met him. It was entirely coincidental that he had attended the reading and that he knew Les. Actually, Les liked his wife a lot. He was not particularly fond of Ralph. Les liked women. I've never known a man who liked women so much.

Even when he was in his seventies?

He liked women. Not only sexually. He just liked women. He liked them as people. He liked their companionship. He liked to talk with them. By and large, he found them more interesting than men. He was very sympathetic to them, very tolerant. And they could do some very shitty things to him. So...where were we going?

Well, you were going to tell me about the book you published after Negligence of Death.

Oh, Ralph LaCharity's book. So Ralph published *Seatticus Knight*. He took full responsibility for it. He did not want it distributed. He had a very unrealistic view of how to sell books. I saw him a few months ago. He's still...a very talented person who is determined to keep his talent concealed. He'll get the book in print and then he won't do anything with it. He will refuse to do anything with it. It ultimately became more than I wanted to deal with. To be talented is just not enough.

So that was the third book. And then Les and I decided to do that book of stories, *Of Great Spaces*. We sold hardly any. Well, now we've sold a few hundred. But at first we sold hardly any. Couldn't get it reviewed. And then Ron Dakron's first book, *infra*, came out at the same time as the book of stories. Both came out in '87. By that time I was becoming committed enough to publishing that I was willing not only to look for investors but also to take more risks with my own money.

161

Are you happy with what you're doing now, in terms of the number of books you publish and the kinds of things you're doing? Or do you have goals that you haven't reached yet?

I would like a partner so that I could do more books. So that Black Heron could do more books. A partner would have to have certain qualities. Would have to like exactly what I like.

Mm hmm. Good prerequisite.

And I would have to be able to get along very well with him or her. I've interviewed a few people. It's not going to work.

You want them to put up some money, right?

Right. They would have to be willing to do high-risk publishing.

Do you think such an animal exists?

No. I was only telling you what I would like. And I would have to be able to trust this person. Because I know what would happen. We would find that each of us has different talents and each of us would start focusing on his particular bent. I would like that. I don't want to be as busy as I am.

Would you trust another person to read manuscripts? Or would you do anything where you both had to agree, like those—?

Probably at first we would both have to agree. But once I gained confidence in that person, I would probably... assuming I gained confidence in that person.

So you're looking for a partner, but one for whom you are the overseer.

I would control the enterprise, right. I told you I didn't think I would find such an animal.

There's no way to realize everything you want for the press, is there?

I may have to modify my desires.

162

You publish your own material. When you're jurying your own work, do you have other people read your work? How do you have that kind of confidence in your own—?

As far as deciding whether or not to publish it, I've always used my own judgment on my own stuff. After I finish something I put it down and maybe I won't look at it again for years. By the time I pick it up again I'm pretty detached. So it isn't just a matter of writing it and publishing it. I've published four books and a chapbook of my own, and I'm sitting on other books that I've done.

Do you apply for grants?

No. My thinking is that if you get dependent on grants you start selecting materials that you think can win grants. I've discussed this with other publishers. They all seem to agree, at least the American ones do. It's just that with those who do go after grants, this twin issue of selection and dependence is not important. So they'll select certain manuscripts instead of others. That seems to be all right with them.

What kinds of grants can a publishing company get?

You can get a grant to publish a particular book. Or a particular line of books.

Like multicultural, or something like that?

It could be that, yeah. Granting agencies have their own standards of correctness. I'm told that you can say anything you want of a sexual nature, but you had better not say anything political. But, see, I'm going more and more into political...call it exploration.

Well, certainly The Inquisitor *was that way.*

Was politically inquisitive? Yeah. And so is *The Confession of Jack Straw* [by Simone Zelitch]. When I say "political" I'm not talking about electoral politics. And I want to do more. I'm working on an essay myself now.... I find myself doing more nonfiction, too.

Personally writing nonfiction?

Yeah. I realized recently that most of the shorter stuff I've published has been nonfiction. Essays. And that's what I'm working on now. It's an essay about approaches to pacifism. Given my military background, that might seem anomalous, but it doesn't feel anomalous. I'm just questioning different things and they seem to be leading in the direction of pacifism.

Do you keep a journal?

I do when I'm troubled about something and trying to figure it out. It helps just to put something down. When I'm troubled or when my life is so intense that I can't think about what I'm doing, I put it in a journal. It gives me some detachment. Although some things can be so intense that I can't write about them.

I want to get back to what we were talking about earlier about when you were nine years old and writing your first story and how good that made you feel. What in your life up till then, do you think, made you want to write a story, and to view it as something that was a positive thing to do?

Well, I wrote the story because it was an assignment from school. It gave me a deep sense of pleasure to do it.

Were your parents readers or writers?

My mother had written short stories when she was a girl. I didn't know that when I was growing up. She told me years later, when I was an adult. My father had written some professional articles when he was working for the Atomic Energy Commission. Years afterward physicists from various universities were calling him, trying to get copies of those articles. Although he's not a physicist himself; he never finished college. But he definitely has writing talent. Both of my parents had literary talent. And there were books. Lots of books. And my mother read...[laughing] easily forgettable novels.

Like supermarket paperbacks? That kind of—?

164

Yeah. Of course, thirty years ago you could buy books in those stands that were better quality than what you find now. I remember my parents reading *From Here to Eternity*. A popular one was Herman Wouk's book, *Marjorie Morningstar*. But they didn't read Hemingway or Steinbeck. Their books weren't available on those stands, I don't think. I take that back. Some of Steinbeck's were. But my father had two cloth-bound editions of Mark Twain. I have one of them now. Complete as of the time he bought them in the '30's. I don't remember seeing him read, but he talked about books.

So you do come from—?

Yeah. In their own way they were encouraging. Although shortly before my mother died she told me that when I was in high school she had asked one of my teachers not to encourage my writing. I had a teacher named Miss Berkey, Elizabeth Berkey, whom I valued and who was very encouraging, and my mother called her and asked her not to encourage me, because my mother felt I could not make a living at writing. I remembered Miss Berkey's attitude toward me changing suddenly. She seemed to distance herself. I never understood why until twenty-eight years later.

What prompted her to tell you that?

My mother? She was dying. She was saying things. I don't remember what particular thing led up to it. It must have been part of a larger conversation. She did also say that she wished I had not continued with my writing.

I was going to ask you if your parents read your books.

They read *The Negligence of Death*. When *The Inquisitor* came out my mother was already dead. My mother read the story collection, *Of Great Spaces*. My father didn't, until recently. He's remarried and his wife read that one and told him that there's one in there about him, and so he read that one. My master's thesis—actually, my mother tried to help with that. She talked about it to one of her neighbors who, it turned out, wanted to be a movie producer. He and his partner offered me a contract that was so heinous I turned it down.

What was your master's thesis on?

It's a description of a conflict in an antipoverty agency that evolved to shooting, arson—

Is it related to The Inquisitor?

Almost everything in the first part of *The Inquisitor* is taken from life. Though in real life nobody was killed. In *The Inquisitor* people were. But in real life one man put five rounds into a teacher's trailer, missing her and her child by inches. In the book, of course, she was shot.

And, also, how it happened is taken from life. There was ethnic conflict and class conflict and a charismatic leader playing one group against another, some of the staff trying to cover their tracks because they'd been embezzling, all this stuff. The producer wannabes wanted the manuscript, but the contract they gave me simply assigned all rights to them. And then if it was going to be made into a movie I would be hired as a technical advisor at the going rate. I thought, Well, there's no way I'm going to sign the rights away.

I guess my mother was of two minds. She saw I was having a hard time as far as gaining recognition for my writing was concerned. She was proud of what I was doing but wished I wasn't doing it; I guess that's the best way of putting it.

Do you think writing is therapy? I mean in your life.

Oh yeah. I'd be insane without it. Now I'm considered merely eccentric. But I think I would have gone around the bend long ago. It's a real need. And it isn't just any writing; it's fiction. Fiction is the need. The nonfiction—I'm not inventing anything. The need to invent. To create. I couldn't live. I think I would have killed myself. It's been my way out of some very difficult situations, emotionally. I'll probably never have to face losing writing. If I suddenly burned out like Conrad did his last year or two—he kept writing anyway, and I probably would do the same thing.

166

Thatcher Bailey
Bay Press

"... that's part of the responsibility of the publisher—to get the books into people's hands. That's, in fact, eighty percent of the responsibility. You're trying to get this stuff out there. 'Cause it doesn't do anybody any good, including all the trees you kill, to have this stuff sitting in a room someplace."

After graduating from Amherst, Thatcher Bailey returned home to Seattle, stayed for a year and a half, then went to Paris for six months. After returning to the United States he rode his bike from Seattle to New York where two of his best pals from high school were living. "Actually, I went back to come out of the closet, I think. My dad had died, and my mom had died earlier, so I had this sense of freedom, among other senses. And I just was a kid in New York, you know, and had fun." He stayed in New York for five years. He worked in a museum and a bookstore and he worked for a publishing company for a while. In 1982 he decided he had had his fill of the city. "I didn't want to be on Wall Street or be an artist, which seem like the only reasons you could possibly want to live there. So I moved back here."

I interviewed Thatcher Bailey at the office of Bay Press just south of Seattle Center and east of Elliott Bay on a cold, sunny day in early January 1993.

I first got involved with publishing in the fourth grade. I started a newspaper. I've always been kind of fascinated with turning things into something printed. But the first book was in 1982 and it was a children's book and it was an error. It was almost a practice project and I did it with my best friend in New York.

We shouldn't have done a children's book. It wasn't a great

book. I didn't know what I was doing. But it provided me an opportunity to go through the processes of putting something together, learn some things. Also it provided me this sort of weird excuse to—I was moving back from New York to Seattle and I put a bunch of these books in the back of my car and kind of took this endless zigzag trip across the country, stopping at every children's bookstore in America. It actually sold a lot of these books. I think people thought it was so—you know, they felt sorry for me or something.

And so the next year I did another project with the same guy, Hal Foster, who actually has a reputation as a critic and a scholar and shouldn't have been doing children's books. And it turned out to be the book that started the whole thing going, this book called *The Anti-Aesthetic*, which continues to be a big, big seller year after year after year. Ten years later it's still a standard course book. So that was very, very fortunate.

It was this book that developed a series of positions and arguments that were floating around at the time, and became this thing that a lot of people responded to with other projects or other discourses. It established an audience immediately. It sold well right from the beginning and it was about a series of issues that were of real interest to me, and I was learning stuff.

We kind of knew who we wanted to market it to. It was a somewhat academic, urban, somewhat left-leaning audience. But, 1983, it was just when the discussion of post-modernism was in contention in academic circles. Like, "What is this about?" "Who is going to own this term?" "What are the ramifications in thinking in terms of a break with modernism or the evolution of modernism?" "What is all this, what's going on?" It was a very hot issue at the time, and the people that we were able to put together were very respected thinkers who were grappling with this.

Hal put it all together. And it was a piece of cake to sell. I mean it was like the bookstores, just because of the people in it, automatically took it. And then it started to sell. It got reviewed everywhere. It was remarkable because I was—it's not a very nice-looking little book, and I had a full-time job in Port Townsend, working at Centrum, and was doing this from four in the morning till six in the morning, hand-packing every book, and it was kind of overwhelming. I really didn't know what I was doing, and it still worked. So if I'd known what I was doing, it would have been fantastic.

In America it sold a little over fifty thousand. And then there are British and Japanese and Spanish editions that probably are another twenty-five thousand. If you could sell between ten and fifteen thousand copies of a book, you could make some money. You could actually make it work.

But you don't do that with every book.

Oh no. No. But I'm not sure that with most books I couldn't. I really believe that I'm hitting about half the market at best. I think that's true of a lot of publishers. We get a third of the market, a quarter of the market. We're always trying to figure out how to get more books out there. And you have to squeeze it through the filter of the reviewers. So it's taken a long time to build up relationships with reviewers. We've had only two books in the *New York Times,* and that's very, very important to get. The *Village Voice* is our main—they review everything, they even put us on their lists. But that's a very distinct audience. It's kind of, in a way, our audience. But we want to get beyond that a little bit.

What did your parents do?

Actually, my dad had a newspaper, so I guess it was malignant. He started with a paint business, but just hated it. I mean he kept it, he did well with it, but he was bored with it, and he bought this newspaper, *The Argus.* It had just about died by the end of the '70's, 'cause he died and it lasted about—it had some permutations and then it collapsed. It very much had my father's personality. It was a time in which a small group of white men felt they ran the city, and basically did. And the city's changed. David Brewster worked at *The Argus* and then went from there to start *The Weekly,* which addressed another era.

Does Bay Press have a mission, a particular reason for being?

Well, if I had to write down a statement of purpose I would say I publish books on contemporary culture and leave it at that. As far as my sense of its purpose, it's very personal insofar as I really have seen this as an opportunity for me to engage in some issues that are of interest, to kind of continue my education. Most of the people I publish are really extraordinary thinkers, much of whose work is actually a little bit beyond my ken. It's been like this graduate course for me, doing this. And I really, really appreciate it. Then it's the opportunity to help put these projects together. So that would be, you know, why I've stuck with it. Usually that's sufficient reason to continue on.

I'm constantly struggling with, like, what happens next. Business has gotten to this certain point now, which is this really good point, but it needs other energy or some other.... It really needs to be bigger, there need to be more books, there needs to be a little bit more focus.

I have a whole other life outside of this in terms of being involved in community projects. It's of real interest to me. I know that I'm not going to want to give that up. I know that I can't do both. I'm sure that a lot of the publishers you talk to spend sixty hours a week doing that work, and I don't spend anywhere near that. So I've been kind of winging it and it's, you know, I haven't done that many books. Yeah, eighteen books since 1982. It's sort of accelerated over the last— it's not like an equal number of books each year. But, still, to make this work, I need to be doing eight or twelve books a year.

It actually comes down to vision. I had this notion that what I need to find is a twenty-four-, twenty-five-, twenty-six-year-old who's gone to college for this kind of stuff but who's onto another set of discourses. Someone young, with energy, with a different edge, who could come in here with that kind of passion that would push it in another direction.

What's happened over the last ten years is that there are so many presses now—I should say in the last three years—doing these kinds of books—you know, there's this explosion of cultural criticism—that I just feel that it's time to do something else. It was interesting to begin with, but now it's just one of a pack, and there are a lot of better-financed and bigger people in that pack.

170

So why not try to get a little bit more of an edge someplace else. I don't know if I can. I feel as though it's a generational thing. I'm not saying I couldn't do this myself. I'm saying I'm directed toward a certain way of approaching issues and certain kinds of ideas, and I would love to have someone else here to make this thing bigger, to really concentrate on it, and to offer a different perspective.

Also, I have a health issue. I'm HIV-positive and I kind of need to figure out what happens if I get sick. 'Cause, as you know, you can't just stop this because there's all this stuff happening, because of the orders and the courses and this and that. There's this funny responsibility to kind of figure out what needs to happen. If I drop dead, could someone else come in here—they couldn't come in here and figure out how to do it.

Do you have employees?
No. Everything is jobbed out. I had someone until about a year ago. He went to New York to start a coffee business, which was a very smart move. Since then, instead of having a full-time marketing person, I have Marcia Alvar—do you know her?—who just takes books on as projects. She's terrific. She's just what you need to deal with all those guys in New York who don't like Bay Press or small publishers. She's done a very good job. I realize that that's not what I'm good at, and if I have to do it I don't do a very good job of it, and I think it's the most important thing. I mean that's part of the responsibility of the publisher—to get the books into people's hands. That's, in fact, eighty percent of the responsibility. You're trying to get this stuff out there. 'Cause it doesn't do anybody any good, including all the trees you kill, to have this stuff sitting in a room someplace.

Can we talk a little about your community involvement?
Sure.

I know you were involved with setting up Artist Trust.
Yeah. There were a couple of us who put that together. I'm actually off the board now. I was involved very, very intensely for five

or six years. What interested me about that project was—it's sort of antithetical to what most people think Artist Trust is—it was less about pointing out artists as a special group than creating a situation whereby artists are much more integrated into people's—all of our—lives. It's not about economic marginalization or cultural marginalization, but about the issues that we allow artists to deal with, which is, you know, confronting a situation without any rules and trying to figure out how to negotiate through it. It's something that we can all learn from.

Maybe we should define it.

What Artist Trust is? It's a statewide organization that provides financial support for individual artists working in every discipline across the state. It also serves in an advocacy capacity in terms of articulating needs and issues that are central to various arts committees. It's also taken a leading role in freedom-of-expression issues which have been key in state and national debates over the last couple of years.

Artist Trust, oddly, was kind of a bad organization for it because we have this focus on the individual, because we have this focus on freedom-of-expression issues, which made larger arts organizations uncomfortable. During all the battles around the NEA [National Endowment for the Arts], we really took what I considered to be a very extreme stand. I have no regrets that we did that. But we isolated ourselves somewhat. We hurt ourselves in terms of funding. We were specifically told at times that some of our actions were inappropriate.

There was a wonderful luncheon that the Corporate Council for the Arts puts on every year. All it is, as far as I can tell, is an opportunity for various corporations to feel good about the few shekels they hand out every year to arts organizations. And this particular one had as its guest speaker John Frohnmayer [then head of the NEA] who, in a meeting with a group of activists right before the luncheon, indicated that he would have to face up to political realities, a statement he denied, but which has since been confirmed he made. And we—in protest, actually—when he got up to speak, walked out on the luncheon, which jeopardized our Boeing money pretty significantly.

And then, two days later, he vetoed the famous four grants. He came back to be a part of the Goodwill Games and we organized a protest which was really a positive protest. It was sort of saying, "These Goodwill Games are fantastic. We're concerned that under the present climate many of the aspects of these games would not have been funded through the NEA. And we just want people to be aware of that."

And so, opening at the Opera House was the Bolshoi. And we were pointing out that while the Soviet Union is now struggling and celebrating a new-found freedom, we're worried about what's happening in this country. All the most prominent arts patrons were coming there and we had an extraordinary group of people handing out these leaflets. We weren't blocking anybody. And it really left a bad taste in a lot of these patrons' mouths. It was very odd to think that people who were this supportive of the arts didn't see what issues were at stake.

But nonetheless, that was the kind of role that Artist Trust played, and I hope it continues to play in the future. Kind of a little bit of a conscience. When you think about it, it's the organization devoted to the people who are making the stuff. Who are, in a way, the workers. Which is always, of course, the group which is less recognized and a little threatening to the status quo.

I've worked more on social issues recently. I was very involved in the development of the AIDS Housing Project in the Madison Valley. And I'm currently involved in helping out Hands Off Washington, a preemptive campaign to keep out an Oregon-Colorado-style, anti-gay-and-lesbian initiative. It hasn't started, but they've vowed to do it. Our campaign actually is about raising a lot of money across the state from all the different groups, and saying "Don't even think about coming in here."

It would be kind of like the AIDS Housing Project which was a way of taking one issue that had been isolated in people's minds—you know, AIDS was about a certain group and a certain problem—and what that project did was just the most wonderful thing. Basically, the whole city got behind it, and the day we opened the facility there we are with about twenty-five hundred people there and they're from all over the place, all different kinds of groups, and everyone had the sense of, like, owning this product. It really made me feel terrific about the

173

possibility of what a community can do.

I think, in the same way, the Hands Off Washington campaign is this extraordinary coalition of people way beyond gay and lesbian groups, working not in reaction, but to articulate a position of respect and tolerance. So I'm kind of looking forward to this, and I think it'll be a very good thing. Although in Oregon the battle was very bruising and left a really bad taste in people's mouths. We want, if at all possible, to avoid the extreme of what happened there. Even though in Oregon the bad guys lost, it was nonetheless a situation where even now there's this residue and bad feelings on both sides, and you just don't want to have that happen in this state.

I recall it being a close vote in Oregon.

It was closer than it should have been. It was like forty-five—fifty-three. Our side spent two million dollars; they spent seven hundred thousand dollars. There was no piece of media in the state that didn't ardently and continuously advise people to vote against the ballot measure. There was no politician from any party who didn't get up and vociferously rail against the initiative. Nonetheless, there was an extraordinary number of people who voted for it.

How do you account for that?

Technically, one of the things that happened was that the campaign strategically concentrated its efforts in the most populated areas. It just didn't feel it had the resources to get out into the smaller communities.

I think, too, there was a—you know, this is why it's such a good issue for these guys. I mean, it's not their only issue. They'd just as soon establish a theocracy, and they'd pretty much eliminate any kind of difference. And, you know, homosexuality has not got a lot of support. There's a very tenuous kind of tolerance nationally that people have for gays and lesbians. And these guys can tap into that well of uncertainty and fear that surrounds that.

Also, their misrepresentations are egregious but they're difficult to counter. It's partly because so many people are closeted that in

174

many communities no one thinks they know any homosexuals, and so they're going to believe these very extreme and threatening kinds of images. And it's a tough battle. It really is. That's why the closet is so important to people like this. Because as long as people are invisible they [anti-homosexual groups] can enforce that invisibility.

You said "theocracy." Do you think the churches are behind the—?

Certain churches are. There's a very specific, kind of right-wing, fundamentalist bent to it [the anti-homosexual initiative].

Right. The Jimmy Swaggarts and Jim Bakkers. And yet their own sexual proclivities seem to be unusual.

Well, we live in a culture where the ability to be comfortable with your sex life is impaired for most people, and, clearly, for some people it's truly impaired. I mean these guys are just fascinated with female sex. They're just fascinated with it. So there's some level of real confusion there. And if you are a completely charitable person there'd be a lot of sympathy for these people, because you can't have that much hate in you unless your sexuality is troubling you.

But it's also about any other kind of difference. It's all this notion that the day of the rapture is no longer something that will come and there [may not] be a kingdom in heaven. Now there just needs to be a kingdom established on earth for you to be claimed as a member of the kingdom of God. So there's this whole shift that's happening in apocalyptic thinking, and you can't have a discussion about it because it's about a certain faith, it's about a certain belief. We can only try to unite and recognize the threat and stand up to it.

That's kind of a repeat of where anti-Semitism comes from originally, back in medieval Europe. There was that shift of apocalyptic thinking then, too. It wasn't going to happen in heaven. Here we were at the millennium and it didn't happen; we didn't all rise and meet Jesus in heaven. How to account for that? The way you just described the rationale behind being against anybody who is different sounds exactly like what's been described in some of the scholarly work that's been done on what happened at the end of the first millennium. Of course, we're now at the end of the second millennium.

Yeah. So we'll put a lot of effort into that campaign. It seems like a worthy thing to do.

Is there any kind of national effort, any coordinating council—?

There are a couple of national organizations attempting to coordinate—nothing like the Christian Coalition with, you know, those deep pockets. The ACLU is interested in these issues. People from Urban Way. National Gay and Lesbian Task Force. Human Rights Campaign Fund. To some extent it's all been coordinated. I was just in LA at a big conference in which this was a primary topic. And it was recognized that these guys are trying to get into thirty other states, and we have to be prepared. I mean we have to be really prepared. Oregon did a good job, but they just were hit with this obscene initiative. And they were reacting the whole time.

It passed in Colorado.

That's what's a little scary, because in Colorado one of the reasons it passed was it didn't talk about removing books from the library, it wasn't about making homosexuality a horrifying, illegal act, but it was about preventing municipalities and other governmental jurisdictions from adopting civil rights legislation. It was actually this no-special-rights conversation, which is the line that they use—"no special rights"—and of course it's really not about special rights. No one is asking for special rights.

It's signifying something else that they don't want to bring into the open.

Right. And it's likely the Colorado way will be a much more effective way to get into a community. On the other hand, these guys aren't necessarily going into these states to win on these initiatives. They're going in to raise money, they're going in to organize, to get a

176

huge network set up. This is what they do for their living. They run ballot initiatives. And they're not good people! The leaders, I mean. I can't get too upset with the voters who vote that way, because it's all about a kind of ignorance and fear, for the most part.

But there's some manipulation at the top that is scary. I mean connections to skinhead groups and violent, extreme fringe groups. We had a security person come and brief us on what we need to worry about here in terms of bodyguards and bars [on the windows] and, you know, where you place your office and unlisted phone numbers and all these terrible things. So it'll be interesting.

A lot of the kids I work with are gang kids. If I say that to somebody who's not black, then that probably means black gang kids. And some of them are. But they're all colors, and they're boys and they're girls. And they are all connected. The skinheads know the others who do similar things, and they may say that they hate... well, these kids aren't going to say they hate Blacks, because they don't, I don't think. They're too young, many of them. They haven't really developed that yet, though they know there is a color boundary that partly defines them. But because they do similar things and know each other, many of them, know each other's families—it's not that they're neighbors, but that they're criminals together. Different gangs may do favors for each other. (Of course, some of the so-called gangs are so unorganized as not to be able to get together to do anything as a gang). Nominally they're antagonists, but on certain occasions they're allies. It's a mirror of the big world, the world of adults.

What am I getting at? I guess I'm just making conversation apropos of the threat of fascism. Because these kids—they are potential fascists. They don't use that vocabulary, of course. They're the disorganized poor that supported Hitler. Except that those were adults. But that's where these kids come from and that's what they'll return to. That kind of poverty. I don't see the world becoming less hate-filled. I don't see the United States becoming more tolerant.

Let's talk about grants. You're on the board of directors of—
Copper Canyon. I mean there's a press that's working in that

way we spoke about earlier. You know, sixty hours a week and everybody committed. They've been doing this for twenty years now. And poetry, without argument, is something that requires additional support. I still, in a way, hold that if I was doing this full time, and did a few more books and focused a little bit more, this press could support me. The books I do can sell enough to do that.

I don't know. I'm intrigued with the nonprofit thing, but there's also something inside of me that really wants to believe that it's not necessary.

Do you regard Copper Canyon's going nonprofit as a form of defeat?

No! I mean I'm kind of ambivalent about it. And that ambivalence comes from some weird thing from my past—the voice of my father or something—speaking to me. In a way, I guess I feel that nonprofit status should be reserved for situations that truly would benefit by it, truly require it. And I'm not convinced that this [Bay Press's] mix of books truly requires it.

There's a press, The New Press—do you know that one? It's nonprofit. It's always kind of bothered me they're—I mean, they publish Studs Terkel. I mean, how the hell do they—what is going on here? They do a lot of books. For them it's just a revenue. I guess that's really all it needs to be, but.... I'm just ambivalent philosophically about what that means. One of the problems is your [i.e., nonprofit presses'] books are too cheap, you know? You need to be charging probably three or four dollars more a book when you get right down to it, to build in the proper margin.

That's true, but if you want to attract a larger audience, then—
See, everybody has to raise their prices. That's the thing. I mean books are cheaper in this country than just about any other country, relative to the standard of living. Right?

Yeah. And they're cheaper now than they were two hundred years ago when a book was more expensive than a horse. But part of

178

our national ideology is the idea of egalitarianism: everybody should have access. Whether we allow that or not, it's the way we like to think of ourselves: people who don't have money should still have access to books. This is something I struggle with too. I don't charge enough. I know I don't charge enough.

What's your average price?

About ten bucks. But I live in the West. In the East the same book will go for fourteen. But I can't charge ten dollars in Washington and fourteen dollars in Maryland.

I never thought about the East-West difference for pricing.

I didn't think about it either until I did a book by an author who lives in the East and she told me that her friends were noticing how inexpensive it was: a ten-dollar paperback. So I started looking at prices on books. North Point, for example, did literary books and they did charge three or four dollars more for a book similar to one I might do for nine or ten. Even for a smaller book. So I have a three-hundred-page book for ten dollars that I have to take a loss on. But in my mind is: Who is going to read it if I'm charging fourteen dollars for it?

That's a real act of generosity on your part. I mean, I guess I'm now feeling that I can't subsidize a reading public out there. I can get by without making a bunch of money, but I don't have the money to pump into this. I can't do it. My last book was eighteen ninety-five. I'm doing another eighteen ninety-five.

Well, I know I'm being unrealistic. I know my books aren't going to get to the people that I would like to see have them. Except through libraries. Libraries are still my primary market. Well, who knows. I mean, I get letters from the Yukon. I don't market to the Yukon, but the books get up there somehow. I actually did get a letter from the Yukon. But my prices are creeping up.

Also what happens when you raise the prices is your sales reports—it's amazing how much bigger they get. I mean if you get one or two dollars more per book, it's a big difference.

Do you sell very much in this area?

No, not a lot. I mean, my sister sells a lot. [Barbara Bailey owns Bailey-Coy Books, a bookstore on Capitol Hill in Seattle.] I just take the books up there. Which is really interesting because what that points out to me is that I do have a much bigger audience if I can get to it. Because obviously she's going to take my books, and she sells huge quantities of these books. And you wouldn't think this is exactly the book for that store. It's much more of a general interest store.

The reason she sells a lot of them is because she keeps them out on the table. You know, she gives me special attention. And it makes me realize that there are so many stores in the country where, if I can get put on the front table, I would sell four or five times as many books. Of course, every publisher knows that. But Elliott Bay [Elliott Bay Book Company] sells some. Not a lot. University Book Store sells some. I don't have much of an audience here. It's really mostly East Coast, LA, Chicago. Big cities.

I asked Cathy Hillenbrand the same question and she came up with a similar answer. Her American audience was the Northeast and the Midwest. It is for me, too. Then the question is: If it is the East, why is it the East?

Well, that gets into a sort of really mushy sense I have of.... You know, I lived in New York for a while, and the difference between New York and Seattle is so profound in terms of the way.... You know, New York is purely cultural landscape. Any sense of nature there is a very fragilely constructed one. It's really, in terms of the reading public that I was aware of and hung out with, a life of the mind. People's psychic space is important there. The way they conceive of their lives, you know, they create these structures of lots of schedules and... their minds create the reality, and it's a world where the commerce of ideas is much more prevalent than it is here.

I mean I love it. That's why I came back here. But here there's an outdoors, there's a different tone, it's not quite as urban. I don't—I never have the kind of conversation in Seattle that I have in New York, and vice versa. It's a very different relationship to issues and ideas. And these books are about the relationship you have in New York and not in Seattle.

That doesn't mean that I think that Seattle people are less or more, it's just a different approach. What's great about the twentieth century is you can actually live in Seattle and sell all your stuff in New York. Besides, I really couldn't afford to do this in New York. This office doesn't cost anything; I couldn't have an office in New York.

Cathy said something about the Dia Foundation.

Yeah. That's my other good pal. It was started with oil money a long time ago. And their original mission was to like provide an endless source of support for a certain group of artists. They ended up with this incredible collection of a certain era of work. And then the oil business went a little awry and the management of the foundation got a little screwy and they went through some hard times, and my friend was hired to run it and kind of resuscitated it and raised a bunch more money. They still have a huge endowment, and it's a very flush organization.

But he and my other friend, Hal, and I talked about this series of discussions in contemporary culture whereby Dia would sponsor these symposia and the proceedings would be published along with the conversations that happened after each person's presentation. So the books would be something between a journal and an actual book. We've done eight of them now. Several of them were really wonderful books because they're very kind of of-the-moment, they have a certain—they're not finished arguments, you know, they're kind of in-process arguments, and they're constantly honed by these discussions. It's interesting, because a lot of other institutions have started to do the same thing. It was a great idea. It worked.

Do you resent—?

Oh, not at all. It wasn't exactly like someone else couldn't have followed up. It's just—it was a way for certain institutions—it was a time when museums were feeling increasingly beside-the-point. And it was an effort to engage more in some of the more political kinds of issues that artists were beginning to deal with. So, how does the museum enter into that? The catalogue seemed sort of useless, so these became these other kinds of projects.

Okay. For posterity, what else would you like to say or talk about?
My gosh. I feel like I've been babbling on. I'm not sure I deserve any more space in posterity.

[Thatcher Bailey sold Bay Press in August 1993. The new owners, Sally Brunsman and Kimberly Barnett, intend to continue to publish cultural commentary.]

Anna Johnson
Open Hand Publishing

"I don't feel hopeless! I guess if I felt hopeless I would give up."

I interviewed Anna Johnson at her office on Third Avenue near Seattle's Pioneer Square on a pleasant but drizzly day in early January 1992. On the left-hand side of the room as I came through the doorway, set in blond wood shelves against the wall, were copies of the books Open Hand has published. Along the opposite wall were a computer and monitor, a telephone, paper-strewn tables—it was a working publisher's work area.

Johnson was born in Niagara Falls, New York where her parents owned and managed a construction company. She went to a small liberal arts school, Colby College, in Maine, where she majored in philosophy. "At the time I was very interested in existentialism."

She married, moved to Sydney, Australia, came back to the United States, returned to Australia, finally settled in Seattle and became a publisher. Open Hand Publishing started up in 1981, twenty years after Johnson first left the United States. That year she published James Forman's Self-Determination.

The original idea was to publish books that promoted positive social change. We started out doing books based on African-American issues and I had envisioned doing books related to the civil rights movement and also to the peace movement, because I see those two movements as related. It was difficult to choose when to go into books about the peace movement, but there was a book that was a bridge, *Mississippi to Madrid*. It's about a black veteran of the Spanish Civil War. And so I thought, Well, that opens the road to books about the peace movement.

183

So very shortly after that we did a book called *Surviving the Fire: Mother Courage in World War II*, which is about German women and children during the Second World War. That's a marvelous, very, very powerful book. But I was unable to sell it, and I think part of the reason I was unable to sell it was because we had gone out of our track of doing African-American books, and we'd developed that audience.

Also at that time I was publishing a novel called *Love, Debra*, about a fifteen-year-old homeless girl. Anyway, I also had a great deal of trouble selling *Love, Debra*. At the time...well, you learn so much, and you see it all in hindsight. But now I see that the distribution mechanism for fiction is very, very different from nonfiction. And so, because of doing two books, one on top of the other, that virtually didn't sell, it was very, very difficult. So, for the time being anyway, I'm pulling back and just doing books related to African-American issues until we become much stronger financially. Maybe I'll feel I can branch out again.

How many copies of Love, Debra *did you print?*
I believe five thousand. Four or five thousand.

Do you usually sell that many?
Yes. That's what we usually do in a first printing. *The Black West* is the book that really keeps us going. I think we've sold between fifteen and twenty thousand copies of that now.

How did Self-Determination *do?*
That sold very well. We've reprinted that three times. It's still selling. It was eleven years ago. And it's a hard book. It's not an easy book. It's not something you can just sit down and read casually. It's really political science. The other two books that we've done by Forman, *The Making of Black Revolutionaries* and *Sammy Younge, Jr.*, were both books that he had published before with major publishers. Macmillan had done *The Making of Black Revolutionaries* and Grove Press did *Sammy Younge*. But they were out of print and so we bought them back.

184

But if I were going to do it again, and I started with no knowledge whatsoever about publishing, I would do more books more quickly. But what I thought at the time was, Well, we'll do one book and we'll make a success of that, and then we'll do another book and we'll make a success of that, and it just doesn't work that way.

Okay, here we go: the big question.
Uh oh.

Why did you get involved with publishing? [Both laugh.]
Well, I had lived for seventeen years in Australia. In Sydney. And prior to going to Sydney I had been active both in the peace movement and the civil rights movement. And all the while I was in Australia I was not politically active. And also I had no intention of coming back to the United States. But I made a visit here in 1976 and while I was here I really had the impression that things were changing and there was some opportunity to work in a positive way for social change. I wanted to do that. So I made the decision to come back here. And I did come back in '78, specifically with the idea of becoming politically active. But I didn't have an idea of exactly what it was I was going to do. And so I spent a couple of years looking around and seeing where I might fit in.

At that time I was here in Seattle and I became involved in the Crabshell Alliance, working against nuclear power. And I decided to write a book myself about being a migrant, or an expatriate of the United States, since there's a lot of books written about the immigration into the United States but there's not much written about the exodus. It's certainly something James Baldwin talked about a lot. And there have been a lot of Americans who have migrated to other countries, but it just isn't dealt with very much.

Yeah, I found out only recently that about a fifth of the Europeans who emigrated to the United States around the turn of the century went back.
Mm hmm. That's interesting. I never heard that figure. I'm sure

there would be a lot, yeah.

Why did you go to Australia in the first place?
I was what was called a "nuclear migrant," though I didn't know that phrase.

A nuclear migrant?
A nuclear migrant. [Laughs.] In the late '50's and 1960 the Berlin Wall was just being built. That was at the height of the Cold War, and I was in SANE, the Committee for Nuclear Disarmament, in Boston. And it looked like a war between the United States and the Soviet Union was imminent.

Maybe that wasn't what the worst of it was. At that time there was a big movement to build bomb shelters, and the whole mentality seemed to be getting crazier and crazier, and people were building bomb shelters and then mounting machine guns on top of the bomb shelters because, you see, you'd have a bomb shelter but your neighbors wouldn't, so you'd—

The survivalists, right.
Yeah. And it all reached a point where it just seemed so insane that a lot of people began to think about moving to the southern hemisphere. The reason for the southern hemisphere was that there would be a lot of radiation in the air and the separate air currents.... So I was just getting married at that time and my husband and I decided that we'd move to the southern hemisphere and of all the places in the southern hemisphere, we picked Australia. And then after we got there we learned that, in fact, there were thousands of people, many thousands of people, from the United States and from Europe, moving to Australia and New Zealand for the same reason. And all those people came to be known in Australia as nuclear migrants.

And eventually you came back and you got into publishing, which is what we were talking about before I sidetracked you.
So anyway, I was writing a book and I also.... James Forman was

186

someone I had known much earlier, in the late '50's. And when I saw him he was writing his master's thesis and he.... Somehow when we were talking about work with Crabshell I said something about printers here in Seattle, and so he asked me if I would get his book printed. And I said, Well, I'll look into it. And so I came back and I talked with printers here at Workshop Printers. They were a cooperative and they were right on this street here, on Washington Street. Just half a... just two steps away. And so I talked with them about printing the book and the whole project got under way, and that's what I was doing. And I realized somewhere along the line, Well, the book needs more than to be printed, it needs a title, it needs a publishing company, it needs.... I learned about an ISBN, which I didn't know about before, and so it just occurred to me, I was really publishing this book, and so that's how I became a publisher. [Laughs.]

So the purpose of Open Hand remains social activism?
Yes. We've put an emphasis on books that will be appealing to children, and we've developed a children's line of books now. I think it's very important that there be material that is attractive to young people, that will keep alive the history of the civil rights movement which is just being lost so rapidly.

Your audience is primarily Black? Or do you know?
Both.

Black and white?
Mm hmm. I personally think that it's important for white people to know the Black history of the United States because it isn't just Black history, it's everybody's history. And what's happened is, as American history has been written, Blacks have been written out of that history. And so nobody knows the role that they've played, and that's just incorrect. That's bad for everybody.

So you intend the books to be read by people regardless of race or ethnicity. But do you have any idea who actually does read them?

187

Well, both read them, yeah.

Where do they get the books?

What's interesting is what's really just developing so rapidly, book buying in the Black community. And this is a phenomenon. It's just taken over like lightning the past five to six years. Because Black people traditionally have not had access to bookstores. They simply were not allowed to go into the areas of town where there were bookstores, and so, as a habit, that hasn't developed. Black publishers started maybe twenty years ago developing markets in the Black community, going into the churches, going into the health food stores, making books available where they weren't available before. And so now there's a whole distribution network of Blacks and of Black literature, and there are more and more publishers of these books. The whole thing is just growing. And people know, Black people know, that there are books available for their children that have pictures of Black children in them, so it makes more sense to them to be buying these books, and the demand is just phenomenal.

And then about three years ago a new organization, called the Multicultural Publishers Exchange, was started, and that's a coming-together of all of the publishers of multicultural books and their distributors. And actually the person who's responsible for getting this all going is Charles Taylor and he's going to come to Seattle next month and give a talk here. He's the publisher of Praxis Publications.

My reason for asking is that I've noticed.... Well, my academic training is in anthropology, and I did field work in the South Pacific and the United States. And I've lived in Central America. And I find that the hunger for knowledge, which means books, just stands up and smacks you in the face in the Pacific countries and Central America and the poorer, or more isolated, parts of the United States. But I don't see it among urban whites, not generally. I'm talking about real books, not pop psych or self-help or romances. Where I work now, it's the Black kids who ask me to get them books. They don't know who they want to read, but they want to read. [See my comments on this interview in the

188

"The interviews" section of the introduction to this book.]

Mm hmm. There's a tremendous hunger there. When we were distributing all our own books, before we were associated with Talman [a major book distributor. Since this interview, Open Hand has changed distributors. Open Hand books are now distributed by The Subterranean Company.], we'd get returns that were slightly damaged, so we always made them available to prisoners for free. And we'd just get endless letters from prisoners begging us for any book we could possibly give them. And then sometimes we'd get thank-you's and people saying how much they want this material. So this need is there, there's no question.

Looking at it cross-culturally, as I seem to be impelled to do, I think it's related to their wanting some control over the world they live in. Their societies are changing. They recognize that the possession of knowledge has practical consequences. I don't know how far to carry that out, but even those who don't read have a great respect for reading. For knowledge. I don't know how your table is at Bumbershoot [i.e., the small press fair at Bumbershoot, Seattle's annual arts festival], but I have to put up with a lot of insults from people coming by and saying "Oh, writers!"

Oh, really?

Oh, yeah. I don't know why they come into—
Oh, I've never experienced that.

Really?
No.

I actually had somebody hit me with a book once. [Laughs.]
You're kidding me!

No, I'm not kidding. [Still laughing.]
Oh, I would never even think of that. And so why is there this hostility?

I think in that case it was because of the topic. It was a novel

189

about Viet Nam. She picked it up and said, "What's this about?" And I said, "It's a novel about the American war in Viet Nam." And she threw it at me, hit me in the chest with it.

No!

And then she said, uh... actually, it was one that I wrote, too. [Both laugh.] But she didn't know that. Well, maybe she did know.

Oh, that's terrible.

Because she said, "Surely you can think of a better way of spending your talent." That's what she said: "spending your talent."

You know, I've never met with any hostility about the books. And one book I expected to.... Well, we published a book on the Ku Klux Klan. *The Invisible Empire.* And the Klan's very active here in Seattle. And I just didn't know how that was going to be received. But I have not been aware of anything happening to me that has any relationship to that. Nor has the author. Knock on wood. I feel, you know, lucky, if that's the case.

Yeah. A number of times, especially my Viet Nam stuff—I have two Viet Nam war novels out and a third will be out in March. I wrote one and this other man, David Willson, wrote two, including the one that will be out in March. I'm planning on another one, done by a deserter, a memoir but in novel form. And there's some real hostility from all points of view. Except I don't get any hostility from veterans. They're interested—

Yeah, sure.

—in reading everything. But one man came up to me and said, "That war should never have been fought." This was an older man, I would guess in his mid-seventies. And I said, "Well, I'll go along with that." And he said, "Another war that shouldn't have been fought was the Civil War." And I said, "Oh?" And he said, "Because it freed the slaves."

You're kidding me!

No. This was at Bumbershoot about 1985 or '86. I didn't know what to say, so I turned my back on him so I'd have a moment to think, and then I turned back again. I thought to myself, I can't let him get away with that. But the only thing I could think of to say was, "You're talking to the wrong person." And I asked him to leave my table. He was standing in front. And I asked him to leave. And it took him a moment, but he did leave. He didn't say anything more.

I see. Well, with all of our books being on Black subjects.... It used to be, I would go around to bookstores and oftentimes the bookstore buyer would simply say, "Well, no, we're not interested." Not any of the major bookstores, because we've had tremendous support from Elliott Bay Books and University Book Store and Red and Black Books. They've just been absolutely wonderful and so supportive. But there have been a few small bookstores around that I've gone to and they just say, "Well, you know, we're not interested." Well, now, maybe they think, Our customers are white, they're not going to be interested in books about that subject. But, you know, I would beg them to try at least taking one or two, but they just were not interested and that's it. So that's a negative reaction. But I haven't met with any kind of hostility ever.

Well. Change of subject. Do you apply for grants?

I haven't, but I'm beginning to think maybe we should take that route, and I'm beginning to search out.... But I still have doubts because the amount of time it takes to apply for grants, I don't know if that time wouldn't be better spent trying to promote the sales of our books. It's just such a time-consuming process, but I definitely have not ruled it out and we do spend time now looking for grants, but I haven't received any yet. Although the two authors of a book that's coming out soon, called *Sylvia Stark, A Pioneer*, received support from the King County Commission for the Humanities.

Do you submit books for awards, like the PEN awards, or...?

I haven't done the PEN awards. It isn't something I spend time on, searching around for awards. Maybe I should do it. The Before Columbus awards are really nice. And I do submit books regularly to that.

I have a question about something you said earlier. You said you saw the peace movement and civil rights as being related. How do you see that connection?

Well, I think Americans have to come to terms with having been a slave society, with having been a culture that was nurtured on slavery, and that had it not been for the free labor of the slaves we never could have developed economically the way we did. And I think certainly that has to be looked at from the economic standpoint. But more than that, I think there's also a psychological conditioning that is just inherent in Americans. That people are treated as slaves.

People generally?

Yeah. It's a way, it's a heritable way, of looking at people. Of treating people. And that if we had not had slavery in the first place, our psyche would be different.

Some other societies have hierarchies but don't have a history of slavery. At least not recently.

Well, when you get further back.... I don't think we should lose track of the fact that we're a slave society and I think that it should be something that is really examined to the point that we're able to somehow come to terms with it instead of just denying it. But it isn't going away. And the way that we dealt with the Viet Nam war, I see that as also related to the way that we dealt with the slaves.

In terms of policy?

In terms of policy and in terms of how people are treated. And we certainly behaved.... We had a very different relationship with the Vietnamese in that war than we did with our enemy, the Germans, in the Second World War. And the Germans in the Second World War were treated differently than the Japanese. And I think these things are just so

192

tied up in a knot that we've got to spend time untangling all of it.

I think even if we didn't have racism as we know it, we would still have war. And I don't hear you saying we would not have war.
No.

I think the implication of what you're saying is that war would take on a different character.
Mm hmm. Well, what I'm talking about is the way I felt in 19— ... you know, early on. But at this point, at this level of sophistication, of war technology that we have, we cannot afford to have a war. Because we can easily destroy the whole earth. I mean it amazes me that we're still here. I can't comprehend how we're still here. Because I didn't think we were going to be here beyond 1960. But we are here. And people have begun to talk about dispute resolution. And this is something we're going to have to develop.

Instead of trying to defeat the other party, you try to resolve the issue?
Yeah. Taking the issue and dealing with it in a way other than sheer brute force. And I think this is something that people are beginning to understand.

But obviously people can want to go to war. We just had another adventure [i.e., the war against Iraq] *and some people got very excited about it. About doing it. Wanting to do it.*
Well, you can drum that excitement up. You can stir it up. But I think that we really have reached a point where we have to deal with things in ways other than through strength. And we can do that. I really believe we can do that.

I don't think humankind has reached that point. There're lots of places I've been where aggression is considered good. It has a positive value. I see people who otherwise may be very nice people, but when given the opportunity to take something of their neighbor's, they'll do

it. Indonesia—
    East Timor, yeah.

I approach the issue of war by asking who benefits from it. Who's fighting it and who's benefiting from it. In Viet Nam I didn't see Blacks or other minorities benefiting from it. But I do see poor people benefiting from military experience in that the military provides jobs and allows people to raise their social status. If they could have the military experience without war.... [Laughs.]
    But we don't have to have wars for people to benefit. I mean, the whole horrible condition that the schools are in today, and here we are spending more money on jails than on schools.... And suddenly we feel that we have—I don't know if I should use this word "we"—the society feels it has to do something with all the criminals. Well, we created the criminals. [Laughs.] And if we would only treat these children decently as children, we wouldn't need the jails. [Laughs.] I think it's only getting worse and worse and I don't see how we can pull ourselves out of this cycle of what's going on in the streets, the violence in the streets.

Did you read Do or Die?
    I haven't read that book.

It's really a fine book. But the author also feels hopeless.
    Well, I don't feel hopeless! I guess if I felt hopeless I would give up. I don't see what's going to turn it around so it isn't like this on the streets anymore, but on the other hand, I think that there is some answer and we've got to keep looking for it.

Well, I don't have any hope. But I think it's possible that I'm wrong, so it's worth going ahead—
    Yeah. You feel hopeless but you haven't given up hope. [Laughs.] Because once one gives up hope, I mean, you stop and you're—

I'm not aware of having any hope. But I think one has to go

194

ahead anyway.
Uh huh. I guess it becomes faith at that point.

Yeah. All right. Not hope but faith. I'll go for that.
Yeah. Yeah. [Laughs.]

Kent Sturgis
Epicenter Press

"I don't really have a big message. I'm just trying to make a living from book publishing."

Kent Sturgis grew up in Fairbanks, Alaska, the only child of a Massachusetts-born father and a Florida-reared mother. His father, a B29 navigator during World War II, had a choice of assignment following his training in Florida: Guam or Fairbanks. As he couldn't find Guam on a map, he chose Fairbanks. In Alaska, he was part of the crew that made the first confirmed flight over the North Pole, having newly developed navigational equipment to verify it.

Like many former military people, Sturgis's family stayed in Alaska after the end of the war, his father establishing an independent insurance agency in Fairbanks and his mother becoming secretary to the publisher of the Fairbanks Daily News-Miner. *Sturgis remembers himself as being "a competitive little bastard when I was in grade school. I recall that in the early grades—first, second, third and fourth—we were always reading in class. It was always a race to see who could read the most books. I think I started reading books for competitive reasons, to get a gold star on the board."*

He spent a year at the University of Alaska, then transferred to the University of Washington to pursue a journalism degree. Eventually he went to work for the Associated Press, quit school, and returned to Alaska for the AP. "Mostly," he says, "I was less than a serious student." With Lael Morgan, another Alaska journalist, he founded Epicenter Press in 1988. We talked at his house north of Seattle on a pleasant day at the end of April 1993.

Well, I've done a little bit of everything. I started hanging around the *Fairbanks Daily News-Miner* in grade school. My mother was the publisher's secretary and I started writing columns in junior high school and then started working part time after school. I was a junior in high school and the sports editor turned yellow one day and they sent him to the hospital with jaundice and I was sports editor for a while. I got a lot of experience early.

Well, I came down here, worked for the *Seattle Times* for about six months and then the publisher in Fairbanks helped me get a job with Associated Press. I was with them for a couple of years and then they sent me to Anchorage as—we opened up an office there. I was a correspondent in Anchorage and I went back and forth between Anchorage and Juneau. I flew down to Juneau and helped cover the legislature during the winter. And then AP brought me back to Seattle where I was Assistant Chief of Bureau. And then the Chief of Bureau was promoted to New York and I was Chief of Bureau for the AP for several years. And then I went back to the *News-Miner* in Fairbanks to be the managing editor. Did that for about twelve years and kind of got burned out on it. Kind of got tired of the murder and mayhem of daily journalism, so I took some time off.

The murder and mayhem that you covered in daily journalism or are you talking about the news room?

The coverage. The kinds of things you're going after. Got kind of tired of that. Took a break. And then I went back. I worked at the *Seattle Times* a couple of times, on the news desk and on the city desk. I worked part time for the *Everett Herald* and I did a temporary stint at the *Bellevue American* and I worked for the *Alaska Fisherman's Journal*. The guy who owns the *Alaska Fisherman's Journal* and I started the *Alaska Oil Spill Reporter* which was a newsletter that we did after the oil spill in Valdez. And I did various freelance, wrote a book, *Four Generations on the Yukon*, did some magazine articles.

Who published your book?

Epicenter Press. About that time I joined with a partner, Lael Morgan, who also had a journalism background and also had a book. We published her book and published my book and two other books in 1988. And so we started publishing books. Actually, before that, Lael and I—it was Lael's idea that we get into book publishing. I didn't have a burning desire to get into book publishing. But she thought it would be a lot of fun.

We were at the *News-Miner* together. There was a disastrous flood in Fairbanks in 1967 and we were both at the paper at that time. You sort of get to know somebody pretty well in that kind of situation. We've been friends ever since. In about 1986 Lael and I were part of a group of five people that were negotiating to buy Alaska Northwest Publishing Company. Bob Henning down in Edmonds. At one time he had *Alaska Magazine* and *Northwest Living* and he did the Milepost travel guides and he had a huge book list and various other things. He'd sold the magazine and he had the books, including the Milepost which had been around for twenty-five or thirty years. And five of us made an offer and it just wasn't enough. We didn't have the muscle to do this thing. So our group fell apart and Lael and I got together later and we thought, well, we'll just start our own company, and we did.

We were very naive in the beginning. We thought we might do sort of a job share. I'd run the company one year and she'd run it the next year and we'd just sort of job trade. This is before it required full-time effort. And we tried that a couple of times but it didn't work out too well. She got on at the University of Alaska, Fairbanks. She's on the faculty there. And so I've been, I don't know, running the company now for about four years.

She sold back half of her—there were two of us and we—Lael and I get along but we shout at each other a lot. You know, when you have a fifty-fifty partner you can't divorce him. You can get divorced easier than you can break up this fifty-fifty thing. So in recognition of the fact that I was running the company and willing to make a long-term commitment to it, she sold back half of her stock to the company to sort of break the fifty-fifty deadlock.

Then later, as the value of the stock went up, we brought in some other shareholders. Both of them are in Fairbanks. So we have a three-member board of directors now—myself and Lael Morgan and another

198

fellow who I've known for many years, B.G. Olson. He has a background in media law, mass communications, journalism, et cetera. The fourth partner is a fellow named Stephen Lay. He works for the Cooperative Extension Service in Fairbanks. In fact, Lael and Stephen and B.G. are all associated with the University of Alaska in one way or another.

Are all the partners working partners? I mean working with the press?

Yeah. They're active. B.G. and Lael sort of have other careers and I've been doing it full time. Stephen's not active so much. At this point he's just a shareholder. I think B.G.'s going to be spending more time in the months to come. We're starting to grow and there's more work. We're growing in numbers of titles, growing in dollar sales, growing in other ways. Slowly but surely.

We do books in three categories. The original mission of the first category was Northern nonfiction. Alaska and western Canada. We've done histories, biographies, adventure stories, nonfiction stuff.

And then we had an opportunity to buy a little series of regional travel guides called Umbrella Books, which we picked up as an imprint. We picked up, I think, five titles. And we've since published four more. *Bicycling the Oregon Coast, California Lighthouses, Washington Lighthouses, Southeast Alaska, Northwest Natural Hot Springs,* various titles like that. So that's the second little niche.

And then the third area is art and photography. We've got a series of art books going by contemporary Western artists. The first two happen to be Alaskans but we're looking for other Western artists. And we have a book called *Wild Critters* that includes the work of a well-known wildlife photographer in Alaska, Tom Walker, and a well-known writer, Tim Jones. Wildlife photography for kids, sort of, with Ogden Nash-style verses.

What's the difference in the Fairbanks operation and the Seattle operation? Or is there a difference? Why do you have two locations?

Well, we're an Alaska-based corporation and Fairbanks is our corporate headquarters. Which is an office in Lael Morgan's home. We ran the company from Fairbanks for the first couple of years and our inventory is all up there. Until recently we'd get new books from the printer and Fairbanks would get some and there'd be a little bit here and a lot of it would go to the distributor. So we'd been doing most of our fulfillment out of Fairbanks. We're kind of phasing out of that a little bit because it's unnecessarily expensive. We were shipping books from Fairbanks to everywhere, and that's why we decided to kind of limit our fulfillment up there. Because we were shipping books to Alaska, then shipping them from Alaska to somewhere else, and paying all this freight—it was ridiculous. So what we have in Alaska now tends to be stuff that there's a fairly good demand for, fairly close at hand, and Alaskan titles only. Our regional travel guides don't sell very well up there. We have only one travel title that's devoted exclusively to an Alaskan subject.

We realized early on that it's real tough to sell books from Fairbanks. You're just so out of synch with everything. You're out of the network and you're out of the time zones and all that stuff. You can't manufacture books up there. You can't afford to. I guess if we'd gotten into desktop early on and spent the money and trained ourselves or found somebody to do it, we probably could do prepress in Fairbanks. But basically I came down here to sell books to the outside world and produce books as efficiently as possible. But Alaska is a real important market for us. A majority of our books have some sort of Alaskan theme and we sell a lot of books in Alaska. To Alaskans and to tourists as well.

But Fairbanks is the heart—you know, that's where Epicenter Press comes from. We put Fairbanks as the name that comes before Seattle on our logo. So that's the heart of it. We place a lot of value in having our roots in interior Alaska. We call this [Seattle] our remote outpost.

How does the market in Alaska differ from the market here?
Tourists. That's probably why there aren't many publishers up there with any money. Because there's not enough population to produce the kind of sales that you need. But there's a lot of tourists.

There's about a million people a year that come to Alaska. Probably three-quarters of them come in June, July and August. And so our strategy from the very beginning—well, not from the very beginning; we weren't thinking much at all about marketing in the very beginning. But when we started to think about it, we tried to develop titles that we thought would be of interest to Alaskans. But when that market had played itself out a little bit, it would also have a recurring sales to tourists. I mean it's like a new crop of customers every year. It's worked out all right.

Do you personally continue to write?

Sort of. I'm actually overloaded a little bit right now. I have three book contracts, one with Epicenter, two with other publishers. The one that I'm excited about is with Epicenter, which I think is going to be a fun book and, I hope, a successful book. It's a title called *Dog Heroes*. It will be a combination of illustrations by a wildlife artist named Jon Van Zyle, who's from Alaska and whose first art book, *Best of Alaska*, we published. Our intern last summer spent all summer researching the great dog heroes of all time. Well, the twentieth century. From Europe to Asia to North America, South America—

You're not talking about film dog heroes, but real dog heroes.

Real dog heroes. So we're combining text with paintings. Lavish illustrations. It's going to be kind of a gift book. I think it has all the potential of just being—it has universal appeal. Great dog stories. And these stories are just amazing. There're different categories. Great service dogs, seeing-eye dogs. How seeing-eye dogs came into being. You know, some remarkable seeing-eye dogs and other service dogs. Police dogs. Acts of heroism. Loyalty. Dogs that explored. War dogs. Entertainment dogs. You know, Lassie, Rin Tin Tin, et cetera. There'll be a couple of dozen dogs. Great stories. Some amazing stories about the Saint Bernards. How they got their reputation. Some terrific stories.

What about Lael? Does she continue to write?

She does. As a matter of fact, of our two fall books, she found one title and developed it and helped with the editing, and the other title is her own. The second title is called *The Earthquake Survival Manual*.

That should be popular up and down the whole coast.

Well, the focus is California to Alaska. We hope to sell elsewhere but we're really concentrating on the West. Lael's been working on this for years. It's a terrific book. It's not only factual and well-checked—we've had all the experts read it—and has a lot of useful information and covers a lot of ground that you haven't seen anywhere else, but there's also quite a bit of humor in it, and personal anecdotes.

I'll bet Dan [Dan Levant, Madrona Publishers] *would appreciate that one. You know he did the St. Helens book. Is he aware that you're doing that one?*

Uh huh. Yeah.

Why did you get involved with book publishing? We approached this earlier in that Lael kind of talked you into it, but do you think that's a complete answer?

Well, you know, I kind of fell into it. I'd left the *News-Miner*. It happened to be an employee-owned newspaper and I'd been there for the vesting period and so I had some cash when I left. So I had some money to invest. Thank goodness I didn't have any more money than I had because the first few titles we had were, you know, not very commercial.

If we had it to do all over again, I'm not sure I would do it. Boy, I've worked harder the last three or four years than I have in my whole life, and I've always considered myself a pretty hard worker. But, you know, the pressures of small business and being responsible for.... Oh, right now things aren't too bad. It's been a real tough winter for us. I wake up in the middle of the night worrying about how to pay bills and whether I'll have to go out and look for a job. I'm in my mid-forties and a white male. I'm not exactly in great demand today.

I think I've learned—the approach we've taken and where we're coming from is that we're trying to figure out how to—I'm trying

202

to figure out how to make a living from book publishing. I don't really have a big message. I'm just trying to make a living from book publishing. I've been at this for going on six years and I've only taken a salary for less than two years and let me tell you, it's peanuts. I've been poor for years. My wife works real hard, has a nursery school. She's been carrying most of the load these last couple of years. I like drawing a salary and I hope that it will increase. Our first several titles were just not very commercial.

I read somewhere that for a general nonfiction trade publisher doing fairly commercial stuff, every title needs to be successful. Every title needs to pay for itself. Maybe one out of every six or seven can kind of be a mission book that you select without regard to profit potential.

If it's a mission book, how would you define the mission?
It's a book that needs to be published. Ironically, a book that I thought was a mission book is probably going to turn out to be the book that turns our company around. It's a book that we're publishing this fall, *Two Old Women*. The subtitle is *An Alaskan Legend of Betrayal, Courage and Survival*. It's written by an Athabaskan Indian woman up in Fort Yukon, Velma Wallis. It's a story about two elderly women before Western culture came to Alaska.

I remember you telling me about it on the phone. Left to die, and then they didn't.
They didn't. And it's the story of what happened to them over the next four seasons. And it has kind of a surprise upbeat ending. We've been messing with this thing for going on two years now, trying to figure out what to do with it. And suddenly things are starting to happen. Native American values seem to be coming into their own. People are more interested in Native American titles, which has been good for this project. Also, it's the '93 winner in creative nonfiction in the Western States Arts Federation book awards. And we wound up selling reprint rights to HarpérCollins for a trade paperback to be published in '94. We had an auction. Simon and Schuster, HarperCollins—

Did you have an agent who held the auction?

Elizabeth Wales. Just did a hell of a job. And it was just amazing. This thing has sort of taken on a life of its own. We're going to print about five thousand hardcover copies in the fall. The Western States Arts Federation, they really work hard to promote these winners and so we hope to sell a lot of hard covers. In the meantime there's a subsidiary income. This comes at the perfect time. I felt like we were about ready to go down for the third time. So that's been real good for us. Initially we didn't think there was going to be much of a market for that book, and we were wrong. Although I must say Lael Morgan has believed in this title from the very beginning. I loved it too, but I didn't think it was ever going to make any money. But I was wrong.

So I fell into book publishing. I don't have any great burning passion to publish literature or history or anything like that. I just kind of fell into it and now I'm struggling, trying to earn a living and trying to create a retirement for myself, basically, by publishing books. But it's a lot of fun and I like the independence. I haven't punched a time clock for anybody since I left daily journalism in '86, and I don't see myself ever holding a standard job again. At least I hope not.

Linny and Denny Stovall
Blue Heron Publishing

"What do these publishers want? They don't know."

At the time of this interview, Blue Heron Publishing published Writer's Northwest Handbook, *a resource directory for writers,* Writer's Northwest, *a quarterly newspaper focusing on books and authors,* Left Bank, *"not quite" a literary journal, according to Denny Stovall, and reprints of children's books by Walt Morey of* Gentle Ben *fame. In 1994 the Stovalls sold both the handbook and the quarterly.* Left Bank, *one issue of which had been put out when this interview was conducted, is published semiannually.*

Unlike most publishers, whether or not associated with independent presses, Linny and Denny Stovall came to publishing from a labor (as opposed to a managerial or professional) background. Denny has worked as a truck driver, a ranch hand, a tunnel builder and a crane operator; both Stovalls spent almost a decade as organizers in Pittsburgh's steel mills. Toward the end of his time in Pittsburgh Denny worked as a freelance writer.

Denny matriculated at the University of Oregon Honors College ("The University of Oregon what?" "Honors College." "What is—?" "That's to train professors. Little professors." "Ah. Little professors."), taking a BA in political science. Linny attended Antioch College in Ohio. They met in "'73 or so," according to Linny ("Seventy-three or -four," says Denny) and moved to Oregon, Denny's birthplace, in 1984. They currently live in Hillsboro, Oregon, about twenty miles west of Portland, and operate their publishing company out of their house.

The interview took place in my apartment in north Seattle late in the evening of November 22, 1991. They were in Seattle to attend the annual convention of the National Council of Teachers of English.

Linny Stovall: We moved back here in '84 in the fall. And about a year later was when the *Northwest Handbook* started.

Denny Stovall: We started it in July of '85.

LS: And then six months later we started on the second edition. Really, that was the focus of the publishing company, was this one book.

How were you earning your living at that time? Certainly that one book wasn't bringing in enough income to live.

LS and **DS:** No.

LS: I was working as the director of a nonprofit during that first year we had the publishing company. That helped, you know, to have one of us working and one of us starting this company. But actually there was something that helped me there. We did publish a directory. That was my first experience in something related to publishing. It was already an ongoing project, so I could just plug into it. But I didn't contribute very much to the first handbook. That was done by Dennis and his cousin.

Oh, there were three of you. What was your cousin's name?

DS: Doug. Doug Freeman. Younger than me by about ten years. We actually did the handbook because when we moved back here and I started to pick up freelancing again—it had been a good business in Pittsburgh but I had trouble getting off the ground back on this side of the country because there were so many more writers and so few decent-paying gigs. I began putting a list together of all of the outlets, and it was really a resource for writers. Doug was a writer here in the Tacoma-Seattle area for a while, and we teamed up in our freelancing to sort of get going together there.

You were doing freelance journalism?

DS: Yeah. Feature writing. We were also doing contract writing.

Feature writing meaning for newspapers and magazines?

DS: Magazines, yeah. And also looking for any writing that we

206

could get. We figured that the business side of the writing was probably the more lucrative and had the greatest potential for a steady income, so we started looking for companies that wanted histories written and people who needed product descriptions, that sort of thing. We did a real short-term gig for the Boy Scouts. The regional council in Portland had been doing the seventy-fifth anniversary edition, had contracted it out, and the person they had given it to had failed, so Doug and I actually wrote the whole thing on a weekend. Wrote a whole book. For which we were never paid. [All three laugh.]

[Still laughing.] *The Boy Scouts.*
DS: Yeah. Got stiffed by the Boy Scouts.

Be trustworthy, honest—
DS: Yeah, and also be cheerful and, boy, tough to collect from. But once we started the publishing company Doug and I started going in different directions. And Linny was ready to leave what she was doing and it just made sense when he left that we picked it up and went with it because the *Handbook* was clearly a useful tool, had a good market, and was developing a better market. It was also putting us in a very good position in relation to other publishers. We had access to people. And information. So we were getting a pretty good view of what was going on, seeing why other presses succeeded or failed. Which was one of the real benefits of doing that book.

When you say "succeeded or failed," you mean in financial terms?
DS: Well, financial and other, but certainly financial. Because that's, as you know, a real problem with anybody who attempts to live off of this business.

Na-a-ah. [All laugh.]
LS: We traveled a lot. That's the other thing. So we got to meet people who were publishing and talked to them personally. We traveled because that was the way to do research for the book as well as sell it.

That's how we started. That was another thing. Doug didn't really want to travel. I don't think he wanted to be a publisher. He didn't want to travel. I think he wanted to be a freelance writer and he heard us saying, "Hey, let's go beyond this. Let's have a little more control about what's being published." So we started writing grants to the arts commissions so we could go even farther afield and travel to Montana and Idaho.

So you became involved in publishing when you returned to Oregon.

DS: Although when I was writing in Pittsburgh, when I was doing contract writing and ghost writing, that involved brushing up against publishing and sort of helping somebody through the process and learning it as I went. Though I wasn't actually publishing I was getting some training.

What do you mean, "process"?

DS: How is a book put together? Who do you talk to? What role do printers play? What does a typesetter do? That kind of thing. The stuff that you sort of know is there, but it's still mysterious.

This was when you were freelancing?
DS: Yeah.

Not all freelancers do that though. How did you get—?

DS: I was looking for base-income kinds of writing jobs, and those turned out to be things like ghost writing and technical writing. Long-term contracts, steady income.

LS: To answer that part: because you had to take that book through to the printer. Two books. Two books that were ghost-written, so he had to learn the process beyond it.

I see. These were books that were self-published by the people you were ghost writing for.
DS: That's right.

So you essentially brokered them.

DS: Well, I just managed all of that. I was a liaison rather than a broker. I didn't know enough to be a broker.

LS: So those were the first books you published.

DS: Yeah. I even did one for the Department of Romance Languages at the University of Pittsburgh. It was the proceedings of a conference on Portuguese literature. Current Portuguese literature. Since the revolution in '75. And I had to type it all in Portuguese. It was pretty bizarre. I had no idea what was happening.

I assume you're not writing as much now as you were ten years ago.

DS: No. No. This business takes up so much time. I'd actually started off writing. Linny gave me a year's leave to learn how to do fiction, which I had always wanted to do. We were both working in mills. Her mill job was better than mine. But it was clear that if I was going to stay in the mill I was in, I had a career choice coming up. That was either to stay there and work through my seniority far enough to get a job that wouldn't hurt my back—I have a congenital birth defect in my back—and that would be another four or five years there, and I could have probably won the presidency of the local or something, or I could have gone into the Steelworkers Union on the international level. That was sort of an option. But I'd always wanted to do the freelance writing full time.

But what I was most interested in was developing novels as a way of working out things in the world, talking about the world. So Linny said that I could have a year with her support while I learned craft. So I quit smoking and—that was the other part of the deal—and, uh, started writing. But six months into that period her mill went under. She and I had to make a living now. And at that point I figured out how to make a living. As a writer.

You were labor organizers, weren't you?
DS: Yes.

Have you found that your experience as organizers has carried over into your publishing? Or has it mattered at all?

DS: It's, in a way, important, because it informs a lot of what we do and how we go about organizing our publishing activity. The background we had as organizers, I think, was important to us in figuring out how to do things as quickly as we could once we decided we were going to do them. But when the mills closed....

LS: They really should write a book about the Mon Valley. I mean, they bought out a steel mill. Collectively. And that thinking was just antithetical to how people were feeling two or three years previously. It's fascinating how things can change. But back to publishing. Like Dennis said, we were applying for grants to the arts commissions and we started traveling and we kind of made ourselves known in a fairly short period of time. There were two of us and we were on the road and our kids were grown. We have to think about that. Somebody said to us, "How are you guys doing this? I mean, how is it that you're doing this?" and suspected that there was something in our background. Weird.

DS: "Where did you come from?"

I think you come from vast amounts of disgusting money. [Uproarious laughter.]

LS: I wish. That would have been easier. And so we said, "Well, we've had experience organizing in the community or in unions" or whatever, and that made sense to them.

The granting agencies were asking this?

LS: Well, actually to themselves. We only found out later when we became friends with some of them and they just kind of wondered how we were doing this. It's not that we'd written a lot of grants before. I had written some grants for the unemployed. When we were working with the unemployed in Pittsburgh we got quite a few grants. But it was the fact that we were willing to go out and give ourselves away free, travel somewhere, do a workshop. Hopefully expenses were made. Usually they were and that was about it. But in the process we talked to tons of people. You know, you found out what they were doing and they found out what you were doing and we spent a lot of time and energy doing that. You have to have that contact with folks, no matter what it is, whether it's publishing or....

I think for most people it's antithetical to writing, that kind of lifestyle.

DS: I don't know. It seems to me that it winds up informing writing. It's more difficult to write when you're caught up in a hectic schedule. I started to mention that one of the things Linny did which helped us when we got into the grant stuff was a video about the end of women's role in the steel mill. The end of the era. It's called *Women of Steel.* Which she and three other women who had been in the mills— they raised grant money, they went to school and taught themselves video, apprenticed and did all of those things and, actually, in about a year and a half did a video which won awards and was on PBS nationally and.... It was an interesting weave. It was similar to the weave I was making, going into doing the writing full time.

LS: Changing careers very rapidly.

Why did this happen, with both of you at that time?

LS: Well, I think, as Dennis said, we had both gone in the same direction together, we both were working in an industrial environment and we were interested in unions and whatever. At a certain point, the economy changed. Industrial organizing changed and, in a way, threw you out into another career. Unless you wanted to stay in a dying union and a dying industry and talk about it. Continue to make films like *Women of Steel.* One of the filmmakers is doing that right now. She stayed in Pittsburgh, she got a regular labor show on one of the TV stations and she's making another documentary. We did have those options but I guess we were both up for following our—I don't know if you could say our hearts and sentiments—you know, at a certain age you say, "Okay, what else do I want to get done in life? What else do I want to go away with?" And Dennis, as he mentioned, wanted to try his hand at writing and find out if he could do it.

I wasn't so clear about what I wanted to do. I fell into it, more or less. Dennis and his cousin had started the business and I.... I studied English in college and I.... I didn't want to write, I don't have the writing skills myself, but I enjoy it and I've come to the point where I read a lot. All the time. It couldn't be better.

Do you do that now?
LS: I do it all the time, yeah. Being an editor, having to read, is just a wonderful job. I wish I could say that I really chose it. [Laughs.] I went kicking and screaming into this business. Really. I mean Dennis has always been more directive and optimistic about being able to make a living at it. And I have more insecurities about living on...hardly anything for the past six years. And watching things around you disintegrate. You know, like your roof and your car. I mean that's what happens. We had high-paying jobs in steel mills and so we were able to make a certain transition. We had a house and a car, and so you live the life of those things and, you know, for a certain period of time, and, uh, they're just disintegrating now, so.... Hopefully, things will be a little.... But, if you look for why I think.... If I looked for why I was able to change this, or at my personality, or even Dennis's, we're both willing to take a lot of risks, which you have to do. Both of us, he more than I, are willing to live on the edge. To live with ambiguity. To live with uncertainties. It seems like a lot of people in writing and publishing are. Maybe that's why I enjoy it, too. Part of the same life. That's not to say there aren't rich publishers. We met some the other night. They're starting a new magazine.

Do you consider yourselves entrepreneurial? Would you use that word?
DS: I wouldn't have at first. But at this point...uh, not so much being entrepreneurial as being willing to take risks. We might make mistakes but we aren't going to make mistakes that will kill us or anything. We'll be able to back out of the mistakes we make and take another shot at it. And ultimately we can make it work. We're pretty close to that.
LS: What do you mean by "entrepreneurial"?

212

DS: We like controlling this ourselves. I mean there's that aspect to it. We do enjoy the personal involvement, the satisfaction of seeing something that's our brainchild come into being, become tangible, have a presence for us as well as for other people.

Okay. Do you want me to try to define what I meant by "entrepreneurial"?
LS: Well, do you mean like hustlers, or...? [All three laugh.]

Well, that was a possibility.
LS: I guess I think of entrepreneurs as, you know, figuring out how to hustle what they need. But I also think of entrepreneurs as having had more business experience, so they know where to go to get the loans and the funding and how to sell ideas to other people.

What I was trying to do was draw a dichotomy between corporate life, which you were both in, even if you weren't managers—and it has certain advantages: security and health care and...various types of security—as opposed to being out on your own and trying to create something that's yours. I suppose one of the things that I consider to be entrepreneurial is creativity, though not necessarily in an artistic sense. Organizational creativity.
DS: We actually were saying to each other while we were eating dinner that one of the things we like is that we don't do things exactly the way other people do them. We come up with our own solutions to problems that are fairly common for publishers.

Well, you know there are problems in American publishing that have never been solved. And there's no indication that they ever will be solved. Distribution has always been a problem. The same things that are wrong with it today were wrong with it two hundred years ago. That's the major problem, I think.
DS: And then the problems created during the Depression of the '30s when the big publishers decided to underwrite bookstores' inventories and passed that burden on to small presses. There was no right of

213

return before that.

I didn't know that.

DS: Yeah. That was instituted by, I think, Putnam, and then the others followed suit because they were frightened. They were scared stiff that the small bookstores wouldn't be able to stock their titles. So they said, We'll essentially underwrite you. You have longer to pay and if the books don't sell you can return them for credit. It had always been just like any other business. You bought the books if you were in the bookstore business and if you couldn't sell them it was your problem. It wasn't the publisher's. It was the big publishers who were able to afford that. They probably put a lot of small presses out of business. I have no idea if that's really true, but I would imagine that it was just catastrophic for small presses.

Do you know John Bennett? Vagabond Press?
DS: No.

He's kind of a legend in the small press scene. He's been around since the '60s. I was telling him a couple of years ago that I had finally come to terms with myself, that I was simply going to lose so much money every year. And what I had to do was budget so that I didn't lose more than that. [All three laugh.] He said, Yeah, that's being realistic, and that he'd had to come to terms with himself several years before. That's just how it is.

DS: Well, see, we couldn't afford to accept that as—

Well, you're trying to make a living at it. I never had any expectation of making a living. My agents keep telling me how unusual the stuff is that I publish. See, to me, it is not unusual. [Laughs.] I think this is standard stuff. I have no idea what they're talking about. [All three laugh hilariously.] I don't understand why everybody isn't doing this. The agent who represents me in Europe is frustrated. He thought The Confession of Jack Straw *especially would be snapped up by an English publisher.*

214

DS: That could be the economy, too.

Yeah. But he says fiction is still strong there. In the United States nonfiction is the staple. That's fairly recent. That's only post-war.

LS: Yeah, that's right. How-to books. As the society falls apart an awful lot of people want to know what to do to put it back together again.

Do you think that's what it is?

LS: Well, there's an awful lot of that. I don't know if that's all of it.

DS: Yeah, the personal self-help stuff is certainly—

LS: But how to do everything! I mean Americans want to do things for themselves. I'm not saying it's just the how-to and get-better, but how-to-fix-your-house and fix-your-toilet and whatever.

DS: I think Linny's right. We're a nation that reads how-to. How-to-love, how-to-sell, how-to-fix. And then read another set of books on it. That's true in the writing business. You look at *Writer's Digest*'s booklist, how many books can you write on how-to-write-a-query-letter? But there are dozens of them, and the same writers will buy all five or six or seven of them and read all of them and still want to know how to write a query letter.

Let's talk about your press. Let's talk about Blue Heron. You know, I get lots of calls—people confuse Black Heron with Blue Heron. I always tell them that I was first.

DS: And we describe it as the battered birds—the black and blue herons.

You've got Left Bank now, and this is a literary journal.
DS: Well, you know, people will call it that, but—

But it's not true. [All laugh.] It's not really words.
LS: *Aliterary: A Literary Journal.*

DS: It's a magazine in book form. We were inspired not only by the number of writers we come in contact with and what we felt was a wealth of available material, but mostly by Linny's reading of *Granta*.

Right! That's a wonderful...whatever it is.

DS: Yeah, whatever it is. And that was it, was whatever it was, and we thought we could have a whatever it is that we want to do. And it doesn't have to be fish or fowl. It doesn't have to be a literary magazine. It doesn't have to meet anybody's expectations. And it can probably succeed by rising to its own level.

LS: We're using reprints and originals and, uh, I guess we'll continue doing that format around a theme each time. Mostly nonfiction. A little fiction and poetry, but not much.

Are you giving more weight to Northwest writers?

LS: It's all Northwest. Which makes it pretty tricky. But hopefully the themes will be universal. But another thing that's unusual about it is there will be more science than I think people are used to. Because a lot of contemporary situations in the world require more understanding of the scientific world and the natural world.

DS: And people writing in unexpected genres. So you take somebody who's known for writing fiction and see if they have something to say in essay form, where they're not used to writing essays. For example, Paul Zarzyski, a cowboy poet who writes only poetry, we got him to write a good solid essay. We're also looking for people who write scientific work, sort of like the Stephen Jay Gould school of science writing where they're involved but they're also reporting.

LS: There is a thread here. There's a continuation of the essays from four *Handbooks*. Having done four *Handbooks* and having a lot of contact with people who write essays in one form or another—poets who write essays, like Sharon Doubiago wrote an essay for the *Handbook* and we put it in *Left Bank*—so, having seen how many people were writing in the Northwest, we decided we could cull them out and have them in a separate vehicle, outside of the *Handbook*.

DS: We've sort of evolved certain themes to the publishing. There are the books for teachers, writers and librarians, with the *Handbook* having formed the center for that. But now it's broadening with the booklet that we did called *Fine Art of Technical Writing*, which has a much larger market than the *Handbook* ever will because the *Handbook* is regional.

Do these books have anything to do with the reason you're attending the English teachers' convention?

DS: Well, our purpose there is to sell our children's books. And our writing books. But it's also to research a book that will go back to that same market a year from now, and that's the one on classroom publishing. That's grown out of the workshops we've done which really themselves came from going to the schools and seeing that there was a vacuum in the way kids were taught to be literate, that it's presented in very elitist forms in the public schools.

Kids can be in journalism class, that's probably the most democratic. If there's a literary magazine, there are very few kids and a teacher. But it's always writing and editing. It doesn't include the kid who might be a good graphic designer or a good typographer, or have a photo essay in mind. Perhaps even be a bookseller, or a librarian, or a teacher. So we're going back in and saying you can promote literacy across the curriculum by publishing. You can involve the art department, the social science department, the English department, and someone can be just as active in the creation of a book from any of those angles, any of those talents, as they could be in something else.

So that's what the book will be. We're looking for the experiments that are going on around the country. Some teachers are already taking a lot of risks. They've involved the community in products and programs. We ourselves were approached by Artists in Education in Portland last year to do two pilot programs in the public schools. We flaked out. We just didn't have the time to do one more thing. Had we done it, we would have established two ongoing programs in middle schools that would have been for-profit publishing companies. In the schools. Internships in the community, involvement of teachers and parents and the administration of the schools. That side of book publishing would sort of take the lessons we've learned and give them back in some way.

Do you have a mission as a publisher?
DS: Not exactly.

A purpose? What holds it all together? It seems to me that Blue Heron goes off in different directions.
LS: It has quite a few directions, that's true. We're flying in quite a few different directions but there are several themes here. One is that everybody we publish is in the Northwest. We are a regional press. And we consciously made that decision this year because we've been getting lots of submissions from all over the country. And we decided that we were going to stay regional. There's enough to be done here. The rule was that we weren't going to do cookbooks or travel books, but we were going to stay with promoting the people of the region. There's that area. That's *Left Bank* and our newspaper and all that.

Then there's the children's fiction books. We have two lines now. We have two authors. And there I think that the classroom publishing book kind of pulls those two together in the sense that they are children and they're young writers but it teaches them how to publish. I mean it's still kind of a bizarre company. We're still kind of all over the map. But there's some subtlety about.... There's something pulling it together. [Laughs.]

DS: There are our interests. We came on to Morey because he came to us and offered us his books. We realized that if we were going to develop some national books—and we care about kids reading good books—that this was an opportunity to break out of the region in terms of markets. So taking that on is also strategic thinking in that if this man is still well known and his most famous books are still in print with E.P. Dutton, there's a library shelf available for every one of the ones that we pick up. The name's right there in front of them. They'll all know it. Bookstores and librarians and school teachers.

218

So he did for us what we could not do for ourselves, which was open up national markets. And having looked at how other presses had failed to develop backlists that sustained them through the ups and downs of their new releases, this was an opportunity to almost instantly develop a backlist. A small one but a fairly potent one. And that's been borne out by the reports our distributor has given us. They've told us that our backlist books are like most of the other presses' frontlist books in terms of sales and continued sales. So it seems that that decision was right.

Then we started looking for ways to link them. As Linny said, this new book takes things a step further toward bridging the gap between the children's books and the writing books. Because writing and kids weave a new link.

Then *Left Bank* comes along as another opportunity out of all the contacts we made through *Writers Northwest Handbook* and the newspaper. This allows us a forum as editors and publishers using other people's voices to talk about a lot of subjects that are important. And *Left Bank* is sort of a creative outlet. We have few restrictions placed on us there. And we can talk about things like, uh, one of the ideas we're tossing around for a theme is men and women and sexuality, but we would give it the subtitle of "Junkies."

"Junkies"?
DS: "Junkies." Because we're all junkies to these chemicals.

I don't understand.
DS: There's a progesterone problem, there's an estrogen problem.

Oh.
DS: And maybe, you know, take all the Robert Blys of the world, or something, and have at it. So *Left Bank* is a way of showcasing the fine writing that we see being done here, and it's an opportunity we could take only because of the fact that we have national distribution. At the same time, it's a way for us to kind of let

off steam and have a little more room to play. Particularly Linny.

LS: I get to play.

DS: We were interviewed by Paul Pintarich of *The Oregonian*. The interview came out last weekend. He asked us what we were thinking of doing, and one of the things that this opens up—*Left Bank*—is that out of all of these contacts with these authors, new and established, we're going to wind up with some opportunities, we're going to see what people are doing long before they go in search of someone to publish it. And we may be able to find some fiction that we never intended to do, or some creative nonfiction that we'd love to pursue. Just because we're in touch.

LS: In a way, it's like scouting. People start telling you what their ideas are. That makes it exciting, and the opportunities open up because, like Dennis said, we're in contact with more writers.

How do people know what themes you're looking for or what themes you want to develop, as far as Left Bank *is concerned?*

LS: We have guidelines.

In the magazine?

LS: Uh, no.

DS: Yeah, actually we—

LS: Oh, I guess it is in there, although it's misleading. But— [All laugh.]

There are guidelines but we don't mean it.

LS: Right.

DS: We have misguided lines. [Harder laughter.] Misguide lines.

LS: Read between the lines. [Still harder laughter.] What do these publishers want? They don't know.

Well, you have to have the writing. Do you determine the theme and then solicit the writers?

LS: Both. People write in for the guidelines and ask what the next theme is. But it's also solicited because, I mean, face it, it has to make money. It has to live on its own or else we have to drop it. So we have to have some well-known names. So we've got to solicit those people and you have, somehow, to get them in there. Or else, as far as we can tell, it won't work. It would stay within the region and we just.... There's a lot of other magazines that do that. And that's not what we want to do. I mean if we're successful, then we've taken writers and been a transmission for them. And the people whose names are—for instance, the next issue is going to have Barry Lopez in it—but that will help other people to tag along. I wouldn't tell his agent that, but if she's smart, she knows. They know.

You keep alluding to fiction. You wanted to write fiction and you tried it for six months until circumstances didn't permit it any longer. Fiction is extremely difficult to sell. In the major houses, the editors will say that it's too good for them to do. They've told me that. An editor at [a mass market paperback house in Manhattan] told me that he's been instructed not to acquire anything written above a fourth-grade level. They're explicit. Fourth grade. I mean newspapers aim for sixth grade!

LS: Boy, Jerry, that would make a great article for our newspaper. I'd love to see something about what New York really says. Wouldn't you?

DS: Yeah, but—

LS: Well, he could keep it anonymous.

I've talked to a number of editors over the years, trying to sell reprint rights, and I keep running into the same thing. Well, getting back to Blue Heron and fiction, I've noticed that you keep alluding to it.

LS: I think Dennis does. I mean I think that since Dennis writes fiction, he would—

You are writing fiction now?

LS: He's in the middle of two books. Um, he'd probably like to do it more than I would because I prefer to see more nonfiction. The essay. The creative type of nonfiction. It just seems to me we'd have to be farther down the road to take on any fiction that was new. If it was new, I wouldn't be doing it. It's real risky.

Na-a-a-ah. [All laugh.] *You just have to make up your mind that you're going to lose three thousand dollars a year.* [Continued laughter.]

LS [Still laughing]: What about my retirement fund?

DS: Yeah, what about it?

LS: Forget it. See these holey socks?

DS: Yeah, there's holes in those socks.

But God will love you for it. [Hilarious laughter.] *I've never been interested in building an organization. I think you are. I'm not being critical. It's just that I've fallen into it accidentally and it keeps being accidental to me. I regard myself as a writer first and a publisher by chance.*

LS: I think what you're saying is that we're building something because we're trying to make a living. And that would be different. Like you said, that's not what you want to do. That gives you a lot more leeway.

Yeah, I joke about it, but really, I'm prepared to lose a certain amount of money every year.

LS: Mm hmm. You're subsidizing the press, so you can do that. And it's possible that we could do that in the future. If we establish ourselves well enough, and have a foundation of, say, Morey, and perhaps we'd get some money from the government. It's possible now to get a grant because we're getting more literary and that's what they want to see. We could just say, "Well, we're going to use that money to showcase new writers." I'd like to get to that place, but I don't think I'd want to publish fiction before I had some kind of actual subsidy, whether that would be from the NEA or whoever. I don't care who gives it to me.

DS: But we've also figured out that in order to survive we have to do other things. So all of the skills that we have as publishers we turn around and try to use to make income to subsidize the press to the point where it starts to make a profit. And it did that this year for the first time. It took six years for it to break even.

Then you know what I'm talking about. You've been subsidizing it.

DS: Oh yeah. We've been subsidizing it with loans. See, we didn't have an outside job. And as Linny said, we let the house wear. The car got—it doesn't run very well, as a matter of fact. But it took...it took...well, Consortium [a major distributor] was evidence that we'd reached a critical mass. They wouldn't have taken us on had they not seen an opportunity themselves. Because they and Publishers Group West and Talman [other major distributors] and a couple of others came out here all at the same time.

It did give us an opportunity, but at the same time it raised the ante. Because it meant that we really weren't regional anymore. And we had to start looking at the way we did our books, and doing our publishing entirely differently than we had before. We just did books when we could get the cash together. You know, we had plans but that didn't mean the book happened.

Now we do a catalogue six months in advance, with the titles that will be there next year. And we have to fulfill that obligation. But we're also, because of Consortium, seeing the sales in advance. Four, five or six months in advance. Which means by the time it comes to press we have some idea of whether this book is going to sell or not.

How many copies of Left Bank *did you print?*
DS: We did five thousand.

You think you'll sell five thousand?
DS: Yeah, I think we will. [Linny shakes her head no.]

No. No, you don't. One does and one doesn't.
LS: Maybe three thousand. I think it was a little.... Anyway.... We're trying to get subs. Subscriptions. We're selling subscriptions. As well as putting it into bookstores.

DS: You didn't ask me how long it would take. [Linny laughs.]

How many hours per week do you put into publishing?
LS: Probably ten-hour days.

How many?
LS: Seven.

Seven days a week?
LS: Well, six or seven. Sometimes we take a day off. We've been getting better at it.
DS: We were going over eighty hours a week for a long time. But we cut back. We're probably closer to sixty.

Well, that's all I have. I want to thank you. Anything you want to—
DS: Yeah. Why the hell are you doing this, Jerry?

Richard Cohn and Cindy Black
Beyond Words Publishing

"In ten years, one of the things we see is that our company is awarded the Nobel Peace Prize, the Nobel Prize for Peace, for the work we have done...."

The interview took place on the morning of April 2, 1993 in the large farm house that is now the residence of Richard Cohn and Cindy Black and the offices of Beyond Words Publishing. I had spent the previous night at the Stovalls outside of Hillsboro, Oregon. I'd planned on a short run down the mountain in the morning but fog at the top of the mountain and highway maintenance trucks all along the secondary road that connected to Highway 26 doubled the time I had thought I would need. Cohn and Black were gracious about my tardiness, Cohn explaining that he had used the extra time to get some work done.

He is a "fifth generation Oregonian. My family came across as pioneers and settled along the Columbia River." His father's side was in the furniture business, starting a firm in 1898, selling it in 1981. His mother had studied to be a concert pianist but gave up the possibility of a career in music to raise a family and help her husband in business.

In college Cohn studied "actually, a lot of foreign languages" and then went on to Johns Hopkins School of Advanced International Studies to prepare for a career in the diplomatic service. "I thought that was where I was heading. But with the Vietnam war and graduating from graduate school in 1968—my draft board had given me two years to pursue graduate studies—I applied for various military programs. I was willing to go into anything with the idea that becoming an officer or entering some program was better than being a front-line combat draftee. My name came up on the Coast Guard list and so I went into the Coast Guard." When he got out of the Coast Guard he went to work with his father in the furniture business and stayed there until 1981.

"When the firm was sold, we closed out the business and then

225

I met Cindy on a blind date. She was visiting Portland—this was in May of '82—and in October she moved back to Hawaii, so I went with her. And stayed."

Black's grandfather was an engineer who emigrated to Honolulu in 1910. Both her father and she were raised in Hawaii. Her mother is a Californian and met Black's father in San Francisco—a trans-Pacific romance.

Black's father is in the construction business. He is musical and used to sing. She herself "took ballet and did a lot of things with art." After high school she went to Mills College in Oakland, California because "it had a good art department. And I was an art major." When she returned to Hawaii after graduation she went to work for a development company as "an interior coordinator who would coordinate and install the furniture in the apartments they were building, and sell them to very rich tourists. And then I ended up being in the real estate business as an outgrowth of that."

Cindy Black: I was living on Maui at the time. After graduation I got married and went to Maui with my husband and started with this company and then the real estate started happening. So I ended up working for a general real estate company for about five and a half years, and then decided that I wanted to take a leave of absence. And during that—I'd been divorced—I met Richard. And we moved back to Hawaii together and I decided I wasn't going to go back to Maui and we started a little business. We were selling tee shirts with a man who had a concept—it was a very local Hawaiian concept of...they were funny designs. So we started a tee shirt company. And in the midst of that— I should let Richard tell the story of how we got into the publishing, because something kind of unusual happened that got us involved with the publishing. He was the beginning of the publishing part, so I should have him tell you that.

Richard Cohn: If any of your readers have seen the movie *Field of Dreams*, they'll understand what happened. I got a phone call from a photographer named Richard Cook. And he had been taking a morning meditative walk, he said, and he heard a voice. And the voice said, "Call Richard Cohn and ask him how he can help you publish your book."

Had you met?

RC: We knew Richard's sister who lived in Hawaii. Richard lived in Eugene, Oregon and was visiting Hawaii. And, walking on the beach, heard the voice. He said it was as loud as a loudspeaker. To him. And when he called me, I thought, "I know absolutely nothing about publishing. But maybe God is speaking to him. It could be something important. So I should at least pay attention." And he brought his photography to me.

CB: He was a *National Geographic* photographer. He was a really good photographer.

RC: And so he brought his photography for me to look at. After the first image I was mesmerized by what I saw. Again, I didn't know what to do with it. So I said to him, "Why don't you find a real publisher and I will be a business adviser for you." About two weeks later he came back. He had found a publisher who was willing to look at it. And so I went to a meeting with Richard Cook and his wife and this publisher. And out of that meeting came an agreement. This was in August of '83. Over a two-month period we formulated a concept to work together and created a partnership to produce a book called *Molokai: An Island in Time.*

During September, October of that year, another book came to the publisher. His name was Charlie Fields [fictitious name]. And the book was called *Within a Rainbowed Sea*. That book was much further along. So *Within a Rainbowed Sea* was brought into the partnership and it became our first book.

The partnership, now, was between whom?

RC: The partnership was between Charlie Fields and Richard Cohn. The photographer for *Rainbowed Sea* is Chris Newbert. So we worked on the project and—

CB: You were responsible—

227

RC: My responsibility was to raise the money. So I got a line of credit at two different banks and we formed a limited partnership for each book, invited family and friends to be limited partners, and we raised the money to produce the books.

How did you ever get a line of credit from a bank? Is that what you got, a line of credit, or a loan?

RC: I got a personal loan just from my background. I had had a line of credit, a signature line of credit, at the bank, at two different banks, and those had been paid off. And so I was able to go back in and borrow again.

CB: Some of our vendors, though, also acted almost as a bank for us. We are still in the process of paying that off.

RC: Then in July of '84—

CB: Go back, because what happened is Charlie had been in the publishing business and he thought, "Well, let's try Waldenbooks. Let's see if they'll buy a quantity of books."

This is before the publication?

CB: Yeah. Before the book was published. Because we didn't know really how to distribute it.

RC: Right. Charlie wisely said that we should presell as much as possible before we go to press. And so Charlie had some connection with a New York publishing house—I believe it was Doubleday—and he went back to speak with them. And while he was there he was waiting in the lunchroom for his meeting and there was one other person in the lunchroom. And that man asked if he could sit down with Charlie. And they talked. And Charlie told him why he was there and the other man said, "Well, if Doubleday doesn't go for this project, you should call Waldenbooks. I used to be a sales manager for Walden. I've just left them and I'm coming to interview here at Doubleday. But I think that if you called Harry Hoffman"—the president of Walden at the time— "he would go for it."

So Charlie did his presentation at Doubleday. They liked it but wanted to change it radically from the concept that we had. Charlie and

I then discussed inviting Harry Hoffman to come—we would fly him out to Hawaii and put him up for a week and he could see the photography and make a decision. So Charlie got on the phone and called Harry Hoffman, and Harry Hoffman answered the phone. It didn't even go through a secretary. He just picked up the phone. And he was flattered by our invitation but said that he really didn't have the time to fly out. However, he would arrange to have all the players together for a meeting if Charlie would fly back there and make a presentation.

So Charlie did that. All we had in hand were some three-by-five photographs, color prints of each book—

CB: No text.

RC: We had no text in hand and we had no mock-up or dummy of the book. We just had this little pile of prints and a concept, a nice story. So Charlie made the presentation. Harry Hoffman said, "I like it. We'll do it. We want to order—"

CB: We also pitched it as the first two books in The EarthSong Collection.

RC: It would be a series of books celebrating life on earth. And Harry asked for two books a year for ten years.

CB: Yeah. Harry liked the concept so he said, "I want two books a year for the next ten years."

RC: And Walden would have an exclusive on it.

CB: Yeah. He wanted an exclusive.

RC: So Charlie came back and Harry asked for—he was going to order twenty thousand copies of *Within a Rainbowed Sea* and twenty thousand copies of *Molokai*. Charlie at that point made what was in hindsight a tactical error, and he said, "Well, don't take twenty thousand. Just take ten thousand. We'll back you up with ten thousand." My father had taught me that, in the furniture business, when someone wanted to buy something, you didn't discourage him from buying it.

What was in Charlie's mind?

RC: I'm not sure, actually. I think what was in Charlie's mind was that twenty thousand was too much for them. And ten thousand would be the right amount. And he didn't want them to get stuck with

229

books and then not want to do the other books.

CB: But he didn't think about us.

RC: He didn't think about the fact that we would have produced and paid for ten thousand extra of each and not have the ability to sell them because we had an exclusive contract with Walden. So that was what happened. And then during the course of conceptualizing the book and starting to work on the design of it, Richard Cook introduced us to Robin and Heidi Rickabaugh who are designers here in Portland. So we met them and we really liked them. They agreed to design the books. They introduced us to Dynagraphics who printed *Within a Rainbowed Sea* and *Molokai: An Island in Time*. So we wound up having a really fine team of participants. Cindy's former high school English teacher became the editor of the books; he's a creative writing instructor. So this team created a synergy. A magic happened in the sense that something was created that was far beyond what any one person could have created on their own.

CB: The photographer actually came and lived in the designer's house. It was part of the photo selection and had input for the design and a lot more than— Other publishers will not allow that kind of thing to happen. They just take the photography and make the book. And so I think that was part of the magic that happened with this book.

And we really didn't set a budget for the book. I mean we were going for the best that we could possibly get on this book. We had the feeling—I mean the photography was incredible, especially in *Rainbowed Sea*. But we spent, on the two books together, over a million dollars, didn't we? Yeah. It's a lot of money.

RC: The books were done in three different editions: a standard hardcover edition, a signed and slipcased author's edition with a set of frameable prints, and a collector's limited edition, hand-bound in leather and hand-made paper. It came in a koa wood box with a dye-transferred, limited-edition print.

CB: Our partner felt that there was a built-in market out there for the limited editions, and we really didn't think to just make a few samples. We made almost the whole edition and it was over seven hundred and fifty of each that we made. We have sold most of it. There

230

are still some of those copies available. But it's something that you don't see, ever, anymore. It's an old-craftsman type of binding. So it was a lot of money for all that production. And then what happened was Richard and I—we were coming back and forth from Hawaii to here at the time. When was it, Richard, in the summer of—?

RC: In the summer of '84. We got married in July of '84 and Charlie Fields fell in love about that time and took off. And we didn't see him for a year.

Took off? With his woman?

RC: With his woman. Uh huh.

CB: Sort of left us holding the bag.

RC: So we had a purchase order. And we had competent printers and designers. Binders. But we had no—

CB: No experience.

RC: —experience. No prior experience. Now that's either good or bad. But, in this case, it gave us an indoctrination.

CB: It was an opportunity to learn publishing by the seat of our pants. We had to learn very quickly. Luckily, we had people who were honest and really wanted it to be as good—they saw the potential for this book, for these books, to be showpieces for their work.

And I think we were blessed with not knowing what we shouldn't do. I mean this man had had publishing experience, but one of the things we didn't know was that he had never really made a profit. That was one of the important questions we didn't ask. But if we had known what we were doing we wouldn't have spent the kind of money we did and gone for the kind of quality we did. And so, as a result, *Rainbowed Sea* and *Molokai* both won incredible numbers of awards. *Rainbowed Sea*, specifically, won just about every award you can win for typography, printing, design....

RC: It was selected as the finest printed book in America by the Printing Industries of America. It won the New York Art Directors Show, which is the Academy Awards of book publishing and graphic design. It won Best Photography of the Year and Best Book Design of the Year. The White House used it in a limited edition as a presidential gift of state from President Reagan to the Emperor of Japan. And it won thirty international awards, besides. So, as Cindy said, the secret to our success really has been that we didn't know what we shouldn't do and we made an agreement among ourselves that we would not compromise. Even in the printing of the book, when the background of a photo was supposed to be black, and the color separation came in just almost black, and it printed almost black, we took it off press, reseparated it, made a new plate, and printed it properly, even though that cost extra money to do. So the integrity of the final product was very important, that we met our commitment to the quality and excellence that we had seen in the original images.

CB: The book has been printed multiple times and we've now sold about seventy-five thousand copies of it. Every year we sell somewhere around—

RC: Around ten thousand copies.

CB: —ten thousand copies.

RC: And it's a seventy-five dollar retail book. So it's a fairly expensive book. But the quality—it was a hundred-dollar value, at least, when it was done. It's printed with nine-color reproduction instead of the standard four-color. Our printer, Dynagraphics, actually took up the slack on the money that we didn't have and they allowed us to defer payment over a number of years.

CB: So it was, you know, a real learning experience. And what happened was Walden had the exclusive for—was it six or nine months, Richard?

RC: Well, they actually had it for a year.

CB: But didn't they give it up after a period of time?

RC: After about nine months I met with them and explained that we had all these books in the warehouse and—

CB: Because you printed—how many?

RC: We printed twenty thousand of *Molokai* and, again, Charlie Fields had this thought that while—

He was back now?

RC: He was not back yet, but this was when the decision had

232

been made to buy the paper and print the books. He thought, "Well, if Walden is going to order twenty thousand, we can probably sell forty thousand." So even though he changed their purchase order to ten thousand, he went ahead and backed them up with another ten and we printed another twenty. We didn't bind them, thank goodness, but we printed them and held them until eventually we needed them. So it was a real expensive learning experience.

CB: So after nine months we got the rights back from Walden and we—Charlie Fields was still, you know, occasionally he'd call us, but he was not actively involved in this.

He was off-island though?
CB: I don't know where he was.
RC: He was traveling all over the United States with this girl, and then even when he came back he wasn't really—
CB: A part of it.
RC: —a part of the process.
CB: He wasn't choosing to participate. We were actually, at that point, operating out of our house. Our apartment. We hadn't gotten it into the bookstores yet. We didn't know anything about distribution.

Well, where were you living now?
RC: In Hawaii.
CB: Still living in Hawaii. In an apartment, yeah. So this is— I guess we're up to '85 now. And so we decided—Richard's parents lived up here and we had all the books stored at Dynagraphics—that we needed to get these books placed in bookstores. So Richard's father let us use his Jeep station wagon. We loaded it full of books and we started going down the coast, selling books to bookstores. And they would give us checks. And we thought, Well, this is great!
RC: The very first bookstore—we didn't know they would give us checks—but the first bookstore we went into bought one of each book and said, "Here's a check." So we thought, This is good! So from that point on, we just asked for a check with each store. What we would do is, we would drive into town, we'd stop at a pay phone, get

a Yellow Pages, and we would call every bookstore and we'd make appointments to go see them that day. Cindy and I would flip a coin to see who would have to go in. It wasn't—

CB: Something that we knew how to do exactly.

RC: We really didn't know how to do it but we would just alternate or flip a coin. Finally we had worked our way down to Santa Monica. And we'd been really successful. We'd had more books shipped down to us along the way. And we were in a bookstore in Santa Monica and the owner said, "These books are gorgeous. But you should not be out selling them. You guys are publishers. You need to be creating more books. And there is a sales rep in the store who sells books." He was in the store at that time.

And so the owner introduced us to this book salesman who was really a nice fellow. His name was Charles Morrell and he was the St. Martin's Press rep for the West Coast. He looked at the books and immediately saw dollar signs, I think, and great commissions that he could earn. So he said, "Look. You guys go back home and I will sell the books for you, and I will put together a national rep network, using St. Martin's reps, and I'll have them sell your books." So he did. And he and the other reps sold close to ten thousand copies of the book. *Within a Rainbowed Sea.* So that got rid of the bound inventory that we had remaining. And they sold *Molokai* as well.

So that really put us over the hump, as it were. It got us distribution all over the country. We didn't realize then that book reps have to have new product every year. It's like a hungry animal that we have to feed.

CB: We had never read "How to Publish" and that sort of thing.

RC: We thought that if you published a high-quality classic it would continue to sell, and of course the reps would continue to sell it. Well, that wasn't the case. They basically only sold new things. They would sell some backlist but they really wanted new. We didn't have anything new. And we couldn't afford to have anything new.

Did you have a name for your company at this time?
RC: It was called Beyond Words Publishing Company. We

234

incorporated in 1988. Because of the debt that we had incurred in producing the first two books—we did not want to impair future projects by the past debt. So Beyond Words Publishing Company remained and Beyond Words Publishing, Incorporated started in March of 1988. And under that umbrella we started producing soft-cover books in the health and self-help area, children's books and other photographic coffee-table, gift books.

Are we making a leap now?
RC: We just made a leap.
CB: We just did.

Is there anything in between, or is there just—?
CB: Oh yeah. There is. Yeah. We—
RC: We moved to Oregon.
CB: Well, we—yeah.
RC: In June of '86 we moved to Oregon and in October of '86 we purchased the farm where we have our offices. What else happened? We continued marketing *Rainbowed Sea* wherever we could....

CB: Well, I think what happened is that we found out after a while that the sales rep wasn't going to push it for that long, and so we connected with Publishers Group West [a major book distributor]. What year was that, Richard?

RC: In 1987, through a man named Hal Kramer who is publisher of H.J. Kramer, Inc. Hal said that we should talk to Publishers Group West. Charlie Winton was the owner. And so we did. So, again, it was a fortuitous happening, because just as *Rainbowed Sea* and *Molokai* were new for the St. Martin's rep, they were new for Publishers Group West. So Publishers Group West went right back out into the same field as St. Martin's and reintroduced the book. They sold another ten thousand copies. They called on some stores, I'm sure, that St. Martin's had dealt with but, in turn, they called on new—

CB: Also the other chains. But I don't know what ever happened with the other chains.

RC: They called on B. Dalton at that point. So we were able

235

again to move—of the forty thousand first printing, we had already sold off ten to Walden and ten to St. Martin's reps. Now we were into that next twenty. We started binding those and selling them. So Publishers Group West carried that through the season of '87. And then in '88 we started adding new product. Again, we didn't have any money. I was not drawing a salary. Cindy was working a second job full time.

CB: Well, I wasn't—I was helping some with the publishing, but I had another job.

RC: She was working a full-time job so that we could stay alive and pay our rent, and then working extra time with me. But the first soft-cover book we did, a health book called *Seeing Beyond 20/20*, by a doctor of optometry—he had an American Express card and we had a Visa card and we each got cash advances enough to print the cover of the book. We rented a target mailing list of doctors and people who would be interested in the book, we designed the book and typeset it on our computer, and had just enough money from the cash advance to print the cover. We used the cover as a mail-out post card and we mailed out ten thousand cards and we got back a thousand orders. At twelve ninety-five each. That gave us enough money to pay for printing five thousand books and pay back our Visa and American Express cards. So that's how we published our first self-help book.

Why did you go from—?

CB: Coffee table to that? We realized that the coffee table books sold mostly during Christmas. And you can't rely on a book that's only selling three or four months. The other books came out in other seasons and would bring in some more cash. Also we had some personal interest in alternative health types of things. This book is about how to improve your vision in a natural way.

We also had an author approach us about a children's book. We had never thought about doing children's books, but we really liked the concept. It was a beautiful book and he came down and saw us and we told him we liked it. He didn't hear that because he had been turned down twenty-nine times before. He heard us say no, you know, we'll send back your stuff. We ended up doing his book, *Davy's Dream*. And

236

Paul Lewis is one of the most popular children's authors in the Northwest. He does a lot of school presentations. And that book has sold about forty—?

RC: Forty-five thousand.

CB: Yeah, forty-five thousand copies. So that was our first children's book. And so we now had three categories that we did.

RC: As Cindy said, it gave us a continuity of cash flow during the whole year. We have now published five books with Paul Owen Lewis. We've done one a year, each year. And we've added, of course, to the other lines as well.

What ever happened to Charlie Fields?

RC: Well, Charlie Fields came back at a certain point, apologized for his lengthy absence—

When he came back, was the girl still with him?

RC: No. The girl was no longer with him. He is now married to a different person and he has his own publishing company in Hawaii. The partnership was basically dissolved in 1986 when we moved here. Charlie assumed financial responsibility for the *Molokai* project and paid back the bank. We assumed responsibility for the *Rainbowed Sea* project.

CB: We aren't doing things together anymore. Our styles are different. But he really helped us get into the business by his leaving us. [She laughs.] So where are we? Nineteen ninety? PGW selling *Rainbowed Sea*?

RC: In '88, '89, we started to do self-help books. And we started doing three or four a year.

CB: But we started doing coffee table books again.

Now Walden had wanted two a year for ten years, right?
CB: He never—
RC: But they never—
CB: I think you checked back with them, didn't you?
RC: I checked back with them and they'd had a change of

thought. In '88 a photographer approached us about doing a photographic book called *The American Eagle*, on the bald eagle. And that became the next book in The EarthSong Collection. It was one that we did ourselves. It has sold about forty thousand copies to date, thirty-nine ninety-five retail.

In '89 Cindy saw an article in *USA Today*, a little two-line article mentioning that photography of Native American elders would appear in *New Age Journal*. We went out and got a copy of the magazine, took a look at the first two photos, said, "This is a book we have to publish." Even though it said in the article "From his forthcoming book," undaunted, we proceeded to call him. His name is Steve Wall.

Just prior to the meeting with Steve Wall a photographer came to us. He was an artist and a photographer and wanted to do a project called *Pacific Light* which was photography of rare earth metals, scratches and high-voltage electricity touching the metal, causing it to discolor and change shape and form. This particular photographer brought with him a funding package. It was not something we could afford to do on our own and we formed a partnership, a joint venture, to do that. *Pacific Light.*

Steve Wall's book is called *Wisdom Keepers*. He had an unlisted number. Richard Cook, the *Molokai* photographer, got us his number through *National Geographic*. We called him—and this was kind of an interesting conversation—we called Steve Wall and said we're interested in doing your book, and Steve said, "Well, I haven't really done a book. I just told *New Age* that it was going to be a book."

I said, "Well, thank you, because we had hoped you hadn't done it. We would like it to be part of a series of books we call The EarthSong Collection."

There was silence on the other end of the line. And I said, "Is something wrong?" And Steve said, "Nothing's wrong. It's just that a year ago the *tadodaho*, the chief of chiefs of the Iroquois Nation, Leon Shenandoah—"

CB: The Speaker of the House, that's what *tadodaho* means.

RC: He had said to Steve Wall when Steve was interviewing him, "Steve, you will publish a book for me, and it will be called

238

EarthSong." When we told Steve Wall it would be The EarthSong Collection, we hadn't talked to Leon Shenandoah. We didn't even know him. Then Steve said to us, "Well, I guess I don't have to look further for a publisher." So that was in the fall of 1989 and the book came out in October of '90. We printed fifteen thousand copies. We took some major design risks and printed the book with recycled paper. It was the first coffee table book in the country printed on this paper. It's called E-s-s-e. Esse. Designed by Robin Rickabaugh for Gilbert Paper Company in Menosha, Wisconsin. We did four-color, black and white. We used soy-based inks. And the fifteen thousand copies sold within four months.

CB: It also came out the same month as Kevin Costner's movie, *Dances with Wolves*. We had no idea that that was coming out. So the timing was pretty good.

RC: In April of '91 we printed twenty thousand more. Thus began a process where we're now about to be at a hundred and seventy-five thousand copies in print. So it's been a major, major seller for us. It is used by the American Indian Movement, by AIM, as a gift when they have a donor they want to give a gift back to, which really gave us a tremendous feeling as Anglos, to produce something that Native people would use as an expression of their thanks.

It has been a book that has changed people's lives. We've gotten letters from people all over the country who have—one woman in New York left a high-paying corporate job because she realized that she wasn't living her truth, her passion, and she moved out to work with Native Americans in the Southwest. We've had Native people write us who did not have pride in being who they were, and after reading the book they totally changed their lives around. They put their artifacts out, or their family photos, and felt really proud to be who they were. So that was the fourth book in The EarthSong Collection.

Then in 1991 we published a book called *Light on the Land*, by a photographer, Art Wolfe. It is a collection of landscape photography from all over the world, with native writings. In '91 we did a regional book called *Cattle Kings of Texas*, about Texas ranching families. Again, it's a black and white photography book, recycled paper. Then in '92 we did *Quiet Pride*, the sixth book in The EarthSong Collection. The subtitle is *Ageless Wisdom of the American West*. Elder Americans from Nebraska west. Text in their own words. Recycled paper. Soy-based ink.

And then we did a book called *Life Cast: Behind the Mask*. Photography of life-castings of celebrities. The text was the experience of being with the celebrity as he or she was being cast. The masks themselves became part of a touring exhibit that would go all over the country for the next six years. Artist Willa Shalit who did the masks is Gene Shalit's daughter, from the "Today" show. Willa has been doing life casting for about ten years. It's a benefit. Willa has a nonprofit foundation called The Touch Foundation and the royalties from this book go to The Touch Foundation as a benefit for the sight-impaired.

CB: This is a mask that she did of me. You know, when someone goes into a gallery they can touch and feel, and it's the only way that blind people can tell what someone looks like. So she has a traveling exhibit of about seventy of those that people can touch and feel. When we promoted the book we gave each of about fifty bookstores—there was a mask that they could have on display with the book so that the customer could come in and touch it—Whoopi Goldberg or Robin Williams or someone.

I'll go back just a little bit. You were talking about all the books that we've done so far and we got up to *Life Cast*. At this point in 1992, through our going down and seeing Publishers Group West twice a year for our meetings and that sort of thing, we were learning how it really worked—the scheduling, you know, creating new books for each season and all that. We were getting pretty good at it by that time, and I left my job.

I was working as a wholesaler for a mutual fund company out of New York. I did that while we were in Hawaii, and then when we moved to Oregon they started a fund here at the same time. The same company. So I was able to move and start my new job here right when we moved. I did that until the middle of '91. That June. And I was just about to lose my mind because I was trying to do both, half of the week there and half here, and I had to quit. And it was really scary. I think a lot of people who are small publishers go through this. A new firm growing—you've got to let go of what you think of as security that you have with a regular job. And to trust that what you're doing is going to work, and that you'll be able to sustain yourself on the income from the books. And so I just decided—I was almost forced to, with my health and just my well-being, to quit the other job and to do this entirely.

So in June of '91 I started working full time for Beyond Words. That was a stressful year for us also because in the previous year, '90, we had hired someone to help us with the running of the company because we were growing so quickly. We had originally hired this person to create a plan for us to be able to raise finances for the company. It was—what do you call it, Richard?

RC: We recognized that we were going to be growing. We were already growing. And to underwrite that growth, we really needed to fund it properly. So we hired this man as a consultant. He then came to us and said, "I prepared this plan for you. I would like to suggest that you hire me as your CEO to implement the plan." And so in the fall of 1990 we hired this man to do that.

His title was CEO?

RC: His title was CEO. The learning experience for us was that if you're going to be on the line as a publisher, or in any business, then you're responsible for the financial aspects of the business and it's best not to give your power away. We did give our power away. And by March of '91 we learned that this person seemed to have another agenda in life, which was to start his own publishing company with our authors, and bankrupt our publishing company so that he could then just take over.

You think he intended to bankrupt your company?

RC: There's no question in our mind. He may have a different truth of this, but at this point there's no question. So we terminated our relationship with him in March of '91. And Cindy and I worked diligently throughout '91—

CB: We found that he had done a similar thing to, not other publishing companies, but other kinds of companies twice before. But since he had started out just doing a business plan for us we had not checked him out thoroughly enough before he began with us. He kind of eased himself in. We weren't prudent in really checking him out thoroughly.

RC: Due diligence is important when hiring anybody.

CB: Yes. A good learning experience.

RC: So we worked very hard in '91 and we made a profit. We were able to pay back all of the losses that were created during the time that this man was with us and have operated profitably ever since.

In June of '92 the next major change occurred for us as a company. We were approached by some business coaches. They are two women who have a company called Carnahan, Smith and Gunter. They're looking for—Cindy, would you say they're looking for people that are making a—have the potential to make a paradigm shift within their industry?

CB: Yes.

RC: They saw us doing and publishing things that look very different from what most publishers are doing. They said, "Don't be surprised, if you choose to work with us, if your staff changes. Some people may quit and move on, because what we represent is change. And, consciously or unconsciously, people will know that." That was June tenth.

CB: Can we go back, please, just a little bit? What happened is, when this man came in—until we fired him in March—the trust level within the company just totally disintegrated. Among the employees. But he even had contacted some of our authors and had said things to them. So he was trying to erode the trust that we'd established with our employees, with our vendors and with our authors. We didn't know all of this at the time. He was doing this in a very underhanded way. And so what happened, especially with the employees, is when we—he actually tried to have like a coup. It was just amazing. He wanted me, as the owner of the company, to fire my husband. I mean this was an incredible event. This is after we had been gone for a vacation, came home, and we had this meeting. We could feel that something was

242

wrong. Something was coming, we just knew it. And he asked me at this table, with everyone around the table—and he wanted them all to say why I should fire Richard, too—to fire him. I mean it was just incredible.

What did the others say?

CB: Well, they—he was very manipulative, too. He'd convinced these people that this was really important for the company. He had told them that if we didn't do this, there wouldn't be any money and they would all be out of a job. They would have nothing. They'd be out on the street, basically. He told some of them they'd better look for another job, things like this. I mean it was incredible. It was like something out of, uh....

What anxiety it must have—

CB: Yeah! Oh, yes! I mean you're talking—it was an incredible thing. Anyway, we knew that this man was a little bit dangerous, too. He sort of looked to me at the time like Jack Nicholson in *The Shining*. And so I knew we had to handle this very carefully, and we did. And we removed him. But the trust level between us and the employees had totally eroded. We had about, what? Five, six people at that time? We had really puffed up the employees to the point where we had way too many people. And a lot of them were his people.

People he had brought in?

RC: People he had brought in, yes.

CB: Yeah, he brought in people. But we never were able to reestablish the trust again. It was really hard. The communication wasn't good. And we had never been owners before. Here this thing was growing and we really didn't know how to be owners and how to handle growth and the things that come up for you, you know. And we were hoping this man could help us. But he totally betrayed us.

Anyway, by June of '92 these people [Carnahan, Smith and Gunter] approached us and said, "We would like to work with you because we recognize what's happening within your company and you're doing some unusual things. You seem to have a real mission behind your work. We would like to help you with your growth." Of course we were a little skeptical and wanted to really check them out before we proceeded, because we had had this experience with this man. So I checked with people that they had been working with, and they had been working with the Washington Park Zoo with Sherry Sheng. They had been working with her for two years. And I talked to some other people and they were all very pleased with their work, so I knew that it was a good thing.

So we started working with Marcia [Gunter] and Karen [Carnahan] from Carnahan, Smith and Gunter—there is no Smith, so if you're wondering who Smith is, he's a man who started it a long time ago and he's now traveling around in his motor home. So we started working with them and within a couple of days the woman who had been here the longest, like for the last five years, had not been happy even before the man had come in and all this had happened, left with no notice—she was our office manager—no notice, like at two in the afternoon she walked out the door and just gave us a written "I'm going." It was two days after we had started with these people and they had told us that things could change, but we had no idea it would be that quickly.

RC: One week later the receptionist left.

CB [laughing]: There were only, what? How many of us? Five?

RC: There were only five of us.

CB: What had happened was, we had started consciously—it's hard to explain in a logical way—

RC: It's not logical, but—

CB: But we had decided to make a shift in where the company was going and how—and the corporate culture and the atmosphere in the company.

Did you talk about this with your employees?

RC: Not at that point, no.

CB: Not—they just—it's like when things change, people know whether they can stay or not. You know, it doesn't have to be that

244

you tell them about it and all that. Things can change, and our experience is that the people who are ready to move forward and go that way are going to come with you and the others are going to fall away. They're going to do something that they're comfortable doing, or want to do. I think that's what happened.

But within two days?

CB: Two days. One of them did it in two days, but she—

RC: And one of them did it in nine days.

CB: Nine days. But she was a friend of the other one. And then we had another one who really wasn't working but wasn't willing to look for something else. And so we had a conversation with her. And with the help of our coaches, because they really are like a...a football coach for us, a business coach—they helped us help her find something she'd be happy doing.

RC: She had pretty much worked herself out of a job. She had been hired to do a specific task and she had done it. There was really nothing else for her to do. And then the last employee took a sabbatical, fell in love and took off. So we started with a whole new staff.

CB: In July [of 1992]. Whole new staff. And the company is so much better and happier, and people have purpose to their work.

What we did in the very beginning of working with these women was we did a session—we asked for input from vendors, employees, authors, investors on what they saw were the values of this company. And we came up with a mission statement and a set of values for the company. This was through three sessions that we came up with this, with the help and guidance of the business coaches. And our mission is "Inspire to Integrity." "Inspire to Integrity" means that through our work, through the actions we take every day, our mission is to inspire people to wholeness through the books we publish. When we are operating we try to keep in mind these values, and whenever we're doing something or something comes up, we go "Well, what value are we operating under now?" This is like the core essence of the company. So this is what we did in July and August.

The way they explained it is, a company is like a diamond. On one side—I'll draw it for you here—you've got the structure and you've got the resources. On the other you've got the mission and the passion of a company. Now where we were was, this was really big but this was really tiny. Now what you want is a balance of the two sides. You want them to kind of balance out. Most larger publishing companies are really strong on the resources and the structure. They know how it is and how many people they need to do it. But they have no idea of why they're in business. And we were strong in this area, so what they're helping us do is—

By "this area" you mean passion and mission?

CB: Yes. We are more from this side, and what they're helping us with now is our structure and our resources and getting that area clear so we can succeed in our growth and move forward. You know, what are the areas of accountability? Who do we need to fill it? What are the intended results? Setting up our cash flow. And we're getting a new computer system now. And we've set goals for our company. Where we want to be. How big we want to be by the year—we have it out to 2008. What we want to have accomplished by that point. Instead of working toward the future, looking from today and going forward, what they have us do is go to the future and work from it. And so you map out what you need to do—

And see how to get there.

CB: Yeah. Every day, when you're doing something, [you ask yourself]: "How am I reaching this by my actions today? How am I going to be in the future with these actions?"

And also what we do is, we work with our employees and every week, at the beginning of the week, we all go over our intended results for the week, what are we going to accomplish and do we need to make any requests of anyone else on the staff. We also have a luncheon meeting together every week where everyone has the opportunity to vent a frustration they've had that week, to tell everyone of something they've accomplished for the week and then also of something they'd like to be acknowledged for.

246

I think in most companies the reason people aren't happy is they don't get to vent frustrations. No one knows what they're really doing and what they're proud of. They don't ever get acknowledged. That's really important to people. I think more so than the money. So the company is just so different now, it's like day and night. And I'm really proud of that, that we've been able to move it from that space.

Did Carnahan, Smith and Gunter—did they bring a certain spirituality into the company, or was it already there?

CB: I think it was there already. I think what it is is demonstrating your own personal values through your work. I really think that that's what most people want to do in their work, but they don't know how to do it.

One of our goals is to set a new paradigm for the publishing industry through the kind of books we do. They are very different and sometimes they're ahead of the marketplace. But they're [Carnahan, Smith and Gunter] not doing it for us. It's coaching. It's guidance. And they really don't want to do it for us. They want to coach us to where we can do it. And by mentoring under them it just becomes easier and easier. It's great. The company has shifted so much in the last year, it's just incredible.

RC: It's really helped me. Not having had prior experience in publishing or owning a business, I was doing a lot of things by the seat of my pants, a lot of things intuitively. And they weren't bad things. In most cases the intuitive thoughts were good ones and they really helped us to be in the right place at the right time. But as one grows—we've grown to a point now where those things need to be put on paper, and we need to be able to delegate, or I need to be able to delegate, to others to assist in that growth.

CB: Yeah. Hopefully nothing would ever happen to him, but, you know, if it wasn't on paper we'd be in trouble.

RC: Plus being able to function in a businesslike way. We're at the point now where to project cash flow out over a year and do budgets and cost analyses for each book, where we will have probably a fifty percent increase in volume this year—just to deal with that level of paperwork and orders coming in and producing ten to twelve books a year, it's got to be organized.

Is that what you're doing now?

RC: That's what we're doing now. We did that last year and we're doing it this year.

CB: I mean it took us nine years to get to thirty, and this year we're going to do ten. It's a little overwhelming at times.

RC: This year, not only are we doing between ten and twelve new ones but we're doing twenty reprints. It's a major amount to manage.

CB: And the other thing we're working on right now is getting into other markets. I think depending on just the bookstore market is so risky. So when we look at a book for consideration we look at the other markets for it as well. We're really making concerted efforts now to get into the gift market, which we haven't been in before. We have been doing corporate and premium incentive work and we're doing more of that.

RC: And catalogues. Catalogues and corporate probably represent between fifty and sixty percent of our volume. Bookstores are maybe thirty to forty percent right now. The advantage with corporate and catalogue is that they pay for what they buy.

CB: Quickly.

RC: Quickly. The disadvantage of bookstores is that they pay slowly and it's on consignment.

CB: And then you get them back all damaged. Not all, but a lot of them. You know, people are just shocked when you tell them how the whole bookstore thing works, with things on consignment for up to a year. They cannot believe—I don't think there's any other industry that's like that.

No. It's only books.

CB: Yeah. It just seems that maybe that structure needs to be looked at, because I think it's encouraging a lot of waste. I hear stories about Simon and Schuster heating their warehouse by burning books.

248

Maybe it wasn't Simon and Schuster. Let me change that. I heard Random House. And that really shocks me. It makes me ill to think that's what they do. They overprint to justify the advances they pay these people and then they just bring them in and burn them if it doesn't work.

RC: Or stripping the covers and having people just toss the books. Buying shelf space in stores by producing twice as many as what the public would consume. Makes no sense in the waste of trees and the cost to our environment.

CB: I think it has just inflated the whole thing, too. The advances have just gotten way out of kilter. And it's fed the whole inflationary thing. But we try to be very conservative in the print runs that we do. We take our distributors' projections and we add a little bit more for what we think our needs will be. And we also will order, if we can, custom-size sheets so that there's very little wastage. When you do it that way, you keep it.

RC: The paper companies will actually trim the paper right to where you need to be. So when they manufacture that paper there's no wastage on the manufacturing end either.

CB: We use recycled paper if we can.

RC: I think Cindy said that the publishing business for us now is really an expression of our core values as individuals. We are living our truth, walking our talk, to a great extent. And with a mission that says "Inspire to Integrity" anything that's out of integrity comes up immediately.

CB: We're not perfect. We're working on it.

Where do you want to be in ten or fifteen years?

RC: We've actually sat down together and visioned that. What we see is that there will be a radical shift from the photographic coffee-table gift book as an item that someone will purchase to experience what a photographer experienced. I think that the industry will change and in will come things like virtual reality or video, audio or CD-ROM, so that the individual sitting in the comfort of their own home can literally experience what someone experienced when they were taking all these pictures.

We see that we are not in the book business as publishers. We're in the information business, in the business of conveying knowledge. So if there are other ways to do that, we will look seriously at them. We're now in discussion with companies that do things other than in print form. We are about to produce our first CD-ROM with a coffee table book, a book that will come out this fall. The book, as envisioned now, will come with a CD-ROM of all the imagery and text. I think that all big books that we produce in the years to come will come that way. And we're open to technology that doesn't even exist today. Because just as CD-ROM is relatively new, there are things that I'm sure we haven't envisioned.

CB: It's kind of amazing. I think when you really go to the future and you—some of it's hard to imagine because you don't know what you're going to be doing in fifteen years. The technology could really change. But if you have some kind of a picture about it—and after we've done that we've had calls from people that we couldn't have imagined would be calling us to do things. We've had calls from Microsoft that wants to do things with us. We are going to be doing some things with Apple. The opportunities just started coming. But it's making sure that it fits within what your mission and your values are.

RC: Growing up, we had been taught that we work toward a goal, that it's important to set goals. And the coaches had said to us that while it's important to have goals, it's important to stand in the future that you vision. And the moment we did that things started popping. Within twenty-four hours we started getting phone calls, unsolicited. Within seventy-two hours we had appointments with major record companies, CD companies—things that we couldn't have imagined happening happened.

CB: One of our values is "Unlimited Thinking is Fundamental." I think it's really important that we open ourselves up to all the possibilities. It's like you're going to be somewhere in the future, but the way it happens—I'm not fixed on how it's going to happen. It can happen in a multitude of ways. I didn't think we would be doing things with the computer companies at this point, but if that's the way it's meant to be, then we'll see.

RC: Another aspect that I don't know that we've mentioned, that's really important to us—it tracks with the value that we have about "Trust and Stewardship are Integral to Fulfilling Dreams." But stewardship in the sense where we give back to life as life has given us.

From the very beginning, with the first book we did, we did something positive for the environment. Like with *Rainbowed Sea* and *Molokai*, we planted a tree for every book we printed. So there's sixty thousand trees in the ground for the sixty thousand books we printed. With Native American books, people can send in contributions that go to nonprofit Native American self-help groups that help to teach traditional ways to children, not turning them into Anglo children, but allowing them to be who they are. The eagle book—we helped fund organizations that released eaglets into the wild in order to help rebuild that population that's been decimated by DDT and by indiscriminate shooting. So we do have a very strong social conscience that goes along with our publishing conscience.

CB: I'm just grabbing this to show you: "You work from what your accomplishments are during this period of time. We are a profitable and vital company and we create products that impact people's lives in a positive way. We set standards and trends in a new paradigm for the publishing industry. We create an environment where people are contributing and...work as partners...." And then what we do is, we set—"During the year, what are the intended results of what you do to meet these things?" And then we just made some notes on where we wanted to be by the year 2010, some of the things we wanted to have accomplished by then. This is not all final but this is what we're working on right now, is setting our goals. And then taking that to the employee level so that they all know what's expected of them to help us reach these things.

RC: We've certainly learned a lot in ten years. August will be our tenth anniversary since the inception. When we began the publishing business we didn't have a business plan. We didn't even have a signed business agreement. But what we had was a "joy prospectus" where all four of us, the author and his wife and Charlie Fields and myself all agreed that this process we were about to embark on, this adventure called publishing, was to be a process of joy, and that communication was essential. I don't remember the wording exactly, but communication was essential to everything and as long as it was fun to do, we would do it. Thus began a great adventure and learning experience for all of us. And it's an ongoing learning experience. I don't think I have all the answers, or perhaps even as much as two percent of the answers. I know a little bit and I'm learning all the time, and I told Cindy and I told our employees that if I ever take myself too seriously to please tell me. I want to leave this lifetime with no regrets and I want to do the best job I can in publishing to help make a difference in the world. In ten years, one of the things we see is that our company is awarded the Nobel Peace Prize, the Nobel Prize for Peace, for the work we have done, the contribution we have made, in helping to bring the world together as one.

Maureen Michaelson and Rhonda Hughes
NewSage Press

"I am continuously learning about people different from my-self. For instance, *Women and Work: Photographs and Personal Writings*. When I started editing that book I was feeling pretty smug, like I really understood working women and what was going on. I mean I read the books in college. I'm a working woman. And I was humbled. I was humbled by what I learned from these women who worked in factories for twelve hours a day, who worked three jobs supporting their five kids by themselves. I mean I really learned a lot from their, you know, down-to-earth living of life."

We had attended Literuption, Portland, Oregon's annual literary arts fair, on Saturday. Afterward, we met at the Heathman Hotel lounge, walking distance from the Masonic Temple where the fair was being held. Maureen Michaelson and Rhonda Hughes are the publishers of NewSage Press, kind of. Actually, Michaelson is the publisher and Hughes is the managing editor. On the other hand, Hughes is the president of Print Vision, a print brokerage, and Michaelson is the vice president. Decisions concerning either company are made by both women. "We work closely together," Michaelson says, "but Rhonda would make the final decision in Print Vision and I would make it in NewSage." "We have never not been able to agree on something yet," says Hughes. "Which is nice."

Michaelson was born and raised in Los Angeles. She attended Loyola Marymount in Los Angeles and graduated from California State University in Los Angeles. Her degree is in journalism. She did some graduate work in political science but didn't finish this degree—a victim of boredom.

Hughes was born in Olongapo, Philippines, beside Subic Bay where her father was stationed. She was a year old when she returned with her family to San Diego. She went through the mandatory twelve years of school in San Diego and started at Mesa College. She moved to San Francisco where she attended San Francisco City College and then Mills College in Oakland. "It's only taken me ten years to get to be a senior. I go, I quit. I go, I quit. I go, I quit. I was going to Mills College and I was finishing up a degree [in art history] when the opportunity to work with Maureen came up, and I decided to put my studies on hold."

The interview took place at the Heathman lounge on a warm evening at the beginning of March 1993 amid the clatter of dishes and the noises of a growing crowd.

When did you start Newsage?
Maureen Michaelson: Nineteen eighty-five.

Were you involved with publishing before NewSage?
MM: My background was in journalism. I was a reporter for *Time Magazine* out of their Beverly Hills bureau. I did that for about five years and then I went on to be editor of *Glass Magazine*. I did that for another four or five years. It was an arts publication, specifically glass art. Sculpture, stained glass, blown glass. But I got to a point where I really wanted to be in business for myself. I was intrigued with the idea of publishing books. I saw a lot of subjects that weren't being covered by mainstream publishing that I thought were definitely worth exposure. And I wanted to do that. And I felt that I could do it just as well as anybody else.

What subjects did you feel weren't getting exposure?
MM: I was very interested in women's subjects. They're very near and dear to my heart. And I wanted to put out books that had quality not only in the presentation, the actual printing, but also in the content. And I was also very intrigued with photography. I love photography as a medium. I think it's very powerful. And I wanted to combine the photographs and the text to make a statement. And I felt that the two together in the right combination could do so very well. And I wanted

254

to be making the decisions. I wanted to decide what was going to be in a book, what the book was going to be. I could probably work for another publishing house for years and never be able to do what I'm doing now.

Do you think your taste for text and photos together comes from your experience with Time?

MM: Oh, sure. It definitely does. In fact, one of the editors that I chose to work with me on what were actually the first and second books that I published was a photographer I knew from *Time Magazine*. We had worked together at *Time*, we had a good friendship, and that really helped develop my interests and my understanding of photography. So, yeah. And I just know how I feel when I look at a photograph. I'm very moved by the medium.

Are you a photographer yourself?

MM: No, I'm not. I take photographs, but no, I'm not a photographer.

As a journalist, you—

MM: You'd go out on assignments with photographers. I mean that would be the usual. Go cover a story with a photographer. I would do the reporting and the photographer would take the photographs. I'm really used to working with that.

Before you got into publishing—what did you do before you got involved with publishing?

Rhonda Hughes: NewSage Press is really Maureen's creation. I sold printing and that's how I met Maureen. She was one of my customers. I've been part of NewSage Press not even a year yet. In a couple of weeks it'll be a year. So it's really Maureen's creation, and only in the last year have I been on board.

You sold printing?

MM: Actually, all of NewSage Press's books have been printed overseas. Part of that is that most of the books are duotones. Duotone photographics is a two-color process. And then there was a four-color book, *Exposures*, which Rhonda had printed for me overseas.

RH: I was Director of Sales for this corporation.

MM: So that's how we got know each other, and she oversaw the printing of my book, *Exposures: Women and Their Art*. With Rhonda's background in art history, she was very interested in the subject anyway and she had contacted me and we started this business relationship that eventually turned into a friendship. We just liked each other very much, we liked working together, and Rhonda just has a lot of background in printing and understanding the printing process, which was very important to me because—

I mean I went on my first press check in 1985 and just really went by the seat of my pants, just went and asked a ton of questions. I went over to Japan and I asked these guys twenty million questions, what does this mean and what's that, and that's how I learned. It wasn't something I learned in journalism school. They didn't teach me how to do press checks. It was really an on-the-job just-do-it. And when you're printing photographs and duotones, there is a lot to know about the printing process. Is it being done correctly, and if something's wrong, what's wrong.

RH: I'm coming into publishing from a printing background. I'm Print Vision. Print Vision is printing books still. In other words, I left the corporation where I worked as Director of Sales, and Print Vision was begun by Maureen and me. And so we're printing books and publishing.

MM: There are two arms of the business.

Where did you learn printing? Not from art history?

RH: No. When I graduated from high school and went to college I needed to get a job. So I got a job as a receptionist in a printing company. And I saw proofs going across my desk and I saw sales reps coming in and out, and it seemed like they had the life of Reilly and they were making a lot of money and I thought to myself, "I can do that." And so I continued taking classes and working. And classes for

256

me were always at night, always part-time, and that's why at thirty years old I'm a senior. It's taken that long to get through.

Were either of you in the military?

MM: No. I protested against the Viet Nam war. That's my association with the military.

That question derives from an hypothesis I had, that an innovator comes to whatever field innovation occurs from something else. I found in my first interviews that I was interviewing older men who were in the military during the Korean War or shortly after. So they'd lived abroad. One had stayed abroad after his service. Then they'd come back and gone into publishing. But this hypothesis doesn't work with younger people.

MM: Yeah. We're the next generation down. But an interesting hypothesis.

It might still work in general terms, but the military is too specific. At least the hypothesis might work for Americans. I don't think it works for Canadians. But I still think you come in from something else. You bring something to the field to make that field different. Whereas the Canadians have an education system that can slip them right in. At least the younger generation of Canadians have an education system that will put them right into publishing. Those of, say, my age, those who are in their forties—I haven't met any older than that—their background is similar to ours. They came out of other things.

MM: But, see, there wasn't any opportunity in the small press for your generation or, really, even mine. Small press is really something that came out of the '60s. Before that there were large publishing houses in New York. That's where they were. And you had to go through the ranks of a major publishing house. What the small press really came out of, I think.... I definitely think the gay and lesbian press, needing to get their work out there—major houses wouldn't touch it with a ten-foot pole—the women's movement—women wanted to

257

write about things that major publishing houses said "It's not going to sell. Who's going to buy it?"

It really came out of filling a need. You think about alternative life styles that came out of the '60s. That's really where the small press came from, was filling that need. And the voices that needed to be heard that the large publishing houses were not paying any attention to because they weren't going to sell books. You notice how they jump on a book. You know how they jumped on the New Age books as soon as they saw that they were making a lot of money. They didn't print the first New Age books though. It was small press. So you look at these different voices trying to be heard, they had to create their own presses. And I think that's where a lot of that has come from.

When you say "small press" in the context that you're using now, are you talking about small press as something that a person can make a living at, or just getting a book out?

MM: I think it can mean many different things. And I think that somebody trying to get a book out and what they need to live on in their twenties is not somebody that needs it [i.e., to make a living at publishing] in their forties when they've got a mortgage payment. I think there's a wide range of definitions of what's a small press or an independent press. And I think that some presses that—like Ten Speed: Ten Speed started out putting out a bicycle book. You go to a conference now and you see Ten Speed, my God, they've got hundreds of books on every imaginable subject.

RH: They're very eclectic.

MM: Very eclectic, yeah. And very successful. It was like "Let's put out a bicycle book," you know, or "Let's put out a book on how to repair Volkswagens." That's where all that came from. Even within that category of small press there're many variations.

You know, even back in the nineteenth century, Mark Twain formed a small publishing company. In the early twentieth century many people, both in the United States and England—Robert Graves and Laura Riding had a small publishing company.

258

MM: Yeah, that's true. But I'm thinking in modern terms of distribution, getting into bookstores in a big way. You're right. The small press has been around a long time, but I guess I'm thinking of it more in contemporary terms where it's really taken off in a big way, where we have everyone like you who's working a full-time job and publishing your books to someone working out of their garage to Rhonda and I who have this nice small office with a staff of four or five to Seal Press which started very small and is now very well recognized in the Northwest as a women's press. Calyx has been around twenty years. Look how much they've grown.

Do you continue to write?
MM: Mm hmm. Yes, I do. Not as much as I'd like to. In fact, just this past summer I took a writing workshop for a week called "Flight of the Mind" which Ruth Gundle and her partner started. It's a wonderful women's writing workshop where you go to this beautiful retreat on the Mackenzie River for a week and you sign up for different groups. And you meet with that group throughout the week and you write. They supply all your meals. You don't have to do anything, just write. It was just so wonderful. I think it was really especially wonderful for me, both as a working person and as a parent, to have a whole week to myself to write and...just to have to myself. Most of my time, though, is spent editing. I edit a lot of other people's work right now. But I also really like to write. It brings me a lot of personal satisfaction.

Do you write book-length stuff or articles or—?
MM: My writing is for myself. I don't write with the thought that I'm going to publish my book. I have published two books that I've edited and I'm certainly interested in doing that, but it's not—
RH: You could see that as a possibility.
MM: Yeah.
RH: Down the road.

Two books. You mean anthologies that you've edited?
MM: Well, I suppose you'd call it an anthology. I edited *Women*

259

and Work: Photographs and Personal Writings. It was kind of like an anthology in a way, yeah. A working woman's anthology.

RH: Exactly.

MM: Then the very first book that I ever published, *Pasadena: One Hundred Years*, which was—

RH: You wrote that.

MM: Yeah. I wrote the text for that.

RH: I can see you writing another.

Did you publish that through NewSage?

MM: Mm hmm. That was the first book I ever did.

Do you write, Rhonda?

RH: No. I'm not a writer. I'm just a reader.

MM: Just personal. Personalized. She loves poetry. She lo-o-oves poetry.

RH: I'm a poetry lover. I've kept a journal since I was nine years old. So I write in my journal on a continuing basis. I've written some pretty bad poetry in my time. That's about it.

MM: She's the one that buys all the poetry books in the stores. Somebody has to buy it, so Rhonda does.

RH: That's right.

What kind of work did your parents do? Did you live with both parents?

MM: Yeah. Yeah. Lived in the same house for eighteen years. Let's see. My father was a college graduate and he went to law school. He graduated from law school. He did what you'd call white-collar work. In fact, he did a lot of contract writing. He did a lot of writing. And I think that, yeah, I got a lot of that—

RH: Did he enjoy that?

MM: I don't think my father—well, who knows how happy they are, doing that. But I can remember him helping me with my writing and my editing. What I realized later on in my life was that my mother was also a writer. But she was primarily a homemaker. Having

260

a family of six children, she was exhausted by the end of the day most of the time. But I realized in her later years that she wrote a lot. Her writing happened in the way of a lot of personal letters to people. She would write, I mean literally, to hundreds of people. That's how her writing took form. So I came from a pretty literate family, in terms of paying attention to writing and reading. Like that was always encouraged.

Did you grow up with both parents also?

RH: Until I was nine. My parents divorced. Reading was most important in my family. Everybody read. When I say everybody I mean my father, my uncle, my mother, the whole family as a clan. I have one brother. And then my grandfather taught me how to read when I was two with flash cards. I was the first one born, and so out of all the cousins—

MM: That's incredible. At two!

RH: Yeah. It was a very big deal and he went through the trouble. He was retired and we lived with him in this big, huge house. My father's father. And he would cut up pieces of cardboard and write words on them. I remember "rhinoceros" was one of them and everybody's name was on there and so it would be show-and-tell time when the relatives came over and he'd hold up the flash card and I would say whatever the word was. So by the time I got to kindergarten I could read. And I think that's what instilled this love of books and reading.

MM: She has an incredible library at her house. I mean just books and books and books.

Did your brother have that—?

RH: He's a younger brother and he's very much interested in photography. I think if he had his choice he would definitely be a photographer if he could make a living at being a photographer. But he's unable to do that at this time.

MM: Yeah.

What about your siblings? Do they also have the love of books

261

and reading?

MM: Well, they're all very literate. I mean most of them graduated from college. That was really encouraged in my family. I don't necessarily think of them as, you know, loving books and reading all the time. Probably my younger sister more so. She's an artist. She graduated from the Art Institute of Chicago. She's a painter. But she reads a lot. But I don't think of my brothers as great readers. I have four older brothers. It's not that they can't read. I'm sure they read. Hopefully. I don't know what.

RH: Lorraine is a great artist though. I love her work. Her younger sister.

MM: Oh, great. She'll love this.

RH: No, she is.

MM: Yeah. She is.

RH: I really like her work.

You went into publishing because you wanted to do it yourself. You wanted to have your own business and—

MM: Well, I really liked the idea. I think this came from my journalism background. And seeing even like an article that would come out in a magazine. And seeing how that would affect a person's life. I also did some freelance writing. I've written for *Ms Magazine* and a couple of other publications on a freelance basis. And, you know, talking to editors and hearing that they got sacks full of mail about an article that was written. So I saw the power of the printed word. I experienced that as a journalist and I really liked that. I liked the idea of creating greater understanding in the world through communication. And so what I wanted to do was take it to another level. I wanted to do it with books. Books that would be around. Books that would go in libraries. Books that would potentially be here a lot longer than I'm going to be here. I mean I love it when I know one of our books is in a library. Because somebody can pick that book up years from now and be touched by it.

One of the really fun things that happened—the very first book I ever published was called *Pasadena: One Hundred Years*, and it was on the community that I lived in for about eleven years, Pasadena. And I tied it in with the centennial. That was my peg. And it was very rich history, and lots of wonderful old photographs. And we had photographers go out and photograph the community in 1985. You know, like a hundred years later. And the city of Pasadena asked me to put one of the books in a time capsule that was going to be opened in a hundred years for the bicentennial. And they asked me to inscribe the book. It was a wonderful exercise in thinking "What would that be like when people"— hopefully there will be people here a hundred years from now—"open this time capsule? And they'll take this book out and I will have written something in there and they'll read it." It just gave me a thrill. I just wrote, "I hope you have a great time. I'm sorry I can't be here."

I asked David Brewster—David Brewster is the president of Sasquatch Publishing; they do Sasquatch Books and the Seattle Weekly—*I asked him where his immortality lay. And he said he hoped his company would last for three generations.*

MM: I would really hope that NewSage Press would be independent enough of me someday that if I were to get sick and die it could go on without me. That's really what I would hope.

RH: I would love to think of NewSage Press as being passed to Alexa.

MM: Yes. My daughter Alexa. She's three and a half. She'll get all the bills.

RH: Yeah. But to think that this company that we created will continue to work would be great.

Rhonda, you came to NewSage Press because of your relationship with Maureen. But why did you go into publishing from printing?

RH: I worked with publishers as a printer. All my customers were publishers. I've always been interested in publishing. I got into printing by accident. I didn't plan on being a printer. I fell into printing and it was very lucrative. And I worked with so many publishers that I began thinking I would really love to do this. But publishing doesn't make as much money as printing does. But I got into publishing because

I'm interested in using publishing as a means for social change.

MM: Yeah.

RH: To educate, like Maureen said, people who haven't thought of a particular idea, a political ideology or whatever the subject matter may be. Usually something that benefits women or a particular minority group or people that don't have voices. I'm interested in getting voices to those people that don't have voices in the mainstream press. And that's exactly what Maureen's been working on since 1985. So our values are the same. I had been thinking about leaving this corporation to form my own printing company, and then Maureen mentioned, "Have you ever thought about combining our two companies and utilizing both talents, because you're interested in publishing and I'm interested in printing and we could help each other and make a nice partnership." So I started to think about it and I thought, "It's perfect."

Which leads us to the next question: What's the purpose of your press? I think you just approached that. Do you want to refine that in any way?

RH: Yeah, I think we kind of said that.

MM: Yeah, I think Rhonda said it very well. It really is to create greater understanding in the world. At the risk of sounding cliché, that's really the point. For people to pick up our books and to read about somebody different from them, and to learn something.

RH: Right.

MM: To broaden their understanding of the world and people in the world. One of the things that is very important to us in our books is that there is a lot of diversity and experience in age and ethnic background. We really pay attention to that.

RH: I want to say something to that issue. We had a great manuscript come in, a submission that I was crazy about. It was wonderful. It was about women, powerful women, that were poets or artists or writers, whatever they were. Powerful women. And Maureen said we couldn't do the manuscript because it didn't include enough women of color. They were all white women.

264

MM: It was a pretty white, middle-class book.

RH: Right. All of them.

MM: Or upper-middle-class.

RH: I mean I saw the submission and I got really crazy about it because it's all the women I have known and admired for years. And I thought it would be wonderful to do this book. And Maureen said, "Well, there's not enough women of color and I would want to include them if we're going to do a book of this on the subject." And so Maureen went back—I think you went back to the writer and said, "Well, you need to come up with some women of color that we can include in this."

And I was just very impressed by that. And I, at first, was pushing her. "Well, why? Let's just do it. It's good enough." And she stuck to her guns and I came to realize you're right. I'm glad we didn't do that. And the author has yet to come back to us with women of color in that book.

What if she doesn't? Will you regret having lost the book?

MM: No.

RH: No. Not at all, because there'll be another one—

MM: Yep.

RH: —that will represent NewSage Press better.

MM: You know, I think some of that sensitivity comes from having sat in hundreds of story conferences at *Time Magazine* where there were maybe two women in a room full of twelve men, and seeing what was decided as being important. What was the quote reality unquote that we were going to report on this week? It usually wasn't on any topic that applied to women specifically, or to people of color. That was a pretty stark realization because I went in as a pretty wide-eyed, optimistic journalism student, thinking that, of course, you report on everything and we're going to be fair about this, and seeing that it was biased from the beginning, biased from the editorial decision on what was going to go in the magazine and what wasn't.

And seeing that the only way that's going to change—well, there're a couple of ways. One is for me to be more sensitive. And also to have journalists of color, women journalists, journalists from different backgrounds, different ages, reporting on the world's events. When you have an older, white male perspective always being presented, that's all you're going to get. And I'm not saying that's bad, but I'm saying that's just one perspective, and there are many perspectives out there. I am continuously learning about people different from myself. For instance, *Women and Work: Photographs and Personal Writings*. When I started editing that book I was feeling pretty smug, like I really understood working women and what was going on. I mean I read the books in college. I'm a working woman. And I was humbled. I was humbled by what I learned from these women who worked in factories for twelve hours a day, who worked three jobs supporting their five kids by themselves. I mean I really learned a lot from their, you know, down-to-earth living of life. It's very humbling.

How many titles a year do you do now?

MM: Well, this year we're doing what? *Stories of Adoption—*

RH: *Stories of Adoption, When the Bough Breaks,* two others that we're not quite sure of the titles yet. That's four.

MM: In *Stories of Adoption: Loss and Reunion,* those are stories about adults who went back to find birth parents. They were adopted out as babies. Or birth parents trying to find their children who are now adults. Or adopted parents. So these are not all happy stories. These are not, you know, "Adoption is wonderful and we're all happy." These are people who were very pained for many years. A lot of the birth mothers were having babies at a time when society did not accept single mothers, and there were no resources, and adoption was like, you know, give your baby up if you love your baby.

There was one woman in the book, she had been interviewed, she had signed releases, everything, when she read her statement she said, "I can't do it. My own family doesn't know some of this stuff." As a publisher I'm not going to say, "Yeah, you're going to do it. You signed a release. I don't care what you think." This is her life. I'm interested in getting the truth but I'm not interested in stealing the truth. If somebody doesn't want to give me the truth of their life, that is their choice. And I have to respect that. When she said that we were very

266

disappointed, because the photograph was extremely strong, the story was very strong, but you know what? That was her life. And so we had to let it go.

RH: That's another thing I learned in working with you. Because I wanted to use that. And never having been a publisher before, I said, "Well, why can't we use it?" And you said, "You can't really do that."

Well, you probably could have, legally, but you wouldn't want to.

RH: That's what I mean. Legally you could have, but it just really brought a consciousness to me that I didn't have.

MM: I'm not interested in the book being successful at her personal expense. And there were enough people in the book who did speak very honestly and told very difficult stories.

Grants. Do you apply for grants?
MM: We're for-profit.

Do you have any intention of—?
MM: No.

Why not?

MM: Because then you don't own the company. When you become a nonprofit, your board of directors can kick you out. I know there are ways around that but I don't want to spend a lot of my time doing grant writing either. Not that I don't have my moments when I wish I could get a big hundred-thousand-dollar grant. I'd love to. We just need to know how to publish books that sell.

RH: Right.

MM: That's what we need to know how to do.

RH: And still publish books that we're interested in publishing. What we need to know is how to sell those books we want to publish.

MM: There you go.

RH: Instead of finding out what sells, we want to learn how to increase the sales on those books that we want to publish. That's where we are now, is figuring out how to maximize sales on those titles that we have recently published. Even the backlist, right?

MM: Of course.

With the books you've done, did you do market research first, before doing the book, or did you publish a book and then try to figure out how to sell it?

MM: I did a fair amount of market research on the very first book.

The Pasadena book?

MM: That was an expensive book. That was a fifty-dollar book in 1985. But it did very well. It sold out. Unfortunately, I did only three thousand [copies]. I probably could have sold six, eight thousand. I don't know.

RH: But a book on Pasadena for fifty dollars a copy!

MM: That book now sells for like two hundred and seventy-five dollars. There's only a few around. We're sold out, for all intents and purposes. On the second book, *Women and Work*, I didn't market. That came purely from the heart, from what I wanted to do. In fact, we published the book and said, "Oh, isn't this a nice book? Now we get to sell it." I mean we did it all backward.

RH: You won a library award.

MM: It got selected for the American Library Association's list of best books for young adults. See, now that we're represented by Consortium [a master book distributor], they do presales. You know, six months before the book comes out, they're out selling it. I didn't do that back with *Women and Work*. I didn't have the sophistication. I didn't know. And nobody will take a one-title publisher. Consortium is not going to pick up a one-title publisher. So it's kind of Catch Twenty-two there. You've got to keep coming out with the books but you can't have anybody selling them. So, you know, you put them with Bookpeople and Inland [regional book wholesalers] and you work real hard.

268

I don't have any more questions. Is there anything more either of you want to say?

RH: I think the most important part about publishing for me is using publishing for social change. To give voices to those who don't have voices, and hope they're brought into somebody's home. If somebody can get those kinds of lessons that I've gotten from Maureen by picking up one of our books, then it's worth it.

MM: We've gotten wonderful letters from people who say, you know, it's great. Sometimes you feel you're operating in a vacuum. You're in your office, doing your thing on the computer, and to go write us letters or call [and] say, you know, "Your book just really touched my life. I loved your book. I sat down with it for a couple hours, I expected to spend fifteen minutes," that is just wonderful. And that's probably why NewSage Press will never be really good at how-to books. We're more interested in doing books that speak on a deeper level. An emotional level, a level of experience, human experience and the richness of that. Yeah. I think that's it.

[Maureen Michaelson and Rhonda Hughes are now independent of each other, a result of NewSage and Print Vision each becoming increasingly successful and requiring greater attention from their respective owners.]

Scott C. Davis

Thatcher Bailey

Joe Matthew Singer

Jean-Louis Brindamour

Top: Ed Varney
Bottom: Jerome Gold

Tree Swenson

Top: Karl Siegler
Bottom: Tim Lander

Top to bottom:
Robert and Lysa McDowell,
Ruth Gundle, Denny and Linny Stovall

Top: Rolf Maurer
Bottom: Barbara Wilson

Top to bottom:
John Ellison and Lesley Link,
Anna Johnson, margareta waterman

Harald Wyndham

David Brewster

Top: Catherine Hillenbrand
Bottom: Margarita Donnelly

Dan Levant

Robert McDowell
Story Line Press

"When the average sale of a book of poetry by a poet with, say, five books out, who has won five or six awards—when the average sale of a book of poetry by a person like that is fifteen hundred copies in paperback, there's something wrong. With a country this size, with this population base, there's something wrong there. The same poet in Ireland will sell ten thousand copies in a year. In a country the size of Rhode Island."

I talked with Robert McDowell, poet and publisher of Story Line Press, in his warehouse, a converted equipment shed set to the side of the farmhouse he shares with his wife (and SLP designer), Lysa, and their two young sons, on April 1, 1993. The afternoon—it was a little after five when we got started—was brisk with a hint of sun lightening the clouds in the western quarter of the sky. In the background was the near-constant tapping of SLP marketing director Joseph Bednarik's fingers on a computer keyboard, the noise broken only by the greater noise of the linked printer.

McDowell was born in Alhambra, California and lived there until he was eighteen when he went a few hundred miles north to the University of California at Santa Cruz. There he studied literature and writing with George Hitchcock and James B. Hall. He graduated from Santa Cruz in 1974 and went on to Columbia University where he received his MFA in 1976. After Columbia he returned to California and spent a year in the Mojave Desert. "I wanted to be in the desert. As a writer, that location made possible my first breakthrough, I believe, toward understanding my material and seeing what I wanted to do in poetry." A few years later Chowder Press published McDowell's chapbook, At the House of the Tin Man, *and in 1987 Henry Holt and Company published his full-length collection,* Quiet

Money. *"Many of the poems in* Quiet Money *are narrative, and I began to understand that kind of poem in the desert."*

Following his Mojave experience, he went to Evansville, Indiana as an assistant professor of English and writer-in-residence at Indiana State University. The teaching load was five courses a semester with occasionally two in summer school. He taught creative writing, literature, and composition. He spent six years in Indiana, from 1978 to 1984. "In '83 they were threatening to turn my position into a tenure-track position and give me tenure. I gave it hard thought and came to the conclusion that if I were to get tenure I would be there for the rest of my life. I had trouble imagining my entire life spent in Indiana on the Mason-Dixon Line. So I resigned. I like to think that my decision was a good one."

McDowell returned to Santa Cruz and stayed until 1989. That year he and Lysa moved to Brownsville, Oregon. Why Brownsville? "We started having children. In mid-'89 we finally just got in the car and drove north. As soon as we hit the California-Oregon border we started looking for places. We wanted something more rural, small-town, than anything we had in California. We had high expectations [but] had them dashed at stop after stop. Culminating with the best real estate person we'd found in Eugene, who got us lost on the freeway, then, as she broke down sobbing, confessed to Lysa that she couldn't read a map. After we got her back to her office she asked us in desperation, "What places have you seen that you did like?" Lysa mentioned Oakland, about an hour south of Eugene. And the woman said, "Oh, well, if you liked Oakland, you'll like Brownsville." We'd never heard of it. The only Brownsville we'd heard of was in Texas. She told us where it was, but she wouldn't bring us up because it was too far out and nothing was available there anyway.

"We already had decided to drive north to spend the weekend with my sister in Lacey, Washington and on the way we spotted the turn-off for Brownsville and decided what the hell, we'll go down and see what's there. It was going on six in the evening, so everything was closed. But we did look at the real estate office window and saw this place listed for sale. Lysa decided to take a flyer, so she crossed the

street to a pay phone and called the agent. Even though it was a weekend he offered to come out and show us around the next morning. And we checked into the Pioneer Villa Truckstop-Motel down here at the highway. Four days later, we made an offer on this place. Seventeen and a half acres. After we closed the deal we managed to dash back to Northern California in time for the Loma Prieta earthquake. Which was a most convincing punctuation mark to our leaving."

Described by another interviewer (Alice Evans, "Story Line Press: Keeping the Stories of Our Time Alive," Poets & Writers Magazine, *November/December 1994) as "a large man of aristocratic demeanor," a description with which I agree, McDowell seems at the same time both engaged and detached. I discovered, in the course of the interview, three subjects he attends with passion, either understated or full-blown. These are: the weight of history as it affected his mother's family; the person who was his father; and the writing and publishing of literature, particularly poetry. McDowell will expound on the last at some length below. But here I want to give him a few moments for his family.*

He has a brother, an attorney, and a sister, recently retired. A second sister committed suicide in 1982. "She was the family's live wire, the cut-up, the prankster. We miss her levity." McDowell's mother was born in Graz, Austria, and came to the US as an infant. Her parents were escaping World War I. They died of influenza in Cleveland, Ohio during the epidemic of 1915-1916. A few years later her only sister died, also of influenza, in another epidemic.

My mother was alone and came under the care of nuns. She also went through a series of foster families. [She] was married three times that I know of. For a time [she] was a ceramist in California. Had her own shop. And then, years later, became a business manager for a group of doctors. Before that, in Cleveland, she was actually a singer. I'd kid her about that. Tommy Dorsey tried to hire her to sing with his band, but she turned him down to marry my father and have children. I always wondered if she thought of giving up singing as one of the great mistakes of her life. Her life was fascinating, especially the early years. Her childhood parallels that of one of our authors, Colette Inez, whose own incredible childhood is explored in the poems in *Family Life* [which] we're bringing out.

My father had a very privileged childhood. He was very pampered and led a very good life. His mother was an actress in New York. A Broadway actress. I mean his godfather was Walter Winchell. I certainly remember a lot of stories about 'Goddamn Walt.' My father was a gambler. He was a confidence man. He was a crook. He was a raving drunk. He was great card player. A great horse player. And he disappeared without a trace—oh, it must be thirty-five years ago. His car was found abandoned in the desert halfway between L.A. and Las Vegas. My brother once said he was consumed by demons he couldn't overcome.

It was an atypical family in some ways. On the other hand, in some of the ways we look at family today, we'd fit in classically as a dysfunctional, broken family, a family plagued by alcoholism, a family certainly plagued by various -isms represented by every pathological behavior my father exhibited. I suppose the family could be understood very much in typical middle-class American terms. I mean the one great component that's missing in younger families now facing these same problems is the parents [not having gone] through something as traumatic as the Depression. And, of course, in many dysfunctional families the mother cannot look back to a completely traumatized childhood like my mother could look back on.

I'd like to talk about publishing now, if that's all right. Story Line started in—when?

Nineteen eighty-five we published our first two books.

When did you go nonprofit?

Well, it's interesting. We started out as nonprofit because we grew out of a magazine which Mark Jarman and I founded. It was called *The Reaper* [and it] went for twenty issues, 1980 to 1990. The magazine argued for the resurgence of narrative in contemporary poetry. It was a very incendiary magazine. It was highly polemical, known probably as much for its criticism as [for] anything else. Provoked a lot of controversy. And I think that had a lot to do with why we can now pick up literary magazines and find long poems in them. Before the mid-'80s you had a hard time locating a long poem, or a narrative poem, in the pages of literary magazines anywhere. Few poets, critics and readers seriously discussed or considered the use of storytelling in verse. *The Reaper* was a catalyst in changing all that.

That magazine was a nonprofit corporation which we added the press to, basically, when we started it. For a couple of years in California we decided to try to go for-profit with the press, but this failed. But because we had this other organization that we had never closed down, we closed down the for-profit corporation and consolidated all operations under Story Line Press, Inc.

Why did you start the magazine in the first place?
Well, the magazine's a result of two young poets, two young poet-critics who were old associates, living in a remote area, strange to them—I was in Evansville while Mark lived and taught in Murray, Kentucky—looking at the scene of American poetry and being very dissatisfied with it. Specifically, American poetry at the time seemed limited, clubby, suffocating. Taking their cues from confessional poetry, from surrealism, most writers produced uniform, short poems that turned on unlikely images and often delivered mundane accounts of the writer's daily life. The verse—and I use the term lightly—was usually free. Such poems dominated poetry publications and workshops. Drama and storytelling were almost impossible to find. Jarman and I launched *The Reaper* to call attention to these essential but forgotten elements of poetry. And we ran that for ten years.

For most issues, Mark and I wrote lead essays together under the pen name, The Reaper. The essay in our first issue pilloried contemporary poetry criticism. But there were also essays that discussed seriously, for the first time, the influence of Frost on American poetry, the influence of Stevens. In one issue we published the "lost" correspondence between Homer and Dante in which the two giants argued about storytelling and music in verse. In another issue we ran a long, satirical interview with the popular married poets, Sean Dough and Jean Doh, about their aesthetic tastes and the American scene, [and] who were effusive in their praise of practically everybody. One of Jean's better lines is often quoted back to us in our travels, even today: "You feel better about people's poems once you've had a drink with them!" Indeed. The essay in our third issue put forth The Reaper's ten non-negotiable demands—ten things that poets could no longer do, and live. Our last essay together proclaimed dead the small, personal lyric and made the case for Louis Simpson as our greatest living poet. Meanwhile, we were publishing the best poems we could find to support our arguments.

This was the sort of magazine *The Reaper* was. As I say, it provoked a lot of controversy, a lot of commentary. The "Letters" columns were frequently the most interesting aspect of the magazine, because we heard from the famous and not-so-famous, most of whom were pissed off about one thing or another that we had written about, some claim we had made. We discovered an interesting thing: even though many people assumed they were going to be attacked in *The Reaper*, those especially were the people you could count on to buy it. People, if they know they're going to be attacked, can't resist getting a copy.

Do you miss it? You sound as if you do.
Well, I don't know. Let me think about that for a moment. Do I miss it? I suppose I miss the innocence of that time. The sheer energy of that time. I mean, when Mark Jarman and I were camped out in his attic, writing essays on Frost and Stevens and the problem with contemporary American criticism in poetry, that was fun. Looking back on it, it was incredibly simple, too. It was easy, in some ways, compared to what we're doing now. Book publishing is much more complicated. As the years go by, as you add books, as things, expand, it gets harder and harder.

I suppose I miss it. I don't know. I had a very real sense, when we decided to close it down, that it was time. Both Mark and I felt this very strongly, that *The Reaper* had said what it had to say and had helped to correct some problems we thought were unbearable, and it was time to go on. I mean the history of good literary magazines in this country is that they come and they go. They die when it's time to die. Of course, with a wonderful name like *The Reaper* it can always come back.

Reaper Redux.

Right. So the magazine sort of carried us into publishing. I think I, more than Mark, always had some interest in publishing books if the situation were right. Now how that arose was really a complete accident. In 1984 Edgar Lansbury, Board Chair of the Nicholas Roerich Museum in New York—he's a very well known theatrical producer; he produced *Godspell*—Edgar approached Frederick Morgan, editor/publisher of *The Hudson Review*, and told Fred that the museum was interested in funding a new national poetry series and would Fred be interested in overseeing that, since the museum knew nothing about the poetry world or poetry publishing. They just knew that they wanted to do this. Fred declined; he had other things he was doing; he was very busy with the magazine. However, he could recommend two poet-critics in the Midwest who had a small, lively magazine of their own. We held some preliminary discussions over the phone, and when Lysa and I returned from a summer in Wales and Ireland, I had lunch with Frederick Morgan and Edgar Lansbury, the first time I'd met Edgar. And Edgar asked me what it would take to publish two books of poetry and begin a press.

I thought it wouldn't be that different from publishing a magazine. I was naive. I stressed that we had no experience in book publishing, though we did know something about printing costs and other aspects of production. So he asked me to write that up and send it to him for the museum's board meeting. Which I did.

I pretty much forgot about it. Five or six months went by. Lysa and I moved to Santa Cruz, and one day I opened the mailbox and there was a check from the museum and a note from Edgar saying go to it. And that started a relationship that continues to this day.

It's a model relationship in the field of literature. A model relationship in the sense of a private foundation investing money in a

276

literary enterprise. Ours lags behind every other discipline in funding. The funding base is extremely fragile. You don't find that in the other arts, not to this extent.

Anyway, that was the beginning of the press. We didn't know a thing, really, about what we were doing. The only thing we were confident of was that we could get authors, specifically poets. We knew, we felt, probably most of the poets in America, in one way or another. Given the tenor and history of *The Reaper*, there were purely perceived visiting camps—you know, those who were for us and those who were agin' us.

But we knew we wanted to have an established poet and a first-book poet. So we contacted Vern Rutsala and we asked if he had a new book and would he consider letting us publish it as the first book by this press. He agreed and we published what was his fifth book. Then we published a first book by an Alabama poet, Dennis Sampson, called *The Double Genesis*. He has since gone on to publish his second book with Milkweed Editions in Minneapolis. But that was the start.

We didn't know anything about distribution. We didn't really know how to job out printing or handle the management of the business. We really had no sense of what the business was. I suppose we were trying to run the press in its very beginning as we had run the magazine, which was our hands-on experience. The only other model we both had—you see, both Mark Jarman and I were students of George Hitchcock's at UC Santa Cruz in the early '70s. And we were there when he was publishing *Kayak Magazine* and Kayak Books and, in fact, we worked quite closely with him as helpers through the process of many a title and many a magazine. And what we knew about book publishing we essentially learned from George.

Story Line doesn't publish poetry exclusively.

We did in 1985 and 1986. In 1987 we began to diversify, very slowly, publishing our first book of fiction. No, we are no longer strictly a poetry press. We have a library of Irish authors. We're publishing work by Irish and American-Irish writers. We publish memoirs, we publish literary criticism.

A number of presses specialize, in whole or in part, in writers of a particular ethnic group. What's the attraction for that? Why are you attracted to Irish writers?

I suppose it begins with a love of country, for one thing, and a love of language. In the best of all worlds I'd be living there.

You've spent quite a bit of time there?

I've spent time there. My younger son was born in Galway while we were living in Connemara in 1992. The music and mystery of Yeats, the drama of Synge and O'Casey, the stories collected and published by Lady Gregory, the Blasket Island tales preserved by one of the purest storytellers who ever lived, Tomas O'Crohan, the songs passed on to us by Joe Heaney, the Clancy Brothers, Tommy Makem and the Furey Brothers and, later, the tough ballads and bittersweet lyrics of Patrick Kavanaugh have strongly influenced my ear and sensibility, if not my subject matter. My father's people came to this country from Ireland in 1798. When we lived there in '92 and helped a son a-borning, I felt as if we were completing a circle. Developing an Irish library, a series of Irish authors, completes another.

That's our interest. I can't speak for other editors or publishers. I imagine it's a similar sort of thing.

I asked David Brewster, who has Sasquatch Publishing in Seattle, "Where's your immortality?" He says he wants his organization to last three generations. So where's your immor—well, you're a writer, though, and that's separate. Or is it? Is it separate in your mind from publishing, or is it two aspects of the same thing, or—?

Well, I used to think that publishing was an extension of my life as a writer. This is something that a founder of an organization like this is bound to feel if he's also a writer. But I have since begun to imagine the press existing without me. Therefore, I no longer equate it so closely to my life as a writer. My career as a writer. That's probably a good thing. More and more I think of my writing as a safe haven, an escape, some place I can go where I can stop being Story Line, stop

278

worrying about Story Line. You know, you can't carry that over into your own work. It'll strangle you.

So I see a greater gulf now between the two sets of ambitions. And the challenge has become how to juggle those successfully, how to keep them both going, how not to cheat one for the other. That takes constant reappraisal. I'm asking myself that question almost every day: Am I spending too much time with this, or am I neglecting that?

As far as where's the immortality, I don't know. That doesn't trouble me as much now as it did when I was twenty, or even thirty. Because I tend to think now that there is no immortality. I think ninety-five percent of what we do here is bound to be forgotten as quickly as we pass. And that's probably well and good. There's nothing wrong with that. Few remember the gorgeous oak, seventy-five feet tall and four feet thick that stood in this field once but is gone now without a trace. Yet that was a magnificent thing.

I mean a question like that always makes me—I guess I suddenly flashed on the Woody Allen line, you know: The universe is expanding, so what's the point? You know, why do the homework? In two or three billion years there won't be any planet anyway. Everything we've made, even Shakespeare, will be blown to bits. So I don't know. In the short term, it would nice to feel that the press is contributing in some essential way to the development of the literary arts in this country. And, perhaps, abroad.

That depends on talent and luck, but also on money. Doesn't Story Line receive funding from the Lila Wallace-Readers Digest program?

No, SLP was rejected by Lila Wallace-*Readers Digest*. But in 1990 the Andrew W. Mellon Foundation did select Story Line, along with eight other presses, to participate in its seminal program to support the literary arts. Those nine presses, in December of 1990, each received fifty thousand dollars. This was phase one of the Mellon program. For most of us the money was targeted for organizational development. Updating systems. For some of us, putting in systems we never had. Developing a long-range business plan. Hiring consultants. That sort of thing.

The second phase, which was funded in October of last year, was for a number of different projects, depending on where each press was. We received thirty thousand dollars to support marketing initiatives, the most important of which was Joseph Bednarik's promotion to marketing director.

The third and final phase of the program is due to be implemented in October of 1994. What that will be is still taking shape, both in the minds of the Mellon supervisors and representatives of the presses. I believe that for Story Line probably something with a marketing emphasis will be called for again.

It's been a fascinating experience. The Mellon Foundation support has inspired a lot of growth, a lot of improvement internally, but it has also clearly defined for us some of the major problems in the field, and certainly some of our own problems here at home.

What are the major problems in the field?
Well, we have a field that basically is very poorly organized.

You're talking about literary—
Literary publishing. It's very poorly organized. If you take out CLMP [the Council of Literary Magazines and Presses], which is undercapitalized and spread too thin, there is no really potent national service organization that serves literary publishing in this country in the same way that music is supported, opera is supported, theater now is supported.

Much has been made of the theater model. Many people have made the argument that theater in this country before the mid-'50s was in the same boat that literature is in today. And the field of theater became galvanized. It focused, directed, and created national service organizations, took care of business, defined itself for funders as well as for an audience, and, therefore, theater is much healthier now than it was thirty-five years ago.

In some regions, yeah.
Yes, but it's very healthy regional theater. And I would say that

that model does have many valuable lessons for literature. One of the arguments we once made in a *Reaper* essay was that the history of great literature is the history of the great literature of a region. All great literature is founded in some region. Faulkner makes us know a part of the South so vividly that none of us might have ever experienced firsthand.

I like to say that Manhattan publishers are just too provincial for me.

In most cases they are. But then we're talking about commercial trade publishing, and the problems of that field are not our problems. As our board president pointed out recently, what we are really in the business of doing is providing luxury items. We are selling a kind of literature in the way that people sell chocolates. Or fur coats. We can put aside the PC element for a moment and think about luxury items. You know, hundred-and-fifty-thousand-dollar cars. That's the kind of thing we're doing really.

Maybe we are, but there are people for whom good reading is as necessary, as least psychically, as food.

Agreed. But the problem is, where do you find them and how many are there really? That is the problem we have to face as a field. When the average sale of a book of poetry by a poet with, say, five books out, who has won five or six awards—when the average annual sale of a book of poetry by a person like that is fifteen hundred copies in paperback, there's something wrong. With a country this size, with this population base, there's something wrong. The same poet in Ireland will sell ten thousand copies in a year. In a country the size of Rhode Island. Now something's wrong. There's something wrong with the way literature is perceived in this country by the general populace.

But we have to take some responsibility for this. There's also something wrong with the way we do business. Both as literary artists—as writers—and as publishers and editors. We're all doing something wrong. We're doing several things wrong. I certainly don't have all the answers but I do begin to see a need for coming up with them if presses like this, like your press, like so many of the presses we know and respect, are going to survive.

What are some of the things that are wrong?
Well, we do not really know how to market our products. We're terrible at marketing. We're neophytes. We're imbeciles about marketing. We generally do a terrible job of identifying our audiences and getting to our audiences.

Do you think it's possible to identify our audience on a national level?
It's very hard. It's damn hard.

I did market research for my own press in Seattle and some of its suburbs. I sampled zip code areas that represent certain demographic characteristics. What I came up with, and I feel very confident that it's right for my area, doesn't match at all with what—I think it was CLMP who did something similar on a national level. There was no match at all. For example, CLMP found that professionals typically read more than other demographic categories. In Seattle I found that people with two or three years of college or university—in other words, those who had some college but had not graduated, may, in fact, have dropped out of school—read more than any other category. Those who read least were the very poor and the professional class. Professionals read what they needed to in order to keep up with their profession, but they did not read much beyond that. I remember one woman telling me, "My husband's a doctor and we don't have time to read." My favorite was the young man who told me, very patronizingly, "My wife and I graduated from the University of Washington and we don't read." I love that one because it can be interpreted in different ways.
Right. I think you're onto something valuable. One of the things we have to do is exactly what you're suggesting. We have to pay attention first to our own regions. At the same time, if we publish books nationally, as we do—

282

You can't not publish books nationally. That's the nature of distribution. Distributors distribute books nationally.

Exactly. Exactly. But whether we're seeking national or regional audiences, I think we, as a field, have been very bad at developing those audiences. As writers, for example, we have to take more seriously the responsibility to sell our own books. And we must also take more seriously the relationship between the writer and the publisher. Traditionally, writers tend to look at publishers as—"Well, I did all my work. I wrote the book. Once you take it, it's your baby. Sell it. Make me famous. Make me money. Do these things for me."

That's a naive view. That doesn't work. Writers have to become partners with their publishers. In independent publishing, in literary publishing, we have to begin to think like that. The writer must be willing to make personal appearances, be willing to sell the book, and be willing to sell the press that published the book. Because if you don't make that connection you're not doing anything to further the development of that press, or to ensure that that press is going to be around in two or three years, perhaps to publish your next book. A lot of authors don't understand that.

Do you find that some authors are hostile toward you, their publisher? Not you personally, but you, the publisher.

Oh, sure. Sure. We've certainly encountered that problem before and, no doubt, will again. One has to guard against the assumption of an adversarial relationship between author and publisher. This is a rusty knife that can cut both ways. As an author, before I became a publisher, I had my own moments in which I viewed my publisher with suspicion and hostility. But that's a no-win attitude. Some writers fall into that trap because they don't understand the publishing world, the particulars of their own publisher's business and struggles. I'm just saying, from where I sit now, the perspective I have now, I think all of this gets in the way of the work that needs to be done.

It's sometimes uncomfortable. Still, it's a fact that publishers sometimes let their authors down. Authors also let their publishers down. In doing so, they also damage their books. We all have to get

283

better at working together to get the material out there. Make the book successful. Make the authors more recognizable. Make the presses more recognizable. The burden is on us to define our field. Of course, that definition must account for the tremendous diversity that exists in the field.

The field being literary publishing.

Literary publishing. The literary arts. Right. If it is true that the Lila Wallace-*Readers Digest* and Mellon programs are harbingers of things to come, or if they are test cases that may lead to a broader funding base, then our field had better be in a position to talk effectively to future funders.

I would say this: If Lila Wallace throws out several million dollars to thirty presses and magazines, and five years from now they're basically doing the same thing they were doing six years before and they're still floundering around, and if the Mellon nine screws up, it's unlikely that other major foundations are going to say "We've been funding dance for years, we've been funding theater for years, we fund the opera every year, we fund the ballet every year, why aren't we funding our local press [that has] a national reputation?"

That's not going to happen if we're not more successful in providing them with an attractive product. By the product, I don't mean the individual books. That's a given. By the product, I mean the presses. The publishers.

They're going to want to see some sort of quantification, aren't they? They're going to want to see sales figures or something on that order.

Eventually they might want to, yes. But what's ultimately more attractive to funders is a plan. A coherent plan. They want to see that all of your systems are in place, that you know how to do business. It's not unusual for them to want to be reasonably assured that they're not flushing their money down the toilet. These are all things we need to do, and literary publishing in this country has just not done that.

284

Can a publisher develop a realistic plan without being able to define its audience in any kind of demographic or geographic terms?

We can make some educated assumptions about our audience. In a country of two hundred and fifty million, for instance, should we not be able to say that our audience consists of at least ten percent of that population? That's a large audience.

Lewis Coser did a book called Books. *Did you read it?*

I haven't seen that, no.

He examines university presses, though he's not talking exclusively about them. He links books to education, to funding for libraries, but also to the quality of education and the training of librarians. That makes sense to me.

That does make sense, but mainly from a university-publishing point of view. I would argue that nonprofit presses must think of education as something much broader than education in the schools. In the colleges. Or just the libraries. You know, there's secondary education, there's grade school education. There are educational programs for communities. We have to recognize that we can't feel too close to educational institutions. We are different animals. A model program that we're trying to develop here is something called the "Rural Readers Project." SLP is located in a rural area. We thought it would be interesting to attempt to galvanize similar areas, setting up authors to appear in smaller communities at libraries, schools, bookstores and reading clubs. The program tries to reach communities where readers live but where books are not always available. A lot of times there are not even bookstores in these smaller towns.

I hadn't thought of it in these terms, but I'm coordinating a reading series once a quarter. The series lasts a month and takes place in a bookstore. The readers are Viet Nam veterans who have published, or who have works in progress and expect to publish. At the first meeting of each series, we have a couple of short readings just to give the audience a taste, but also I present all of the books then and I encourage the audience to read the book first so that later, at the more extensive readings, they'll be better educated as to what questions they might want to ask the authors. It works. Not everybody reads the work first, but many do.

That's a good example of the things we can do. That builds an audience not by hundreds or thousands, but by tens and twenties. I think that's what has to happen more and more. Too often we've ignored the individual reader. That's easy to do because all independent presses are understaffed and working hard to appeal to the largest possible audience. I recently received a letter from John O'Brien of Dalkey Archive, and he asked this question: "How can you stand back and assess when you're so busy *doing*?" That's a real problem.

What other problems do you see?

I can't stress enough the importance of coming up with a clearer message for potential funders in our field. We certainly can't count on government funding. The budget for the NEA literature program is an international embarrassment, and there's no indication even from the present administration that the situation will improve.

It wouldn't be stable anyway. It could last for a short time and be taken away. Ruth Gundle [publisher of The Eighth Mountain Press] was saying that's why she's not nonprofit. She doesn't want to learn to be dependent on an unstable source of income.

Right. Right. That's a good point. That cannot be argued with. Survivors among independent, nonprofit publishers must learn that. The lesson is often painful.

What Congress giveth, Congress can taketh away.

Yes, and it can hurt people and close down institutions. If independent literary publishers all die, then most of the best books of our time will remain in manuscript on authors' shelves, and many of the community programs that enrich our lives will disappear. Making sure that doesn't happen is worth fighting for.

John Ellison and Lesley Link
Broken Moon Press

"Having been a social worker has served me very well in being at Microsoft where there's incredible stress and incredible pressure, but they're not life and death issues. It's important stuff and it's important to meet deadlines and it's important to do the very best job we can do, both there and at Broken Moon, but we're not dealing with life and death issues. I have worked day to day with people who are facing life and death issues, and it really does put it all into perspective for me."

I interviewed John Ellison and Lesley Link, publishers of Broken Moon Press, on an evening of soft, cool rain in early May 1993 at their offices in the Wallingford district of Seattle. Broken Moon publishes trade paperback books and has recently started an audio book list.

Ellison is from Tacoma, Washington. He attended Tacoma Community College where he received an associate of arts degree in communications and took his BA in communications at Pacific Lutheran University in nearby Parkland. His mother, retired now, worked for many years as a reporter and writer on the base newspaper at McChord Air Force Base.

Link was born and raised in Denver, earned her BA at the University of Puget Sound in Tacoma and a master's degree at the University of Washington. For her undergraduate degree she majored in psychology with a math minor. Her master's is in social work. All of this is "absolutely appropriate to being a publisher," she laughs. Her father was a general contractor. "They did sewer and water and public utilities for a lot of the growth in Denver, for the suburbs, for a lot of the ski resorts in the mountains. He created things out of nothing. What I learned from watching my father build a business has been incredibly useful for helping us do this. There are times when it's just so worrisome and it's just so tiring, trying to do this, and then I think, oh, this is nothing compared to what my father did to support a family of six and a crew of twenty. And, you know, he started with nothing the same way we did. So that actually has been very helpful for me."

Both Link and Ellison are senior editors at Microsoft in Redmond, Washington.

I take it you're not able to make a living at publishing. Or, if you are, you choose not to.

John Ellison: I would say that we choose not to. The organization is strong but our focus was not to create a business that we could work in and then subsequently leave Microsoft. We were looking for compatibility rather than one world or another. It was compatibility of worlds rather than exclusivity for the worlds.

Lesley Link: John and I have always done multiple things. When we talk about what we did as children and when we talk about how we went to school—we both worked full time and went to school at the same time and did things like that. We both love being at Microsoft. It's very interesting work. It's very stimulating. And it really is wonderfully compatible with Broken Moon, so I feel like I have the best of both worlds, that I don't have to have just kind of an aesthetic business world or a technical world. I could have both of them. Which I feel like, intellectually, I need.

Are there conflicting demands on your time?

JE: There are times when Microsoft requires us to do more than an eight-hour day or a nine-hour day. And Microsoft always gets its time over Broken Moon. And that does create some conflicts. But they're mostly personal conflicts. What we found is that when I'm under heavy deadlines at Microsoft, Lesley generally is not. And when she's under, I'm not. And that pattern's been pretty consistent. There're a few times it hasn't been that way, but most of the time it's that way. And so one of us can more or less take the day-to-day demands of being a publisher off the other person for a short period of time. But there are conflicts and Microsoft always gets, obviously, top priority because it is our primary livelihood.

LL: That definitely says it. The conflict is really just when we're both under heavy deadline pressure. We just don't sleep much. I mean you cut out what you can cut out in a twenty-four-hour period, and usually the last thing that you can cut out is sleeping. So when we're under heavy deadline we just don't sleep much. But it's usually pretty balanced. And it's been really fortunate that we both work there. Because we both understand the demands that we're under at Microsoft. So it's not like one of us is demanding the other person to be full-time at the press or really focused at the press when it's really not possible. I think we understand the worlds that we move in and out of. And so it makes it actually pretty easy.

Do either of you write for publication?
JE: No.
LL: Mm mmm.

Why the smile?
LL: Because that's a question almost everybody asks us. When we first started the press it was like, "Oh, you're a writer. That's why you got into being a publisher." That's not why we started this.

I asked [an author-publisher] *the same question and he said, well, of course, he writes but that wasn't why he started the press, and then it turns out that two of the first five titles were his.*
LL: Yeah.
JE: Statistics are hard to get around. I used to write poetry in college and fancied myself a poet. But I didn't pursue it beyond my discovering publishing in college. I saw compatibility, perhaps, because we started out with a letterpress focus and I thought maybe that was a way to publish myself and/or the group of student friends that I hung out with. But nothing really came of that. And then as publishing—as we began doing what we're doing here—I had no notion of it. We toy with ideas of writing projects, but they're not in the same—it's not like poetry or fiction. It's not that kind of writing. It would be more

nonfiction writing.

LL: And we're editors. I mean, I think we think like editors and—

JE: Yeah. It's our training.

LL: Yeah. It's—

Camus was both.

LL: I do both. At Microsoft I do both. You know, there are times I write and there are times that I edit. Primarily I'm an editor, but I find that—certainly for the press, I feel my biggest contributions are as an editor and as a production person and as the bookkeeper and, you know, whatever else we do.

JE: I think editing can be practiced at a variety of levels. It can be a fairly straightforward process of just assembling something or a very creative, involved process, as you probably know. It can be as demanding, in a different way, but as demanding as writing, and as time consuming and tiring. We involve ourselves editorially with all of our books at Broken Moon and we do the same at Microsoft. And it's very emotional, very draining work. So, speaking for myself, I find that I can't imagine the two at this point in time—the demands of being a writer and trying to be a good editor—would be compatible. 'Cause there's not enough hours.

LL: You write great letters.

JE: I write tons and tons of letters, and I feel like that's somewhat creative, but at this point—and I would love to find the time to write more. I'd love to write essays, expand some of the ideas in letters into essays. But at this point, the last half hour of the day I like to sit on the sofa and look at the paper. And then pass out.

Do you have time to read things other than what you're involved with in publishing?

LL: I feel like I read twenty-four hours a day. I read in the bathtub, I read in the car when we drive to work—

JE: You have great tricks for reading.

LL: I read out loud to John when we're in the car. We commute

290

for what? About an hour and a half a day? In the morning it's about thirty minutes and at night, depending on what time we leave Microsoft, it can be as long as an hour to get home. So, yeah, we read in the car, I read at lunch sometimes—

JE: I even buy books on tape and listen to them as I fall asleep because at least I can get a little bit more, a little bit, you know, for fun.

LL: But we have books at home piled up next to the bed, you know, so I feel like we read all the time.

JE: In publishing, as you know, there's not a lot of room to read as one of our readers might, where maybe there's time to really map out a program of—I don't want to say leisure reading, but of more casual reading, and drift however you want through books. There's always an agenda of reading we have to do, kind of a core for our jobs, and then there's peripheral reading that we're each doing, of course, for what projects we're on.

LL: And when I'm really tired I read children's books. So I still read, but I find—like we read *The Little House on the Prairie* series last winter and it was wonderful because it was, you know, it's good writing, it's really pleasant reading, but, you know, I need to read all the time but it was about all I could handle at the time.

You mentioned having a letterpress focus, but that was in the context, I thought, of you and some friends when you were in college. Did I understand that wrong?

JE: No, that's right. When I started the press, I started it when I was in my last year at TCC [Tacoma Community College] and first year at PLU. At Pacific Lutheran I studied communications and took the publishing course there, and studied from Tree Swenson [then of Copper Canyon Press]. And then I audited the class a second time a year later. And I bought my first letterpress from PLU while I was there. It was one that was rusting and out back in the yard where they kept the trucks and the maintenance equipment. And I attempted to set it up for a couple of years, up to about 1983, '84. At that point it became too difficult to do. We simply couldn't get the space, we couldn't get, you know, a place that had a roof on it that wouldn't leak. So then at that point I stored it and I thought, Okay, the first thing I've got to do is get a job and resituate myself. And it went into storage for about three years, till I got to Microsoft, and then I met Lesley. And of course I had acquired all of this stuff for publishing anyway, a lot of reference materials, and I always rented two-bedroom apartments because one was full of the stuff that traveled with me.

LL: You had all of your lead type and your type drawers, ink—

JE: All of my type, all of the type drawers, ink, paper.... It was massive. I had this massive amount of stuff. And then when Lesley and I first started Broken Moon we actually acquired a couple more presses. We acquired one that belonged to Scott Walker [then of Graywolf Press] and then we got one from Bleitz Funeral Home and restored them.

What did Bleitz use it for?

LL: Funeral announcements.

JE: Yeah. And our first press site was at 619 Western in this old funky art building.

LL: It's a warehouse.

JE: It's about six stories. It's been condemned several times, this really funky art building full of studios. And we had this shotgun studio, this big, cavernous room, and we set up our presses there. And that was really the last attempt to do what we—

LL: They were wonderful to play with and we really liked it, but we were not good at it. I mean we were just playing with it. And when we decided to do books rather than broadsides or chapbooks, we realized that the only way we were ever going to be able to do books was to do trade books.

You had been doing broadsides and chapbooks?

LL: Just playing with it. We never published anything. We just played with it really.

JE: We had set some type and.... Yeah, the press behind you now is the only remnant we kept. That belonged to Adrian Wilson and Joyce Wilson. Adrian Wilson was a great letterpress mentor at Press At

292

Tuscany Alley in San Francisco. People like Clifford Burke learned how to print from Adrian. Adrian Wilson was the master printer and his wife Joyce did children's books, and she did them on that machine. That was the last press that we acquired. And then when we realized, about the time *Passport* [by Sam Hamill] was well under way, that we weren't going to do any letterpress, we gave away the equipment.

LL: And we saved this and we saved some of the type. That's all.

JE: Actually, we took one to Canada, up to Barbarian Press.

LL: They do beautiful letterpress.

JE: They're really a fine.... They're a vibrant kind of self-sustaining little printing family. It's Crispin Elsted and his wife Jan. They have two children and they have this wonderful, beautiful, letterpress studio. It's like a letterpress printer's dream studio.

LL: And so we gave them the press from PLU that you restored.

JE: We gave them the PLU press. We took it up and...barely made it.

LL: On the trailer the press was in, the hitch broke on the freeway and we almost lost the press. And it's—

JE: And it's pouring down rain. Pouring.

LL: Horrible, horrible rain.

JE: Like the sky opened. And the studio was being built and there was no driveway and it was down a slope to the studio.

LL: Solid mud.

JE: Solid mud. No slab had been poured for a driveway and we took the press off and it was a sixteen-by-twenty-two-inch C and P [Chandler and Price], which meant it's the biggest—you could do newspapers on it. And immediately it hit the mud and just went—'cause it weighed almost a ton.

LL: A huge thing.

JE: It was this huge press. And we were well understaffed to retrieve it from the mud. So we worked for probably four or five hours, shimmying it, lifting it, sliding it, moving it, inching it, cajoling it, arguing with it, all in this torrential downpour. And we're soaked. We're just getting soaked by the hour. Several times it almost fell over in the mud, but we did finally wiggle it in there. It was just ridiculous.

LL: But it's very happy there.

JE: It's happy there.

LL: We've seen it since then.

JE: They fitted it for a motor and it's printing like it's happy.

LL: It's printing, yeah.

JE: It's happy.

LL: It's very happy there.

JE: Took it about, I don't know, five years to go from its rusty beginnings to being a functional machine.

LL: Yeah. And it's really loved there. Crispin and Jan both love printing and they're very, very good at it and it's the kind of machine that needs to really be tended.

JE: So anyway, that was sort of the close. At that point we got rid of our letterpress studio and gave two of the presses to a couple of our interns.

LL: And decided to make trade books.

When was it that you decided to make trade books?

JE: It actually happened when *Passport* came out.

LL: The spring of '89. When John and I first met each other at Microsoft he talked about being a publisher and, you know, we talked a lot about books. And one of the things that we both discovered as we grew to be friends was that we both loved what we did at Microsoft but that it wasn't enough. That we wanted to do something lasting. You know, technology changes so rapidly that it's really disposable. And so we would work really hard on the release of a product and then the minute that it was done, you know, you start on the next release of the same product. And we just found that to be tiring and not satisfying at a really core level. So we started talking about books and one day we just kind of looked at each other and said, you know, we ought to make books. And you actually gave me half the press, a half of what he had acquired as Broken Moon, and said, "Join me as copublisher and we'll make books." And I said, "Sure. Why not?"

Was this something you had thought about before?

LL: I hadn't thought about being a publisher so much as I had thought about just doing more work in...something with books. I had toyed with the idea of doing children's books. In my background in social work and teaching I had worked with children and families. So I had written workbooks and I had done a videotape training series for parents. I'd done a variety of things.

You were thinking in terms of being an author or an editor.

LL: Being an editor and pulling things together, or perhaps of writing a children's book. I've never thought about writing an adult book, but of perhaps writing a children's book. I just wanted to do something that I could put my hand on and say, "This is something that's going to last." And when John gave me half the press it just kind of ignited all of my creativity and his creativity in terms of what was possible, what we could do together. And we set out to make one outrageous book, which we did.

I don't ask this question of everybody, but you seem to have set it up here: Where lies your immortality? You're talking about something lasting. Are you speaking in spiritual terms, or psychic terms, as well as material terms?

LL: Yes to all of the above, I think.

JE: If you mean immortality in the sense of doing something with my name on it, if that were the question, I would say no. That's not the—it doesn't lie in Broken Moon. Broken Moon, to me, is a community of people doing something that they all have a shared value in. It happens that the end product of that is a book, and that we keep making books. But I actually think the goal of the press is to build a community of friends, a community of like spirits, like-minded people doing good work together. Broken Moon isn't just Lesley and me. It's a group of people, some of whom have been working in books all their lives. We started this because we wanted to build a community of friends, and as I've done it more and more, I've found that's the greater value of it to me. That's the lasting thing.

LL: Well, the lasting thing for me, too, is the—I very much feel that we're a vehicle for something, that we're a vehicle to what I call "get the word out." To publish people who ordinarily would not get to be published. First poets, first novelists. Multicultural writers. People who New York is not going to publish, but people who have very valuable things to say and a major contribution to make. I feel sometimes like we're a vehicle for the work of these people to get out. And the immortality is that the word gets out, people read the work, they are moved by it, it affects their lives.

I want to be able to affect culture. That's part of why I got into social work; I wanted to do something to make the world a better place. That sounds real sappy, but there is that motivation. And being able to do it through books, which are physical objects, which may be beautifully done so that it feeds my creative and aesthetic side, and, most important, to be the vehicle to get the word out, to touch people—I don't know if you call it immortality but it has an effect on culture and, you know, it makes a contribution.

What John was saying about us doing it as a community—to me, that's been this just wonderful discovery. It's very clear that we can't do this alone. This is community work. From the very beginning, when John shared the press with me, it was immediately "Oh. Well, if we're going to design books, then we need to talk to so-and-so who's a designer. And, oh, we need to talk to so-and-so who knows how to set type. And to so-and-so who's an artist." And it just immediately began to expand inside of us.

JE: I very much like that aspect of publishing. It's what was communicated to me when I got involved in this, that it was people who weren't in it for money. It was sort of acknowledged that you wouldn't do it for money, because there isn't a lot of it. And you wouldn't do it if you didn't want to work hard, because the work was hard. And you wouldn't do it if you wanted stability, because it's not a real stable kind of thing to do. When you look at the kind of people who are drawn to this work, they're generally very committed and energetic. Like is drawn to like, so you find that community just sort of naturally evolves. All of the great small presses that I read about had that element of community that sort of gives you a place in literature in a time when it's hard to find a place in literature.

Have either of you lived overseas?
JE: No.

LL: I lived in Europe one school year when I was in college. I went to school in Rome. I studied art history and sociology and so on. It was not an exchange program but we had classes with the faculty from Loyola University in Rome. We lived in Rome and also toured around the continent. That was my sophomore year in college.

Do you think that experience—living abroad—changed the way you look at the world?

LL: I don't know. I've had other experiences of being in Europe and I have friends in Europe that I've gone and stayed with on extended vacations. That has changed me more than living in Europe because I lived with a bunch of American college students who, many of them, were incredibly close-minded and complained a lot about not being able to get good American food and, you know, all the stuff that people talk about with Americans in Europe. And it was a very cliquish group of folks. We didn't go out and meet people in the community. When I have gone over and stayed—I worked in Germany and in England where I've had friends—and you actually get to meet the natives, you know, people who live there. I've learned more that way, in terms of how people think about culture and about America.

As far as its affecting your life: Do you think your life has been affected by living abroad?

LL: I think my life's been affected by everything I do. Actually, what's really had a very major effect on my life was being a social worker and working with disturbed kids and their families, and working with families where there had been generations of sexual abuse and generations of physical abuse.

Where were you working?

LL: I worked in Luther Child Center in Everett for a long time, and I worked at a private agency in Tacoma. It was actually a United Way agency in Tacoma. And I worked at Children's Hospital for a little while. You know, when you're working with children who are at risk of being beaten, and you're working with families where there's been generations of incest, and you're working with families where people are marginally getting by, the concerns of a publisher, you know, the concerns about what color a book cover is going to be, I mean it kind of puts it all in perspective for me in terms of what are the life and death issues. Having been a social worker has served me very well in being at Microsoft where there's incredible stress and incredible pressure, but they're not life and death issues. It's important stuff and it's important to meet deadlines and it's important to do the very best job we can do, both there and at Broken Moon, but we're not dealing with life and death issues. I have worked day to day with people who are facing life and death issues, and it really does put it all into perspective for me.

What kind of work did you do after you graduated from college?
LL: I worked in a residential treatment center with boys who were eight to fourteen who were so dysfunctional that they couldn't be at home. It was a twenty-four-hour-a-day residential center.

Dysfunctional in what way?
LL: Everything from children who banged their heads through walls to children who were assaultive to children who, you know, children who bit people and threw chairs at people's heads and...these are behaviorally disturbed slash emotionally disturbed kids. Yeah. I worked with pretty disturbed kids and their families for almost twelve years. And then I just woke up one morning and knew I couldn't do it anymore. All the joy of doing it was gone. When I did it full-focus, I really loved it. But it got to the point where it just was too hard emotionally. And I looked around at what I knew how to do, because I knew I needed to change careers. This was the year I was thirty. And I looked around at what I needed to do, and what I could do. And what kept coming up was writing and editing.

I had done a lot of manuscript preparation. When I'd worked at the U. I'd done some journal-writing, professional journal-writing, and editing of textbooks and indexing of textbooks for several professors, and I really liked that work a lot. And I'd done grant-writing, that kind of thing. And there was an ad in the newspaper for a proofreading position at Microsoft and I answered the ad and they hired me. And that was really my first step into publishing as a living.

Tell me again about the goal, or the purpose, of your press. Now it's not nonprofit; you're for-profit.

LL: Yes.

JE: Right. Our purpose was to publish works of an international nature that would promote human understanding. I think that's still very true. When we wrote it in 1987 we didn't know really where that would take us, but as I look at our list today I think that that is very much true. We're publishing Native American, Chicano, gay and lesbian authors....

LL: Korean, Japanese.

JE: Korean, Japanese. In translation. From the very beginning we did translations. But we didn't group them in a serious format as we do today. When we did them before it was just individual books. Now we're focusing a series on looking at the world through translation. This year alone we're adding four books to that series. It's a very important part of what we do, that international focus. But also international in the sense of multicultural—we're doing more cultures. Native and Chicano work particularly.

LL: I think we really have been true to our statement of purpose. One of the things we've been talking about recently is wanting to be sure that we're very focused on our statement of purpose, or of adding a layer to our statement of purpose. I think that's because we've been in business now for a while and we've gone through this real growth spurt and we're just kind of wanting to really focus once again. But that has been the underlying ethic of the press all along, to do work that will—you know, we talked about doing work that's provocative, work that causes people to think. We want to do work that will promote increased understanding among different peoples.

You did your statement of purpose in 1987?
JE: Yeah. The first book then came out in 1989. It took that time to organize the system. As you know, it's not an easy system to work out. But that was the time we used to learn for ourselves how we would make books, the process we would use.

How many books a year are you doing now?
JE: We're doing thirteen books this year, and two audiotapes. That's probably not the norm. I think it's probably going to shake out to about twelve. Ten to twelve. We sort of had this growth spurt when we went from four titles in our first year—
LL: We did four, then seven—
JE: And then we just kind of exploded. I can't even remember what we did last year in terms of title count.
LL: We have thirty-four books in print.

Do you keep them all in print?
JE: Oh yes. So far. Well, it's such a young organization, yeah. Our goal is to keep everything in print. We're looking for books that have that quality. We're also building a backlist. So we're trying to find a viable, sustaining backlist as much as a frontlist. And then we've added audio material that we're doing as a sideline. That'll grow to probably four tapes a year. And those won't necessarily be books we're doing. We're negotiating rights on books that are published by other houses.
LL: The books, I think, fit the statement of purpose, but they also reflect John's and my eclectic tastes. Poetry and fiction and nonfiction and multicultural voices—it's the kind of material we buy to read.

When you say poetry and fiction—this is something I wanted to get at when you were defining works of an international nature. You didn't mention the type of thing you were doing. You mentioned,

300

rather, who does it. The category of person who does it. Now you're talking about poetry and fiction. Is it important to you who writes the book? Is the book the thing? Or is the author?

JE: Both. If you mean by "who does it," you mean categorically, like if it's a Chicano versus a Native American person. Or do you mean just as a meaningful person to work with, whoever they are?

I mean categorically because you mentioned categories earlier.

JE: Oh, I was just trying to classify what I meant by international. It's like saying "multicultural" today. What does that mean to anybody? It's a buzz word so you try to—when I think of multiple cultures I think of everything from Native American to the gay and lesbian communities, because they are culturally different and have an integrity that's separate. But when we select our list we absolutely do not have a percentage assignment that says we have to do twenty percent Chicano, twenty percent Native American, twenty percent gay/lesbian. We always look at what we have on the table, what looks really good.

LL: We always start with the manuscript. We always start with the book itself.

JE: Yeah. In that context, that's the answer to your question. The book is the most important. The book has to be well written and be making an important statement. That's where our major focus lies.

LL: And then we talk with the writer and find out whether the writer is somebody we can work with. Because we have a real belief that certain writers belong with certain presses. It's kind of like the personality styles fit. Because making books at our level is such an intensive process and it takes, you know, a year to do and then a year or more to promote. We want people with us as part of the community, people we trust, people whose integrity we can admire, people that we feel we can work with compatibly. We send out author questionnaires and we ask authors—for example, if an author refers someone to us, we require that the writer of the manuscript also be in contact with us. We would never accept a book on referral without having some contact with the writer him- or herself, to know whether this is somebody we want to work with.

301

What types of question are on the author questionnaires?

JE: Well, the questionnaire goes out at the contract stage. By that time we've kind of worked our way up to the stage where we want to put paperwork out. And the questionnaire asks for a lot of very general information about the author, about the way they see themselves, the way they see their work, basically what contribution they think they're making with this book, who cares about this book, who do they see as the primary audience, how do they see themselves promoting this book. It's kind of a broad range of textbook questions, not so much to elicit the perfect answers, but to get some insight into areas that we never seem to touch on conversationally, like "Who is your audience?" That's a very revealing question in how it's answered. That questionnaire gives us a lot of tools to use when we're designing the book, promoting it, writing catalogue copy, that kind of stuff.

Something Lesley said that I think is really important—I really do believe that not all authors can work with the same house, that there is a like energy. One of the most important parts of our community is the authors—the community that we have built—because many of them become our good friends. We correspond with them and we visit them when we're in their cities. You know, they're good people. We admire them so. They're very much an important part of that group.

LL: One of the things John and I talk about in terms of how we live is that we don't really make a distinction between Microsoft, Broken Moon or anything else. It's all us. I mean it's what I do from the time I get up in the morning till I go to bed at night. And I feel like we lead very integrated lives in that way, that what we're creating is a life for ourselves. We're building a life which involves this wide group of people and a variety of tasks that we do every day. We work a lot and it seems fine. We both really like it. I don't think of my life in kind of little compartments. I think of it as this is what I do. I make books. Sometimes I make computer manuals and sometimes I make poetry books. But I get to work with words, I get to work with production issues, from the time I wake up in the morning till I go to sleep at night.

JE: For me, I feel like I've undone the American dream which is that everybody pretty much hates what they do by day and only feels like they come alive Friday night and Saturday night and Sunday.

That's not the American dream. That's the American way.

JE: That's not the American dream, that's the American way. Thank you. The American dream is to do nothing and to get lots of money for it. You're right. I actually like what I do. It is really exciting. I correspond with an outrageous group of people. I get up in the morning and I'm actually glad to be getting up in the morning. I'm glad I have this whole list of things to do. I keep legal pads and I write down all of my things for the day and I toodle off and come here for a couple of hours and then go to Microsoft to work and then we come back here in the evening and—

LL: And I love Saturdays because then I can work here all day.

JE: Or even sometimes we go out to Microsoft. In fact, Les will be working this weekend out there. But it's great, you know. We just decide where we're going to go and we go.

Margarita Donnelly
Calyx, Inc.

"...only crazy people do this kind of thing."

On a warm, gray day in early February 1993, Margarita Donnelly and I got together at the Stauffer Madison Hotel in downtown Seattle. The Women's Caucus for the Arts was holding workshops in the hotel that week and Calyx, as well as other women's presses, had tables set up in the Washington Room to display and sell their books. I met Margarita there a little after nine in the morning and we went looking for a quiet place to conduct the interview. We finally decided on the registration table, which was now vacant, on the floor below. There were two problems with this: because we were the only people seated at the table, Caucus attendees looking for sundry events assumed we knew where they were being held; also, around the corner was a piano which eventually drew a pianist.

Donnelly is one of the founders of Calyx, along with Meredith Jenkins, Beth McLean and Barbara Baldwin. Currently, Donnelly is the managing editor of both Calyx Books and Calyx the Journal of Art and Literature. *The two together come under Calyx, Inc., a nonprofit corporation.*

I'm what they call a *caraqueña*. And I'm named after the island of Margarita. Margarita Island off the coast of Venezuela. That's where all the beautiful pearls come from. So I was my mother's little Venezuelan pearl. See, "margarita" is another word for pearl. Well, I think it is. Maybe I'm wrong.

My parents were really musicians, is what they were. But my mother was.... See, my family is really weird. My parents were first cousins, number one. It's the same family. And both my parents were musicians, but my father had to make a living. And so he worked for oil companies in South America.

Mainly he had a band at night. I mean that was his big thing, was his music. He always had a band. And he was always doing music. But he ended up becoming a safety expert. And he was in charge of safety, which was horrendous. I mean they had awful, awful, ghastly accidents. I mean it was like a battle. One time he lost thirty-five fire fighters in one fire. He was the head of safety for Mobil. He had to train the truck drivers that drove the oil rigs. He was an interesting person. Anyway, he worked for Mobil and he never got very high up in the ranks because he didn't have a degree, and his first love was music and he always had a band.

And then my mother was a musician. She was a concert pianist and a conductor and a mezzo-soprano. And she had studied at Juilliard and she had a bunch of degrees and she had been the first woman to conduct a choir at Saint Patrick's Cathedral in the choir loft. They had to write a papal dispensation so that her choir could sing for Cardinal— this cardinal who became Pope Pius the Twelfth. And she was quite an incredible individual who then left all of that and went off to South America and raised four kids in the boonies away from all her— When we were in Caracas she was very, very happy because they have the greatest symphony in the world. And she conducted "The Messiah" over Christmas, and she started the Red Cross in Venezuela. They wouldn't have a Red Cross if it hadn't been for my mother. But when we moved to the interior she got really isolated and it was really hard on her. My father and all of us kids loved it. 'Cause we lived this wild frontier life. Hunting and fishing and piranhas in the rivers.

I was stationed in Panama in the '60s before I went to Viet Nam. And some of the American soldiers who were getting out of the service or retiring in Panama—one or two of the oil companies were hiring them to patrol their pipelines against the—
Ooh, that's interesting. Against who?

Guerrillas.
Colombian guerrillas?

No. There was a guy in Venezuela at that time—Douglas Bravo? Do you remember him? He was a Castroite. He was later killed by the Venezuelans. If I remember correctly, they—the guerrillas—were kidnapping executives, holding them for ransom—

That's right! They were holding them for ransom. See, my father retired in '62. So at that time he came back. He just couldn't take it anymore. He said it was really getting bad. You know, 'cause he loved Venezuela. My family was really different. We weren't like the ugly Americans. You know, my mother sent us to Venezuelan schools. I didn't speak English till I was six. We loved the music and we loved the culture and we worked with Venezuelans and we didn't do that ugly American stuff.

So your father mentioned that there were executives being killed, or—?

No, he just said it was getting rough because the anti-Americanism had developed at such a high level that even he who got along with all the Venezuelans was beginning to feel it, and it was hard to take. He took an early retirement 'cause he didn't want to go to Saudi Arabia. That was what was happening, was Saudi Arabia.

Okay. Let me get some more biographical data and then we'll get into the publishing stuff. Okay?

Okay.

Okay. Let's see. Date of birth?

Nineteen forty-two. Why do you need my date of birth?

Because when I first—

That's an invasion of privacy.

You don't have to do this. [Both laugh.] *When I first started doing this I wanted to do some demographics to see if there was anything common to publishers. And actually there is. And age is one*

of the common things for US publishers.
That's interesting.

There's a difference between the US and Canada in this respect.
Oh, that's interesting.

Place of birth?
Caracas, Venezuela.

Married, or ever been?
Not really. Not officially. I was found null and void. I actually, you know, thought I was married once. But the judge found us null and void when we split up.

You have children though, or a child.
Yeah, I have a grown daughter. Yeah. She's twenty-six. I raised her alone, pretty much.

And you live now in....
I live in Corvallis. That's where Calyx is based.

What were you doing, or what were your parents doing in Venezuela?
My father went down there in '28, during the Depression, and he ended up just staying in South America. Well, he started before the Depression. My mother went down with him. It was the beginning of the Depression in '28. Times were rough in '28. It just crashed in '29. He was there for thirty-five years. And he worked for different oil companies.

There were four children?
Yeah, there's four of us.

Where are you in that order?
I'm the youngest. I'm the baby.

Yeah, I could tell that. I knew—

Hah! You didn't know, man! Come on! You "could tell that."

Um. Did you go to college?

Yeah. I have a whole bunch of degrees.

Ah. What are some of them? You show me yours, I'll show you mine. [They laugh again.]

Well, I got a bachelor's in anthropology from...I ended up...I went to eight different universities before I got my bachelor's, so it's from San Francisco State University. And then I did part of a master's at U of O [the University of Oregon] and never finished it, and walked away during the Viet Nam era. And then I got into a special program that was in Portland but accredited at OSU [Oregon State University]. So I actually have a master's from OSU but I never attended the university.

Is that in anthropology also?

No, it's a Master of Education and Counseling. I was a counselor.

Hmm. I got a Ph.D. in anthropology.

You did? You're kidding!

No.

That's what I wanted! I wanted a Ph.D. in anthro. That was my great love, was anthro. And they wouldn't let me into the graduate program 'cause the guy I moved to Oregon with, Russ, he was in the Ph.D. program and he was a big politico—he was an antiwar-movement leader—and he got into a lot of hot water while we were at U of O. And he got on the blacklist and they gave him a terminal master's, something they had never done in that university, to get him out of the Ph.D. program. And then while he was still in the Ph.D. program, I tried to get into graduate school and they—that was before feminism—and they refused to let me in because we were together. Oh, we had split up by then, but they thought we were really married and they said they wouldn't let a divorced woman in the same department with her ex. And so I didn't get into the Ph.D. program. So then I had to roust about 'cause I had this foreign fellowship and I was going to lose it.

You had a fellowship for—?
I had the fellowship to do research in Mexico, but I was going to lose the fellowship if I wasn't a classified graduate, 'cause I was an unclassified graduate. So I thought of this CSPA—Community Service and Public Administration—and they let me into their program. And that's the master's I never finished, because I hated the program. And so I did all this marketing stuff in Mexico, when my daughter was three. So we were down in Mexico—

Who were you working for, doing marketing?
It was this fellowship I had. I was doing market research. There was a special market research program, man, at the marketing program of U of O, funded by the Ford Foundation. So I went to Mexico and did all this research in Monterey. When my daughter was three. That was pretty wild.

How long were you down there?
I was down there part of a year. It wasn't a real long time but it was really something, being a single parent doing this research with a three-year-old. I love Mexico, so that wasn't the problem. It was just trying to do it all and be a mom and everything. It was pretty amazing.

I wanted to do my field research in Mexico originally. Chiapas was where I was going to go.
I went to Chiapas. I did research down there.

Oh, did you?
Yeah. As an undergraduate. Yeah.

But I wound up going to Samoa instead.

309

Oh, really? You went to Samoa? You did your research in Samoa?

Yeah.

Wow. I had a friend who went to Samoa. Claire. I don't think she really did research there. She did a little bit, but she was out there for a little while and she loved it. Is that your thesis?

Yeah. My dissertation.

So why don't you work as an anthropologist? There are not jobs, right? Or did you give up on it?

Well, I never applied for a job. I became convinced—I'm still convinced—but I became convinced late in my graduate career that because I had been in Viet Nam there was no way I was ever going to get a job in anthropology. I'm still convinced of that.

That's because you're a Viet Nam vet?

Yeah.

You think that anthropologists are all that bad? Is it a liberal bent, or what?

I don't know about a liberal bent. I'm the liberal. I think there's a real.... Among those my age and older, not twenty years older, but those, say, ten or fifteen years older than I am, who control the departments— Put it this way: these are the people who made their careers through their anti-war politics. And they are invested in their careers. They still establish their credentials by saying what they were doing in 1968.

Really?

Yeah.

That's interesting.

In fact, there were a number of veterans who entered the

program at the U of W [the University of Washington]. *Only two of us stayed with it. Right after the other guy graduated he apologized to me because he had lied about what he had actually done in Viet Nam. He had acted as kind of a clown while at the U of Dub. It turned out he had been in combat, but he had lied about it, saying he had been sort of a rear-echelon malcontent. And he apologized to me for letting me take the brunt of the faculty's wrath by myself. So it wasn't just my perception.*

Well, you know, that's interesting, Jerry, because I was a graduate student during the Viet Nam era. I mean I started the graduate program at San Francisco State, and then Russ convinced me to move with him to the U of O and I had to stay home and be a wifey-poo while he did graduate work in anthropology, and I did nothing but take care of the baby. And then we split up after that year because it didn't work too well for me. [Laughs.]

But I functioned as a T.A. [teaching assistant] for about a year after Angie was born, 'cause this wasn't Russell's baby, it was somebody else's baby; I never married her dad. And when I was grading papers I learned the politics about what the hell was going on. It really outraged me. I can remember one guy deserved a D or an F on one of his papers and I gave him that grade, 'cause I was the T.A. doing the grading in these classes. And this professor switched all the grades on me. So I went up to him afterwards and he said to me, "Do you want him to be drafted?" So I really learned a lot about the politics....

I just loved anthro, and this whole thing about—see, my war was this pregnancy—me getting pregnant when I wasn't married, and what that did to my life and my daughter's future life, which I had no idea how it would affect her. And coming to grips with all that, and coming to grips with the politics of what went on. Like in the anthro department, they were so supportive of me through my pregnancy, and then I found out they had all expected me to give away the baby.

Why would they expect that?

It was 1966. You know? When I came back after the—I almost died, having her. I mean everything that could have possibly gone wrong went wrong. I was doing natural childbirth, luckily, and that saved her. And we both survived. Both of us almost died. So it was this really difficult thing that I hadn't expected. And I got very, very ill, and I had to drop out of school for awhile. And that was a big decision. She was born in February and I was in school when she was born. I was taking classes. And they—I stayed home with the baby for six months. It was my wonderful aunt and uncle who let me live with them and not have to worry about anything. And then, once she was six months old, I went back to graduate school.

But it was like when I called up to drop out of classes, and Jim Hirabayashi who is now a big-time anthropologist—he ran the Ethnic Studies program; he left anthro and ran Ethnic Studies at San Francisco State—and I called up and he goes—he was shocked that I was keeping the baby, and I said, "What did you think I was doing?"

They all thought I was giving the baby away, so when I kept the baby there was this freak-out in the department. Then what was funny was I came back six months later and they were so sweet. They saved me plum jobs. They waited for me to come back and they saved me plum jobs. I came back nursing the baby, 'cause I nursed her till she was sixteen months. The funniest thing was—these are all anthropologists, right?—I come to graduate classes with the baby and I nurse her. I was giving a presentation, Angie was about three months old, very quiet, she was the best baby, and I had everything covered and I noticed that all these men—Schuyler turned every color but beet red while he was giving—and I'm thinking, "These are anthropologists? And they can't take a normal, red-blooded North American woman nursing a baby in a classroom?"

This was someone on faculty?

No, this was one of the graduate students. And I showed up at one of my research meetings—this is a really funny story—I show up for this research meeting, I've been down forty-five miles away visiting my dad and family, and I had a meeting on this research project I was working on at the school, and I rushed to get there and Angie got hungry on the way up, she was about six months old, and she was screaming all the way in the car. And I kept going "I can't stop, I can't stop, I'll feed you as soon as we get there." And I was a mess. I walked in, I had to change her diaper and she was starving and I had to nurse her. So I'm talking to this guy, he's one of the head guys, he's an anthropologist, he's a big professor, he's gone off to study the Hoochiegoochie, so, you know, he's supposed to be used to all this. I say, "You don't mind if I handle this baby while we talk?" So I proceed to start nursing and changing her diaper at the same time, and having a serious discussion with him.

He about died. It was the most hilarious thing, with my revelation that the problem with all these anthropologists was that they could take it if they were out in the South Seas or Mexico or West Africa, but they couldn't take it on their home turf. And I was breaking every more. Not only had I had this child out of wedlock and kept it....

And they were real supportive of me. I mean like the head of the department gave me the use of his office and I did all my research, I worked in his office late at night with the baby and I'd come to school the next day and he'd go, "Oh, you're turning my office into a nursery." There'd be all these baby things I'd thrown away in his trash. He was real nice about it. But they had such a hard time accepting it. It was really bizarre. And they were the ones that pushed me into this marriage I never should have had. You know, they found this guy in the department, and I went trotting off with him, you know, [though] we were never really legally married.

You know, it's such a brutal system, getting the doctorate. Getting through the program. I had a harder time than most. Other graduate students were amazed at some of the shit I had to do to get through, because they did not have to do that.

Is it because you were a vet?

I believe so. It wasn't only the political fact that I was a vet, but also they assumed that anybody who was a vet was stupid.

So it was a class thing as well.

Yeah. As a matter of fact, one guy on faculty admitted that he had a bias against me because, he said, I looked like a truck driver. He couldn't figure out what I was doing in graduate school. The same guy told me that when he wrote his dissertation he hadn't looked at any of his research notes. He wasn't interested in whether anything was true or not; what was true was what was in his mind. But, yeah, it really was a class thing.

Well, you know, the whole thing over Viet Nam, nobody's come to grips with it. I was in Contra territory, in Nicaragua. We went out and stayed with Witnesses for Peace on this place that had just been decimated by the Contras. And it was really moving, but the Contras started activating while we were there and they were just a couple of kilometers away and nobody knew if they were going to attack us or not. And the Sandinistas—there were only about twelve of them, and we were supposed to be pacifists, right? And I was the leader of this group. I was supposed to be this big-time pacifist and I've known all my life— 'cause my father taught me how to shoot when I was eight, and I'm a pretty good shot. And so the people who live on the cooperative asked just before we went to bed, they said, "Look, does anybody here know how to do...you know. We've got plenty of guns, we just don't have enough people." And I looked at the guy and I said, "Well, I used to be a crack shot but I don't know how to shoot an AK47." And he said, "I can show you." And I remember everybody was furious at me, but I just thought, "Shit, man, we get attacked, I'm not gonna sit here and let them massacre these people. I'm not gonna let that happen."

And I'll never forget the terror of that night. I thought I was pretty courageous, and I slept outside all night, and it was a really creepy night 'cause we did not know what was going on. The Sandinistas disappeared. What they did was they went way out and got out about ten kilometers, or five kilometers, to try to keep any battle far enough away. And then during the night a storm hit and these pigs started fighting with dogs over this carcass.

A human carcass?

No, they had killed a cow that day. And I thought it was the Sandinistas getting massacred and I thought, "I'm the biggest chicken in the world 'cause I'm lying here and I'm not helping." And then I realized it was just the pigs and the dogs fighting over the stupid cow. But I got really scared that night, and I'll never forget that 'cause it was a taste in my teeth I had never experienced, and I learned what a chicken I can be. And I really had to come to—I never slept all night. I was the only one outside. Everybody else went inside and I couldn't stand to be inside. I didn't want a grenade thrown at me. 'Cause that's the way they hit these houses. They had blown up three young kids with a grenade and their blood was all over the place. I just thought, "If they're gonna come, I'm gonna be outside when they come." But I'll never forget that terror. It was an amazing revelation, what a chicken I could be. And, as it was, they never came. They disappeared into the night. Everything turned out okay. And it was just pigs and dogs fighting over a carcass. I don't think anybody knows.

To feel the fear doesn't mean you're a chicken.
It's just reality. Right. Well, that's all I'm saying. That was an extent of fear I had never felt in my job or in anything else. You know? It was like this real palpable thing in the mouth. That was the thing that really got me, was what my mouth did for me that night.

Back to publishing. You earn your living from Calyx now, right?
Right. Four years ago I quit my regular job.

What were you doing then?
I was an editor down at U of O. At the ERIC clearing house. That's an acronym for Educational Resources Information Center, the biggest database in the world. It was fun. I didn't know I'd like it, and I loved it. And it was a regular state job with benefits and everything. It was really great. Anyway I took the ERIC job and I quit it so I could be full-time at Calyx. I took a huge cut.

Before you got involved in publishing—and you got involved with Calyx in '76, right?
But I also started Women's Press down in Eugene in '69. During

the war. When I became a feminist. And it's still going strong. We set it up as a collective and when those of us who started it all petered out, it was successful and it kept going.

Do you still have any connection with it?
Yeah. It was really neat. They came and looked me up. They want to do books now. Yeah. I still am connected and they know where I am now. God, they must be twenty-three now. Twenty-four! They're gonna be twenty-four! 'Cause Angelique was a baby. That's right! She used to doodle things and we'd put 'em in the paper. So, yeah, they're twenty-four. God, they're almost a quarter century. Yeah, they found me when they hit ten. Back then we didn't put our last names on anything 'cause that was patriarchal. And so people have trouble figuring out who the first names are. We didn't keep good archives, either.

You said they want to do a book?
They're gonna start doing some books. So they came and talked to me, the women who are editing it now, about doing books. It's really nice to see them growing.

In '69 what else were you doing besides Women's Press?
Well, I was supposedly a graduate student.

At the U of O.
Yeah. And I was a real activist. I was very involved. See, my involvement in the anti-war movement got me into feminism. And then, you know, the sexism in the anti-war movement was so horrendous. It was just awful. All these SDSers [Students for a Democratic Society]. And I got involved and started the women's movement in Oregon, basically. Helped found the first NOW [National Organization for Women], the Women's Political Caucus, Women's Press, and then some of the radical offshoots. I was doing all sorts of things. I was going to Mexico a lot, too. Getting away from it all. I was poverty stricken, trying to survive. Angie's dad never supported her, so I

316

was always really struggling.

What is she doing now?
She's an engineer for AT&T. [Both laugh.] She's a yuppie. After all our years of poverty.... She's getting married in July. She's a wonderful young woman.

When you got involved with publishing, you were an activist. You were a radical activist. And publishing was an expression of that?
Well, with Women's Press it was, yes. That was how I got into Women's Press. And then later, when we started Calyx—that was quite a bit later. That was a good eight years later. It was '76, so.... By then I had mellowed and then what we were about was that women weren't getting published at the rate they should be, and that the kind of work that we like to see, we hadn't seen.

What do you mean by "kind of work"?
Just themes. In terms of things women would write about. And we wanted to see more of that, and women's arts. So it had a political base too.

The same idea, the same purpose or mission, continues with Calyx today?
Yeah, except it's literary. Women's Press wasn't literary. It was just a radical newspaper.

Okay, Calyx publishes a semiannual journal—
We used to be triannual but we switched three years ago to twice a year.

And you publish books aside from that. Now the journal itself is book-length. It's perfect-bound, right?
Mm hmm. It's a question: Is it a journal or a book? 'Cause it sells like books. It does pretty well. We started the journal in '76. And we only did journals until '86 and then in '86 we started doing

317

books as well.

The books are always fiction?
No. We've got a lot of poetry.

Are the books always imaginative literature?
Yeah. Well, we have one that's essays on China. And we've got one coming up that's the experience of a woman who went to Nepal. That's real moving. It's her first book. It's not like fiction or anything. It's sort of like a self-exploration.

You get grants.
We get grant support.

Could you do what you're doing if you didn't get grants?
No. We never had any money. Calyx is a real miracle; we started it with no money. Absolutely nothing. Nobody that started Calyx had any money. There were four of us and none of us had any money. We all worked. We started with a small grant from the Women's Resource Fund in Portland. They gave us eight hundred dollars. We got the first issue out that way. So we had funding from the beginning. And we've really relied on that over the years. I think it would be very hard to start a press like we did without money. I mean ours is really different. When you look at all the feminist presses, there's been this real interesting, different sort of thing. We're one of the few that's collectivized, where decisions are not made on the basis of one or two people reading everything and deciding. We have an open collective that does the decision-making of what we publish, and it's a very different attitude.

Okay, lets talk a little bit about that. Do you accept manuscripts over the transom?
Mm hmm.

So a manuscript comes in. How is it decided whether or not to accept it?

318

Well, there's about eight of us reading these things, and two people have to read everything at least once. Two of the eight. And two people read it and say yea or nay, hold or not, on the first reading level. One person can hold. It takes two people to return it, to say no, we don't want to consider it any further. Then, when it gets held, everybody reads the "whole." I mean, we do it through consensus.

How long does that take?

We're speeding it up in the journal, but it is slow. It can take six months. We're trying to keep it at three to four for final decisions. And we're averaging about four right now. But it can take six.

That's for the journal. What about the books?

Yeah, that's for the journal. For the books it takes us a whole year. We just lost two manuscripts this year 'cause we were too slow. We finally accepted 'em and found out the authors had given 'em to somebody else and hadn't told us. So we're trying to speed the books up. We hope it will never be longer than a year. And that we can get through the first readings in the first four months of the year. 'Cause we're only open for two months.

In which people can submit, you mean?

And that we'll select the wholes during that period and then be able to make the decisions in the fall. We're open January first to March first, I think, or fifteenth. Something like that. I can't remember if it's the first or the fifteenth. And we don't want to see a complete manuscript on first reads. We just want to see a sample.

Okay. Let's see. You initially started with a grant. There were four of you. Could you tell me how Calyx evolved. You're getting big grants now. And there're eight of you.

Well, no. There's twenty-five people involved in Calyx, but there's eight on the journal collective and then there's a separate book collective and then we have a board and we have interns and volunteers and it's a pretty large organization now. We have staff now, something we never had for ten years.

How many staff do you have?

We have four and we're hiring a fifth this month. We've got an editorial coordinator half-time, we have an office manager twenty-five hours a week that does all the bookkeeping, we have an administrative assistant who is three-quarter time, and we're going to have a promo person three-quarter time. And I'm three-quarter time.

How do you decide when you need to hire—?

Money. We've always needed more people but, unless we get grants—like we just got two grants that are allowing us—the administrative assistant came as a result of Lila Wallace [a Lila Wallace-*Readers Digest* grant], and the promo position we're hiring for is a result of a Lannan [Foundation] grant.

When you hire someone you apportion work to that person, and you know in advance what that work is going to be.

Well, what happened for us is we got into the NEA Advancement Program back in '89, and that was really good for us because we had to write a plan. So we have a long-range plan for the organization now that we update every year. And the plan has been remarkable because it made us think out everything. And then part of what we did for Lila Wallace was we wrote a marketing plan specifically for the journal. All these consultants came in as a result of these two grants and helped us with administrative and organizational issues. And that helped us clarify for ourselves what it was that we needed. So now we have a really good plan for the—it's like a small business plan.

Your long-range plan: it includes long-range goals?

Mm hmm. Our plan was interesting because when we got into Advancement we realized how overextended we were. The consultants came in and took one look at us and showed us how overextended we were. So we consolidated. So instead of trying to get bigger, we're getting smaller in terms of what we're doing. So our long-range plan

320

basically is to maintain the quality of what we do and to not try to do too many books a year, but to do them well. Our plan will include growth in a couple of years, but right now it's maintaining what we're doing, beginning to spend more money and time on the infrastructure of the organization, getting the staffing, getting enough money to have decent equipment and decent working conditions, treating the authors as well as we can and beginning to improve author payments. That kind of thing.

So our goals, okay? our statement of purpose—where's that catalogue I gave you? It's right there in the beginning. This is our mission statement. We exist [quoting from the 1992 Calyx catalogue] "to nurture women's creativity through the publication and wide promotion of women's finest artistic and literary work."

One of the things that we do is we not only publish books but we keep them in print. Which is really rare. We're committed to keeping a book in print as long as we can possibly sustain it economically. That's why we have to keep looking for support. When we went through Advancement we realized that on the journals we lose about twenty-five cents on each sale, and on the books it's somewhere around thirty-five cents on each book. That was when we realized that there's no way we're ever going to break even on the books we produce, 'cause we put so much into them. So we have to find more grant support and do more fund raising to make up the difference. Okay, what else?

Actually, that's it.
That's it?

Yeah. Is there something else you want to say?
Well, you know, I've been thinking about it a lot. Having gone through Advancement, having gone through all this stuff, reaching fifty, having had some problems with a couple authors over the years, it finally hit me that only crazy people do this kind of thing. Being in Advancement and being around a lot of the other publishers—

I don't know what you mean by "being in Advancement."

321

NEA Advancement is a special program that twenty-five presses have been through so far. I think there're four more just got in. And it's a unique process where they provide arts consultants to help an organization grow. It's a long process. And going through the Lila Wallace program was really interesting 'cause we had all these meetings together, everybody that was in it this last year. And I just feel that only people who really love literature, people who really care about the written word, are the people who get involved. And there has to be a certain element of craziness, dysfunctionality, and only people with a certain sort of craziness in their personality take this on. They're somewhat self-sacrificing and they're sort of Pollyannas to do it, to begin with.

I also have some concerns about presses that aren't collectivized. I mean, I think we have to have room for everything, but it's really interesting that there are very few collectivized presses, you know, with multicultural boards making the decisions about what gets published. And the fact that there're so few presses available by people of color, and I'm very concerned about that. And I think it's much harder in the '90s to do what we did in the '70s, to start from scratch with no money.

And we're really rare in the sense that there was no wealthy person involved in starting Calyx. I know there have been people who thought there was some wealth behind Calyx and who have no comprehension that there wasn't, that there was just a lot of ingenuity, a lot of guts, a lot of care, a tremendous amount of commitment. It's not just me, it's a whole big range of people that keep Calyx alive. The authors, and the artists who are real generous with their work, and then all the volunteers. At any given time there are twenty-five to thirty-five volunteers helping to keep that organization going.

That's in addition to your twenty-five—those are the people involved with Calyx? You said there were twenty-five.

There're twenty-five officially involved, in all our collectives. And then there's more beyond that. People who read for us and all of that. And, you know, we have interns all the time. It's just this huge amount of work that's done for free that keeps this organization going.

322

It's a tremendous amount of time and energy that it takes to do these publications. All the editing, all the proofreading, all the copy editing. 'Cause we work with developing writers. We take unfinished work and help a writer finish it. If we like it. And that's really rare. That's not happening a whole lot anymore. We also do book reviews in the journal. It's a tremendous amount of work.

I interviewed Ed Varney up in Vancouver, British Columbia. He was one of the founders of Intermedia. They were an artists' collective. Both literary art and visual. Lots of different things. And he said the advantage of a collective is free labor. He said without it, you can't be a collective.

But there's more than just that. The other advantage to the collective is that we get such different decision-making things—I mean if it was just me doing Calyx, we'd have a hell of a lot of sheep poems.

A hell of a lot of what?

Sheep poems. I mean it would just be my peculiar little bent, you know? But because it's this broader group—I mean there're these wonderful, magical things that happen.

Oh, I don't think Ed would deny that. But he would say that you have to have free labor.

Oh, yeah! You have to have free labor. There's no other way. How could any of this have been done? Any of these small presses, they started off that way. It was free labor for years and years and years and it still is. I mean those of us who aren't paid something as an income— it isn't a real income—we're subsidizing the organization. 'Cause we do so much for free. I want to be sure that that's clear that it's—

The other thing that's really hit me over the years is the naiveté of many writers who have never been involved with publishing and who do not understand the tremendous amount of work that's behind it. And that is something that we're striving to educate authors about when they sign a contract so that they understand better what it is we do for them, and what they do for us, and how they could work with us to help promote their work.

I try to do that too. I want to work with the author. But I've been wondering lately whether it wouldn't be easier for me if I just didn't keep the author as well informed as I do. I think sometimes that the more the author knows about what I do, the more he or she tries to manipulate me into doing something I really don't want to do.

Huh. That's interesting. I could see that that would be a problem. I think it's easier for us because it's not just one person. We have this larger group that they have to cope with. But the relationship between author and publisher is set up for conflict. It's an adversarial relationship. No matter how much you love them and how much you do for them, it's still adversarial, and that's unfortunate. You know, our idea was not to be that way, and we hope not to be that way, but it's a problem because authors, even the most educated, surprise me with their naiveté. The people I would think would be the most sophisticated, the most understanding of what it is we do for them, have a total misunderstanding of what's involved. I mean we work very hard not to have that. But unfortunately the world isn't perfect, and even amongst feminists the reality is that there is this separation between publisher and writer. I hope we can bridge it, but it's not an easy thing to do. Although writers have been incredibly generous with us. And we have pretty good relationships with most of our authors.

So that's all. I just wanted to put that in.

Barbara Wilson
Seal Press

"... it wasn't anything very serious in the beginning.We certainly didn't say, 'We want to found a large feminist press that will support eight people.'"

Barbara Wilson's house was once a boathouse. It is long and narrow and it sits on the eastern lip of Lake Union in Seattle. On a gray, damp day at the end of October 1992 Wilson and I sat at a table by a window overlooking the lake. Inside, where we were, it was warm and dry. Wilson is one of the founders of Seal Press and the author of several mysteries published by Seal and other feminist presses. She is also a translator and has translated a number of works from Norwegian. She is able to earn her living now from her own writing and from her work at Seal.

I haven't had another job since 1984. Up until then I definitely had to work elsewhere.

Before you got involved with publishing, what kind of work were you doing?
Oh, I did a lot of things, like most people, I suppose. I traveled quite a lot, so I worked at a variety of jobs for short amounts of time. For instance, I lived in Norway for about a year, and I worked on a boat, and I worked in a laundry, and I worked taking care of kids, and I worked in a store. And then I worked in Spain, teaching English. And in the States I did all kinds of things, from factory work to nurse's aide. Really, anything. Usually I wanted to work only part time because of my writing.
And then in '74, when I moved to Seattle, I was told that

325

working in hospitals would be a good idea for me because they paid pretty well and you got benefits and it was flexible work. So I trained a little bit as a ward clerk, or unit secretary, and went to work at Swedish and worked there for about a year, and then Providence for about a year, and then I worked for Group Health for eight years. And I worked on pediatrics from four to eight every day for a number of years. And then the last few years I just worked every other weekend. It was good, you know. I didn't need very much money and it fit in well with my schedule and I could get medical benefits.

Did you have confidence then that you would eventually be able to give up wage work for writing?

Well, I wanted to, but I didn't know when that would happen. Fortunately, I'd never had a lot of money when I was growing up, and I didn't have a lot of requirements. I didn't have a car. I always rented. And, you know, I just didn't miss what I didn't have. I mean now I would find it very hard to go back to a more poverty-stricken way of living.

But everybody seemed to be living the same way back then, especially in the '70's. So it seemed fine. And when my income began to go up, it just seemed like it was appropriate and at the right time. Now I've never been able to make it totally as a writer, but then I've never worked totally as a writer, either.

It seems to me that I once saw, in a private library, a chapbook that Seal Press did. I think it may have been stories by you, but I'm not certain. The binding was either staple or string. Does that sound right?

Yeah, we did a children's book early on. It was just a children's story that I did that was bound that way.

When did Seal Press start up?
Nineteen seventy-six.

And it was you and—
Yeah. Rachel da Silva. She lived in Seattle and was working as a printer and was interested in printing. And had just bought a letter-

326

press, an old Tramline Harris clamshell, and a lot of type. She had installed it in her mother's garage. And she had been printing some broadsides and she'd been doing some sort of paid work for people. She was calling [her operation] Seal Press.

I ran into her at a party and was taking a printing class myself at Seattle Central [Community College] and just asked her if I could come over and take a look at it. So I did and got really interested and printed something that first day, which was very thrilling, and said, "Oh, we should print a book."

We didn't know exactly what to print though. I had been in a literary journal with this woman, Melinda Mueller. I liked her poetry a lot. So we found her name in the phone book and called her up and asked her if she wanted a book, and she said, "Sure." [Both laugh.] So we got her to put in forty dollars and Rachel and I each put in forty dollars, and that's what we started with.

I mean, we had no money. I think we might have bought the paper, but I think the money actually went towards printing the cover, because we printed the cover offset, and we just—we might have gotten the paper donated or we might have bought it. Rachel was able to get a lot of free things.

So we did that that summer, and she moved up to Bellingham to go to Western [Western Washington State University] in the College of Visual Arts and Sciences, or whatever it was called, to do design and things. And so for the first couple of years we mostly just printed very small things, like at Christmas when she came back, or in the summer.

And eventually we started to do some offset. She was working at a printer's up in Bellingham and I would— We had a friend who worked in some insurance agency and she would typeset everything for free and then I would paste it up on a borrowed light table. Then I would take the Greyhound up to Bellingham and we would start on Friday night and I'd make the plates and she'd print and we'd just stay up the entire weekend. And that's how we'd do it.

But early on— Now, it wasn't anything very serious in the beginning. We certainly didn't say, "We want to found a large feminist press that will support eight people." We were just futzing around and—

Now, I put my address in the book because I thought we should have an address, you know. And Melinda's friends who were poets began to send us their poetry, which we hadn't quite thought about. Then we realized we actually had to sell the book, so I would go around to the bookstores and tell them about it and they would say, "Well, great, I'll take three copies. On consignment." [Laughs.] So it wasn't like we were making a lot of money. But it was kind of fun.

I wasn't that aware, in the beginning, of the feminist press movement. I was somewhat aware of the small press sort of movement. I think I'd read a book called—it was the first Bill Henderson, *Publish It Yourself*, or something like that. [i.e., *The Publish It Yourself Handbook*, edited by Bill Henderson, published by Pushcart Press.] And he talked about Anais Nin and Virginia Woolf and—

You know, in the '70's there was a whole sort of movement getting going. And so Rachel and I got to know Scott Walker, from Graywolf, a little bit. We went up there and visited. And Tree Swenson at Copper Canyon. And then there were a few other people around.

I think Scott published the Tess Gallagher book right around that time. Either '76 or '77. Because I remember he was just finishing *Instructions to the Double* one day when we went up. I think that was his first book and he was printing it by hand on a letterpress in the back of his house, and we just went there and looked at it and he gave us a copy. [Laughs.]

And we knew some other people around Seattle who were printing and publishing. I don't think any of them are still doing it. But at that time there were quite a number, and a lot of readings, and some small bookstores that don't exist now that sold that kind of thing. So we were part of that. We weren't part of any kind of national movement. We didn't know anything about distribution. In fact, there were no distributors, really, that would take our kind of thing on, or that were really big, like there are now. Like Bookpeople and Inland. So we didn't really meet anyone outside of Seattle for a pretty long time. And also we were too poor to travel.

But we did start getting in contact with some of the other feminist publishers. Feminist publishing had started around '69. There

328

were a handful of printers and publishers and we got to meet a lot of them in 1981 at the Women in Print conference in Washington, D.C. We both decided to go to that and there were probably about two hundred and fifty women there, some of whom were publishers and writers and editors. And from that we became much more hooked into that network.

How did you know other feminist presses existed? Or how did they know you existed? I'm curious about the mechanics of it.

Oh, just from seeing their books reviewed and seeing them for sale in the bookstores. And they were somewhat aware of us. We were still doing poetry and kind of futzing around for a long time. Well, we had started doing some fiction, too. So I don't know exactly how many books we published before '81. 'Eighty-two was sort of a big transition year for us. But I think that we probably had done something like fifteen, maybe twenty. And a lot of those were chapbooks.

We applied to the National Endowment in '78 for the first time, and got probably five hundred dollars. And then sort of got more ambitious and applied for more money and sort of accepted projects contingent on getting some Endowment money. And so that's really where we got some capital investment.

I mean neither of us— We worked for free, so we didn't pay ourselves. We didn't pay rent because it was all still in my apartment. And we had very low expenses because usually we printed everything ourselves. Or had some kind of donated this or that. And we were lucky in some ways because Rachel was a printer. We didn't have to raise thousands of dollars to get things printed. She could do a lot of really wonderful work with very little money.

So that's how we kind of went along for a number of years, and there were just the two of us. We did have a lot of volunteers who helped us, and we had to collate everything by hand, and we had to sew the chapbooks and so on.

Where did you warehouse it all?
Well, a lot of it was in the closet in my apartment. And then,

increasingly, in friends' basements and closets. In '81 we got our first office. In Pioneer Square. And Rachel, by that time, had moved back to Seattle and was working with a printing collective, Workshop Printers. And so we, Seal, subleased a small office from them. They started out closer to the Kingdome and then in '81 they moved to the Kaplan Building at 310 Washington Street in Pioneer Square, and Seal built itself a little front office and paid some minimal rent. So that was an important step, in getting it out of my house, for one thing—

Did you have enough revenue coming in from sales to—?
Oh, yeah. We had, you know—

Of course, you weren't paying printing bills.
Yeah. We had a few thousand dollars coming in by then. We were having to use it for various things but we certainly had enough money by then to get a phone, and we got some second-hand furniture. And so then we would both work down there.

But it was a little bit— It was stressful in lots of ways because there were only two of us doing the work. We worked well together but Rachel's primary loyalty was to Workshop Printers, and so she didn't really have that much time for Seal. So it was necessary for us at that point to get some others in on it, because Rachel had always had a somewhat more ambivalent attitude towards it than I did. I mean she always considered it a hobby, and she was interested in a lot of other things in life. And I was very, very focused on publishing. And the more I learned about it, the more interested I got and wanted Seal to take on more and become more than it was.

And a manuscript came to us that year, in '81, that was a handbook for battered women. And we decided to take it on even though it needed a lot of work, and I worked on that really hard with the author. And at that point we began to get volunteers, including a woman named Faith Conlon who had moved here from New York. She had worked for Anchor Doubleday and then she got a job here in Seattle, working for Madrona. She was very interested in Seal and helped us in a lot of ways as a volunteer.

330

I interviewed Dan Levant [Madrona's publisher].

Right. Yeah. So she worked for him until his business went bust and then in '82 she came to work for Seal full time and has been there ever since. I only ever worked part time but my heart was very much in it and I was, in fact, obsessed with it for a number of years. [Laughs.]

I was going to ask you about that. You started out in the mid-'seventies, saying "Let's publish a book." And then by '81 you're very focused on publishing. What happened between '76 and '81?

Yeah. I think I had learned to see the world. I had learned to see that publishing was actually a powerful thing, and I had learned to see the world somewhat in terms of these units of information, which are books. And to see how things, ideas, whether they are practical or creative, could be turned into books.

I think it's just kind of a bug, you know? I've seen it happen to a lot of people, where they just think, "I'm gonna publish this one thing," and the next thing they know, they're embarked on the whole business. It's probably because of the risk factor. You get hooked on that. You think, "I think I could really sell a lot of these," and then you do, and then you get feedback from people that they love it and they want more. And people send you manuscripts and you think, "This one's really good. Let's go with this."

But I also think that I must have gotten a glimmer of being able to help support myself as a writer through publishing and working in a publishing company where I could get paid something, and also do that kind of work as my meaningful political work in life. And that came true as the money began to come in more.

We started paying ourselves around '79, '80. And I think that that's what I was partly working towards, too. Certainly with the publication of *Getting Free* and selling three thousand in just a few weeks we saw that we were launched in a whole new way.

You must have had distribution by that time, to sell three thousand in a few weeks.

331

Yeah. I can't quite remember when Inland started. But Bookpeople definitely was there and we were dealing with them. And we had done a lot of advance mailings to all the shelters and crisis clinics, and then the book got reviewed in the *New York Times* and so the phone was ringing all the time and we ended up selling a hundred thousand of that book over the years. So that really was the backbone of Seal and supported it and enabled us to go on.

Ginny NiCarthy is the author?

Yeah. So from that point on it was just sort of steady growth, and a lot more commitment. Faith and I were very committed and she was working there full time, so that was great. And we just got more ambitious.

Rachel was involved up until 1985. And there was another woman, Sally Brunsman, who was involved for about a year and who is now the managing editor at Microsoft. She had just moved out to Seattle and worked with us. But then she left to go to work with Microsoft, and then Rachel decided to leave, and Faith and I just sort of restructured it. We had been sort of very loosely organized and we just formalized it more in terms of ownership so that Faith, Rachel and I owned it, but Faith and I managed it. And then Rachel stepped back.

And we just kept publishing, starting with about four books a year, and then working our way up to eight and ten. And we were still funded by the NEA for literary and translation projects, and we did get a bunch of money from the Norwegian government to do an anthology of Norwegian women's literature. We got twelve thousand dollars with which we bought our Xerox machine and another typewriter. [Laughs.] In those days we didn't have computers, we did all of our paste-up ourselves. Workshop printed most of our stuff. So we went along like that for a while.

And then we had another big expansion around '86, '87, because Metro was putting in the bus tunnel downtown and the start of it was going to be right near where our building was. And so they were paying everybody to leave the building and to sort of help get them relocated. So they did that and we moved briefly up to Capital Hill, into a not really satisfactory space. But at that time we kind of joined forces with Cathy Hillenbrand [publisher of Real Comet Press]—you interviewed her? Yeah—so we were both sharing the space on Capital Hill.

And then the people on the other end of the bus tunnel—it was Brocklind's Tuxedo—decided they needed a space and Metro thought they should move them into our building and that we should leave. So we got into a big fight about that with Metro, and Cathy, being a lawyer, wasn't going to stand for this.

But then she and I—Cathy and I—happened to find this spot when we were driving by. We were looking all over for something because the place where we were on Capital Hill didn't even have a warehouse. We were still using our warehouse down in Pioneer Square. But we were driving by the Northwest Industrial Building down where Denny and Western and Elliott all sort of moosh together and we saw this space for rent, and we went and looked at it and it was great. It was huge, had a warehouse with a loading dock, there were a lot of artists and warehouses around there. And so we took it and it was gigantic. And Cathy had a friend who was an interior designer who agreed to do it, and Metro was going to pay for this whole thing.

In the end they didn't pay for all of it, but they paid like about thirty thousand dollars. And we got walls! We got carpets! We got phones! You know, we never had separate offices before, Faith and I. We'd all worked in one big room. We had one typewriter and one telephone. And all of a sudden we had more stuff.

It wasn't all through Metro. I mean it was just sort of this idea that we needed to expand. I think by that time we had three employees. We had a graphic arts designer, part-time, and we had a book packer, part-time, and a full-time kind of office person. And then we had some accounting help. And from there we just started growing again. I mean we got sort of used to having employees. Some of the books that we were doing were selling well enough to, you know, support this operation. That probably was the end of '86.

We joined Consortium [a major book distributor] along with Cathy. And even though Consortium wasn't perfect, that was a big step for us, to have sales reps for the first time. And also to start going to New

York twice a year to meet with the sales reps and to meet on a much more regular basis with reviewers and editors, and just getting to know the publishing world more.

We had started going to the ABA [American Booksellers Association conference] in '85. And we got pulled into the commercial publishing world more and more. Faith had been part of it a little bit when she was with Anchor, but being in Seattle, you know, and not having very much money, we hadn't participated. But increasingly, you know, we were a part of that. So that's kind of continued.

At this point there are nine people working there, five of them full-time. And I think we're going to be hiring one more. But we've added on slowly. Some of the people have been there ever since we started our expansion, like our art director. And then another young woman who came in as an intern and then was a book packer and then did the production and is now an editor. They've both been there about four years.

How do you select a manuscript? You must get thousands each year.

Yeah. Well, we've kind of gone through different criteria. One of the things about having gotten so big—I mean at this point our gross sales are about seven hundred thousand dollars, and the overhead is much greater with the rent and the salaries, and now we pay benefits to people. So we can't do some of the things we used to do. So we have sort of pulled back.

We stopped being able to get money for the translations from the National Endowment several years ago. This is kind of a little aside. So we actually formed a nonprofit called Women in Translation, which I run, and has gotten some money from the Endowment. It rents part of the Seal space and has done five books in the last couple of years. It used to be a series of Seal Press and now it's a separate nonprofit.

It's done some great books, but because translations are so expensive—because you have to pay the translator—and they don't really sell that well, they can only be published with a subsidy. So Seal

334

couldn't afford to do them anymore. And we didn't want to turn into a nonprofit like Scott Walker did because, for one thing, we still wanted to own the press, and for another, we were very interested in the nonfiction books that we did on social issues, and that's not the kind of thing you get funding for from the NEA. So we had to pull back from the literary stuff, as much as we liked it.

At this point we're probably only doing one to two novels a year, and we're rarely publishing short stories. We published a couple of books of poetry in the last couple of years, but it's not usual. So, increasingly, we've turned to nonfiction books where we know what the market is and where we can sell ten thousand and charge sixteen ninety-five so we can make more money. Because we need more money if the whole operation is going to survive.

So when we get manuscripts in, or queries, we kind of look at them to see, you know, is it a subject we're interested in? Is it an author who seems like she's got it together and could do the book, especially without an advance? And is it something that would fit into our areas of publishing? I mean people are always writing to us and saying, "This book should fit Seal perfectly." But that's not always our idea. So we don't take very many manuscripts over the transome. We develop a lot of projects ourselves, and we also work with authors who have published with us before who are on their second or third books.

We've got a lot of books on abuse, domestic violence, incest and so on. And health—we did a Black women's health book that sold many thousands. And now we've been doing more books on women and sports, and women and the outdoors, which is sort of a new departure. But there's a definite need for it and those books are selling really well. Yeah. So we look at everything.

We haven't done a lot of political stuff. You know, essays and so on. We did do a book on bisexuality this spring that has a lot of theory in it and sort of gender studies and so on. But generally we don't do a lot of theory. We did a book on prostitution a few years ago to enter the international prostitutes-rights movement, and we also copublished a book called *Good Girls, Bad Girls* with a Canadian press, Women's Press, in Toronto. Some of those books have sold okay. *Closer to*

Home, the bisexuality one, will probably do well, but most of them haven't for us. So we've kind of stuck to self-help and change.

Is that satisfying for you? For you personally?

Yeah. Because I know that all those books we published on abuse have been incredibly helpful to women and that the shelters use them and have used them and, you know, we've gotten letters about women who have managed to get out of really dangerous situations through reading them and relying on them. So I always did feel really good about them.

I actually feel good about everything we publish. I feel somewhat bemused sometimes by how badly some of the fiction does. For instance, the translations were always my big thing. And, you know, it's sort of sad that in a country of two hundred and forty million you can't sell two thousand copies of a book even though it gets brilliant reviews and everyone who reads it loves it.

I've been interviewing Canadian publishers too, and a number of those I've interviewed are about the size of my press, the size of Black Heron. They'll print, say, two thousand copies of a book where I will print one thousand copies of a similar book and not be able to sell those thousand copies. Yet they'll sell all two thousand copies of theirs just in Canada, which has the population of California.

Yeah. They do support their authors and presses up there. And here there's just so much competition. There're so many books published. It's hard to break in and make people believe that they have to read it, that it would be important to them.

Well, I don't know that people take fiction seriously in the United States. Where is your best market for fiction?

The lesbian novels that we publish sell the best, and we sell most of them through the feminist bookstores. But we also publish some books that have been picked up by women's studies and also English departments and African American departments. We published a book from Zimbabwe called *Nervous Conditions* which is a brilliant novel, I

336

think. And we've sold thousands of that. It gets ordered like a thousand copies a quarter, two thousand copies, because some department will decide that this is going to be a text. So that's really done well for us. And then a book that was translated from Norwegian that's a satire, a role-reversal satire, we continue to sell year after year to all kinds of classes as well. So if they get into course adoptions, then we can sell a book forever. And, actually, a few of the mysteries have gone that route too. Otherwise they sell best in feminist bookstores, and then, to a lesser extent, anywhere that we can sell them.

Do you know which part of the country is your best market?

I can't really say. I mean I would assume that the East, Midwest and West Coast are the best and the South is probably the worst. And the Southwest. But it depends. We put in these little blow-in cards every once in a while, and people can write to us asking for a catalog and there's room for remarks and things like that. And they're really great to read because people will tell you, you know, "Hated this book," or "I love this book," and they will write down where they're from. And these cards come from all over the place. That's sort of amazing, you know, especially people in small towns that you never heard of.

Right. They take books seriously in those places. It's a connection to the world.

They do. And people get stuff out of the libraries too. Our books turn up all over the place in libraries. You know, librarians are very good people, and they tend to be pretty progressive. So they're on our mailing list and they recommend them and they get into all kinds of funny places.

Are you able to separate your work as a writer from your work as a publisher? Or do you see a separation?

It's been a struggle at times. I'm no longer obsessed with the press. I used to be. And I think it's partly just that I'm older, but also it's actually easier than it used to be. I mean, we had to work so hard for so many years, and we just killed ourselves. Like generally I put in a ten-, twelve-hour day between my writing and the press and the translation and all this other stuff, and I just can't do that anymore.

But fortunately that coincided with a general rise in our fortunes. I did book packing up until '84 when we hired somebody. I was still doing production until about '87, and then somebody else took it on. I did publicity until '88, and then we hired somebody. So gradually my role became part-time managerial and editorial.

I thought that editing was something I would never want to give up, but in fact I've also backed away from that because I feel that there's a limited amount of energy I can give writers when I'm working on my own stuff too. But, once again, we've been training this young woman, Holly Morris, to take on projects and she's proved to be a really able editor. So between the three of us, Faith, Holly and me, we kind of get everything edited. And I want Seal to succeed. I really believe in it. But it's not so tied in with my, um—I guess I just think it will succeed without my being there every single second. I've learned to delegate and I've learned to step away. Some of that is because I travel a lot, but also because I need that separation.

I guess I've been lucky in a way because I always worked with other people. I never worked alone on Seal. I worked alone on Women in Translation sometimes, and that is a little bit too much at times. But I was really lucky in that I worked with Rachel for a long time, and Faith is—that's Faith's thing, is publishing, and now there are a lot of other people working there.

The people I know who do the publishing single-handedly get a lot out of it. You don't have to manage a staff, you don't have to worry about meeting payroll, or having people around that bug you. But on the other hand, it's a complete drain. I never could have done Seal on my own. I knew that. And I think that's why Rachel didn't leave until Faith came along and other people started to materialize. Because she knew, too.

I really believe in small publishers, in independent publishers. I know why people publish with New York and I never try and hold anybody back if they want to move. And some of our authors publish with large publishers in addition to us, or they started with us and then went on to the mainstream. And I've thought about it myself, too. There are a lot of things that New York publishers can do that we can't.

But I think it is important for people to understand how publishing works. Publishing in New York always seems sort of controlled by these mysterious beings. It's alway going to be controlled by somebody else, and I think it's very important for small publishers who know their markets and who have passionate feelings about things to continue to publish good, attractive, well-designed books and to get them out. I think that regional publishing and noncorporate publishing, publishing owned by the people in publishing, that's dedicated to distributing to people of color and women and different minorities, is essential. And that's not going to be found in New York.

New York tends to look around and see what's interesting and say, "Oh! Oh! Sandra Cisneros! Okay, let's publish an Hispanic woman." Or Amy Tan. "I guess it's about time for an Asian woman." Or whatever. But they won't do it unless we're publishing it first. I don't think New York is ever very cutting-edge. The real innovation and imagination and actual love for publishing comes from the small, independent publishers, and it's very important work that we do.

David Brewster
Sasquatch Publishing Company

"I wanted to live in Seattle and I wanted to work for a publication I enjoyed and respected. It became clear to me that that would have to be created. I think that in the process of doing that I discovered that I liked to start new things, that I have that side to me. I honestly didn't think I had that. I thought I was creating it because I didn't want to work at the *Seattle Times*."

I interviewed David Brewster, president of Sasquatch Publishing Company, which publishes Seattle Weekly, Eastside Week *and* Sasquatch Books, *at the offices of* Seattle Weekly *in downtown Seattle in the late afternoon of March 3, 1993. It was a gray Seattle day, as usual.*

I was at Yale for eight years. I majored in English, got a bachelor's degree, and then went to the graduate school, got a master's degree in English and finished all but dissertation for a Ph.D. And then came out here, expecting to finish my dissertation while teaching at the University of Washington, but never did. So I didn't receive a Ph.D.

But you taught for a while at the U. of Dub?
Yes, I came out here in 1965 and taught for three years in the English Department. Assistant professor in the English Department back in the days when junior faculty actually taught. Taught a lot of freshman, taught a lot of composition and a lot of survey courses.

When did you become involved in publishing?
Well, let me go through a little of that. I taught for three years at the U. and I found that I was not that fond of teaching. I had worked

for five summers at newspapers in New Jersey—one newspaper in New Jersey—as a summer job, so I had an alternative skill as a reporter. Vacation fill-in summer reporter. Moved to a different beat every two weeks. And so I got a job at the *Seattle Times*. I was going to take a few years in journalism and then decide whether I liked teaching better than journalism. And my first job was with the *Seattle Times*. I was an editor. I was a copy editor and did some writing. Some reporting. Mostly on the copy desk.

Then I got a job at *Seattle Magazine*. I was there 1969 and 1970, the last two years of its existence. It went out of business in the big Boeing crash of 1970. That was a great job. That was a terrific magazine. And that's what made me want to be in journalism rather than teaching, and stay in Seattle rather than go back to the East Coast. Until then I didn't really think that we would stay in Seattle. It was kind of a way station.

Had you worked for a magazine before?

No. I'd worked for newspapers and then this magazine. When that went out of business I worked for KING-TV in the newsroom as an editor. Of course, KING owned *Seattle Magazine*. And then I worked for four years as the editor of *The Argus* which was an old cracker-barrel weekly, politics and art.

When *Seattle Magazine* went out of business, I and a bunch of my colleagues, we all said, you know, we'd be back, we'd start something to replace that. And various people moved away and gradually it fell to me as the sort of leader of that band. So I was thinking that I would eventually start a monthly. But working at *The Argus*, I found that weekly is more satisfying than monthly. You could be more on top of things, you could review plays that people could still go to. It was more forgiving.

So I decided to start a weekly. And I did that. In 1976 is when *The Weekly* started [Brewster frequently refers to *Seattle Weekly* as *The Weekly*]. So my circuitous course was through newspapers and magazines, a little bit of television, and then a weekly. Just as my very first job in journalism as a high school senior was at my hometown weekly in New Jersey. Hermitsville, New Jersey. So I went from weekly to weekly.

Was that in your mind at the time you started—?

No. No, no. But weeklies have a wonderful history to them. They're close to the community and they have more of a literary side. So I'm comfortable that that is the way to do it. But the mid-'70s is the time when many cities were starting city weeklies as they're usually called, as opposed to community weeklies or rural weeklies or national weeklies. I actually got the inspiration to start *Seattle Weekly* when I was down in Portland, working on the best-places book. And that came out before *The Weekly*. I was simply the hired author to do that for Madrona Publishers. Dan [Levant] had that idea and hired me to do that. And so I was down hanging out in Portland, going to restaurants and gathering information for that part of the book. And I was hanging out at a new newspaper called *Willamette Week*. And they were good enough to show me sort of how they did it and some figures and all that. And that inspired me to come back and finish the book.

And then I left *The Argus* and put together the investors and the team, drawing from *The Argus*, drawing from *Seattle Magazine*, drawing from others around. *The Seattle Flag* was a weekly that had gone out of business before us. And that amalgamation started *The Weekly*. Our first issue came out the day the Kingdome opened. A famous day in Seattle history. March 31, 1976 was the opening of the Kingdome and the first issue of *The Weekly*. Yeah.

You weren't in the military?
No.

I ask that question to get at something else. I had hypothesized that entrepreneurs, in politics or business or whatever, have some sort of relevant experience elsewhere before coming home, or before setting themselves up wherever they set themselves up. And in the United States I thought the military would be important. I think it was important following World War II, but I don't think it is any longer.

342

Well, you know, entrepreneurs are usually sort of rebound personalities in the way that you're suggesting. Many of them come out of Boeing, for instance. They're very tired of a very large organization that stifles their creativity. Boeing is really the mother of small business in this town. It's the reason that Seattle is so entrepreneurial, I think. In my experience, I felt that—at first I desired to buy *The Argus* and transform that, and so I was in a kind of tussle with the printer of *The Argus* who also wanted to buy it, and eventually did. So sort of propelling me on was a kind of "Well, I didn't get that, so"—in the immortal words of every entrepreneur—"I'll show 'em." That's really the driving force. If you've got something to prove—you are balked from getting something that you felt was your due—that pushes you to show them.

Entrepreneurs like to be laughed at, like to be scoffed at. The ones I know, they're always telling me, say, "Remember when I asked you whether such and such"—like starting Starbucks Coffee—"would be a good idea, and you said that it will never work in this town?" That's what they always remember, is the people who said they couldn't do it, because they get their jollies out of doing something that is hard to do and that the odds are long against.

And, you know, you had a succession of good publications like *Seattle Magazine* and *The Sun* and so forth failing in this town—hard town to make it work; that's part of the thing here. You've got a succession of book-publishing companies: Pacific Search, Madrona, and so on, not surviving here. And I'm very proud of how much Sasquatch Books has grown and how it's a thriving operation.

When did Sasquatch Books come into existence?

Well, *The Best Places* was started in 1975 by Dan. It was called *The Best Places: Oregon, Washington, British Columbia.* Then we acquired that single title from Dan for Sasquatch Publishing. Then we retitled it, I think in about 1981, *Northwest Best Places.* And then we went to multiple books within that guidebook thing. We did *Seattle Best Places.* We now have *Portland Best Places. Northern California Best Places.* And then, I think it was 1988 that we decided to become a

343

full publishing company—still a regional, not a national, book-publishing company—and hired marketing and all of that, and then branched into other guidebooks like *Cheap Eats* and *Cheap Sleeps*, garden books, cook books and general, all-purpose, regional nonfiction. Always nonfiction. Books on the Seahawks, books on the environment, books on real estate. And now our latest step is to branch into northern California. Our market is now the Bay Area to Vancouver. And we will do in California many of the same kinds of books that we're doing now. We've also recently gone into children's books and gift books.

But we're trying to be what I call a true regional publisher. That's to say, in a region outside of New York and publishing books by regional authors for the region, not for the nation. While we have some national sales of some of our books, we try not to think about it at all.

That, I think, was one of the calculations that Madrona made and Pacific Search made that led to problems. Because the national market, if you're small, is very tricky. It's hard to gauge it right. You don't know what your competitors are up to. It's hard to get paid on a timely basis. And it's easy to overprint, get a lot of orders and have a lot of them come back.

The other thing is—I remember when we were making this decision about one of our first garden books, *The Year in Bloom* by Ann Lovejoy, and we were trying to decide, should we put into the index where to get a lot of the flowers that are talked about in the book, because that would make it clear that it wasn't a national book. We decided to do that, make it very obvious that it's a regional book, meant for people who live here. We sold thirty thousand copies of that book, which by national standards would be a best-seller for a garden book. I think the thing we were in front of was that if you are confidently regional, and really helpful to people there, and say that you do not care that this book doesn't travel across the Cascades, or across the Columbia, then you can do better. So that's the course that we tried to follow. I'm not sure we'll follow that all the time, but that's what we've done.

You know, we're niche publishers and we try to be one niche ahead, in a sense, trying to see around the corner. The niche in book

344

publishing is, as I've just described it, quality books where you command the market, as in guidebooks. In *Eastside Week*, which is now two and a half years old, the niche is sophisticated suburban readers. That is, I think, an enormous opportunity for publishers around the country. Most newspaper publishers think of suburban readers as escapists, as people who may work in a high-pressure job at Microsoft or in a downtown Seattle law firm, but when they come home they sort of sigh from the heavy day's work and get into bake sales. Our perception is that forty to fifty percent of the market in these edge cities—we don't even call them suburbs anymore because they're so urbanized— are people that love to read the *New York Times* and are tired of having newspapers in their own area, their own community, insult their intelligence. They're very interested in problems of congestion and education and—

Did you do market research to establish—

We did. And I remember one of the things we found was that the percentage of readers of the *New York Times* in Redmond, compared to Seattle, is three times higher. It's also twice as high as in Bellevue. That was an indication of the new wave of suburbs, the outer suburbs like Redmond, which are very influenced by Microsoft. People moving up here from Los Angeles and larger metropolitan areas are very sophisticated consumers of news and are not going to bother with a paper that treats them like they only care about bake sales.

The second thing we did there was to see that the paper is very independent of *The Weekly*, not a zoned edition, not carrying stuff from one over to the other. It has its own editorial policy. It has its own editor. I have no idea what's in one week's issue until it's printed. And it's not in any way, say, the eastside edition of the *Seattle Times*—it's not in any sense a Seattle-produced paper. Even though we do the typesetting over here and we have a common accounting. It has its own staff, its own editorial staff, its own art director.

You're still personally involved with the operation of The Weekly?

345

Yes. That's right. My job here is that of president of the company, CEO of the company, so I look at the overall direction of things and, you know, the publisher of *Eastside Week* reports to me, the publisher of Sasquatch Books reports to me, and the executive vice-president of the company, who runs the whole business side, reports to me. But my roll-up-the-sleeves job here is to edit *The Weekly*. And that's what I spend most of my time at. I edit that paper closely. I'm involved in editing a lot of stories, working with writers, cultivating new freelancers, and writing myself. I've resisted just becoming an executive and losing the thing that made me start the paper in the first place, which is the opportunity of shaping a paper each week and helping to shape the city's debate. But I'm not at all involved, for instance, in titles that are selected by Sasquatch Books or any of the editorial decisions of *Eastside Week*. Those are run by separate publishers. So it's really a company of three publishers, and then one who's more equal than the others.

Your first love is newspapering.
Yes. Yes. Right.

So why do Sasquatch Books? Why did you establish that?
Well, you know, I've got two daughters and it's not a problem to love both. I certainly don't mean to say that in loving *The Weekly* that much I'm not that interested in books. We're a publishing company and our mission is to fill quality niches in this area. I saw that that was an important thing to do.

Secondly, I think this synergy works very well. For instance, the gardening book I was talking about, *The Year in Bloom*. We pretested that. We discovered Ann Lovejoy as a writer. She was a columnist writing every week in *The Weekly*. You could see how popular she was and how much people liked her style and her knowledge. And so that became the basis for the book. And that's where the material is done, where first drafts are written, and then when the book comes out she's already a well-known writer. And then you can run ads in *The Weekly*, of course, at a big discount, to push that. So in terms of generating

346

writers, generating fame, preparing the market for a book to come, it's very helpful.

Likewise, writers that Sasquatch Books develops sometimes will come to me and say, "Look, I'm working on this book and in order to fund my research for this I'd like to sell some of the material. You know, chapters and so forth." That's great. I get that at less than I would have to pay otherwise. The writer is getting more money so that they can take off the time to do the book. And the writer's name is getting known by virtue of the newspaper, so when the book comes out—"Oh, I've heard of that person." So I think it works very well.

And there are certain other advantages, obviously. In equipment that you're buying for production. In accounting, where you can spread your overhead. It's not at all an original idea. *Texas Monthly* has Texas Monthly Press. Chronicle Books from Chronicle newspapers. Atlantic Monthly Press, New Republic Press. I think it works very well.

When you started out, did you start with the idea of filling a niche, or creating a niche and then filling it? That sounds—that's a business decision.

That's a business decision. Well, as far as I can reconstruct the motivations, they go this way. I wanted to live in Seattle and I wanted to work for a publication I enjoyed and respected. It became clear to me that that would have to be created. I think that in the process of doing that I discovered that I liked to start new things, that I have that side to me. I honestly didn't think I had that. I thought I was creating it because I didn't want to work at the *Seattle Times*.

Secondly, when I started being a reporter here in 1968 it was a time of terrific civic change and progress. The fight to save the Pike Place Market, all kinds of change. I was, and still am, very exhilarated by the civic-political climate of this town compared to, say, New Jersey where you can't fight City Hall. Here it's fun to fight City Hall. It's fun to take over City Hall when you make these changes. So I wanted a paper that was an expression of that rising generation of people that had a vision of Seattle as a sophisticated arts center—good politics, sidewalk cafes, Starbucks Coffee, all of this stuff that is on one level

347

a yuppie consumerist version of things, and on another level, making good urban schools and being more civic-minded. I love being in the middle of that and thought the paper could really do that function. Arts included.

I think Seattle is a good entrepreneurial town. I started a pub with some people. It's the Mark Tobey Pub. I started two musical organizations. It encourages the starting of things. It encourages these little crusades. People have fun doing them together. So that's a lot of what I was in love with.

One other thing, which is kind of literary. I've been a journalist and a professor of literature, and in my mind *The Weekly* is an attempt to mesh those two things. Journalism as we know it began in the early eighteenth century in France and England at the same time in which the novel was being created. The roots of journalism are in literature. Addison and Steele, Defoe, Fielding, Dickens and so on. I really think that journalism needs to return to something that is closer to imagination and closer to literary structure. It's, of course, not art. It's craft. But the—

It can be art.

It can be. It's probably done in too much of a rush to be that. And it has a strong obligation of factual accuracy. Of course, realism does too. There are parts of art that have that. But what I mean is, for instance, the structure of a play, the structure of a speech, the structure of a short story, is basically get attention, create conflict, work through the conflict, resolve the conflict, and have the ending be a surprise. Have a nonpredictable, yet inevitable, ending. And that's the way in which I try to see that journalism can be structured. Now, typically, journalism is structured in a way that's very different from that. State your conclusion, state your second most exciting fact, and then let the thing sort of run into the sand as the story goes along. The inverted pyramid. So I would say build to a conclusion rather than fall away from an opening statement, even though you need an exciting way to get started.

Other things: management of tone, management of point of view, management of pace, changes of pace, visualizing things, getting

348

in dialogue and all of that. It's been a lifetime interest of mine to see that good writing gets back into journalism. By which I mean many of the lessons that are drawn from as far back as Aristotle who, you know, originally outlined what is the structure of a speech. How do you hold an audience? At what point do you put in the dry material and still hold an audience?

And Aristotle had that all figured out. He said in about the second fifth of the speech, because you've got their attention in the first fifth, but if you wait until later there's too much fatigue and then the dry material will come in, and so you've got to get that out of the way pretty early and then build to an exciting conclusion, which is, you know, strap on our armor and go beat those Spartans.

The ending must be a surprise. That's very hard to do in journalism. There's a lot of peer pressure on writers. There's a lot of pressure from politicians and everybody else: Don't go out on a limb. Don't get out in an interpretive spot where people are going to say, "I don't think that's true."

My whole thing is to try to release writers to be themselves and to make statements that the audience is not going to assent to right away. And now comes the interesting evidence for it, and so forth. And then to have the conclusion after looking at a lot of the evidence and sifting through it, not to be predictable. Because if it's predictable I'll stop reading long articles. And magazine journalism is the art of getting people to read a long article. You want them to read a long article, first of all, because you love your writing. You know, you're a vain writer. But mostly because then you can get into the shades of gray. You can get into the true nuanced reality of contemporary life. And it takes length to do that. But it takes narrative skill to get people who lead busy lives, and our readers, you know, are the achievement bunch in this town. They are very busy, and so it really is a struggle that way.

But I think that the challenge of reforming journalism and setting a new style that is more personal and so on.... But this is part of my thing, being able to create a paper that is different and not a formula paper.

The period in which you started your paper and just before, say from the late '60s through the late '70s, saw the creation of the personal voice in American journalism.

Right. The New Journalism. Mm hmm. Tom Wolfe. Right. Oh, sure. That was coming in magazines like *New York*, and *The New Yorker* was doing that. Yeah. And many of us were very influenced by that. How to get that in, and how to make it respectable and truth-telling, not just a Tom Wolfe kind of fireworks. And how to make it work for writers who are not Tom Wolfe. For good but not fabulous writers. And how to have that in politics, not just in arts criticism. Not just in sports writing. Have it pervade your paper.

So where does your immortality come from? Aside from your children. Have you thought about that, or do you think about it?

Well, I would like.... One of the versions of that is to create in Sasquatch Publishing a company that has the characteristics of the publishing houses I most admire, and the publishing empires I most admire. Like the *New York Times* and the *Washington Post* and the *Los Angeles Times*. Those are family enterprises. This is not set up to be a family enterprise. I'm only a small stakeholder in *The Weekly*. There are fifty owners of the paper. It's set up to have a lot of owners so that, for one, the editor has a lot of freedom, it's not an expression of a single owner, but also to give it stability. But to see that its mission can continue on and be improved with subsequent editors and writers as come through here for three generations—I would think that would be about as much as one could hope for. And that it remain independent and locally owned, not a chain and not a part of somebody's formula, so that it springs out of the point of view of Seattle and the Northwest. That would be good.

Did you discover a sense of community—your sense of community—here? You made a comment earlier about something not being there in New Jersey but which you found here. I interpreted that as a sense of community.

Right. A sense of civic optimism. Yes. Yeah. Right. Yeah, when

350

I came out here I intended to be an academic, to live in the world of literature. And while I had very much enjoyed those summer vacations away from that by working at the newspaper, and enjoyed newspaper people and writing those stories and seeing murder victims and all of that, I thought of that at the time as material for a novel rather than something that I'd do. Once I started doing it—I sort of backed into it—there was more of a flare for that than I had thought, and more of a feeling for being a figure in the community and being involved in that and knowing the mayor and giving advice about what the school board ought to do.

It turns out not to be that surprising. My father has a lot of that and did a lot of that. So it's in me more than I thought. But I came to it accidentally.

What did your father do?
My father was an executive at RCA. He's an engineer who became a very successful business manager and was in charge of various plants and some overseas operations before he retired. My mother did some secretarial work but was primarily a homemaker and did not have a career.

Did you live overseas yourself, or was this after—?
No. In fact, when he was doing that he was still living in New Jersey. Yeah. No, I've not spent a lot of time overseas. Three or four extended trips. I never lived there.

Seattle being a good entrepreneurial town, and entrepreneurialism being a response to Boeing—
It pushes out entrepreneurs.

What I'm finding—I agree with you, by the way. I'm looking for an explanation for this. It's not a loaded question, it's just a discussion.
Mm hmm.

I find in British Columbia, where I've interviewed six publish-

351

ers, and in Oregon, where I've interviewed three so far...well, in Canada the publishers have the Canada Council; they get money from the government. I'm looking at book publishers now. They reach a point of eligibility, then they get money upon application. Our system is somewhat different, though in Oregon publishers do apply for grants. In Washington it's rare. It's not that people aren't eligible. They just don't do it. I interviewed Thatcher Bailey of Bay Books. He said that he just doesn't want to give up control of his company by turning it into a nonprofit corporation [thereby qualifying it to receive government grants]. He said he'd probably do the same thing that he does now if he got grants, but he wants the company to be his. There seems to me to be the enjoyment of risk here in the Seattle area that I don't find in Vancouver or Oregon. Do you have any comment on that?

Well, Oregon is a more hierarchical and established and traditional culture. Older. More Boston style. In Portland it's important who you know. Seattle is always thought to be kind of a crazy place where Lord knows what schemes they're coming up with next. And that's the Seattle spirit and it's sort of been self-perpetuating here. It's odd that it would be here and not in Portland. I think Portland kind of fell asleep at the tollgate down there. They thought they had a perfect situation with two rivers draining the main area of the Northwest going right by their front door. All you do is put the tollgate down and get rich. In Seattle, probably the greatest thing that happened is that the railroad went to Tacoma and Seattle realized that it wasn't sitting across the tollgate and had to engage in a lot more risky behavior in order to capture the leadership of the Northwest.

The Canadians, I think, are afflicted with an inferiority complex that comes from a certain Scottish temperament and being a small country up against a monster. I was interested once in joining with some Canadian partners to start a Vancouver weekly. It would a great thing to do. You can't do it without Canadian partners and the Canadian partner would have to own seventy-five percent of the enterprise, by Canadian law. It's very protectionist against American involvement in media.

So I was helping them to raise money, and we'd go and show

some people and we'd look at the quality of the competition in Vancouver and I would say how bad it was. I would go through all of its weaknesses in order to build up to promising the glorious new day of our new publication. But I could never get to the next step, which was to talk about how good the new day would be, because the people in the room would get so depressed about how bad the products were that they were producing. And they would say, "Well, what does that tell you about Vancouver?"

And I would say that where there's bad, there's an opportunity for good. There's a strong hunger for good things. It's like here's a town with no good French restaurants, so do a good French restaurant and people will come to your door. They looked at the half-empty glass and said, "Well, it looks like Vancouverites don't have any appetite for quality things," even though the people in the room did. They couldn't think well of their townspeople. And that sort of summed up....

In fact, our frustration about not getting anywhere with the Vancouver weekly is what led to *Eastside Week.* We applied a lot of our energy and some of our thinking about a second paper to one that was right under our noses.

You don't apply for grants, do you?
No, we don't. Of course, we would not be eligible, since we're a for-profit corporation. I suppose there would be some way, in that I've tried occasionally to get an author a grant so he can work on a book project or things for us. But I would add to what Thatcher was saying about that, which is independence. I'm increasingly alarmed at what public funding of the arts is leading to. I think it's just become a branch of politics. The pleasing of the constituency *du jour* has become so extreme that.... Chamber music is European. Even though it's per-formed all over the world and loved all over the world, it comes out of a European culture, so it is virtually shut out of public funding.

What's the reason for its being shut out now?
Because it's not multicultural. Because it expresses European values. Because the audience that goes to chamber music is a highly

educated and, therefore, fairly affluent audience. And it's thought to be a dying rather than a thriving form of art. For classical culture, it's get-in-line-and-wait-your-turn. Unless you're a powerful organization like the symphony or something like that. Maybe that's a valid function of public funding, to give to the have-nots. But I think that judgments about quality, judgments about the conveyance of emotion, of high art and things of this kind, whichever culture they're found in—I think that's just been lost from public funding.

And I don't trust the process. I don't trust the strings. And I think that the kinds of books and other things that one would be encouraged to do would be things that—Thatcher would see it, as I would, as too many cooks in the kitchen. Publishing is basically an individual act. An editor, a writer, a publisher—it's not committee-designed stuff. I don't mind an individual patron that cares a lot about a form of art, contributing to it—I think that's good. But when you get these public dimensions, which are turnstile-oriented and constituency-serving, I think that ultimately everybody gets debased by that. I'm almost at the point of abolishing the National Endowment for the Arts as a good progressive move.

A number of people who regard themselves, or whom I regard, as progressive thinkers would agree with you. So would a number of people on the Right, but for different reasons. But as far as selecting, and the thought process that goes into deciding what gets published and what doesn't.... In the big New York publishing houses, except in rare cases, no one person is responsible, though some of them have individual editors whom they give a lot of authority to. The university presses have that committee system. Calyx Books, which is a pretty small operation as far as national publishers go, although they do a lot for this part of the country, has a committee of twenty-five people. I guess what I'm saying is that multiculturalism isn't the only thing afflicted with that kind of committee mentality. It's pretty unusual, actually, to find an operation that is not an assemblage of committees.

Well, I think committees in book publishing are basically—their perspective is on how to do a good book. The political dimension

354

is not that concerned about a good book. They're concerned about advancing certain values. They're concerned about altering the market. In other words, in both an idealistic way and in a cynical way, empowering people that don't have the money or don't have the position. I think that adds a funny dimension to it.

It's one thing to get a lot of opinions about books, and obviously university presses do a lot of that with peer review. We do a fair amount of that, too. We certainly have a very democratically run decision process for books. Lots of people put in ideas. People talk about how they like covers, whether to publish, and all of that. The final decision is made by an individual who feels free to make that.

Is that the publisher? Chad Haight?

That's right. Chad Haight. He gets a lot of advice, and sometimes he gets talked out of a book or talked into a book. But I think it remains pretty individualistic that way, and I think that's right. Publishing generally is getting too market-driven. Certainly this is the big problem with newspapers. It used to be that a good editor on a newspaper was one who was not safe, who could get high-impact writing out of writers, and who was fairly fearless in taking on the vested interests. There were many examples of that.

Now most people wouldn't define a good newspaper editor that way. A good newspaper editor now is one who is a master of marketing studies and knows how to serve various constituencies. It's driven by what advertisers want in certain constituencies and then what surveys show those constituencies like. That makes for a blander product with a more predictable, pandering kind of feeling to it.

I don't need that. There's no surprise to it. There's no edge to it. It doesn't stretch my mind. What it does is play to my prejudices. That felt good for awhile, but it's really kind of boring. Why do I need to spend twenty minutes a day being convinced that I'm right? I already know that. I say to our writers, "Insofar as you can imagine our audience, treat them with respect. They're all people who see things in many of the same ways we do. But your obligation is to prove that they're wrong. And to prove that you were wrong. You, the writer, were

355

wrong when you went into the subject. And why wouldn't you be wrong? Aren't you going to learn more about it? And in learning more about it, isn't that going to lead you to say, 'Now I see the things I didn't before and therefore I've changed my view'? Get somewhere. Get somewhere beyond your top-of-the-head reactions to things, and take your readers there."

Conventional publishing says, "Find out what readers think about something and then give it to them. Feed it back to them."

That's true of book publishing too, for the most part.

Yeah. Right. What do you want? Okay, I'll give it to you; you give me your ten dollars. My variation of that is that what satisfies people is not what they say they want. It's something that lies deeper than that. And that has a lot to do with the sense of my mind being stretched, or my seeing things in a new way, or my feeling uncertain about what conventional wisdom is purveying, or the way I thought about a problem before I read this article. Or [the fact] that I don't agree with the writer. You've shaken me from where I was before but you haven't convinced me that you're right. And that's fine, and I think the writer ought to say, you know, "I don't expect you to agree with me, but let's consider these things together. And I'll tell you where I come down on it because I've spent some time on it and, in the interests of full disclosure, you have the right to know. But that's just me. You ought to have your own view. And you can read my article, get value out of it, change your mind about something, disagree with me, and be grateful to me as the writer for giving you that stuff."

That's the way. That's the kind of journalism I like.

356

Scott McIntyre
Douglas & McIntyre

"... when I feel bleak at the work load and the bullshit that publishing really is, yeah, I can look at the list and what I believe we have done for the culture of this place. I think if one was to say what is the real contribution D&M has made, it's to take the real voices of this place, often the artists as well as the writers, and make them national or international."

Douglas & McIntyre is, in Scott McIntyre's words, "a classic book publisher." It's organized around two divisions: a children's division, Groundwood Books, headquartered in Ontario, and Douglas & McIntyre itself, located in Vancouver, British Columbia. The two divisions together publish one hundred books a year. There had been a third division, an education book company, that was sold a few years ago. "It just was going to take too much work and capital to sustain the kind of development we need to fight the big guys." At the time of this interview, Douglas & McIntyre was starting up a new division called Greystone Books that would specialize in natural history, sports and guidebooks.

Known primarily for its large-format art books, Douglas & McIntyre currently employees twenty-five people. Its president and publisher is Scott McIntyre. I interviewed McIntyre in the late morning of November 19, 1992 in his office in Vancouver. It had rained earlier— "It was pissing with rain"—and the day remained gray, though beyond the Burrard Inlet north of the city the mountains were blue.

There was, McIntyre says, nothing in his childhood that might, in retrospect, be seen to have guided him toward publishing. "My father was a railway clerk. I grew up in a house virtually without books." For most of his childhood, his mother was a homemaker. "It was a very quiet, quintessential, middle-class, Canadian upbringing. In a nice suburb" of Vancouver. He graduated from the University of British Columbia in 1965. "Honors, fine arts. It's an odd background for a publisher. Art history, primarily. Art history, architecture." He did not go on to graduate school.

Well, in fact, I decided to take a year out and got an offer in an ad agency. I'd been a year-book editor. Got an offer to join an ad agency on the creative side and I thought that was kind of interesting, and so one thing followed another. And, in fact, I'd also done a book while I was at university and had become fascinated by book publishing.

You wrote a book while you were at the university?
Yeah. It was an illustrated book, but I designed, wrote the introduction and met Jack McClellan of McClellan and Stewart, who really was sort of Canada's Knopf. Flamboyant, and an old-style publisher. Strikingly similar in look and style to Horace Liveright, the American publisher in the '30s.

I read his biography.
Well, believe me, that photograph on the cover of the biography is Jack McClellan. Jack hates it when people say this, but.... So I went back to Toronto in the fall of '67 as advertising-promotion manager in McClellan and Stewart, which was then kind of the hot independent. Still is the best Canadian publishing house.

You graduated from university in '65 and you took the job with the ad agency—
I spent two years in an ad agency. To my shame. I started—same old story—I started as a three-hundred-bucks-a-month production assistant—it was a small shop then—and moved up fairly quickly. But, really, my heart was in other things.

So you knew in university, you already had an indication, that you wanted to go into publishing. Or were you thinking in those terms?

Interestingly enough, never. In fact, quite by accident, in grade eleven I was approached by a committee and asked if I would edit the yearbook in grade twelve. So I edited the high school yearbook and then stumbled into the yearbook at UBC and ended up being on it for four years and editing it for two. Had anyone said to me that I would end up in a business that's built around writing and journalism—never, never in my wildest dreams. I was going to be an architect. But I got seduced by the notion of books in university. And a buddy and me spent all our spare time and money for about three years doing a book. It went on forever.

Why were you selected in high school to do the yearbook?
God knows why. Probably because I was a straight-A student.

Okay. What was the book you did as an undergraduate?
It was a photographic book on Vancouver. But it was an attempt to portray Vancouver in a somewhat more realistic way than the post card shots have traditionally got.

Did you sell it?
No. In fact, M and S took me, not the book. They offered me a job but they didn't take the book. And it probably is a good thing that nobody took the book.

Why?
I think the photography was wonderful but the book wasn't going to be exceptional. It was a great process, as they say. And along the way I met a guy by the name of Jim Douglas who was the local sales representative for McClellan and Stewart, and Macmillan. In fact, he is the Douglas of Douglas & McIntyre. And I came back to join him after leaving M and S, thinking life was too short for the fast lane in Toronto. Published our first books in the fall of 1971. Although the company actually was something that he had started as a wholesale company in 1964.

A book wholesaler?

Yeah. He had, in fact—let me digress. Jim Douglas had been a book man all his life. He was in the air force. The Royal Air Force. He's twenty years older than me. Flew in Burma, in fact, out of Australia. Out of Darwin. He had been at McClellan and Stewart but his family wanted to come back here. So he moved back here and was the first, I think, the first commissioned sales rep in Canada, representing Macmillan, the UK Macmillan, and McClellan and Stewart. In fact, he was asked by the principals of those companies and others to open a wholesale company here to try to keep the business that was going south to American wholesalers. So he built that company. Jim was always one to start something, to sell out fairly early on, to be generous to the next generation, but basically to never get too entrapped. Whereas by building a company like this one to the size we are, it doesn't become so easy.

"Never get too entrapped." You mean that was a personal thing with him, not to—

Yeah, well, he'd probably be irritated to hear me say it, but he always was quite clever in bringing young people in and then offering them equity, getting them involved, and moving on. In fact, he sold that wholesale company to another wholesaler here called Harry Smith and Sons. They'd been a toy-and-book wholesale company that this business drove out.

Backing up, you and Jim Douglas transformed his wholesaling company into a publishing company. Where'd the capital come from?

Hah! First of all, the wholesaler was moribund. It was a nonfunctioning legal entity. So we certainly started from scratch, the old-fashioned way. I mean sales the first year were eleven thousand dollars. The next year they were fifty thousand. The next year they were a hundred. The next year they were a quarter million. And, really, we grew—first of all, we took our livings out of doing something else. Really sort of wage work and sales and stunting with suppliers and bank loans. We worked with the bank from a fairly early time. The company

360

was called J.J. Douglas, Limited. It became Douglas & McIntyre, Limited when I joined it full-time. Because we felt that was inappropriate while I was a sales rep for other publishing houses, even though we were quite public about it.

But the capitalization of the company, in fact, was very low. There was some retained earnings in the legal shell. I added some capital. But, effectively, we've built this company on the back of sweat equity and an operating line from the bank. But we've not done what is considered traditional now, which is you take whatever, your parents' quarter million bucks or somebody else's two or three million, and build a company. We built it literally by proceeding cautiously. Much more cautiously than I would have liked. And publishing practical books. And evolving as the company grew. We were pretty pragmatic. We were never a small press in the classic sense of the word, and never a literary press, particularly.

And this started in '71?
Yeah. First two little books in the fall of '71.

How many did you do in '72?
Probably four or five. We always did other things. I mean we distributed—we picked up self-published books. We did lots of unglamorous stuff initially.

Was your goal to build a company, or to do a particular kind of book, or both, or—?
I would say the broader goal was to build a publishing house, rather than—yeah, I was not motivated by publishing a certain kind of book, but by building a general house. So I have perhaps the odd combination of, alas, some real business skills. I mean it's a mix.

You didn't get that with a fine arts degree.
Hah! No, I learned it along the way. School of hard knocks. Certainly my personal passions tend to focus around very beautiful books. Illustrated books. Art. Native studies. My particular bent shows

in the list.

Do you regard yourself as a competitive sort of person?

Competitive in what sense? I mean, yeah, I am by nature a Type A creature. And we are up against other publishers all the time. Mostly eastern publishers. So, yeah, I'm pretty competitive, I think. I would have to say that my curse and my blessing is I take it very personally. I get involved with ideas and I like them, and then it hurts to lose them. I don't think we lose very often though. But, you know, in this business, if you're up against the majors—I mean our competitors are Penguin, McClellan and Stewart, Key Porter, Random House. We get very competitive. But rather than a sort of publisher glaze, where you get fifteen hundred projects a year, or whatever it is we get, and you sit in a meeting and if the numbers look good you say yes and otherwise you don't worry about it very much, I'm inclined to get involved with either the writer or the idea.

How do you mean, you like to get involved with the writer or the idea? Do you help design the book, or do you yourself edit?

No. What I mean is a fairly hands-on approach. Usually a significant relationship with the author. In fact, many of our closest friends are our authors. It's been said that one of the reasons publishers and writers get on so badly is they are so alike. But certainly many of our closest friends are writers and photographers that we've published over the years, and obviously those people, on the whole, whose talent I most respect. But I haven't edited in a long time. And I never really came up the editorial route. I mean I have edited, but I wouldn't consider myself a great editor. I think I've got a good nose for a book. My background is, rather, design, so I'm inclined to be fairly hands-on in terms of the look of the book, the production specifications, the editorial concept. But I confess I don't do a lot beyond that. I often write the jacket copy still. But what I meant by that was we don't have a fancy committee system, where the decisions are made by a committee, which some houses of our size are moving towards.

I like to read something first. In fact, I have a rule, which is I don't want to meet an author until I've read something. Because, you know, you like someone and you have a couple glasses of wine in a bar and the next thing you know, you've made a commitment, when in fact you shouldn't have because you haven't read anything yet. New York was famous for that in the '50s and '60s. That old style of publishing. A couple of martinis in a bar and the whole thing kind of floats along. I mean, hey, one of the things we have done very successfully is popular memoir, and as often as not those are ghosted books.

Because it seems to me that publishing is a fairly personal activity. I think the problem is always, especially in a market like this one where the average book of nonfiction is gonna sell twenty-five hundred and the average novel might sell eight hundred to a thousand—

That's your experience?

Those are industry statistics. That is, Canada-wide, Canada Council statistics. One of the things that distinguishes publishing culture in this country is no American publisher I know of could survive with the kind of market economics we have. Small companies can. On the one hand we have the grants, which are more generous than American grants. Canada Council, Department of Communications, Cultural Services. I mean government relations is a full-time job. So on the one hand we have the grants.

On the other hand, we have restrictive ownership legislation so that, as a foreign national, you cannot own more than forty-nine percent of a Canadian house. And within that bubble of artificiality you've got, I think, quite an interesting publishing culture. Because you haven't had the amalgamation and the mergers and the acquisitions and the building of the global giants that you have in Australia, the UK and the US. So I would argue that you've got an industry that is interesting creatively because most of the companies, almost all of them, are still owned by their founders, by the entrepreneur, and this industry is really regionally and generically quite diverse. The downside is the market is the shits. And we don't have sub [subsidiary] rights the way an American publisher has.

Who has them? The author?

Well, no. There aren't any. There are very few mass paperback houses. There's no independent mass paperback house in this country. The film business has really just started. There just isn't much money in rights. And a large chunk of library purchases go through American wholesalers. We don't have a very protected territory in terms of market. It's gonna become more protected. And, of course, we don't have a discrete language. And we're up against the huge influx of books from the States. So we have to price competitively with New York.

At our size now we feel very strongly about export, and we do a reasonable job. About twenty percent of our volume is export, primarily to the US, but also Africa, Asia and Europe. Everywhere, but certainly the US primarily. And we do our share of rights sales. But on the whole you really wouldn't get publicity internationally without a US publisher in it and a rights sale. And it's very tough in these times for serious writers to travel. They may do it occasionally. Seal Press took a novel of ours called *Disappearing Moon Cafe* which we're very proud of. Author called Sky Lee. Was nominated for a Governor General's. Really one of the first serious novels to come out of the Chinese community here. And a kind of feminist, historical, multi-generational—the real edge. And Seal took it and I think it's going to get interesting reviews. It did very well here.

Now, we would not be known as a literary house. I would say our reputation would extend more to art, architecture—beautiful books. We're known for the kind of regional culture that we do, although the list is becoming more national. And we would be known for children's fiction and illustrated books. But certainly we would be known as a nonfiction house. And the fiction we have published, while we've done some pretty good fiction, we are not known as a fiction house and we would not be respected as a great literary enterprise. I mean, we've Malcolm Lowry, with those we've bought and reprint. We've books like a Sky Lee. I don't want to downgrade the fiction we've done, but we're not New Directions.

Why did you decide to do that novel, or to do Malcolm Lowry?

Well, we do about a half dozen adult novels a year. And the list, in fact, is in the process of becoming more literary. But clearly one doesn't get in this business without wanting to publish the best writing. But we've always had one eye on the base, which has been nonfiction. I think our fiction list is going to get dramatically more interesting over the next few years. In fact, we've just made our children's publisher, Patsy Aldana, our fiction publisher for the adult program. Which means it will be a more personal, riskier list than perhaps it's been. We have a series of murder mysteries, detective novels, and some literary fiction. The commitment is growing, but certainly the house is known more for its nonfiction and its illustrated books and its kids' books than for its adult fiction.

Can we go through the history of your company and your own evolution, your own feelings about what happened between 1971 and now?

Who can remember?

Well, I wouldn't think what it is now is something you antici-pated it would be twenty-one years ago.

I would say what we represent now, relative to the industry in this country, probably exceeds my fondest dreams. I mean I've been the last to believe that. I'm told that often enough by people who I don't believe are sycophants. And I've been going to Frankfurt for twenty years. So when I feel bleak at the work load and the bullshit that publishing really is, yeah, I can look at the list and what I believe we have done for the culture of this place. I think if one was to say what is the real contribution D&M has made, it's to take the real voices of this place, often the artists as well as the writers, and make them national or international. Not in any hugely grandiose way, and I don't know that the names would mean anything to you. But, oh, the architect Arthur Erickson, Bill Reid, the sculptor who did the magnificent piece in the Canadian embassy in Washington, Emily Carr, Paul St. Pierre, Hugh Brody, people who have either written about this place or really are of this place. It's a very particular style. I think that's what we've done best.

We've done a lot of other things. We've done lots of western history and we've done a lot of popular memoirs that have sold extremely well. But I think rather than publishing, say, a brilliant literary list, what we really have done is given voice to the place. We are one of the largest publishers, in fact, on the West Coast. There's no equivalent on the American West Coast, except maybe now Chronicle which is going like crazy. And whether that's good or bad, I think that's really what we've done.

Other than the notion of a publishing house, I don't know that my dreams were very specific. Certainly it's been tougher than—I think if you ever thought about it—it's like writing a book. If you ever really thought about what you were going to go through while you were doing it, you'd never do it.

I don't know that that's a very good answer to that question. I mean certainly there are a number of things that I'm proud of. I like the international stuff. I like to travel. I think cultural policy—I mean in this country, you get people like Karl Siegler [of Talonbooks] who've made a huge impact on cultural policy. I think I've made a significant difference, and I've been involved in a lot of it for twenty years. I find that quite fascinating. It takes away from the publishing house sometimes. Just the time it takes. But, really, I think it's fair to say that, over the years, quite a dramatic amount of leadership nationally has come from publishers based here. Including Jim Douglas and Karl and me. I know this company provided the president of the Association of Canadian Publishers for something like five years out of twelve, until a few years ago.

But I think what we've done is we've really gone through a lot of the swamp without having the problems that most companies who grow like we have go through. Which is they either go bankrupt or they have to reconstruct, or they merge, or they get into deep trouble. Certainly, as a business, we're adequate but we're underfinanced, as all publishers are unless they're owned by Time Warner.

Barbara Wilson of Seal Press was saying they're of a size now

*where they have permanent employees rather than independent con-
tractors, so now they've got to deal with health plans and that sort of
thing. Now they have to worry about the organization—*

Right on this desk. I mean that's one of the problems—the
amount of organization and financial management just becomes huge.
And the danger is that the position gets so waylaid by it that you're
seldom able to go back to what really should count, which is coming up
with a great book idea or reading a great piece of writing and shaping
it into an artifact that brings value.

*At what point does that happen? It seems to me there would be
a point at which you find yourself divorced from the books you publish.
You say you want to get hands-on, and you could do that to some extent,
but I'll bet you don't do it as much as you used to. Or am I wrong?*

Well, I'm thinking about that. Because one of the reasons for
some of these changes is I wanted to get back and do more of it. But the
practical circumstance is, of course, the company's too big. But we're
making some other organizational changes with the intent of freeing
more of my time to go back to publish, as opposed to doing a lot of other
stuff.

When did the company become Douglas & McIntyre?

Nineteen seventy-eight. And then we built this education company, and I took a year to do that. It was hugely successful, but it took
a year. So, really, I've never been full-time hands-on, primarily shaping
the books. I've always done other things, in my view, out of necessity.
I'm still the senior management accountant. We have a comptroller but
I do a lot of the management accounting, and my view of that is I don't
do it because I love it, although it appeals in some strange abstract way,
like a chess game, but I do it because I'm cheap. I can do it at night and
given, like every publisher, our house is still at risk—I mean everything
we have is tied up—one doesn't want to be too far from the financial
side.

There's been no difficulty getting credit from the banks, even from the beginning? I don't think an American publisher can do that.

Our record at the bank, I think, is quite extraordinary by publishing standards. Although we've had our raw moments, and we've certainly fought, and it's taken a lot of time. One of the reasons we've had a very significant line of credit for a lot of years, probably more than perhaps we should have, is that the bank gets a lot of time. And we report flawlessly, monthly. The upside is you get the money. The downside is it takes a significant administrative load to make sure that it functions. We used to look enviously at American banks. We don't now.

But a house like D&M doesn't normally happen without a wealthy parent—I don't mean parent literally, but a parent company or whatever, like Chronicle where there is really someone with deep pockets somewhere—either that or you sell at some point. We've gotten to a larger size than many do without the traditional sources of capital. I think it's a combination of three things. One is publishing more pragmatically than, ideally, one might want to do. Another is the bank. And the third is the grant system here.

On the whole, we've been able to do what we want to do. We've done a lot books like this, for instance, which is a single book on the Bill Reid sculpture that is in the embassy in Washington. It's simply the chronicle of the creating of what I firmly believe is a masterwork. Bill Reid is actually half Haida, and has been significantly responsible for the renaissance of Haida art. And books like that a lot of people don't do. The scramble is always to have enough commerce to pay the bills without sacrificing the books you really want to do. We don't turn down a lot now that we really want. That's 'cause one of the interesting things about the Canadian market now is that serious culture, in fact, works quite well. You take a nose dive, probably more often, trying to do the commercial stuff. We have certainly lost much more money trying to be commercial than we have ever lost being cultural.

Why?

I think when you fall, you fall big. You do a big printing and you pay a big advance and you blow a bundle on marketing, and if it all comes back [i.e., if the books are returned unsold], you can really take a bath. Which is why I think publishing has changed as it has. 'Cause if you're gonna publish a Stephen King, you have to have big sales to fall back on when you screw up. And you're gonna screw up half the time. I think we have made some mistakes trying to be commercial simply because our instincts perhaps aren't as crass as they ought to be.

On the other hand, we've done some very successful commerce. I'm thinking of a book like *Wolves*. this is a book you've never heard of. It's not a bad book, and it's sold a hundred and twenty thousand copies around the world in seven languages in less than two years. Now there's a whole series of clones. I mean that's pretty commercial publishing. But, in fact, the text is serious. And it's not a bad text. But, as I say, I'd like to think that we're respected for our standards, the standards of the craft. The editing, design, production.

Didn't you do something recently with the University of Washington Press?

Well, we have, I think, one of the great horse-trading relationships in North American publishing with the University of Washington Press. We copublish ten to twenty-five books a year, and we've been doing it for twenty years. I mean it's millions of dollars over the years. And certain parts of our list are virtually shaped jointly. That is, the Northwest Coast and Native Studies stuff. Almost always, they take coeditions of our books and we take coeditions of theirs. It's a relationship that I treasure. It's a wonderful relationship. Twice a year we sit down for a day and we go through an agenda of thirty to forty items, and we do everything from shaping books together to neither of us accepting them unless the other one does, to simply buying and selling rights. Not rights so much as coeditions. And the advantage of that is we get the runoff. So instead of us doing three or four thousand copies of a beautiful or complex book for Canada, we do six or seven thousand for North America. We really like the people and it's great fun, and it's what publishing used to be. And it's very practical. I mean, it works.

How would you evaluate your career at this point?

I think at the end of the day, for all the agonies, and publishing is a very—I don't have to tell you—a very difficult business, particularly when you're taking significant risks which are into six and seven figures, I think it's an enormously satisfying business. I still, I must say, at my weakest and most tired, I can look at a book I'm proud of and it still is worthwhile. When you lose that, you get out of the business. But I think you're gonna find in this country that you've got all of these publishers that have built these companies, we're all the same age—

Karl pointed that out to me too.

Karl knows. We've talked about this. And this whole generation of Canadian publishers, we are all within five years of one another. We have all paid the price of sweat equity and personal sacrifice. Some people, like Karl, more than others. And we're all getting to our late forties, early fifties. And I think what's going to have to happen in Canada is what happened in New York in the '60s where people said "Whoa, what do we do now? We can't work twenty hours a day anymore. What are we gonna do about our families? How are we going to retire? What are we going to do about estate tax?" I think you're going to see a restructuring of the business simply because we're going to have to go through something publishing in this country hasn't really done yet. Which is go from the first generation to the second.

Of course, what New York did, which changed US publishing very quickly, was go public.

My understanding is that for the most part American publishers in the '30s, '40s, '50s built out of cash flow. They didn't have bank loans. They didn't use the banks significantly. And when the time came where the pressures of competition were beginning to force banks to come into play, a lot of people wouldn't take the risks. They wouldn't risk their homes. Arthur Wang actually said to me, "We were going to have to get a collateral mortgage, and we said we can't live with that much stress." I mean, Jesus! I don't know a Canadian publisher who hasn't risked everything!

So there was a concern about bank capital, which was a change.

370

And I think companies like RCA, in the case of Random House, having deep pockets—I mean, to me, of that kind of publishing house, I think Random House, the Random group, has done as well as you can do. I know there've been problems, but I find it amazing that Knopf has now gone to its third-generation publisher, and it's still an amazing house.

Knopf has kind of lost out, in terms of prestige, to Farrar Straus, though.
It's interesting you say that, because I know Farrar Straus is the noblest of the independents.

In New York.
Yeah. I mean New York. Sorry.

Well, there is that new generation of publishers like Graywolf and Coffee House.
Yeah. Here I go, typically thinking of New York. But I like New York and I know a lot of people there. I would have said under Sonny Mehta Knopf was coming back. But it's still pretty commercial. Certainly the Knopf list, I think, is better than it's been in years. And I've heard other people say this. I mean the good fiction, Jesus! And the look of the books, the graphic quality, the jackets—I just shake my head. They do so many things so well. But you said the American houses went public—

Yeah. I'm using Random House as an example of that, where Cerf complained that he lost control.
Well, all I know about Bennett Cerf is I read *At Random*, and one hears gossip. But my understanding is that Bennett Cerf regretted having sold it. Because, indeed, he never really got accustomed to the lack of control. In this country, a couple of things are different from the States. No publishing house in this country has ever successfully gone public. Primarily, I think, because the bottom line has never been good enough. And the Canadian market is much more conservative. The mentality, when it comes to speculative investment, is much more

conservative than in the States. You wouldn't know that on the penny stock market here, but generally speaking....

And something that's really been different, and continues to be different, is that you haven't had the largish media groups looking at buying up the independent publishers. Because, on the whole, they have such a bad business reputation. The bottom line is never good enough to really make it attractive to any kind of hard-nosed business person. So I find it interesting to wonder, and I guess I'm going to be in the middle of this, one way or another, what happens now?

What do you anticipate?

I think you'll see mergers and acquisitions. That doesn't mean that we've made any decision, because, in fact, I cannot imagine losing independence. The minute you sell, or the minute you get significant outside—the first thing that happens is you sit around a board table and the pragmatists are saying "Why, these publishers don't know shit!"

Karl made the point that it was his fear that there are not younger people coming up to take his place.

That's another opinion we share. In fact, I would argue that that's the case with nonfiction writers, as well, in this country. If you look at this generation, and you look at what's below, there's nothing like the kinds of individuals with the same kind of motivation and willingness to take risks. And whether some of that was all of us rebelling, all of us growing out of the '60s—

I think this industry, at least in this country, has been very, very short-sighted in its thinking. We should have four or five bright young kids around here, making trouble. And we don't. I think, perhaps, it's for a whole combination of reasons. One is people are more aware of the dollar. You know, they want more than publishing can provide financially. I think it's tougher to get into the business. Although, is it really? You can still have ten thousand bucks and publish books you believe in, and that can still work.

What about people like Brian Lam from Arsenal Pulp Press, and

Michelle Benjamin from Polestar? These are young people. Brian's only thirty. Michelle's in her twenties. They knew what they wanted to do before they ever graduated from university.

They literally wanted to go into book publishing?

Yeah.

That's astounding!

[Laughing.] *I thought so too.*

Although I got hooked on books and the process of making them, the mechanics of making them, I certainly would never have imagined that I was going to end up in book publishing. I just can't imagine—'cause I find kids so practical and cynical—they know about book publishing, at least in this country. I don't know. The fact that we don't see the kids, is that just because we're now—I'm forty-eighty— is that just because we're old and crotchety? Are they there? Do we just not see them? Or is there indeed that kind of gap? Is she that young?

Michelle? She's pretty young. I don't think she's thirty yet. Rolf Maurer is only thirty-seven. New Star Books. So if Karl says he doesn't know who's coming up—

Yeah.

But I asked some people at COSMEP if they could think of anybody younger than we are who is doing these things, and they couldn't.

What's interesting is, in this country, one can look at Expo '67 in Montreal as a cultural symbol. I mean it really was following 1967 that the whole generation of feisty Canadian publishers came into being. There were the old-line houses, four or five of them, and mostly branch plants. But Tundra Books—1967, Talon—'67, '68, Oberon Press in Ottawa, New Press, House of Anansi, Douglas & McIntyre and many others, many of which are gone now, all of these people have gone through the business together. And there has been nothing like that range of houses underneath. There're always new houses. And there're

373

always young idealists.

But moving forward as a generation—is that what you and Karl are talking about?

Well, I think there was a moment in time when a whole batch of people got into publishing and started houses, and because of the grants have been able to, if not prosper, at least grow. And I don't think there's anything equivalent underneath. But I'm open to be told that it's just me being old. Enough babble.

Jean-Louis Brindamour
Strawberry Hill Press

"Oh, who really knows why? I mean, what motivates any of us to do anything that we're interested in?"

Jean-Louis Brindamour founded Strawberry Hill Press in San Francisco in 1974, publishing his first book in 1977. The press got its name because Brindamour was in a bookstore in San Francisco's financial district one day, thumbing through a book on the history of San Francisco, and "I saw the name Strawberry Hill. Well, Strawberry Hill is a little hill on a little island in a lake in Golden Gate Park, and nobody knows that's its name. Nobody. I had no idea. But the minute I spotted it in the book, I thought, That's our name!" He did not know at the time, "because I wasn't that intellectual," that in the eighteenth century Horace Walpole had a Strawberry Hill Press on his estate. "And so collectors today pay tens of thousands of dollars for volumes from his Strawberry Hill Press."

In 1990, Brindamour moved the press to Portland, Oregon "for the lifestyle, basically. It's a lot less pressured. It's a lot nicer, actually. And it's a hell of a lot less expensive." Though he is a fifth-generation native of San Francisco, he found when he moved to Portland, that he is rooted there also. "I knew it, sort of, but never paid attention to it. My maternal grandmother was from a Portland pioneer family. There used to be a downtown building named after—there's a section of the city, Raleigh Hills, named after—I'm a Raleigh on my mother's mother's side. And then there's a Raleigh Street downtown. It's just kind of interesting that I came here and I found this city and decided I liked it and it was only after I moved here that I began to remember that I have roots here. And I have relatives here who I'm sort of getting to know a little bit about. They live way up in the hills."

Brindamour and his partner conduct the business of the press out of their house. It is a large, high-ceilinged house built in the first

375

part of the century. On the main floor is a living room and a dining room and a butler's pantry and a kitchen and a foyer. Upstairs are four bedrooms of which two are used for business and two remain as bedrooms. Then there is an attic and a full basement and a carriage house. We did the interview in the living room late in the morning on a sunny day at the beginning of June.

I'd met Brindamour at the 1992 American Booksellers Association conference in Anaheim a couple of weeks earlier and warned him then that I would be calling to arrange an interview. When we met again at his house in early June we began almost immediately to talk. Soon, even before I had set up the recorder, and to my delight, he had taken control of the conversation and was running with it.

...I don't want to reach seventy or eighty until I'm, oh God, I'm considered an old fart who just hangs on in the corner somewhere. This is—this is not—it's much more than my livelihood. The least part of it is my livelihood. Nobody in his right mind would go into publishing to make money. Well, that's not true. There are people who are very smart and they pick a niche. And if you pick a niche in publishing, you know what you're talking about. Then you can, in fact, make a whole lot of money out of it. Most of us don't really do that.

Of course, since we are not nonprofit, there is no possibility of our getting grants or assistance from anybody. I mean, even.... Well, it's very hard to get a bank loan. You try going to a bank and telling them that what you will give them as collateral are a hundred thousand books in a warehouse. They'd laugh you out the door. I mean, that's absurd from their—what they want is gold, platinum, re- —well, it used to be realistic. Today, no, because the realistic market is in such a bad situation. So banks are not a place that a traditional-type publisher can go to. There are exceptions, of course, but they're rare.

So if you look at our colleagues in the business—again, I mention my classes at Berkeley, and remember, I taught there for fourteen years. And I have all kinds of case histories of former students who mortgaged everything they had. Fortunately, in those cases it worked out okay. I'm thinking, for example, of a couple who are very dear friends of mine, who had no background whatever in publishing but an enormous desire to be in it. Oh, who really knows why? I mean, what motivates any of us to do anything that we're interested in?

And I guess what happened was they got enthused. Enthusiasm is a very dangerous thing; you have to be very careful with it. I'm one of those people who is normally enormously enthusiastic and my enthusiasms carry over to other people. It's kind of like being a charismatic minister or something or other. You can get people turned on very easily. The problem is then you can't get them turned off again. And you have to be very careful that, you know, it's okay if they're young enough to carry it through and if they lose everything they can still go ahead. If, on the other hand, these are their life's savings and they're nearing retirement, well, you gotta be really careful. I mean it's.... Anyway, one carries a lot of guilt, I think, with this kind of business.

See, it's a matter of image. One creates an image. Sometimes one intends to, sometimes one doesn't really intend to, it just happens.

And I guess part of the problem with all of this is you struggle and you hope and you pray a whole lot, if you believe in prayer—I mean, you mentioned the earlier recession in '83, '84. Now we came through that very well. No problem at all. We started—I guess our first book came out in '77. And we've been very lucky. We had one book that sold more than a million copies. It's out of print now. It's called *The Book of Internal Exercises*, by Dr. Stephen Chang.

And by the way, you probably need to know—see, what happens, I'm mentioning niche marketing and also image. You create an image and if you go out of that image you often ask for the trouble you get. Now we started out saying that we were a totally nonfiction publisher, with our strengths being, we thought—and we were right, actually—health and nutrition, biography, history, self-help, inspiration—not religion; there's a difference, from my perspective—cookbooks, a very big area for us, or was. But we were not doing any fiction, we weren't doing children's books, we weren't doing poetry. We did a children's book which, thank God, I just sold to a major publisher at the ABA. Because we're not a children's publisher; we shouldn't be doing them.

And we do fiction. And we've been extraordinarily lucky with our fiction. We've gotten very, very strong attention nationally and internationally. But I want to get away from it. I want to get back to our roots of nonfiction. First of all, fiction costs a great deal more money in terms of what you pour into it for marketing than does nonfiction. And the financial rewards are much more tenuous. You just don't know. You don't know if you'll make it or not.

Now I founded the company in 1974, but that was just a shell. And, as I said, we didn't bring out our first book until '77. Now our first book is still very much in print. Here we are in 1992 and it's a book that we have done very well with. It is a book called *Pinoy: The First Wave*. It's a book of oral histories about the first wave of Filipino immigrants. What happened is the minute we brought that book out we realized there had to be three books because there were three distinct waves of Philippine emigration to the United States. Well, then the author died. The author was my very dear friend and that's probably why we published the book. He and his wife, in the days when I went to San Francisco State and eked out an existence, used to feed me, partly because the wife's brother was my classmate and he would bring me home. Maybe that's how one repays these things; I don't really know.

So we published the book. Dr. Vallangca died. And then his wife decided—his wife is quite a bit younger than he and a very good writer, as a matter of fact. If you look at his book and then you look at the book that followed, which is her book—very, very different in style and form. Because Roberto was a very simple man. I don't mean not well-educated; he just was very simple in his ways.

Caridad Vallangca did the second book, which is called *The Second Wave*, and has much, much, much, much more thrust toward the women who emigrated from the Philippines. Very important for us. Her book is oral history but it's much more than oral history. She delves deeply and rather scholarly into the immigration laws and their meaning and so on. But there's a third book, and she hasn't written it yet, and she's been interviewing people for several years. In fact, while you and

I were at the ABA she had gone to Houston to do yet another interview. These are people, of course, in the third wave. So we brought out, from 1977 to 1992, two out of three books which we have projected, and God only knows when the third book will come out. But the topic won't be complete from our perspective until we bring out the third book.

But going back, we did very well with our earlier cookbooks. Now we had two by the same author. Her name was Josephine Araldo. Her first book, *Cooking With Josephine*, we sold well over eight hundred thousand copies, and then made a terrible mistake. We were doing so well financially that when Doubleday came along and wanted to buy the rights from us and offered what seemed like a large sum of money, we fell for it and we sold them the rights. Well, they brought out a fifty-thousan-copy first printing and they did a second printing of another fifty thousand copies a month or two later. And that was great, that was terrific, that's a hundred thousand copies.

And then the whole thing died. And they kept our rights tied up for eight years. The book was out of print, we could do nothing about it. In the meantime, I had Josephine on, oh, almost every major television show you could imagine, including, oh, who's that woman in Los Angeles who plays golf and used to be the lover of, oh...I just can't think of her name. She's a singer and—Dinah Shore. Yeah.

Well, this is past tense. Josephine died about two years ago at age ninety-four or -five, I think. Well, the point was we brought out Josephine's first book. It did so well that we brought out a second book called *Sounds From Josephine's Kitchen* which even had a record attached to it, sold not as many but about seven hundred and fifty thousand copies of that, planned to bring out a third book but never did for very confused and mixed reasons which I don't want to go into.

It's interesting, I guess, if you go back and you look at how you started out. That is, Strawberry Hill Press. Like almost everybody, we started with one book. And then we had two books, then three books. We made a lot of mistakes. Had a lot of friends in publishing every-where. So when publishers in the east heard that Jean-Louis Brindamour was starting his own company they kind of came out of the woodwork and said, "Oh, let us help you." Not with money, you see. They were perfectly willing to allow me to spend my own money, and you probably want to know that my partner and I have put well over two million dollars into this company thus far.

In any event, a house in New Jersey called. Lodgepole Books. [The name and location of this company have been changed for purposes of this book.] They approached us.

Didn't they do military books?

Right. And it's very interesting that you noticed that because we didn't pay much attention to that. That's exactly correct. General Lodgepole founded it and it's part of a miniconglomerate and a very dear friend of mine was its head at that time. His name is Claude Anders [not his real name]. He has since left publishing but he was very well known in publishing in those days and doing a wonderful job with Lodgepole. And Claude approached us and said, "Look," when he heard—this is before we had any books, "we know your background and all of that and we'd like to be the exclusive distributor for Strawberry Hill."

Well, that was wonderful. That was great. And then we didn't have to be concerned about that side of things. That's what we thought, you see. What we didn't realize was that, in essence, what we were doing was we were selling off our souls. And we were. The way it worked—I don't want you to misunderstand here, I owe an enormous debt to Claude Anders. I don't think I owe any debt to Lodgepole at all, but an enormous debt to Claude because he believed in us at a time when nobody at bookstores knew of us. Know of us? How could they know of us? We didn't exist yet.

So, to have a sizable publisher—at that time they were doing probably four or five million dollars a year; again, we're talking 1976, '77, something like that—that was a very sizable publisher for us who had nothing yet except a bank account and some ideas. But what they did was they tied us in with a printer, a very nice printer, and also did our warehousing and shipping. What in essence was happening was like a funnel. At one end we pumped in the money. At the other end whatever was left they got. And, in fact, the reality was we didn't see any money for years. But it was always for a reason. Or no cash. Which meant that we had to keep pumping in money. Well, in those days it wasn't so bad. In those days I had a whole lot of money.

So at the beginning it was great. When you started out and you had no books and then one and then two and so on, it was really wonderful. I mean I would fly to New York and Miami and Chicago for sales conferences and give these terrific—what I thought were terrific—sales pitches on my titles. It was something I'd already been doing for many years before that anyway, but for others until then. And then the books began to sell. And that was great, that was all quite wonderful.

But after awhile we began to realize that our books and their books were totally different, and really diametrically opposed. See, their books weren't just military history. They were also how to kill and skin a deer. How to trap animals. How to get the most out of your hunting and so on. In other words, they were books about killing, et cetera. Exactly the reverse of what our books were about: love and happiness and...and...fulfillment. So we began to realize—I mean you would go into a bookstore and you would have people say to you, "I won't buy your books!" and you'd say, "Why not?" "Well! Because! They're in Lodgepole's catalogue, and there's a book about how to kill a poor, defenseless, little rabbit—"

How to skin Bambi.
That's kind of the idea. And then also, at that time—this was—I don't remember how many years we were with them, but several years, in any event—but then Claude, for a whole lot of reasons, was getting ready to leave that company. And he was the key for us, of course. So we went for quite a few years—we built a very good reputation as a very dependable publisher, particularly of books on how-to, self-help, health-and-nutrition, et cetera. It must have been around 1980, '81, something like that, that we began to realize, "Hell, we don't get any money from them!" In any event, around 1980 or '81 is when we decided that we needed to cut the umbilical cord and, in fact, not be distributed by anybody other than ourselves.

381

And that was very interesting, in fact, because in several incarnations, if you will, of the jobs that I had I was affiliated with various selling groups. I'm speaking of people who sell books, independent reps primarily, throughout the country. Wherever I went I sort of took them on again with the company that I came in to run. Well, many of those independent repping groups were part of Lodgepole's selling background. It didn't work for us when we went independent. I don't know why. I've never quite understood why. All of those people have remained my friends till today. But none of them, absolutely not a one of them, has ever distributed us since we went independent. They just didn't want to...I guess. Of course, a lot of time has passed now and I don't really—I'm not sure I remember it all accurately.

But anyway, for whatever set of reasons, we did not go out on our own and have those people still there representing us. So we really didn't have sales people. What we had now was Baker and Taylor, which has always been our major wholesaler, and at one time we did probably ninety percent of our business through Baker and Taylor. That's changed quite a lot, of late. And that has to do with the changes that they've gone through, that the industry itself has gone through, the times in which we've lived, et cetera. So we began creating our own accounts, selling by direct mail to bookstores and libraries, working with wholesalers.

It's interesting because I'm a funny person; I'm a very trusting human being. I believe a shake of the hand is all that's necessary. I still believe it. Absolutely. Even though I've been slapped in the face several times. But also I've had all kinds of experiences where it's worked.

So we got into a real brouhaha with Ingram, which, of course, is the other major wholesaler. I'm not quite sure how it all happened. I think actually some of it was left over from the Lodgepole days. But whatever it was, they ended up owing us, oh, I don't know, seventeen thousand dollars, I think it was. And refused to pay it. And so I took them to court. And I got my money. And then they wanted to continue distributing us. And I said, "No, thank you. I never wish you to distribute my line again. Never, never, never. I don't care how much I lose. I will never deal with you again." And we don't. Today

382

we don't deal with them. And I don't think it matters a whole lot. For a while it probably did.

We've gone through, as everybody does, changes of policy, sometimes because you didn't think things out too carefully to begin with, sometimes because the times have changed and have required them. A major one for us has been the discount and return policy. I began to question why—under Lodgepole, for example, we saw that we had tens of thousands of books that were returned from accounts, for which we got these little pieces of paper from Lodgepole saying "credit memo," "credit memo." Well, that was wonderful for them and terrible for us. It meant that what we were doing was selling books. But we weren't selling books. We were sort of giving books, or lending books. And if, for any set of reasons, somebody didn't want them anymore, well, they just sent them back to us and wrote it off. That meant we were the people who were stuck with books that really were nonsalable.

What I mean by that is the reality of a return. See, if you look at any publisher's return policy, it says very clearly that you can only return within a certain time frame. You must also ask permission and you must give background information as to the invoice on which it originally appeared, all that sort of thing. Which, by the way, most of the industry ignores. When people want to return books they simply return them.

But there's another key that's vital to me as a smaller publisher. And that is, they're supposed to be returned in resalable condition. The reality is that ninety percent of the time they're not in resalable condition. See, "resalable" to me means if I go to my warehouse and I look at my books and they have nicks in them, or the color on the cover has been rubbed off, then those aren't resalable. How could I ask you to pay me six ninety-five or nine ninety-five or whatever it is for something that I wouldn't pay that same price for? So it was very simple, very straightforward and simple. We—I guess this must have been about 1983 or so—we just issued a new policy. It was based on discount. If you got a discount of fifty percent or more, which is what you have to give wholesalers, then you couldn't return the books.

383

Well, our business took a nose-dive. We went from—at this point we were probably at about six hundred and fifty thousand, seven hundred thousand dollars a year, I guess. In other words, we kept increasing our sales year after year. It was always on an uptrend. And all of a sudden it took a nose-dive. And Baker and Taylor, of course, who was our major wholesaler, simply wouldn't order books unless they actually had orders in hand for them. So our business with them went, for a while, for at least a year, to nothing. Absolutely nothing. Over time, it balanced.

See, one of the most important facets here is how badly do people want your books? And the wholesaler isn't the key. It's the consumer who is the key. Well, if you were lucky, as we considered we were—we had people like Josephine and Dr. Chang whose books were getting enormous attention, not only in the media but also through word of mouth. Well, Baker and Taylor can't not order your books if they've got people clamoring for them.

As I say, the first year of that new policy we barely breathed. I mean we just struggled along. And, as I said, our sales were dashed to maybe one hundred and fifty thousand dollars from six hundred and fifty thousand dollars. It's a huge amount because, of course, your costs are fixed costs. What you're paying the warehouse for insurance, you know, all those costs that most people never think about but I have to think about all the time because I pay them every day. Those are the things that, if you don't have enough money to survive, then you're dead. You're really in bad shape. Anyway, eventually it began picking up. I guess we hit our first million-dollar year in 1989.

By the way, I should explain something here. I mentioned "million-dollar year." I really referred to our own sales, because, of course, like all publishers, there are other sources of income. A lot of our books are in other editions elsewhere. But we are always the originator of those books, which means that we always get a piece of that income. And so we have a lot of foreign editions of our books.

There are a lot of English language editions in England of a number of our titles. Interestingly, it's all nonfiction. We have Israeli editions and Danish and Swedish editions, I think some French and

Italian and Japanese. And then we also have other American editions, mass market and even just lesser-priced, literally cheaper, and I mean poorer quality, editions of our own books.

There's one book of ours, for example—ah, that book is a godsend—a book on reflexology called *Mirror of the Body*. And there are three American editions besides our own. And then there's an Israeli edition. And a British edition. Fortunately those other editions also supply us with cash.

It's interesting. That particular kind of cash always comes at the time we most need it. You know, if one didn't believe in some higher being who guided you, you'd sort of have to when, you know, you're ready to cry your eyes out and then there's the mail, and in the mail is a check you never even thought about from the Israelis for six hundred bucks or whatever it is. Anyway, it's an interesting business.

I think you need to direct this, 'cause I'm.... Do you want to hear about why do I publish? You ask the questions.

Okay. You went to college?

Yeah. I started at Georgetown School of Foreign Service. I've gone to so many colleges, you don't really want to know. Let's put it this way: I finished my undergraduate work at San Francisco State in, of all things, drama and, well, let's see, what's my BS in? Yeah, drama, I think. Anyway, then I went to Columbia University where I got both my master's and my doctorate in speech therapy. That's my field. And that's when I got into publishing.

Like many people, I.... See, I had two choices: I could have my parents pay for me—my parents were very wealthy people—or I could be what I wanted to be, independent, and manage my life for myself.

Anyway, when I went to Columbia I had to—how was I going to pay for my tuition and live? Anyway, I worked at that time as a clerk-typist in a place called International Social Service, and there was this guy whose name I don't remember at the moment but he's now an Anglican bishop. And he worked at the desk next to me and we used to talk about how was I going to get my tuition at Columbia. And he said,

"Look, go to Columbia University Press. They'll hire anybody." That was exactly what he said, and I tell all my students that and they all laugh.

So I did something that I had never really done in my life. I'd never been pushy. So I went to Columbia University Press and I applied for a job, any job, of course. You know, what could I do? Type and file. And there was this wonderful woman. Her name was Jana—I don't know how to spell it but it was pronounced Ja'nuh—Anderson and she was head of personnel at that time. This was 1960. She was a very nice lady and she would say to me, "Gee, we don't have any jobs for you."

Anyway, I started calling her every day. Every single day I would call her and say, "Jana, did you find a job for me yet?" And I still am convinced that the only reason I really got a job was she didn't want to have me call one more time. Anyway, one day I called and she said, kind of sighingly, "Yeah, we've got a job for you as a clerk-typist."

So I went to work for a wonderful man named Henry Wiggins. And Henry Wiggins was quite a legend in the publishing industry. He was the assistant director of Columbia University Press. And, really, in university presses it's often the assistant director who really runs everything. And that was the case with Henry Wiggins. We called him Wiggy. Of course, to me—I thought he was ancient. Actually, he was probably no more than fifty. But then I was in my mid-twenties, so that's how we tend to look at people.

So I went to work for Wiggy as a clerk-typist. Columbia University Press was an interesting place. When people left, rather than go outside and hire somebody else to fill the job, they would often look within and simply hand the job, or part of the job, to somebody who was already there as another one of your functions. Well, anyway, I was very lucky, and Wiggy took a great liking to me and kind of guided me through the press. And then also its editor-in-chief at that time was a wonderful man named Dr. Bridgewater. William Bridgewater. He's now dead. And Wiggy died about a year ago in an accident. It was a very sad thing that happened.

Anyway, at Columbia University Press, if you were interested in the business, and I found I was fascinated by it—I had no idea, by the

386

way, that I was going to be in publishing. Remember, I was working on my master's and doctorate. But if you were interested in the work, then people encouraged you and they shared with you. And, fortunately for me, the assistant director's office was kind of a central body for everything else. Nothing really happened without the assistant director's office being involved. For example, all contracts came out of our office. All contracts were filed in our office. I remember to this day this enormous green safe with double doors which only I and Wiggy had the combination to. You would open it up and it was simply filled with drawers that were filled with contracts, everything filed by number and all this kind of stuff. No monies could be spent without the approval of the assistant director's office. So you began to see how money worked in publishing.

All rights—and there's a key here involving me; I'll come back to this in a moment—all rights were handled through the office. It was a very small thing at that time. It became enormous under me but, as I say, I'll explain later.

Accountings came through our office. Virtually all editorial correspondence came through our office. So I was privy to virtually all of the facets of publishing. And I began to realize what a wonderfully exciting business this was. And it was just in the days when university presses were beginning, only beginning, to realize that the monies that had kept them going for years and years were no longer available to them.

Remember that in the old days of university publishing virtually every scholar got some kind of a stipend or an award for his or her book to be published, whether you're talking Margaret Mead or Franz Boas or whomever. But, as I say, this was just beginning to change. Those monies within the departments weren't available anymore, or if they were, they were much lessened. And so university presses were having to face the reality that they had to sell their books, it wasn't enough just to bring them out and give them away to people. And so that's when I began first to see the phenomenon of the trade paperback coming out of the university press, as I say, starting in 1960.

Well, anyway, what happened for me was I had an innate

affinity for part of the business that I didn't know anything about, it was just within me. What I began to see was here was a university press that had been publishing for a hundred and fifty or two hundred years, whatever it was, a very long time. It had a wonderful backlist, an incredible backlist. I mentioned Margaret Mead and Franz Boas because they were part of the backlist. And it was dead. It was sitting on shelves, books that were out of print for years and nobody was doing anything with them.

When I say "books" I mean the rights to these books were still owned by the university press, still controlled by the university press. But the books themselves were long out of print. And yet these were materials that many, many people still wanted. It happened to be the beginning of the phenomenon of scholarly reprinting. You may remember there was a whole slew of companies who came along, some just kind of out of the woodwork, some became very well known, some not too well known. But they were the scholarly reprinters.

There were thirty or forty such companies, some of which became enormous in size. Academic, for example, which is now part of Harcourt Brace Jovanovich. Anyway, a lot of them merged with others, and some, by the way, merged and it didn't work out and they bought themselves back later.

But the point I'm trying to make is it happened to be a phenomenon and lasted for about fifteen years. And I was very lucky. I was in the center of it. Partly it was because nobody else at Columbia University Press had any interest in this, and I did. I thought it was fascinating. And I would go to what was called the master library up in the attics of our building, which I think was in the—yeah, it was the Journalism Building at that time; it isn't in that building any more. And I would look at these tens of thousands of titles. And I began to perceive which of our titles could be sold off to somebody else and bring us in money. I eventually created a situation—you have to understand, I was still just a clerk-typist, but I kept adding all these new jobs and I kept learning about the editorial department and contracts and so on. And Wiggy took me under his wing and really guided me through all of this. And at the time that I left Columbia University Press, which was in

1967....

I got my Ph.D. in '65 and I taught—what was happening then was I was teaching at Teachers College, which of course was part of Columbia, and still working at the press. Now I was working at the press not for money but because I loved it. It was just really great. And I just kind of woke up one day and realized I don't want to teach speech therapy, I want to—I am a publisher, that's what I am. I had found my niche.

Well, anyway, at the time I left Columbia I had ensured that for the next twenty years it would get a minimum of a half million dollars a year from its old books that nobody seemed to want. One of the ironies of this is years later I would go to the ABA and meet its then sales manager—I think he's retired now; his name is Carl Hansen—and Carl would say to me, "You've ruined our press." He would say this partly with truth and partly with a joke behind it. And I'd say to him, "What do you mean I've ruined your press?" And he'd say, "Well, because you sold off our entire backlist so we can't even touch those books any more." And I said, "Yeah, but, Carl, look at all the money you made out of it." He said, "Well, yeah, that's true, but...." So, anyway.

Then what happened was one day Wiggy came to me and he said, "You don't know it but Xerox Corporation has been watching you for some time." This was in '67. He said that Xerox Corporation had been watching me and they had approached him to get him to talk me into leaving Columbia University Press and joining them. Now I don't know what my salary was at Columbia but I don't think it was more than three thousand dollars a year. It seems to me that's what it was. And Xerox was offering ten thousand dollars a year. So that was an enormous increase. But I didn't want it. I couldn't imagine going any other place. As far as I was concerned, Columbia was where I was going to stay for the rest of my life.

So Wiggy sat me down and he said, "Look, what you don't know is anything about business." He said, "You only know what you've learned here and what you've learned in your academic training." And he said, "That's what happened to me." He said, "I came here...." I guess he went there in the days of the Depression, and in the days of the

389

Depression if you had a job you stayed with your job. And then the war came along and he went off to the Marines and then after the Marines he came back to Columbia and, as he said, "I never worked anywhere else in my life. And it was a mistake." He said, "I love it here and I'll die here, probably." But he said, "My suggestion to you is go out, take this job, take whatever other jobs come along, and learn about all of the business." And he said, "If you want to come back to scholarly publishing some day, then come back to it with all of this background behind you."

So I went with Xerox and it was very interesting. I was with them for a year and a half and I traveled all over the world for them. I was called "Manager of Publisher Relations"; not public relations, but "publisher relations." Basically, my job was to meet publishers all over the world and tell them what a wonderful company Xerox was.

You have to understand, in those days Xerox was buying up every publishing company it could get its hands on. Of course it later divested itself of all of them. But I was supposed to tell publishers how wonderful Xerox was, which it was in some ways, and that it really wasn't out to monopolize the industry, which was a lie because it was. It was getting ready to buy Bowker; it had not bought it yet, it was just in the process. And that, by the way, if you had a project that you were working on and it didn't seem to be coming together for you, why not let me take a look at it and see if I couldn't perhaps transfer it over from you to one of the Xerox-owned publishing companies and make money for you and them? Well, it was quite interesting. I went to London and Paris and all over the United States.

And I dealt with—I don't know if you remember, well, there is a modern version but it's a totally different thing—*Vanity Fair*, the original *Vanity Fair*, the magazine. It was a mirror of American culture for the period that it covered. Virtually every person who affected Western culture was covered. They either wrote for or were written about in *Vanity Fair* before they were famous people. Anyway, it mirrored American culture for the period of time that it covered, and of course it went defunct just at the time of the Depression.

In any event, one of the projects that I ended up picking up, but

I don't remember from whom we picked it up, was a complete reprint of *Vanity Fair* in hardbound volumes. So this was twenty-eight or thirty-six volumes or something or other on very expensive coated stock. And there were two so-called editions of this book. One was bound in silver and black and the other was bound in purple and something or other. And one of these bindings was for the designers market. I mean people who were designers. And the other was for libraries.

Well, anyway, I had to go to Ann Arbor, which was where—I worked for Xerox Education Division but it was paid by University Microfilms out of Ann Arbor. And they'd just bought University Microfilms from Mr. Powers, its creator, and of course they don't own that anymore either. It's interesting as you see how things have happened in our lives.

But in any event, while I was based in New York I had to spend one week out of every month in Ann Arbor. And the big cheeses from Rochester would fly in and, of course, I was the lowly person on the totem pole, but I would always sit in at these board meetings where everybody would talk about why we aren't doing this and they would talk about what they called their "onion theory." Their onion theory at Xerox was that all onions have layers and you peel it off one layer at a time, except there's always more underneath. Anyway, it was great talk, actually. The reality was very little happened.

And just to give you an aside here, here I was paid ten thousand dollars a year, which was a lot of money, at least to me, and, actually, for 1967 it was a lot of money. And I didn't have a business card the whole time I was with the company. I would go to London and meet the chairman of the board of Grolier and have to write my name on a scrap of paper. It was very embarrassing, actually. Yet I had a 3400 copy machine or something or other. The day I started I was told—I guess I asked for a piece of carbon paper and I was told, "No carbons are used in this company." So I had this very big office, and a very nice secretary whose name I almost remember, and this enormous copying machine. Just enormous. That was all for me. There was nobody else to use it. I always found this very wasteful but amusing.

Anyway, so you go to Ann Arbor—and I'm using the *Vanity Fair* as an example—they would complain about how they had spent a million dollars, pulling all of this material together, getting it printed and bound and so on, and they weren't selling it. The answer was so obvious. And I would just sit there and try to say something, but it was kind of like a little kid—you raise your hand and they'd say, "Go ahead and go to the bathroom." I wasn't raising my hand to go to the bathroom; I knew the answer. Finally one day somebody said, "Well, what is it, kid?" And I said, "Well, I know why you're not selling these books." I said, "You've got these very high price tags on them, and that's not your problem. Your problem is you've got a run of I think it's twenty-six years of magazines and they're primarily for research and reference purposes, but you have no index. And they're of no value to anybody without an index. Who is going to spend that kind of money?" So everybody kind of looked at me for a moment and they said, "Ooh. Oh, we never thought of that. So how much money do you want to make an index?" So I went back to my office and I figured it out and I came back and I said, "Fifty thousand dollars. Give me fifty thousand dollars and I will give you, camera-ready, an index, and then I betcha you'll make millions." So they gave me fifty thousand dollars.

Now, I wasn't going to spend my fifty thousand dollars on hiring people. The first thing I did was I called Conde Nast who were the publishers of *Vanity Fair* and from whom we had licensed these rights and I said, "Look, these aren't selling and you're not going to make any money unless they do sell. So I need some help. What I need is an office and some of your staff members that I'm not going to pay to help us do research." So they said, "Sure. When you come back to New York we'll give you an office." So they gave me an office. I then found a wonderful woman through the New York Public Library. They recommended her. We hired her to oversee the putting-together. And everything else was done on a volunteer basis; I didn't pay anybody except that one woman.

So, I don't know, six months later we had an indexed volume. And that was the key. And it sold both sets, and they sold them all out. So this is what I did. I was kind of a trouble shooter. And it was great fun. I loved it because I had a boss who never had any idea of what I did, never asked me, left me alone all the time, and all he was concerned about was that I was happy and did what I did.

And then one day I just kind of woke up and thought, "Oh, this is very interesting, but I don't even have business cards." I guess what had happened, I had gone to—I am not a drinker and I'm not a smoker and so if I go to cocktail parties I stand against the wall like a wallflower. And I'm also very shy, though most people don't know that because I talk a blue streak.

Well, anyway, I was at this cocktail party of publishing people and standing against the wall, and here was this very distinguished gentleman standing against the wall too. And he sort of turned to me, he was in his late sixties, early seventies, I guess, and he introduced himself as Leonard Davidow. And it meant nothing to me and he asked me what I did and I told him I was with Xerox but I was thinking of leaving and he said—just out of the blue, at a cocktail party; remember, I hadn't spoken to this man for more than ten minutes—he said, "Well, why don't you come to Chicago as my assistant?" And I just kind of looked at him and I said, "But I barely even got your name yet. What do you do?" So he told me they did dictionaries and bibles and encyclopedias and cookbooks and—

Anyway, before I left the party I'd agreed, yes, I'd join the company as his assistant. So I told Xerox who were very unhappy to see me go, and I hired a U-Haul truck and I took my paintings and my books and my cat and I drove to Chicago. This was all on a handshake. And I got to Chicago. And all I knew was Mr. Davidow was president of a company called Consolidated Book Publishers in Chicago which, it turned out, was a part of the John F. Cuneo companies.

John F. Cuneo is now dead, but at that time Mr. Cuneo owned the largest group of printing establishments in the world. They were broken into groups called The Cuneo Press of New England, The Cuneo Press of the Midwest, The Cuneo Press of the West, I guess, et cetera, et cetera. He was an interesting old man. I only met him once; he was kind of scary.

But Consolidated Book Publishers, it turned out, had sixty

divisions and did three hundred and eighty million dollars—this one company, Consolidated—three hundred and eighty million dollars worth of business a year. Well. And I was the assistant to the president of this company.

Problem was I arrived in Chicago, called the company and they said, "Oh, we never heard of you." It turned out Mr. Davidow was at the Frankfurt Book Fair and nobody had heard of me; he hadn't mentioned me to a soul. So here I am with a U-Haul truck and all my possessions and my cat. What the heck am I going to do?

Fortunately his driver, a wonderful man whose name I don't quite remember, who was kind of a Mafia figure, a very interesting guy, Louie something or other—he sort of remembered that as Mr. Davidow got on the plane to go to Frankfurt, he just sort of mentioned, "By the way, I've hired an assistant and he'll be arriving." So, anyway.

Then Mr. Davidow came back and, again, it was very interesting. For my whole time there, I was left entirely alone to do—basically, I was a trouble shooter. I was the head of one division called The English Language Institute of America. I find at garage sales and things these great big, enormous dictionaries. It was the Webster something or other Dictionary of the English Language, and if you open that you'll find my name in there as head of The English Language Institute and all this kind of stuff. Anyway, it was very amusing and interesting.

And so we published dictionaries, bibles, encyclopedias, cookbooks, sort of prepackaged classes—The English Language Institute did that—self-help, improve-yourself, and all this stuff. And a lot of it, by the way, was very interesting to me. Despicable but interesting. A lot of it was door-to-door sales. I was not directly involved in any of that. But there was a very interesting documentary made some years ago, called, I think, *The Salesman*. You see it on PBS once in a while. Well, you may remember, there was a man in there, I can't think of his name right now, who was teaching the salespeople how to sell—Mel Feldman, that was his name—and Mel became a very good friend of mine and was a very sweet and gentle man except when he was with his sales staff. And he just hell on wheels then. Again, it wasn't my part of the business. I was protected from that.

394

But this was an organization, part of which, at least, sold door-to-door, foot-in-the-door, very much, and a typical example was the salesman who would go into a small southern town, knock at the door of a very poor black family, say to this lovely lady who came to the door, "Madame, do you want your children to be as stupid as you are?" Or "as uneducated" or however it was worded. All the time with the foot in the door. And then would con her into— It wasn't that the books were bad. They weren't. But, you know, she'd have to pay five dollars down and five dollars a week for the rest of her life to buy this thirty-five-volume encyclopedia or whatever. Well, it was an interesting business and I was there for three, three and a half years.

And what came out of it was there was another company that they were involved with—they didn't really own it but they had put a lot of money, millions of dollars, into it—called Educational Marketing and Research, EM and R out of La Jolla, California. Its basic theory was a very good one. It would buy books from publishers all over the world, package them for, I believe, elementary school, possibly also high school, although I'm not sure of that, classroom libraries. Not central libraries, but classroom libraries. And it would let them have those books on a lease-purchase arrangement.

Turned out that it was politically and legally almost impossible because what nobody understood was that you could not tie one board of education to its successor, or the successor to the one that preceded it. See, these things worked over a four-year period. Well, boards of education don't last for four years. I may not be using the right terminology but, in any event, you couldn't commit a later group to what an earlier group had wanted to do.

And where the shit really hit the fan was what I did. I thought this was very exciting, by the way. My job was to get to know—it was probably one of the most exciting and creative times of my life—I had to get to know virtually every publisher in the country who had anything that was at all appropriate for elementary and high school classrooms. So that meant Rand McNally and Grolier and Lerner Publications in Minneapolis, almost anything you could think of. Random House and Simon and Schuster, et cetera, et cetera. And Columbia University Press even. I bought twenty-five thousand copies of the Columbia University single-volume encyclopedia. I also ended up with a near disaster on my hands because of it. But, in any event, we bought literally millions of dollars worth of books and acted as a kind of middleman, if you would, placing them in these schools.

Now it was the company in La Jolla that did the actual selling. It was interesting because the day I met the guy who headed the company I just hated him. And he hated me. And it was so clear to me that this man was one hundred percent dishonest, I couldn't understand how my bosses in Chicago could have been conned by this guy. But they were very gentle people, very, very influential and absolutely fascinating.

See, Leonard Davidow was not only a publisher with Consolidated Book Publishers, he had been the owner of—I think it was Parade Magazine— His family created Davidow Suits in New York which are evidently some very exclusive kind of suit for women. His wife was the head of the Girl Scouts of America. She was a lovely, lovely lady, Mrs. Davidow. Anyway, very interesting people, fascinating people. And you learned a whole lot from them.

But this guy, this group in La Jolla, they brought in very naive people, people like me, who were, all of us, really quite naive, who believed that this stuff made sense. And it did appear to make sense. But what we didn't know was they were greasing the palms of the—in other words, they would find a weakness in the person who made the decisions, and often that weakness was money.

So what happened was—what I was doing was, I was, without knowing it, I was giving a cover to all of this. I was hiring major educators across the country to form a board of advisors and governors. Everybody thought this was a wonderful idea. And so some of the biggest names in America began to work with me and with this group, lending their names.

Well, what happened was a huge sale was made to the city of Las Vegas. When I say "a huge sale," it was something like three million bucks for all this stuff I'd been buying for them. And so the company, I guess the one in La Jolla [rather than its parent in Chicago], decided,

"Okay, we'll give a huge celebration." And it seems to me they gave it not in Las Vegas but in La Jolla. Anyway, it was a kind of seminar cum party thing. It went on for three or four days. Ended with a voyage to Mexico. And we brought out all of these educators from all over the country to celebrate this sale. And the last day of the event was when we were handed the front page of the Las Vegas newspaper. And some very smart reporter had just proved that this guy that I was talking about, who headed the company, had paid twenty-five thousand dollars, or whatever it was, under the table to the Superintendent of Education in Las Vegas. The point of it was this sale was suddenly null and void.

And we were stuck—I was stuck—with three million dollars worth of not just books but globes, anything you could imagine, including my twenty-five thousand Columbia Encyclopedias, et cetera. I spent the next couple of years selling that all off. Now all of this is—I had no experience. I simply had nothing to go on except what was in my head. And it probably taught me more about marketing than I could have learned in any other way. I was very lucky and I sold it all for a profit. But it took several years to do.

Then what happened? Oh. That's how I got my next job. So that brings us to about 1971.

One of the publishers I had been working with was at that time a medium-size mass market house. Now notice, I was with a scholarly publisher; Xerox, which was strange and peculiar; Consolidated, which was doing reference materials primarily; and then Pyramid was the name of this company. Pyramid is—what's left of it—is now part of Berkley Putnam. Pyramid Publications was a mass market house. Books and magazines. I didn't have anything to do with the magazine side of it. In fact, what happened was I was hired to head what was called "special publications" and, for all practical purposes, was the health-and-nutrition line and the religious line which at the time I came to the company were not doing well at all. I was now making really a huge salary. I was making more than the president of the company when I went to Pyramid.

But in any event, what I saw right away was I had this very

limited line of health and nutrition books and of religious books. And I also saw immediately that my markets were obviously supermarkets and drugstores. Well, it was fairly obvious that a lot more than just born-again Christians and Baptists went to supermarkets to buy religious books and that, in terms of health and nutrition, you needed the broadest possible involvement. So I began using the connections I had made at Consolidated and began copublishing with other companies. I copublished, well, literally, in my three, three and a half years there, at least six to ten thousand books. I mean titles, individual titles. And I became the largest publisher in America both of health-and-nutrition and of religious books.

In other words, the minute I realized that what we lacked was breadth of coverage, then the answer to it was not to go out and find hundreds and hundreds of new authors, which would have taken enormous sums of money plus a tremendous amount of time, but rather to go to publishers who already had such product but that weren't in those markets that I was reaching. So, for example, to go to the Jewish Publication Society and to go to the Baha'i and the group that Helen Keller used to belong to, which I believe was the Swedenborgians.

Anyway, I began to work with religious publishers and health-and-nutrition publishers all over the country. And taking product which, in many cases, had sold anywhere from ten thousand to a couple of hundred thousand and suddenly increasing the numbers enormously. For example, one book that I had which was called *The Cross and the Switchblade*, by David Wilkerson—well, by the time I left we had reached over twenty million copies of that book.

What happened was I began to see that I'd kind of like to go back to San Francisco. I'd never thought of it before that. What I'd seen in San Francisco, to that point, was that there didn't appear to be a whole lot of publishing there. There were publishers but they were mostly people who had no real experience and just kind of started.

Well anyway, I met a very interesting man that I'd rather not identify because I loathe him. Anyway, he sold me a bill of goods. He talked me into taking a cut in salary—at this point I was making about a hundred and seventy thousand dollars a year and he talked me into

398

taking a salary of twenty-five thousand a year. So I went from a hundred and seventy thousand a year to twenty-five thousand a year to run his company. He made a whole lot of promises, none of which he ever kept. But that's okay. I believed him. This is a very charismatic man and when he wants something he gets it. But in any event, I came to California to run this company and our agreement was that he would go away and leave the company in my hands. I came as vice-president and general manager. And I would turn his company into a first-class publishing house. And I did.

But I stayed there fourteen months. The first seven months I sang at the top of my lungs on my way to work every day. I loved going to work. I loved the company. I loved the people within the company. I loved what they published. And as always, I brought along with me, in terms of sales people and so on, people I was already affiliated with. One always does this. It's part of living. You share with others your successes, and so on.

The second seven months, unfortunately, were the worst in my life because the owner decided he was bored going around the world, spending his money. And he came back. And he interfered in absolutely everything. And so my seven months were spent as a buffer between him and all the rest of the company. It was absolutely dreadful. And I dreaded getting up and going to the office every day. And so at the end of the second seven months, that was the time to leave. I was fired but it was interesting, he said that if I ever said I was fired he would deny it. I was fired because, of course, he and I didn't get along at all.

He would deny firing you?

Oh yeah. Yeah. He has ever since. He's always said, no, he didn't fire me, and all this.

He'd rather people believe that you quit.

Well, yeah. But, you see, it seems to me that if somebody calls you to his home the day before Christmas and says to you, "We must part company," I believe that's being fired. I mean it's very straight-forward and simple. I'm just telling you. Well anyway, interesting.

But I wouldn't have been in California were it not for him. So I owe him that, I suppose. And it's at that point that I decided, okay, I will now turn Strawberry Hill Press, which I set up before I came to California to join this man, I would now turn it into an active company. So that's where Strawberry Hill—so that's my history.

Tree Swenson and Sam Hamill
Copper Canyon Press

"...all publishers, in a way, are maniacal zealots out to transform
the world."

---

*I arrived at Fort Worden, outside of Port Townsend on the
Olympic Peninsula, late in the morning on a sun-bright, but chilly, day.
I had expected to interview Tree Swenson, publisher, and Sam Hamill,
editor of Copper Canyon Press, but upon my arrival Swenson announced that she wanted Mary Jane Knecht, formerly the managing
editor and, at the time of this interview, the marketing director for
Copper Canyon, and Jenny Pettit, the office manager and marketing
assistant, to be included in the interview as they were integral to
Copper Canyon's operation.*

*Although I did not know this—I was not told until a year later—
shortly before the interview took place Swenson had decided to leave
Port Townsend. In the months following this interview she would
negotiate with Copper Canyon's board of directors to remain as the
press's publisher or, failing that, to open a branch office of the press
in Boston. She was not successful and Copper Canyon remains in its
entirety in Port Townsend, Washington. None of this would be announced until the following summer. Knecht would leave also, to return
to film school, Hamill told me, but at the time of the interview she was
still wrestling with the decision to go. The four Copper Canyon staff
and I sat around a table that took up most of what I understood to be a
combination layout and conference room.*

This is April 16th, right?
Tree Swenson: Right. The day after tax day.

Yeah. Friday. Nineteen ninety-three. At the offices of Copper Canyon at Fort Worden State Park.

TS: Before we start the official interview—

Do you want me to turn this off?

TS: Yeah.

[After the cassette recorder was turned on again] *What I tell everybody is that if I ask a question and you don't want to talk about it, you don't want to answer it, just say so and we'll pass over it. If you say something that you regret having said* [There is immediate laughter around the table.], *let me know—*

Sam Hamill: Not if. When.

TS: Would if be possible to see a copy of the transcription and make corrections or deletions at that point?

I can't promise corrections or deletions. I'll take that as advisement. But I will give you a copy of the transcription. I'm not out to embarrass anybody—

TS: Mm hmm.

—and if you feel that you've exposed something of yourself that you don't want exposed, and it's personal, then that's fine. I will delete it if that's what you want me to do. Um, what are the conditions? [This is a reference to something said when the recorder was off.]

TS: Oh, I'm just wondering what the process is. I mean there are times that we've done interviews, and particularly when an article is written out of them—there're some real misinterpretations of things that were said. And even on a factual level it's useful to be able to correct or clarify if something isn't coming across.

Okay. So I'll be sure you get a copy. Um, yeah, I guess everything's open for negotiation if you want it to be. But I'm not going to guarantee that— If it's personally embarrassing, that's not a problem. I'll take it out. The focus of it is what brings a person into publishing. But what happens is that people start talking about—people imply their own identification, their personal identification, with publishing.

TS: Is that what you want as the focus of the interview, is...the personal? What brings people into publishing?

I don't want to be too analytical here. I would rather...I have some open-ended questions. Wherever you go with the questions is fine with me.

TS: Okay.

What I'll have to do is, especially as the women talk, I'll have to clarify who's talking. I'm not sure that I'll be able to pick it up later when I listen to the cassette.

TS: Okay.

The first few questions are biographical. I guess we could just go around from left to right. Place of birth?

SH: Unknown.

Unknown place of birth. Place of birth?

Mary Jane Knecht: New Castle, Pennsylvania.

Okay. That was Mary Jane. Jenny?

Jenny Pettit: Washington, DC.

TS: Seems like a pretty boring way to start an interview. [General laughter among the four Copper Canyon staff.] That's why I asked if it was going to be a straight transcript. Salt Lake City, Utah. I won't be difficult. Not the most important detail, as far as I'm concerned. [Laughing.]

Well.... Date of birth? Unknown?

SH: Nineteen forty-three.

MJK: Nineteen fifty-eight.

Okay, that was Mary Jane—1958. Jenny?

JP: Nineteen sixty-eight.

TS: 'Fifty-one.

SH: Got the decades covered.

Yeah, well. What I've found is what appears to be a generation gap, especially among the Americans. The Canadians educate people into publishing. They go from the university into publishing. At least this is happening in British Columbia, and apparently in Toronto.

TS: Mm hmm.

The Americans are not doing that. People who are going into publishing who are younger than middle-aged— First of all, there's hardly anybody who is founding anything. Some are coming into publishing from an informal internship program, apparently like yours.

TS: Mm hmm.

But there's a disjunction between the craft, or profession, in the United States that does not exist in Canada. What clued me into this were the answers to the questions I was asking about the ages of the people I interviewed. So this type of question is not totally valueless.

TS: So you were finding that people from earlier generations were coming in from more formal training programs?

No. There were the founders in the '60s and '70s. Most of them have not lasted. But even those who are founding presses now are middle-aged. They're founding them as middle-aged people. Young people are not founding presses. The routes by which younger people go into publishing are different. Some are going into publishing but they're following different routes in the United States from those their counterparts are following in Canada.

TS: At least in the Northwest.

Yeah.

MJK: Actually, I see that a little differently. I came into it purely by accident. But now in the States there are a number of publishing schools, like at Stanford and in Colorado and—what is it? Radcliffe or Wesleyan.

SH: Chicago has a program too, I believe.

MJK: Chicago, yeah. And the number of queries we get in here has really increased in the nine or whatever years I've been here, from young people who have gone through the publishing schools.

I get those too. What are they looking for?

MJK: A job. After having gone through the publishing schools.

Do you have jobs to offer them?

MJK: No. [Hamill laughs.] But I'm saying that I have noticed an increase over the years, where I think younger people are being a bit more strategic about getting into publishing.

TS: Yeah, but I do think that it's a difference between the entrepreneurial let's-start-doing-it and—

MJK: Oh, and create training, yeah—

TS: —but there are some really good—I agree with Mary Jane that there are some publishing programs that I think really do lay out what—

Those are the ones that are several weeks long, right? Stanford, Chicago, Columbia.

TS: Yeah.

I get their brochures. Okay. Do you all live in Port Townsend? You don't live here at Fort Worden, do you?

SH: Nope.

TS: No.

Do you all live in Port Townsend?

SH: Near.

Huh?

SH: Well, I don't live in the city proper, but I live near here.

Okay. Do you live in a place that has a different name from Port Townsend?
SH: I live in the county.
MJK: I also live in the county, about eight miles from Port Townsend.
TS: But they both get their mail at a Port Townsend mailing address.

Okay. We're nitpicking again.
SH: Just being accurate. [Laughter on the part of the Copper Canyon staff.]
TS: If boring. [Laughter.]
SH: I don't get to vote in Port Townsend elections.
MJK: Yeah, right. [Knecht and Hamill laugh.]

Years of education. Did you go to college, Sam?
SH: Fifty.

Fifty years of education. What about formal education?
SH: I've been a student all my life.

Mary Jane? Formal education?
MJK: Graduated from Evergreen State College.

When did you graduate?
MJK: 'Eighty-one or '82.
TS: This really—I don't know, I really feel like this is not about Copper Canyon Press. This is bits of biographical data that, to me—I mean, I just don't like to see—

Do you feel uncomfortable with this?
TS: —an interview about the press with this kind of biographical data. I think it's all somewhat irrelevant to, you know, the mission

406

of the organization which, um....

Do you want to skip over the biographical data?
TS: I'd probably rather get down to the heart of the matter.

[To all] *Does everybody else want to skip over the biographical data?*
TS: I just feel like this is— If I were going to read this interview, I would have quit by now. Because it just seems not to be on track.

But I'm the interviewer, and what I choose to summarize and what I choose to leave to the transcription may not be what you're envisioning.
TS: Ah! I see. Okay. That's why I asked if it was going to be a straight transcription or if you were going to edit or, you know, put it into a—I mean, I'm assuming you're going to edit out my curt comments about "Can't we skip over all this stuff that—?"

I don't know if I will.
TS: Okay. That's fine. You can leave it in. [Laughter from the Copper Canyon staff.]

Do you want to skip over this? Does everybody agree?
TS: Yeah. I'm bored.
MJK: I think, quite honestly, there is—you know, it's kind of Friday and we've got a lot of, I mean—
TS: We've got deadlines. I mean we do want to be available and do the interview, but it does seem to take up a lot of time going over stuff that really doesn't get at what the press is about particularly.

Okay. Do you want to talk about the mission of your organization? Is that the term you used?
TS: Sure.

I'm asking Tree and Tree is answering "Sure." Okay.

TS: Actually, we're in the process of redrafting our mission statement. It currently reads—Sam, do you want to give a paraphrase while I find the exact, or—?

SH: Give him the exact if that's what you want to do.

TS: Well, we have actually been rewording a very concise sentence, to try to get it precise about what, as an organization, Copper Canyon has as its focus. And that's part of this process of planning and advancement work that we've been going through. And it's really interesting, sitting with the group of staff and board members in a series of meetings, and every time looking at just exactly how we're stating what it is we are established to do.

The current draft is [reading from a sheet of paper]: "The mission of Copper Canyon Press is to publish poetry and to enhance the understanding and appreciation of poetry as an essential part of our culture." But, you know, it's been through a number of little drafts where we've changed words. We've changed "understanding" or "appreciation," we've changed "essential part of our culture," and it's like we're really trying to craft this one statement into what is at the same time very concise and focused but [which] gives us a very broad sense of what it is that we want to do with Copper Canyon.

When you come up with a draft of your mission statement, who reviews it and critiques it?

SH: We do. Along with our board of directors.

TS: That is, we the staff, along with the board. Because in the way that we're operating now, it's really important that we're all very clear about what it is that we're working on.

"Operating now" as opposed to...earlier?

TS: Mm hmm.

SH: Well, for many years the press was run as a partnership between Tree and me. And when we went nonprofit we had to define exactly what we were doing, and we had to set up fundamental procedures so that things would be orderly. Because we're issuing, each of us, weekly reports on what we're doing, we have boards-of-directors meetings that both Tree and I report at. All of this has to do with defining why we're here and what we do. It's good work but when what you say has to be crafted that carefully, there's a lot of defining and redefining that takes place.

You can redo your mission statement whenever you want to, right?

TS: Well, except that we've been operating since 1990 with a rather longer and expanded version of a mission statement, so this will probably not be revised for three to five years, I would say, at a minimum. It is also reflective of the shift in how we've been doing what we do; for instance, the program I mentioned that Mary Jane has been working on, which is really a marketing program, although it's more than that. It's more than a straight marketing program in that the aim of this is beyond just simply selling copies of the books. We're really looking to expand the audience for poetry in the culture.

What mechanism or mechanisms are you using to expand poetry's audience?

MJK: Well, specifically with this poetry appreciation program that we're launching, the aim is to promote the diversity of poetry being published in this country. And we have different avenues where we're going to be trying to cover different audiences. Right now we're heavily focused on the book trade. So we're, right now, preparing for the ABA [American Booksellers Association] convention in Miami where we will be hosting one of our authors, Lucille Clifton, who's been selected to give a reading. It is a very rare event when a poet is included in the ABA convention. And during the convention we will be officially launching the program with the trade by having in our display a poster and a poetry pamphlet that includes an essay that Don Hall has written.

So let's say you're successful at the ABA, and you convince the trade to stock more poetry books. But the trade is your buyer. The trade is not your reader. So what mechanisms are you going to use to get to your reader?

MJK: We'll be working intensively with a number of book-stores across the country by helping to facilitate in-store displays and poetry readings, and by leading poetry-reading discussion groups. So by concentrating on the trade, our readers are going to be coming into bookstores and exposed to this.

TS: We're—

That was Mary Jane. Now it's Tree.

TS: Yeah. Some of these materials will be used as part of in-store displays. We're working with particular stores to set up special displays of poetry. And not just Copper Canyon books, but poetry as a whole. And that's why it's important to get back to what it is that our aim in publishing is. It's somewhat broader than simply producing books, which I think for a long time really was the focus of the press. We still, I think, take particular care in the production aspects, everything from editorial and handling of the manuscript through typographic design and cover production, to produce a good book. But it's futile to spend all of that effort on production if there isn't a follow-through mechanism to get books into stores. And then from stores to readers. And that is the primary channel of distribution for us, is through bookstores. So that's why it makes sense to focus these efforts on the trade right now. And then we'll work on other areas.

But it's within that attempt to enhance the understanding and appreciation of poetry as an essential part of the culture that goes beyond just the production of books.... And there'll be other kinds of programs within this. I mean, cosponsoring readings and just increased contact with—

Cosponsoring with bookstores?

TS: Mm hmm.

MJK: We're also working on a series of events in celebration of the press's twentieth anniversary. In early November we will be working with different organizations in the Northwest to put on some poetry readings.

410

The press started in 1973 then?
SH: Well, we issued our first title in 1973.

TS: The press actually started—that is, the impetus was in '72, but our first title came out in '73.

What was the impetus?
SH: To publish poetry. [Hamill and Swenson laugh.]

Why in 1972 as opposed to any other year?
SH: Well, I began the press when I left the University of California, Santa Barbara. I had been the editor of their literary journal there. *Spectrum.* And I had won a literary award for my editing job there and used that little bit of cash to buy a printing press, partly for very practical reasons. I wanted to continue to publish in a small way. I wasn't thinking in terms of major distribution and promotion programs. I just wanted, in a very small way, to publish a little bit of poetry. And Tree and I and a third partner really kind of began things.

TS: There were a number of peripheral people who were coming and going and it really—it was very much a product of the early '70s. It was almost a collective effort, but as often happens in those collectives—

SH: This was in Denver.

TS: —it takes more focus than most people—

SH: We began in Denver.

TS: —that a whole group of people—

You began in Denver?
SH: Yeah.

TS: —was in Santa Barbara and ended up moving to Denver.

Were you in Santa Barbara also?
TS: Yeah.

SH: And we issued...one, two, three...four books in just over a year in Denver. Very small editions. Two hundred and fifty to five hundred.

Were these books with spines, or staple-bound, or—?
SH: Both.

TS: The first book actually had a very narrow spine.

SH: The first.... No, we didn't do any chapbooks until we came out—

TS: Until later.

SH: Yeah. And we came here to Fort Worden in the spring of '74. To become press-in-residence with Centrum. And that was when we began to get a lot more serious about how we were doing things and what we were doing and so forth. In Denver we all had outside jobs and we printed in our basement at night and so forth. And when we came here, Tree really began to take over the daily operation of the press. I was often away teaching, to make money to keep us eating. I mean this was really a labor of love for many years. And then the press evolved out of the years that we spent doing our various kinds of business and typographic and editorial homework.

TS: And as the production and quality moved up we were able to improve distribution. As distribution improved we were able to begin to sign contracts with authors who were better known. I mean the whole thing cycled into a much more, uh....

SH: Businesslike.

TS: Well, I wouldn't simply say "businesslike." I mean maybe "professional" is a better term. I mean—

SH: Well, except it implies money. "Businesslike" does too. But you get the idea.

What I see from the perspective of Black Heron is that as I persist, I enter into a kind of synergy that seems to exist between all the elements—from writing to selling the book. Everything's constantly changing. It's a system of covariation. But once you get into that, you become caught up in it. It seems to me that that's what you're describing: you start making more general statements rather than localized statements. Or maybe you were making general statements all along with your poetry.

412

SH: I don't think it's possible to make general statements with poetry.

MJK: Yeah. [Hamill laughs.]

TS: Right. That's probably the—

SH: In fact, the one thing that I would say has been the constant throughout all of this is that we have consistently published a very high quality of poetry. And a poetry that is not in its nature at all general.

Do you want to mention the names of some of the other people involved at the beginning?

SH: No. I mean they were sort of peripheral. I mean Tree and I held this together. I'm not going to give somebody credit for what they didn't do. [Laughs.] It was, in the beginning, a kind of communal sort of thing. People came and people left, people came and people left. And, uh...here we are. We didn't leave. [Laughs.]

When you started, were you publishing yourselves and the others involved, or were you from the beginning—

TS: No, the first books were other writers'.

Writers outside the group.

TS: Right. Writers outside of the group. It was not a co-op established, as a number of publishing co-ops have been, to publish the work of the people in the co-op. We really didn't have a co-op, but.... We did at various points publish a couple of Sam's books, but that was never the intent or the primary focus of what we were doing. I think the aim from the beginning was to establish a publishing house for the best poetry, and, as is often the case with younger writers, you're in touch with a group of writers and there is an impulse to see the value of the work and to want to publish it.

SH: And at that point you're not going to entice a well-established poet to come, even for a small edition, to an unheard-of house. But it didn't take us very long until, in fact, we did begin to achieve what I consider our ideal, and that is a blend of the various ranges of poets. So we've got, you know, Pulitzer Prize winners and

413

Nobel Prize winners and poets' first books and everything in between. And we've always had that as an ideal, to have that range in our authors. Because (a) some poets help pay the rent, and (b) some poets you want to publish not because you're going to make a penny on them, but because you want to publish them. And it's achieving a balance within all of these—and in our case, we also included a great deal of poetry in translation. So we've covered a rather broad literary spectrum within that narrow market called poetry.

Has it been called Copper Canyon from the beginning?
SH: Yeah.

Where did that name come from?
TS: It obviously is all rooted in the Southwest. There is an area outside of Salt Lake City, which is where Sam was raised and where I was born— Now, see, when it's relevant, it creeps in. [She and Hamill laugh.] But then it suddenly fits, that that particular geographic area seems to have ties—it's actually Bingham, but—
SH: It's Bingham Hill.
TS: Bingham Canyon, but it's often been referred to as Copper Canyon. But the entire geography and landscape of the Colorado-Utah—
SH: Arizona-New Mexico.
TS: —area—
SH: Four Corners.

Bingham Canyon, Utah?
SH: Yeah. A huge open-pit mine.
TS: And I think that part of the impulse was with the sense of place, of being rooted in an area. Now, ironically enough, we very soon uprooted and moved to the Northwest, taking with us our rather Southwestern name. But the press was at that point, with just four books out, established enough that we kept the name Copper Canyon.
SH: Well, also, because it's a place name it refers back to when the Northern Utes use to dig medicine jewelry there. So it goes back to

414

myth and ritual and all of those things that inform the poetic.

So from 1972 or '73, from the very beginning, you had clearly in mind what you wanted to do with your press.

TS: No. I think that what we wanted to do with the press has evolved all along. I mean what we have to explain along the way is that the early production methods were split, so that we started with offset equipment, acquired a bit of letterpress type which we used to prepare photo-ready copy, and then eventually shifted over and started doing all letterpress work so that we were doing trade editions, but produced by letterpress. We then shifted, [having] realized that that was an unreasonable sort of production method if we wanted to get books out into the world, and split into really two different programs, one with trade books which were manufactured out-of-house—

You mean printed, I presume. Printed and bound out-of-house.

TS: Right. Printed and bound out-of-house. And limited editions, which were printed in-house.

Did you do your own binding here?

TS: No. We had—we did some binding here. Chapbooks. That's when we started to do a few chapbooks. But that was a—

Sh: We still have chapbooks that aren't selling. [Laughs.]

TS: What was that—from '72—at least ten years that we had a pretty active limited editions program that evolved— Well, in '83 we discontinued that in order to focus on the real heart of what we had always been up to, which was to get poetry to people. And we saw that the limited editions were reaching mostly collectors—

SH: Rare-books stores. [Laughs.]

TS: —and individual collectors and rare-books collections at libraries rather than really hitting readers in a way that was calling forth responses. So we discontinued that part of what we were doing. So no, I wouldn't say that it's always been a clear line of what we wanted to do. Although there is a very definite—Copper Canyon's really about the only press of its size that is concentrating on poetry exclusively. There are a number of other presses that started at around the same time that Copper Canyon did who have since gone on to publishing other genres.

So I think that Copper Canyon's commitment to poetry, and poetry exclusively, is what really distinguishes it as a press. And I think that it's been a decision that, every time we've re-examined it, makes more and more sense. And we've been able to establish an identity among publishers, because one of the problems for small publishers in the whole distribution system is letting people figure out what it is you publish. So we're very clear about what it is we publish. But also just in terms of what it is that we want to do—

I think all publishers, in a way, are maniacal zealots out to transform the world. Why else would we be doing this if we didn't believe in the transformative power of literature? And I think we keep coming back around to poetry as perhaps the most deeply transformative of all the branches of literature. In our sense of things. And as long as that is our sense of things, it makes sense to continue down this path.

I don't know what you mean by "our sense of things." Who does "our" refer to?
TS: Copper Canyon Press.

Okay.
TS: That's why it's so important to look back at this mission statement.

SH: That's a collective rather than an imperial "we."

TS: Do we want to continue to publish poetry, as [per] our mission statement? I mean, that's why we re-examined this mission statement. We discussed it with the rest of the staff. I mean we do have—in fact, it was really kind of insane, the discussion we went through, agonizing [over] whether or not we should launch the Prose Series that we're—

The Prose Series?
TS: Yeah. The book—

416

SH: The one book a year of prose on poetry.

TS: It's called *Writing Re: Writing*. And, really, it's prose by poets, is what's included in that series of books.

SH: It will be basically an in-house series. That is, we will basically draw from our poets for these books.

The poets you've already published.
SH: Yeah.
TS: Mm hmm.
MJK: Mm.
SH: We published several books by Caroline Kizer. She will have the initial volume. The selected poems of Hayden Carruth will be published.

TS: It's prose. *Selected Prose of Hayden Carruth.*

SH: Prose. We'll have a book of prose by Odysseas Elytis. He's what? The '72 Nobel Prize winner?

TS: 'Seventy-nine Nobel Prize winner.

MJK: Translated by Olga Broumas. I'd like to add that his work has had a major effect on Olga Broumas's own poetry.

TS: She's also one of our Copper Canyon authors. We've published three of her books as well as the two translations of Elytis.

As you've taken on more poets have you felt at any time that you're reaching your limit as to how many people you can deal with? How many authors you can deal with?

TS: Well, we've added staff in the meantime as well, so that the organization is growing. And, in fact, we're in the process of talking about yet another what we would see as a series of books. Although we're not at a stage yet to announce it, we're going ahead with it. But it's always something that we're reevaluating. Because of the way we operate now, we really do tend to look at what's needed and how this organization—

What's needed by—?
TS: This press.

417

By whom?

TS: What's needed by—in order to have a thriving literary culture. And what we're seeing is that there really is a falling-off of avenues of publication for poets. Major houses continue to move away from publishing poetry. Even the university presses, which have published a great deal of poetry, have, in recent years, been cutting back. And there's apt to be a real crisis in university publishing this year because of certain funding decisions that have been made. So what we're seeing is that there is a greater and greater need to be filled in publishing poetry. And since that is what we do, and what we do exclusively, we want to try to address the needs and make it possible to publish some very good books that are without publishers, and some very good writers who don't have an artistic home.

SH: In 1988 there were fourteen hundred and sixty books of poetry published in the USA, according to *Publishers Weekly*. In 1991 there were nine hundred. So there's a third fewer books being published. And that will continue to decline as other publishers that began by doing things like poetry exclusively do more and more fiction and nonfiction. And as corporate publishers do less and less poetry, it becomes more and more important for people like us to continue to grow.

Under "corporate" do you include commercial publishers and university presses?

SH: Yeah.

TS: No.

SH: I mean—

TS: I certainly don't.

SH: In this figure I do. Because there is the same trend in that scene, which is to publish less poetry. And that's the only part I'm speaking about now. It's just the sheer number of titles. I think everybody in here knows dozens of poets out there with a track record already established, hunting for a publisher.

Right. [To Swenson] *You don't consider university presses—*

418

TS: Corporate? No.

How come?

TS: Well, because the mission of the university press is entirely different from the mission of a corporate publisher. The *raison d'être* is completely unrelated. They operate differently, their publishing decisions are different. I'd certainly not—

SH: They advertise differently.

TS: I would not put them in the same category at all.

Why did you decide to make the move to nonprofit status?

TS: Well, actually, a better question might be "Why didn't we always operate as a—?" I think in the early years, like any start-up press, we had a notion that, well, we'll just do this and become New Directions. In a few years we'll turn around and discover that we've published the canon and our backlist will be strong and we'll have a list of titles that will continue to sell and, in fact, sell more and more copies and—

SH: And how many millions of dollars has New Directions lost over the years? [Hamill and Swenson laugh.]

TS: Anyway, I do think that there was a sense that, in setting out to do this, we would reach a point where the press would become self-sustaining. But there was never an intent to find manuscripts that were salable. And this is the real difference between corporate publishing, which has as its reason for being the making of a profit, and a nonprofit, because it has as its bottom line changing people's lives. And that has always been the intent here, to publish literature that we felt was important and that might have the possibility of changing people's lives.

When you say "corporate" I assume that the model you're using is a large Manhattan house.

TS: Mm hmm. That's the usual corporate model.

Okay. But Copper Canyon has never—

TS: There are also small publishing companies that have making a profit as their reason for beginning to publish. And they would search out manuscripts that are commercial. And that's never been what we've done. But just the smallness of the organization in the initial years, and the necessity of focusing on how to produce a book, was so overwhelming that the additional organizational sophistication that a nonprofit organization brings in was beyond our need at the time. Or our capability to meet the kinds of requirements necessary to be responsible to a public.

As a nonprofit publisher.
TS: As a nonprofit publisher.

How big is your board of directors? Do you have to have a certain size?
TS: Legally you have to have at least three people on the board of directors.

Not including the publishers or editors.
TS: Right. You could, I suppose, have a nonprofit organization that was composed of two staff people and an outside person. It becomes questionable whether you're really a nonprofit if that's the organizational structure. We have seven board members and none of us are on the board.

SH: Also, in setting all of this up, one has to think very seriously about what sort of board of directors one wants to have. Should a board of directors, for instance, direct? And if they should direct, what should they direct? So we determined that we wanted an active board of directors, partly because we want growth. We don't want just stability, but we want growth with stability. And that requires that our board of directors actually do things. There are a lot of nonprofit corporations out there, mostly the very small ones, that are really kind of totally staff-operated. They don't get suggestions, they don't get direction, they don't get critical feedback. The board of directors just sort of checks over what they're doing and tends to rubberstamp it.

And we didn't want that. We wanted people on our board with some vision of what the press has been, and what it might become.

Because that was a major transition for us. Part of what we're doing is planning for a Copper Canyon Press that will be here after Tree and I are history.

A question that I sometimes ask in an interview, and that I'm going to ask now, is: Where do you see your immortality? Have you just told me?
SH: Where do I see what?

Where does your immortality lie?
SH: Immortality?

Yes. Your immortality.
SH: Oh, it's about thirty-six feet offshore, in the middle of the Strait. I mean this is a question that doesn't make any sense to me.

Okay. [To Swenson] *Does it make sense to you?*
TS: I think that probably people do see publishing as an immortality project. You know, you're going to put the words on paper and, yeah, we'll use acid-free paper and good bindings and it'll be around forever. I think that my sense of what's involved with publishing is much more in the immediate. I like the idea of the old Pocket Poets series.
SH: Little square books with a staple, and they have a shelf life of probably fifteen, twenty years max. But they were read and read and read.

Of course, the high acid content in the paper they used—
SH: And they're folded and stapled instead of bound, and the staples rust. For me, the idea of immortality is a ridiculous idea anyway. I was talking with Hayden Carruth on this, in fact, about an essay he had written which, in writing it, depressed him. And he was pointing out that in the end, it's always in the end. And that extinction is, you know, is part of it, and this whole kind of Zen perspective. And he said to me, "What I never understand about you, Hamill, is when in the middle of all of

421

this you always bring up this issue of mystery. I don't see any mystery in it at all."

I pointed out to him that I've been talking to him for twenty-five years, that the first thing I wrote him was when I was a student in Santa Barbara and I wrote him a letter about how much I loved *The Voice That Is Great Within Us*. Twenty years later he's won the National Critics Circle Award for a book that we published. I've still never met him. And if there isn't mystery in that, and gratitude, what the hell are we doing here? So it's not a matter of what's immortal, it's a matter of what you're in touch with. And for us, I think, the principal thing has been the sense of dailiness, the sense of wanting to do a particular kind of work.

TS: That's precisely the reward, I think. Not that we're publishing because these books will endure and be around long after we will, although of course it's lovely to think that someone might stumble across a Copper Canyon book and be intensely touched by it at some point long after we're dead. But it's very much a sense of the present to think of someone across the country right now picking up one of these books and having, uh...a change—

But not more rewarding.

TS: Not more. No. No. But I think that that's part of the reason. I mean I would rather be involved in the now, and be concerned with what we're able to do at this moment. And also for me, I think, it connects to a sense of the current historical moment. We do live in a particular culture, in a particular time. And that's what we have to work with. And what we can try to effectively change is what happens in that culture now.

Do you have confidence that the direction you want to see the culture change in is for the better?

TS [Laughing.]: I have confidence that if— This I can only take by personal knowledge [of] what is opened through the reading of poetry. How the perception of one's day is altered by the simple act of reading a very fine poem. And I see that as a change for the better. And, therefore, have to believe that if the reading of poetry is a more—I mean I do think it's a very essential part of our culture. I think that our historical memory is carried in poetry. One of the things Don Hall addresses in his essay is that the material of this particular art form—it's the only art form that the material is used by everyone on a daily basis. Sculptors use, as their material, stone. Poets use, as their material, words. Everyone uses words. And yet not everyone makes art out of words.

A while ago you spoke as though early in your career as publishers you were thinking of emulating New Directions. Do I have that wrong?
   TS: I think that most of the presses that I know look to New Directions as an exemplary publisher. [To Hamill] You don't think so?
   SH: Sure. Well, yeah. But that's a different thing than—what was the word you used?

I said "emulate."
   SH: Yeah. I don't think we particularly wanted to emulate New Directions. I think certainly we revered good old Nude Erections.
   TS: That's spelled N-u-d-e E-r-e-c-t-i-o-n-s.

What? [Swenson and Hamill laugh.]
   TS: Sam was using the other pronunciation of New Directions.

Oh.
   SH [Speaking slowly and distinctly]: Nude Erections.

Ah.
   SH: It was Pound who started that.

Oh, is that right?
   SH: In many ways we learned a lot from New Directions. And in many ways Jay and company [James Laughlin, publisher of New Directions] have been a constant source of inspiration.

TS: In fact, we published two of Jay Laughlin's books of poetry. He's a very fine poet himself.

SH: But we never set out to do things the way Jay has always done things. Some of the things that have happened in the history of New Directions are famously hilarious. As with Pound's *Confucius* that was issued with the Chinese on the title page upside down.

TS: We've made mistakes. I do not—

SH: Everybody does. But, to be perfectly honest, New Directions was run to a very large degree on the whims of Jay Laughlin, depending on his ski schedule and other things. And we've never done that. We've always been kind of labor-intensive.

[At this point, under pressure of work remaining to be done, Mary Jane Knecht and Jenny Pettit excused themselves from the remainder of the interview.]

Where were we?
TS: I think we were off on New Directions.

SH: I think one of the primary differences, frankly, between us and New Directions is that we have for, I would say, the last ten years had what I think is the best book designer in the country. And New Directions has never been famous for book designs. Except when Jay was doing those editions printed in Italy.

TS: Mardersteig used to print some limited editions for New Directions which were just exquisite volumes.

[To Swenson] *You're the book designer for Copper Canyon?*
TS: I do design most of the books.

Most.
TS: All.

All.
TS: I design the books.
SH: Well, nearly all.

424

TS: In addition to my other—

Nearly all.
TS: Nearly all.
SH: We've still got some books in print that I designed.
TS: That's true. Superior books. I design most of our books.

What is your initial press run on new books?
TS: It varies. In fact, the most recent book from the press was published in an addition of nine thousand copies. Lucille Clifton's *The Book of Light*. That's the high end of what we would ever produce in a first printing, but our advance sales on that book were higher than anything we'd ever published before. And I think the book is going to do very well, so we decided to do a large initial printing. The Carruth book, which I think was an initial printing of five thousand, is now in reprint. We just got the reprints in today.

That's a lot of copies for poetry.
TS: Well, at the small end, we're around twenty-five hundred.

You're able to draw a living from the press now, I take it.
[Hamill and Swenson laugh.]
TS: The press is now operating as a nonprofit organization with a professional staff, a paid staff, yes.

And you're part of that paid staff.
TS: Mm hmm. But that doesn't mean that we haven't, at times—
SH: Well, I'm technically a part-time employee. A major portion of my income comes from royalties on other books and lecture circuits and other things that I do to supplement my salary as editor. That's not an accident, by the way. When we went to nonprofit I could have become a full-time employee, but I have a writing life outside the press that I believe completely makes me the editor that I am. That is, my outside artistic life is very important to my life as an editor. It

425

informs and relieves me. So, technically, I'm only a half-time employee here.

TS: And technically I'm a full-time employee, although, in fact, I live and breathe Copper Canyon Press and poetry and publishing and the work of what we're doing here. And I have—

Sh: Well, also managing to do others' design work, and so forth.

TS: —for a very long time. And I've also done some outside design work. But just in terms of how the press is operating, we have three full-time employees now, Jenny, Mary Jane and myself, as well as a little outside help for proofreading and part-time bookkeeping and accounting and—

On a contract basis?

TS: Mm hmm. Actually, the bookkeeper is part-time staff as well. And then there are people on contract. That was part of the transition from a concern that was supported by the subsidy of its founders to an organization that now is seen as something that has a much larger, broader mission that's supported by a much bigger constituency.

Its "founders," meaning you and Sam.
TS: Mm hmm. Yeah.

Sam, in the way you feel about writing and editing, do you emphasize one over the other?
SH: No.

Do you emphasize design or publishing one over the other?

TS: I don't think they can be separated any more than it's possible to pull apart the old form and content.

SH: You know, rather than set up—we set these things up as though they were in some sort of opposition. I don't think that opposition really exists. I refer you back to Pound's lovely comment that "a great fabric isn't woven from a single thread." So that one holds in

426

one's hands a number of threads. One participates in different kinds of economics constantly, rather than just dollars and cents. There's spiritual economy and the economy of the gift and all of that. Those things are not in opposition. They coexist and coevolve.

TS: Precisely. So that as one part of the press has developed and evolved, it brings along other aspects of the whole of publishing. It's like water seeking its own level. Things need to be tuned up and adjusted as the vision of what the press is about changes.

I'm finished.
TS: Okay! Let's finish!

Michelle Benjamin
Polestar Books

"... I felt intimidated by good writing. Something I think about in the back of my head is—but right now I enjoy the connection that I have with writing."

Michelle Benjamin is one of only a few publishers I found under the age of forty. At the time of this interview she was six months shy of being thirty years old. She had joined Julian Ross, founder of Polestar Books, as copublisher about a year and a half earlier. Ross "was going to the University of Victoria. How he started out was with a calendar. It was called The Original Student Calendar. *He couldn't find a day book that helped him keep his life in school organized, so he designed one and it's in its tenth year and it's the biggest selling product that Polestar does. And then he did a poetry book when he was in Victoria, moved to Windlaw and continued to run the press from Windlaw." Benjamin has an office in Vancouver while Ross keeps one in Windlaw, in the southeast corner of British Columbia. Each has a part-time assistant. They employ editors and a designer on a contract basis.*

Benjamin was born in Bistroff, France where her father was stationed while in the Canadian Air Force. She graduated from the University of Ottawa in English and Women's Studies. She considered graduate work but "I decided that academics were too removed from the real world."

We met on Saturday morning, September 5, 1992, shortly before the Bumbershoot Small Press Fair opened for the day. Although the building had been unlocked the day before when I interviewed Joe Singer, this morning it was locked. We began the interview at a small table set just off the walkway in front of the building. After a few minutes one of the security people showed up and unlocked the building and we went inside and did the main part of the interview

428

there before the crowds arrived.

I worked in a bookstore part-time while I was in university and then full-time for a couple of years when I finished, knowing all that time that publishing was what I wanted to do. Even when I was in university, I was just...I've always been interested in the business of books. As well as the production and all the sort of artistic and aesthetic values, I enjoy business and marketing and promotion and that whole side of it. So while I loved working in the bookstore, and I expect that someday I'll probably end up back in a bookstore, it always felt like it was training for publishing.

When I left Ottawa I went to Banff, the Banff publishing workshop. The Banff School of the Arts has a publishing program. They have a magazine one and they have a books one. It's a two-week-long, very intensive program. Faculty are all people who work in the publishing industry in Canada. It's a really valuable course. Basically, you set up a publishing house. You publish a season's list of books within two weeks. You learn a little bit of everything. Concentration on marketing and promotion. You learn about production and costing and editing and how the relationships in publishing work. It's really a valuable course and you find a lot of people working in publishing in Canada have been...I guess younger people in publishing in Canada have been through the course. They also, as part of their—a year later they have an editing workshop. And it's a week-long course. Again, you spend a week working with professionals who are people who have been in the field for a long time and who give some of their time to these courses. It's really worthwhile.

You're the fourth Canadian publisher I've talked with. Three of you—yourself, Brian Lam and Rolf Maurer—knew they—you— wanted to go into publishing from at least the time you were in university. To me, that's really unusual. You just don't see that in the United States. In the United States we call publishing "the accidental profession" because nobody intends to go into it.

429

Is that right?

We love it. Once we're caught up in it, we don't want to get out. And those who do leave, I think, have a real grief reaction about having to leave something that's so...consuming.

Yeah. Yeah.

But nobody intends to do it. You don't have that expression in Canada, "accidental profession"?

No. A lot of the people I know that are in the business are here because it's what they wanted to do. In Canada, besides Banff, which is a wonderful, wonderful course, we've got university courses now. They're less practical, I find, and more theoretical and people who take them, I don't think, are as—very generally—aren't as interested in getting into publishing as they are curious about it. Where Banff—it's very intense and it's very concentrated and it's hard to get into the course. You have to show a real interest in the business.

The courses I'm familiar with are those that are put on by universities. Columbia has a six-week course in the summer, I believe. And the University of Chicago has a course. Stanford has a course. All of those are to train people to be editors so they can go be employees of a Manhattan firm.

Right. Right.

But I'm not aware of any course that teaches a person how to be a publisher, how to coordinate all of the activities of a publisher. There may be courses in the United States. But I've talked to a lot of publishers now and I don't know anybody who ever went to one or even mentioned one.

Yeah. Well, that's really what Banff does. The course that I'm a little bit familiar with—I don't know if there are others in Canada or not; I don't think there are—but at Simon Fraser University in Vancouver you can get a degree in publishing. I think it's mostly theoretical. There are some practical courses. As I said, I think you'll find a lot of—especially I think that younger people in publishing in Canada have been through Banff. That could not necessarily be a reflection even of how good the course is. It may be more a reflection of the kind of people that take the course. It's people who are really committed to getting into publishing who, you know, the course is good background. It can't get you in, but it certainly indicates that you're interested and serious about it.

Did you go right from Banff to Polestar?

I was with Raincoast Books for about two years and my job, my official job there, was inventory manager. Raincoast distributes for about forty publishers, some Canadian, mostly American, and some Australian, some European. My job was as a liaison with the publishers, just to make sure that we always had books on hand. Through Raincoast I met Julian Ross and moved into Polestar. He was tired and he needed a break and we just came to a good arrangement and I joined him. Before that I was in a bookstore in Vancouver.

Before Raincoast.

Before Raincoast, yeah. I was hired on a four-month contract as a consultant to set up a new bookstore in Vancouver. An architectural bookstore. I did everything from making first contact with all the publishers, doing the first orders, helping design the store, selecting computer systems, hiring a manager...and before that I worked in the bookstore in Ottawa for three years.

It was that experience that enabled you to become a consultant to set up a bookstore?

Yeah. I moved to Vancouver from Ottawa to get a job in publishing. There's very little in publishing happening in Ottawa. The centers of publishing in Canada are Toronto and Vancouver. There are a number of other attractions in Vancouver but publishing is a career move, so I knew that I would have to do a few things to find my way into it.

431

Have you any idea how you knew or why you knew that you wanted to go into publishing? You say you always did, and it seems since adolescence anyway—

Yeah. I guess it started out as a fascination for and love of books. My whole family are readers. For a long time I thought that was going to translate into teaching, being an English teacher. High school English. At some point during university I realized that wasn't what I wanted to put this book energy into, that that seemed almost thankless sometimes, or it would be unsatisfying. That was at some point during university. I don't remember the exact revelation or how it all came together. I worked on some publications when I was in university, newsletters and things, and got some sense of putting things together, the fun of putting words and thoughts and ideas together.

Do you write yourself?
Not really, no.

Have you ever? Or have you ever had the idea of becoming—
Yeah. Yeah. Mostly I felt intimidated by good writing. Something I think about in the back of my head is—but right now I enjoy the connection that I have with writing, and it feels like what I'm doing now with writing is creative and satisfies any writing urges that I might have. I've got to write catalogue copy, back-cover copy. (Laughs.)

Does Julian write?
Yeah, he does. He's written some children's stuff, not published. And I think he's done fiction and poetry. He has published one book, the *All-Star Hockey Activity Book*. That's a book he wrote with his son who was eight years old at the time. It's a hockey book for kids. Julian is a hockey fan and has a really good eye for a good hockey book. And that comes out of his interest in this. He's got two boys and they're interested in hockey and there's a big market for hockey books in Canada.

Apparently. I saw in your catalogue that you've sold sixty thousand copies of hockey books.

Yeah. We did a book of hockey cartoons last year and the first print run of ten thousand sold out in a month and we had to reprint. Ten thousand in Canada is a phenomenal number.

It is here, too.

Yeah. It's certainly phenomenal for us to do it. That number of anything.

How did you know to print ten thousand?

We watched the back orders come in. And it was the second book that we had done of this cartoonist and the first one sold close to that amount and we knew it was going to go. It was a bit of a risk for us, but it worked out. We're doing a hockey book this year as well. It's called *Hockey's Young Superstars* and it's a fan book mostly for young hockey fans. And we're going to print ten thousand as well. We feel pretty sure that's going to go. The reaction we're getting from bookstores and the feedback we're getting from our sales reps is that it's really going to go.

When you do poetry, how many copies do you print?
Between a thousand and fifteen hundred.

And you sell those?

Yeah. Within the last year we've reprinted two of our poetry books.

One of them is a prize winner.

Yeah. That was one that the first print was last year and we're getting close to having to reprint that one. Kate Braid's book, *Covering Rough Ground*, won the Pat Lowther Award which is for the best book of poetry by a woman in Canada. The two that we reprinted actually were both prize winners as well, in different categories. *Being on the Moon* won the City of Regina Book Award and *Whylah Falls* won the Archibald Lanphman Award. It's real exciting for us to be able to

433

reprint poetry. I think our first run on both of those books was fifteen hundred and I think fifteen hundred of each was the reprint number as well.

I was looking through your catalogue this morning. You publish on a variety of different subjects. Hockey, calendars, poetry, fiction. Does that present a problem in marketing?

No. In fact, I think it probably helps us in some ways. We can reach into a lot of areas. People can always find something on our list that's interesting.

I was talking with Joe Singer yesterday, from Mother of Ashes Press, and he was saying that a problem he has is that every time he does a book that's different from what he's done before he has to learn all over again how to market it, because it's a different niche.

Mm hmm. Well, we're distributed by Raincoast. Raincoast has a huge and very diverse list. Part of our distribution arrangement is marketing and promotion. So, in consultation with us and working with us, they do our marketing and promotion. And they've reached into just about every market, so whatever we come up with they've had some experience with anyway. We're just interested in doing a real range, based on whatever happens to come along for Julian and me that's interesting and exciting to us to do.

There's lots more we'd like to be doing with our books than we have the time and the energy to do. We're really trying right now to get books into the States. We don't really know how to do it. We've got books at Pacific Pipeline [a regional wholesaler located in Washington state], books at Bookslinger [a small press wholesaler which, since this interview, filed for bankruptcy] and Inland [an East Coast wholesaler], but we don't know how to get them out of their warehouses into the stores, and out of the stores into book buyers' hands.

How many titles a year are you doing now?

We were doing ten this year. One has been delayed; the manuscript wasn't ready. Looks like we've got fourteen on the list for

434

next year, which feels like a lot. It's a lot for us to do.

So you're expanding a little bit every year?

Yeah. Not really intentionally. Not really, you know, with it in mind of building the list every year. It's just more and more comes in that we're having a hard time saying no to.

Right. I'm in the same boat.

Yeah.

It's amazing how much good stuff there is out there, isn't it?

Yep. We get a lot of stuff that's pretty easy to turn around, but we get a lot of good stuff.

Does your press have a purpose or a mission?

Yeah. A couple of things we're committed to: first-time writers, first-time illustrators. We see part of our role as giving first-time writers and illustrators a break. Assuming, you know, their writing is of a high standard and quality, which often it is. A lot of the larger publishers won't take chances.

We're committed to good-looking books. We're really interested in the design. Both interior and the cover. That includes our hockey books as much as our poetry books and our children's books. We've got a really great designer who's done most of our covers. I think our covers are outstanding. Once we've made a commitment to a book, we're committed to really being behind it and getting it out there. We can't put a lot money up front for any of our books and we can't pay much in advances. We just don't have the money. So what we can promise is that we will do really great marketing and promotion, and Raincoast will be behind it, and the reps will be behind it, and that the writer can count on us to do everything we can to get the book out there and to keep it out. We push the backlist all the time. We don't publish it and leave it on its own out there. We're behind it. In terms of what we publish, we're committed to stuff that, you know, that sparkles for us. That can be anything. We're willing to take a look at anything that comes in, whether it's biography or children's books or nonfiction. If it shines for us in some way, we'll do it. We'll take a chance on it.

Do you get money from Canada Council?
Yeah.

Everybody does, huh?
Well, yeah. They have a minimum number of books that you have to have published, and minimum sales. But once you've reached that minimum, yeah.

I was looking at SPAN's latest newsletter—
Yep. Small Press Action Network.

Yeah. That newsletter they put out.
SPANZINE.

Yeah, right. They were quoting somebody, an unknown official from the Canada Council, talking about the "appropriation of voice." We have the issue but the terminology is somewhat different in the United States. Somebody talking through another ethnic group's or, I suppose, gender's voice in fiction. Somebody on the Canada Council—it seemed like a pretty open threat that somebody who does that runs the risk of not getting Canada Council money. I'm using that to illustrate a larger question: Is there an implicit restriction attached to the acceptance of that money?
I've never felt so. They have guidelines, and some of the books we do aren't eligible. Like we did a hockey guide this year, a guide for goal tenders. That's not eligible. Guidebooks, instruction books, aren't eligible. We've got a book that's a guide to a region of BC. It's called *Exploring the Kettle Valley Railway.* That's not an eligible book.

So they don't fund the press, they fund a particular book?
Yeah. They fund particular books on your list. It's a point system. The press gets a certain number of points based on the kind of marketing and promotion and how much you're getting your stuff out there. You get a certain amount based on your sales, and then individual

436

titles are awarded points. And those points are awarded by jury. I've never felt—I didn't read that thing in *SPANZINE*. I'd be curious to see some of the background to it. I can't imagine—the Council hasn't seemed to me to be that restrictive. That's, to me, a risk that an individual publisher will take. Or not. To publish a book that is going to stir up that kind of discussion.

Is there other money available for publishers?

Yeah. It's provincial. In BC there's a thing called BC Cultural Services. They give grants to publishers and writers and other arts groups. If you're eligible for Canada Council funding, then you're eligible for BC Cultural. It's much less money. BC is one of the least funded provinces in terms of arts in Canada. Ontario has huge, huge provincial grants, and loans to publishers that are smaller but are very helpful.

Rolf pointed out that there is a sense of—I'm paraphrasing; he didn't use these terms—there is a sense of belonging, or of community, in Canada that he sees us lacking in the United States.

Mm hmm. Yeah. I absolutely feel, especially—well, I haven't been publishing in Toronto, but in BC I really feel like I'm part of this wonderful community. I love being at events where I can get together with other publishers, whether it's at a fair or, you know, we have BC Book Prizes once a year, things like that. It's always real exciting for me to be with these people. We're a diverse group but have pretty strong allegiances and pretty strong connections.

I think we've covered everything. Is there anything you would like to say for posterity? To be known forever?

No. [Both laugh.]

Ed Varney
Intermedia Press; The Poem Factory

"I used to say when I was young that I was an existentialist. The existentialist looked at the world as being absurd, and his response was kind of despairing. And then I became interested in Zen. And I looked at the world as being absurd, but lost that sense of despair, just sort of accepted it. And then later I became interested in Dada where you see the world as being absurd and the only rational response is to laugh."

Ed Varney was born in New Rochelle, New York in October 1942. His father was a machinist, his mother a homemaker. When he was twelve the family moved to a farm upstate. "It became a family farm. I had three brothers, so we all worked on the farm. I really didn't get along with my father very well." He graduated from high school when he was seventeen and went away to college at Syracuse University where he got his BA and MA in English literature. "There were some good people there. Delmore Schwartz was there. And George Elliott. Short story writer. Donald Justice. Poet. There were some good writers there but I thought, Well, jeez, I'm going to have to make a living so I'd better get a degree. Especially with Seventeenth Century, I'd better study literature so I can teach. Never have." He lives now in Vancouver, British Columbia where he moved during the Viet Nam war. "It was traumatic, but at the time it just seemed for me the right thing to do. And I've lived in Vancouver ever since and basically made Canada my home. Just about all of my artistic life has been in Canada.

"I've been married and divorced and married and...my second wife died. Leaving me with five children. Actually, the four older ones have left home. I have one daughter with my first wife and then when I married my second wife she had one son and two adopted sons. And then we had a daughter together. So she died and I had five kids. The older kids were like from about eight to fourteen and my youngest

daughter was two. So the older kids were really helpful. Now they've left home and my youngest daughter is thirteen. So it's really just her and me now. But the older kids were really great. They made it a lot easier than it could have been. I guess I was really lucky. Really lucky. 'Cause they were pretty good. They really pulled together."

I interviewed Ed Varney on Sunday, September 6, 1992, in the morning of the third day of Bumbershoot, Seattle's annual arts festival, in the Performance Room of the Art Pavilion in Seattle Center.

I actually lived in Seattle for a year prior to going up. I had a friend who was going to the University of Washington and I thought, "Hm. Seattle sounds interesting." So I lived here, and I enjoyed my time here. I was associated with the Free University which predated the...whatever it is.

The Experimental College.
The Experimental College. Yeah. And *Helix*, which was sort of a hippie newspaper. You know, I sort of hung out on the Av [University Way Northeast]. So then I went to Vancouver and, um, I was originally, you know, I was making sandals and sort of craft items and I had, um, I have an MA in English and I always had wanted to be a poet. I was associated with a couple of literary magazines in college. And at one point I—actually, I got involved with a really interesting cooperative in Vancouver called Intermedia. Intermedia was based on the fusion of art and technology. And at some point we acquired a mimeo machine that had an electronic stencil cutter, which was pretty sophisticated for its time. And so I adopted that and adopted the name "Intermedia Press" and started....

First I published a couple books of my own. This would be like '69, '70. And I realized, hey, I can publish a book of poetry and sell it as easily as I can sell sandals. You know, if I can sell the sandals, I can do that. So then, of course, you realize quite quickly when you have access to printing tools that you can print other people's work as easily as you can print your own. You can't produce as much writing as you

439

can print. So I just worked away at that, and little by little.... Intermedia Society sort of moved its location a couple of times and we ended up— at one point we rented a church and a manse and I lived upstairs. I was like the caretaker.

Do you distinguish between "Intermedia" and "Intermedia Society"?

Well, there's Intermedia. It was actually a society, which was the structure. And then a branch of it became Intermedia Press. What happened was a bunch of people got together, we got some grant money from the Canada Council, which was very helpful, and we administered this Intermedia for four or five years. And then within Intermedia various groups split off, basically learning to administer themselves.

And in 1973 or -4, I'd say '73, Intermedia Society basically ended but Intermedia Press continued and something called Image Bank continued. And a group of the artists that had been involved with Intermedia formed The Western Front which was kind of the first artist-run gallery/performance space in Vancouver. And the film people formed something called Visual Alchemy.

So Intermedia had been a wonderful melting pot for artists and technologists, and artists in different media worked together. The technology was mostly, you know, baling-wire-and-string technology but some of it was quite interesting. And then people developed their own ability to administer their own trip. So Intermedia Press went through a kind of varied series of changes. People used to come in and I'd teach 'em how to use the equipment and they'd produce their own books and things.

And then in about 1972 we got an offset press. When we first got it, you know, it was a clunker, a Rotaprint. It was a large-format, eighteen-by-twenty-four. When we first bought it, somebody said, "Well, what do you need water for?" You know? Like we didn't know a thing about offset technology. "What do you need water for?" So there were three of us became partners in this, in that Rotaprint. And then we had to buy a little Gestetner to, you know, to use while we tried to learn how to use the Rotaprint, which never worked right.

440

So I would say in about 1973 one of the partners had gotten out. So there were two of us left. We had the press in an old warehouse. And my other partner went to Mexico for a month. And when he came back he had no money, and I hadn't made any money in the time, and the press as a separate entity had no money. Like zero. So here we are, what do we do? We either sell the equipment and get jobs or we get serious. So we decided, well, we'll get serious.

So we had published, you know, a number of books and kind of book-like projects. Hadn't had fantastic success at selling them, but we decided, well, we'll do commercial work as well. So we started doing commercial work and little by little we acquired, you know, sort of bottom-of-the-line equipment, inexpensive equipment. But we had it in our minds to build a shop that could produce books. At one point we found a sewing machine, an old Smythe sewing machine, and we bought a Buffalo book binder, which was a piece of junk, that was. That never worked right. We bought a folding machine. You know, we tried to assemble equipment, using the money we made from the commercial printing. So then we just kept at it. We published as many books as we could, and the truth is we got better and better at publishing books.

We got a Miehle twenty-three-by-twenty-nine-inch press. It was an o-o-old press, but, man, it was a good press. So you could print a five-and-a-half-by-eight-and-a-half format. You could print a twenty-four-page signature, twelve pages on a side. So you were much more efficient than most other printers. And that thing had dead-on registration, you know, if you knew how to do it. So we started printing color covers. We'd print like four covers at a time. And we started buying book paper in quantity. You know, nice, sort of slightly off-white book paper. And we would produce books for other people as well, and publish our own books. But our ability to print them outstripped our ability to sell them. So at a certain point we decided we'd start trying to do commercial books. We had a few attempts. We did a tea lovers' handbook and a coffee lovers' handbook.

The noncommercial books you had been doing, those were poetry?

Yeah. Mostly poetry. We did a Canadian short story anthology. We did two volumes of that. And we did a couple of novels. And then we got a line on a gardening—I convinced this guy who was the CBC Radio gardener to write a series of gardening books. And they sold very well for us because he promoted them on the radio and everybody listened to him, you know? Um, that was interesting. I found that quite interesting.

But then more and more my partner became, you know, was really very interested in the commercial aspect. And so in about '78, I guess, we sort of started dividing. I became the publisher and he became the printer. And he wanted the books to pay their way for the printing branch, shall we say, the same as any other commercial job. And it wasn't really reasonable. We started to part ways at that point. My partner was a really good salesman and he had managed the sales part of the publishing as well. So it was all kind of thrown on my shoulders. And, uh, we went along.

Actually, the publishing grew too. Until about 1981, and we had this distributor and he went belly-up, owing us a huge amount of money. And in '81 there was also a recession. And so at that point we decided to give up the publishing and concentrate on printing.

So I sort of did the publishing on the side. I scaled my ambitions down. I kept all the books, of course, and kept selling them. But I scaled my ambitions down. And at a certain point I started doing *Bite Magazine*, which was a small poetry magazine. And, you know, I still worked at the print shop because we were co-owners. And then in about 1990— '91, I guess—I came up, with a friend, with this idea for The Poem Factory. So we did a series of individual poems. Sort of like broadsheets, really, but they're folded.

And midway through 1991 a friend of mine, Carolyn Zonailo, who had had a press called Caitlin that also published poetry, sold it, and we decided that we'd collaborate on The Poem Factory as a publishing entity, and we'd publish three or four books a year but keep everything really humble, try to keep the books at around five dollars. Sort of the bottom of the market, as far as production values went. Approach it from a, shall we say, cost-effective attitude. So we have our first three

442

books lined up but not produced yet. In Canada there are some subsidies for literary publishers. You have to have two years of operation and, I think, six books. So we're planning to do three a year.

Before, when you had Intermedia, when you were producing books, how many did you do?

I think we did a total of something like sixty-five books.

How big a run for a first printing?

Well, that's interesting. In the mid-'70s, from about 1976 to 1980, we would print a thousand copies of a poetry book and, really, we sold out of a number of them. You could actually sell six, seven hundred copies of almost anything. But by '81 or so, '82, it seemed to—what happened is there was this kind of what they call a "flowering of Canadian literature" in the mid-'70s. And at first there was none, then there was a lot, then there were so many publishers and so many books of poetry and so many books of short stories that the market was just over-saturated. And then in the '90s, as we get through the '80s, there are lots and lots of publishers and lots and lots of books, but not a lot of sales. Now it's tapered off. There are very few publishers in Canada that publish poetry. It's really changed. But there was that flowering in the late '70s in which you could sell about six or seven hundred copies of a book. Now it's down to about three hundred. I was talking to someone from the Canada Council and they said that the average poetry book sells about three hundred copies.

I talked with Karl Siegler from Talon and Brian Lam from Pulp Press. I think they sell more than that. But they're fairly well established, too.

Yeah. Talon's been around since.... I don't remember when Pulp came in. I think '76 or something. Yeah, they've been quite single-minded about it. And I think what's happened is they've developed this kind of—Pulp, in particular—cooperative around the publishing venture, which has really allowed it to flourish.

Cooperative labor, you mean?

Yeah. I think at Intermedia at a certain point I ran against my partner, and it was really hard to keep doing it. And through the '80s, actually, Intermedia Press grew quite substantially. And the commercial printing side grew, and I became the production manager. I actually worked at Intermedia until, I guess, '89. And I quit. And went out basically on my own.

When you say "cooperative," what—?

Well, in a cooperative, I think, you end up with cheap or free labor. Sort of an earmark, in a sense. Donated labor.

Writers are donating their labor? Who's donating their labor?

Oh, I think the authors as well as the—

Everybody involved.

Yeah. Publishing is odd because in many ways it's done as a labor of love. It's an art as well as a business.

How do you earn your living now?

Well, I have two methods. When I left Intermedia I sold my share to my partner and he's paying me out over time. So I have an income from that of which I'm trying to save as much as possible. I also scaled my standard of living way down in the last few years at the press, because I knew I was going to leave. And I do some graphic design work. I've got a computer on which I do typesetting and some design. I do some art work. Actually, I've been selling more lately.

I sort of...in about 1988...I'd always sort of identified myself as a poet first and artist second. I think that's why, one of the reasons why, Intermedia was successful in the printing, was because I was quite a skilled graphic artist. Almost by accident. My poetry always was the most interesting thing to me, but it came harder to me. And the graphic arts and the art skill was kind of facile and I always sort of passed it off. But I really got kind of tired of the small audience that poetry has. I didn't seem to be reaching very many people. I also noticed that it

444

wasn't hard as an artist to have an opening and have two hundred people come and, you know, the papers come and write reviews of your work. And I thought, Jeez, you know, poetry is just not as rewarding. So I thought I'd shift my focus, my major focus, from poetry to art. I guess in some ways it's been easier for me. I haven't given up writing poetry and I certainly haven't given up reading poetry. And maybe it's made me a better poet, I'm not sure.

But I always define success in writing poetry in my own terms. If I could write poems that I felt met my criteria for excellent poems, then I'd be happy. Worldly success wasn't really—I didn't think that was really in my package. But I guess maybe it was. Maybe it was. Maybe I expected some kind of recognition from the poetry that I never got. Or maybe I—you know, I feel in my own mind that I've written some excellent poems that meet my criteria for excellence.

And so, in a sense, I could shift my focus for my identity from poet to artist and feel that I had accomplished what I had set out to do, I guess, as a poet. I think the poetry has always come harder to me. I never had a flashy talent for poetry. It was something I worked at quite hard, and I really appreciated the results. But, I don't know, I guess that's the best I can explain it. So I decided to capitalize on what was my more, in a sense, facile talent. And I've been able to do that.

The art has really interested me. My basic ideas are the same. It's just that the mode of expressing them is different. And I think, really, my philosophy when I was younger—I've always been most interested, really, in philosophical poetry. And Philosophy. My minor was philosophy. When I was younger I had a much more complicated view of the world. As I've gotten older my view has simplified. [Both men laugh.] And so, as a writer of philosophical poetry, you know, I sort of have less to say. [They laugh again.] I always felt that art was too simple, that you couldn't express complex ideas the same way you could in poetry. And I guess I still feel that to a certain extent, but my philosophy has simplified down to the level of art. Really, that's basically the truth.

I thought that as we got older we were supposed to feel more humble because we realize how much more complex the world is than we thought when we were young.

Yeah, I suppose. But maybe—I used to say when I was young that I was an existentialist. The existentialist looked at the world as being absurd, and his response was kind of despairing. And then I became interested in Zen. And I looked at the world as being absurd, but lost that sense of despair, just sort of accepted it. And then later I became interested in Dada where you see the world as being absurd and the only rational response is to laugh. Poke fun at it. And I think that's really the transition of my philosophy. You know, humor and poking fun. Parody. These have become, to me, pleasures. Tweaking the public imagination. Poking fun at institutions. This has really become my pleasure.

I never thought of the laughing Buddha as a Dadaist. [Both laugh.] *The transition makes sense to me.*

I suppose that sense of surreal juxtaposition and all of that has also, I would hope, informed my poetry. I've become more liberated in some sense. I think my poetry has moved to a lyrical or perceptual base from a philosophical base. I've felt like, hey, I've lived through all these different ideas, and I've said it all, and now my view is a lot simpler. My view of life is a lot simpler. In a way, it's a change almost from anger to play.

I think I've been enjoying myself more. I'm enjoying what I do. Sometimes I feel disorganized because I don't have the same structure in my life than with all the kids, and I used to work nine to six. But I still found plenty of time to do poetry and art, even when I was working. I just made the time. I made it. It was important to me.

Right.

You can fool yourself a long time about what you should be interested in, but at a certain point you abandon those things that don't interest you and you pursue the things that really, fundamentally, interest you despite all the circumstances of your life. You pursue them. I think I'd say that about both poetry and art. I've pursued both of them despite what I was doing for a living, you know, how many kids I had. I never really slowed down my activity. I had to find different methods

446

of, shall we say, getting it out. I had to find different methods but I never slowed down my activity.

Getting back to Intermedia for a minute—was Intermedia formed to produce and promote the work of the people who formed Intermedia?

No, I wouldn't say that. What happened is we wanted to produce and, to some extent, write books. And what we did is when our capacity to produce books became a lot greater than our ability to write them, which was right away, we started looking around for poets and other writers who interested us.

See, at first Intermedia was like a co-op of a whole bunch of people from different disciplines. And so there were the poets and there were the visual artists and the sound artists and the filmmakers and the sculptors and the electronics people. And the idea was cross-fertilization. That worked pretty well.

So the Society was the important thing to begin with.

Yeah. And so the poets and the Society, from the need for the Society to have access to printing, and the poets' need for access to printing, formed Intermedia Press. So the press did promotional things for the Society as a whole. But Intermedia Press—the poets' part of Intermedia Press—was a facility and anyone could come in as long as they knew how to use it, could come in and use the equipment. They just did their own thing as long as they didn't destroy the equipment. So that went on for a number of years.

And then as those of us who were using it most became interested in offset, Intermedia Society was beginning to dissipate. So we got together and bought this Rotaprint for three hundred bucks. We each put in a hundred bucks. And then it became like Intermedia was using our press. You know, it wasn't really defined very well, but at that point those people who had their hundred bucks in the press, you know, were the core, and it became a case of ownership in some sense.

So then what happened was we figured out a couple of projects that were like a make-work scheme that went on for four or five months where we had like seven people on it. So the three of us who owned the press were three and then we got four other people to come in. And we had this project where we would do printing for anybody at cost without labor. Because the government was basically paying you a sort of minimum amount of money for labor. You know, it wasn't welfare but it was like training, make-work training, that kind of thing. So we'd print anything for anybody for the cost of the paper and the ink.

But then when Intermedia Society went its different ways, Intermedia Press, which was the three of us, and then later the two of us, you know, we had to move the press to a warehouse and we became kind of the owners. And at a certain point we bought a compugraphic typesetter and we hired someone to be the typesetter. And little by little we acquired employees.

It actually took us a couple of years to get to that point. When we first did that in '73 we paid ourselves fifty bucks a month. I don't know how we lived. I really don't. It was kind of live-in-your-van kind of stuff and for a couple of years I lived at the press itself. My partner's girlfriend had a job so he had a place. So he lived there and I lived at the press. I mean it was pretty subsistence living.

There was a transition there. And I always date it around '73 when my partner and his girlfriend went to Mexico and I was left living at the press. You know, it was like zero zero zero. At that point it became an ownership situation. There had been three other guys renting the warehouse with us. And at that point, for some reason, everybody sort of went their way and I was left holding the warehouse bag. And my partner goes to Mexico and that's like—'cause we owned the press and one part of the warehouse but the other guys, you know, had studios and stuff. So I really see that as the beginning of it being get-a-job or get-serious-and-do-commercial-work-as-well. It was really a turning point.

Jumping ahead now to Bite Magazine—*do you want to talk about your plans for that?*

Actually, we'd been a participant in the mail art network. What I did in about '71, we had this thing called *The Poem Company* and we'd print an eight-and-a-half-by-eleven sheet with four poems on each side, folded down, and that'd fit in a small envelope and we'd mail them off. So we'd print about five hundred copies and we'd mail off four hundred and keep a hundred. And we did fifty issues of that. And at the end we bound them together, so we had this *Poem Company* book, phase one.

Then *The Poem Company*, phase two, was a bunch of monographs. Really, chapbooks. And at one point we bound four of them together to make a book. Sewn binding. Both of them actually have sewn bindings, hard cover. Phase three had a soft cover. But we had a sewing machine. We actually got this old clunker sewing machine for— I think we paid thirteen hundred bucks for it. No, three hundred! He wanted thirteen and we said no, and then about six months later he said, "I got to get rid of this thing!" So three hundred bucks. You know, it's really—it was a clunker. It was a Bremer-Leipzig, pre-World War One, I think. But it worked! It worked. It was an old sucker. But it worked.

It's really fascinating, this stuff, how you had to really get into it. Because when you first got it, you didn't know how it worked, you barely knew what it was supposed to do. Actually, you didn't know. You had no idea. I learned how to do binding. I went to the library and just hung around and asked them how they—you know, they showed me all the binding techniques. So when I was able to sew a book with machinelike precision, then they got a machine to do it.

I was always sort of the production person. And then later we got a perfect-binding machine. Total bottom-of-the-line one, worked good. And for a long time we'd sew the book. And then we did the perfect binding. That's sort of like the universal binding, where it's sewn into a paperback. Makes nice books.

So, okay. Then *The Poem Company*, phase three, was a magazine very much like *Bite*. Same thing, really. The magazines were like twenty-eight-, thirty-two-page, staple-bound magazines. But at the end of it we bound them together. We did seven issues and we bound them together into a book. So that was happening also during the '70s. I was sort of running the magazine and the publishing side by side. So this idea of printing them separately and distributing them separately at first, and then binding them into a book, is something that I've been doing all along.

The way you describe Intermedia—the Press, I mean— it sounds like kind of an exploration into the possibilities of what can be done, given the tools you had access to and the people who were interested. Do you agree?

Not really, no. I think Intermedia in 1973—I would date that as the beginning of Intermedia Press—we knew what we wanted to do. We wanted to make a print shop that was basically specializing in the printing and publishing of books. And we gave that up about 1981. Because, first of all, in Canada we saw the rise of these monster book-printing shops, mostly in Winnipeg where they have inexpensive Mennonite labor. And all the publishers—publishers are incredibly cost-conscious—they go to where the printing is cheapest. Those monster shops didn't start out being the best quality but now they produce excellent quality. So our situation was we had old equipment, clunky equipment, and sometimes inexperienced labor, so we weren't really competitive in book printing. And also we had become more and more interested in color printing.

In the late '70s I started taking night-school courses at the graphic arts vocational school, the Vancouver Vocational Institute, and I learned how to do color printing. Luckily, the Miehle we had was an excellent press. What a great press that was. We actually had two of them; we bought a second one, really cheap. You know, ten-thousand-dollar presses that could print this huge press sheet in full color. Better coverage than the Heidelberg. I mean these are great presses! Really great. The '57 Chevy of presses. Actually, more like the Mac truck of presses. They were good machines.

What would you like for Bite *and for* The Poem Factory *now?*

What would I want for them? What I'd like to do is—I like the idea of *The Poem Factory*. I like the metaphor. *Bite* is pretty well defunct. I like the idea of a metaphor, to kind of crank it out on an inexpensive medium. I would like to do more visual poems myself. And, boy, I'd like to just keep cranking out *The Poem Factory*, slightly modifying the format.

See, the first *Poem Factory* is going to be thirteen issues, and then that format will be wrapped up. But keeping basically the same format, longer poems, figure out some format for visual poems that makes sense. Maybe even post cards. But keep it on a really inexpensive, kind of humble level.

The books make me a little nervous, but Carolyn really wants to do them and so, again, I'm becoming the production person and she's becoming the marketing person, and the editorial decisions we more or less make together. So I don't know. I like the relationship because— I know how to do the marketing but I'm not good at it. I'm a lackadaisical bookkeeper. She's very good at it. She likes it and the production part scares her. But for me, the production is—I like hands-on.

That's really why I like my identification as an artist, because I can go down and turn on the table saw and feel like I'm making things. That's really important to me. It's actually my favorite activity, making things. I don't want *The Poem Factory* to overwhelm me to where it's taking up all of my time But I'm totally willing to devote like twenty-five percent of my time to it. I love books. You know, I love books. I like making them, I like binding them. I like reading them.

My mother is an incredible reader. My father was, boy, he could read, but he was really an unschooled person. But on my mother's side—it obviously comes from that—my mother always said that her father used to, you know, he'd bring home, almost every day he'd bring home a new book.

And I've gotten that way. I probably bring home five books a week, easy. I go to second-hand stores. I stop in at used book stores. Occasionally I read a review or something of a book I've got to have. And then I'll come back from Bumbershoot with several weeks' worth. I mean they just pile up in my house. I've got bookcases and bookcases. I hate to get rid of books, too. I just hate it. I've got an incredible collection of poetry! Because of being in the poetry-publishing field you do incredible trades. So that would be my number one specialty area of books. But I'm not a book collector. I just hate to get rid of them. They're not well organized. One time I tried to put them all by author, but then I changed bookcases.

So I think of myself, in the Greek sense of the poet as "maker," as a maker. I like to make things. That really is my place in life, I think, is making things. But I'm not that great at distributing them after I make them. I make them and I want someone else to take them on. The distribution. And I think at Intermedia that worked quite well. As long as my partner was willing to help in the marketing it worked really well.

But in about, say, '79 or so, he really became much more interested in the commercial printing, because at the end of a commercial job you get paid. For the books, you really don't make your profit until the last ten percent of your books go out the door two or three years later. So from the business point of view the books were less interesting to him. And at that point my ability to produce them had increased. My skills, being the production manager, had increased. But I couldn't hold up both ends. I couldn't hold up the whole thing and do as good a job in the marketing as I could do in the production.

And then there was a recession in '81 in which, you know, as a business we had to look at and say, What are we doing? Where are we going? I could see then that what I was going to have to do was I was going to have to build up my equity in the business as part of my life plan, build up my equity in the business so that when I left I would have something to take with me. And, basically, that's what I spent the '80s doing.

As part of your life plan. What's your life plan?

Well, my life plan was to become, on some level, financially independent. I'm financially independent on a subsistence level now. So I still have the need to work and make money. But I don't see myself ever having a job again. I can't imagine myself applying for or taking a job, unless it was teaching part time. You know, teaching a couple of courses. I could do that. I mean every time you take on a free-lance job, you're taking a job. But I'm not going to take those where I would work for a company or someone else, even if I have to starve.

You've never been someone else's employee, have you? You've

452

never worked for a corporation, have you?

No, except for a corporation of my own creation. When I left Intermedia I had twenty-five people working there. And it becomes a monster with its own life. If you don't show up it doesn't affect only you and a couple other people, it's like twenty-five people are standing around. Sort of like, "Hmm, what's supposed to be happening now?" You're chained. And the chains are stronger than if you're working for somebody else.

But that wasn't what you referred to when you said you could never apply for a job. You weren't talking about making your own job. Or were you?

No. No, I'm not talking about that. Yeah, I'm basically saying that working for somebody else, or...I guess I never have, really. That's interesting. I mean I have it in my mind that I did have jobs before...well, not really. I never had any career jobs before the press. So I don't know. Sometimes I think.... Well, I guess I've been pretty single-minded and I've done what I could do.

You know, if I compare what I've accomplished, say, with Talon, I think Talon has really done.... Because of their single-minded kind of dedication to what they're doing, and their having a single-minded direction, they've really accomplished a lot. And I think what I've accomplished has been much more peripheral. I think the poets that we published and the kind of writing we published is more peripheral, less central, to your mainstream Canadian literature. We published a lot of people who were on the outside, you know. Idiosyncratic people. Immigrants. People that had something to say but sort of weren't in the old guard of writers born in Canada.

So what I've done I'm pleased with. I feel proud of it. And I hope that I'm able to continue at the same level. Hopefully, with what skills I have I've learned to become more efficient and more effective. Sometimes I feel I'd like to do a little more political rabble-rousing. I don't know. It's hard to say. But when I see something I think is wrong I try to be more effective in pointing it out and trying to effect change. As you get older, you know, your abilities to make things happen in the world—you become more able. You know which strings to pull and how to go about it. Pretty amazing, but it does happen. When you're young you exert a huge amount of energy to try to get—you don't get very far. When you get older you're able to exert a lot less energy, but you can apply it in the right places to make things happen. It's wonderful.

Those are all the questions I have. Is there anything else you would like to say?
What I didn't mention is the Museo. My Museo. As an artist one of the institutions I wanted to take on was the museum. So I'd been doing mail art as part of my activity. See, originally, with *The Poem Company*, instead of waiting for people to subscribe we would send it out for free. In the early days, postage was cheap, printing was cheap, and you could communicate with whom you wanted. So, for instance, I decided, well, I wanted to communicate with Allen Ginsberg and William Burroughs. So I got their addresses and I started sending them these things. Then eventually they sent us stuff back and we published it. And so what happened is that, because we published a lot of visual poetry we found that the artists were actually a lot more—somehow were very communicative. So I've been doing mail art trades since the early '70s. So this is like a parallel activity. This is what I was doing as a visual artist as well as designing the books and all the stuff I had to do at the press. The press was very helpful because in down time I could print my own stuff. So I have amassed a huge collection of stuff that's been sent to me in the mails. I mean really huge. It takes up a couple of rooms. So, at a certain point, I had to either dignify it and call it something, or throw it out. So I decided I'd call it the Museo. I made up a museum.

I like your choices there. We'll either exalt it or call it junk.
Well, in a sense you have to, because it starts to impinge on your life. You know, it's like I can't even get into this room. What is it, you know, what's going on in there? So I decided to call it the Museo collection. I've been trying to, little by little, organize it. It's the Museo Internacional de Neu Art. Because it comes from all over the world. I've

454

had correspondence with many in Spain and Italy and France, England, Germany, Holland, Poland, Rumania, Czechoslovakia, Argentina, Brazil, USA. It comes from all over. So I gave it an international name. And I've had a lot of fun with that.

So mail art and the Museo are like my, I don't know, my.... When you first start writing, magazines you send to won't publish your stuff. So you start your own magazine. You say "The hell with this," and then you put yourself in the same position. Even when you get published in magazines and you start to have a list of published poems, you submit them to a publishing house and they won't publish a book of your stuff. So you say "The heck with this," you know, "I'm going to do it myself." And then you learn that these institutions that are set up by society, you can parody and play with them the same as anyone else. So the metaphor, The Poem Factory, the metaphor of the factory, you know, you set up your own factory. It's a beguiling metaphor. And I think the same with the museum.

What's been part of my pleasure is setting up a metaphor and then getting other people involved in it. A while ago I set up something called The Specific Research Institute, which I suppose in some ways is following through on my interest in philosophy. And I have this buddy who, for him, this metaphor had real meaning. So he's like taken this on as an endeavor, and he's got these research projects going as part of The Specific Research Institute. You know, he makes a phone call, he says, "It's Terry Loychuk from The Specific Research Institute." It gives him, you know, it gives him a front. It's like a front.

I guess I like having working relationships with people. And one of the ways I do that, I'm quite clever at creating these kinds of fronts. You know, give me ten minutes and I'll whip up a wonderful letterhead. It's like, somebody else is gonna play this game? Hey, let's get a letterhead.

I've been very lucky in my family and their support. My kids have been great. I think, in my hierarchy of priorities, my family has always been first. Though my work would certainly be pretty close. I wouldn't abandon my family for my work. But I haven't had to.

Rolf Maurer
New Star Books

"...one of the ideas that Canadians have about the United States is that America is a country filled with people who basically feel that they have no real influence over decisions that are made about their lives. In Canada we're getting more that way, especially since we've had a series of small-c conservative governments throughout the last twenty years who don't want to involve most Canadians in important decisions that affect their lives."

I interviewed Rolf Maurer, publisher of New Star Books, on Sunday, April 26, 1992 at his apartment in Vancouver, British Columbia. We had stolen away from the small press book fair at the WISE (Wales Ireland Scotland England) Social and Athletic Club in east Vancouver where we both were showing books. It was an afternoon of intermittent rain and we sat at a table off the kitchen, sipping tea as we talked.

Born, raised, and educated—the University of British Columbia; degree in English—in Vancouver, Maurer is one of six children. "My parents were, to use the terminology of the 1970s Left, classic petit bourgeois. My father had a string of local travel agencies which, along with his hard work, provide him with, I guess, a certain amount of comfort in his old age and a certain set of views and values about how things ought to be. And some of those values, actually, I've soaked up. I've, almost by osmosis, picked up a lot of my father's habits about running a business. I tend to be very conservative in a lot of ways. I think the key to the press's survival is to stay out of debt, and we're managing to do that."

Maurer and a colleague each are able to take a small salary from the press. "One of the great things about not being married is that you're not forced to go and get a job that pays thirty, forty thousand

456

dollars a year, doing something you hate doing. I am able to make my living as a book publisher, although it's a marginal living."

New Star Books publishes six to eight new titles a year and has published at that level all the time Maurer has been with the press, eleven years at the time of this interview. Maurer was not one of the founders of New Star.

New Star actually was started in the '60s as a spin-off of an underground newspaper here in Vancouver called *The Georgia Strait*. *The Georgia Strait*, in the meantime, has metamorphosed into an absolutely, utterly mediocre entertainment-advertising medium. But it started out as an underground newspaper. A number of people associated with that paper wanted to publish literature and originally they created something called *The Georgia Strait Literary Supplement* which eventually turned into an organization that published small books of poetry and prose, experimental poetry and prose, under the name *Georgia Strait Writing Series*, and that became *The Vancouver Community Press*, and that in 1974 became New Star Books. I didn't come onto the scene until seven years after that, in 1981. So the press is actually quite old, by small press standards.

Yeah, it is. Who had it between '74 and '81? Who was publishing it then?

Well, the ownership history is an interesting one because it started out not really owned by anybody. It was just a group of people— it was really a collective effort in the true sense of the term, and nobody took the trouble to look after the legal niceties of registering ownership, registering names, things like that. That only came about in the late '70s when a dispute arose about the direction of the press and whether or not the press should continue to operate. As I understand it from the older generation who was there at the time, the infighting got so bad it got to the point where people were literally fighting over who got the typesetting machine and who got the Selectric. And one of the people who represented a faction that wanted to keep the press operating found out that nobody really, in the legal sense, owned the press, and he took the legal steps to register the company, register ownership, change the locks, get rid of the people who wanted to liquidate the press, and continue the press under what essentially became its current mandate, which is to publish books about politics and social issues, broadly speaking, from a left social democratic, left socialist, perspective.

Did you institute that mandate, or—?

I didn't. That was in place when I got there. I obviously have no trouble with it. There are a relatively small handful of presses in North America that have an overtly political focus the way we do. It's very common in Europe. Almost every country in Europe has at least a handful of overtly left-wing political presses. In North America there's, as I say, a small handful. Probably, in the United States, South End Press might be the one most people are familiar with. In Canada, there are a couple of small ones as well.

What's your role as publisher? Do you have a board of directors you have to answer to?

No. Essentially, when the press was reorganized, or I guess you could even say organized, in the mid-1970s it became something called a limited company. There was one person who owned a hundred percent of the shares and when he got out of that in 1990, spring of 1990, I bought him out. I bought a hundred percent of the shares. It's not a collective or anything like that. In some ways it's basically just another business, in terms of its formal organization. Although that's certainly not the way it operates on a day-to-day basis.

Essentially, when you've got two people working in a little basement, putting out books under relatively lousy working conditions for long hours, low wages, you're not going to be able to publish if there is not a very strong sense of agreement between the two of you about what the press should be doing and how you go about it. And that doesn't change very much if you go up to three or four people as we have been at certain times when things have been better.

So the mandate to continue the press as it was is voluntary on your part. You're not constrained to do it.

Yes. I mean, theoretically I could decide tomorrow, or we could decide tomorrow—Audrey McClellan, the other person—we could decide to do different kinds of books. But essentially we are both committed to doing the kinds of books the press does. Certainly the world doesn't need yet another commercial press or another mystery-novel press or something like that. Or a cookbook press. Not to put those down, but the gap we're filling is political books, books about issues that are not getting a lot of coverage in other media, in other kinds of books, and that's what we're going to continue to do.

What's your average print run?

Generally our first print runs are between two and three thousand copies. Sometimes they're a little higher. But two to three thousand is a fairly typical first print run for our books, and we reprint about one in five books. That used to be higher, actually. We're finding it much tougher now to sell books than it was five, ten years ago.

You expect to sell, then, two or three thousand copies over time? Not in a year, maybe, but over time.

Yes. Over time, yes.

That's good. How's your distribution?

Getting better, actually. Ironically, I think our distribution was much better ten years ago when we could still do our own fulfillment to bookstores. However, like a lot of publishers, there's been a lot of pressure on us in the last five or ten years to move away from that model of direct fulfillment and to move to a model of meeting the booksellers' needs through larger distribution networks. And we do now have national distribution in Canada, a good regional distributor out here, and we're in with two US distributors, Inland and Bookslinger. [Since this interview, Bookslinger has gone out of business.]

Getting back to 1981 when you began with New Star Books,

what was your role with them then?

Well, it's interesting. As you're probably aware, or anybody who's involved in small publishing is probably aware, there's very little specialization in small publishing. When you work for a small publishing company you do everything from reading unsolicited manuscripts to packing orders and sending them off to the bookseller. Everything in between as well. At various times, and quite often at the same time, I've read manuscripts, been involved in deciding which books get published, did substantive editing, did copy editing, did typesetting, did design, did production, proof reading, promotion, marketing, order soliciting, order fulfilling, invoicing, tracking down unpaid invoices, filling out application forms for government grant programs and things like that, organizing author tours—there literally is not an aspect of book publishing that I have not performed.

How many people were doing this?

Well, the reason I got hired, actually, is up until 1981 the press had one full-time employee, and that person generally hired people for shorter stretches of time. Now in the fall of 1981 the person who had been there for the summer was leaving that job to go back to school. She was a friend of mine. Lanny Beckman was the guy who owned the press at the time. He was looking for somebody to replace this friend of mine. This friend knew that in the job I had at the time I was getting stale, it was time for a change. She suggested to Lanny that he give me a call and see if I would be interested. He phoned. I immediately recognized the phone call as destiny calling, and on the spot knew that I was going to take that job. And I took that job. It was a matter of being in the right spot at the right time. It was also, very fortunately for me, the time when Lanny decided he needed a second full-time person. So I got that job and became one of the two factotums at the press.

What kind of work were you doing before you—?

I'd come from a journalism background. I'd worked on student newspapers at university, I had worked, directly or indirectly, for both of the daily newspapers here in Vancouver, *The Sun* and *The Province*,

I was—In the late 1970s there was a long strike at *The Vancouver Province* where I was working. During that strike I got a job at the local teachers union, the BC Teachers Federation, putting out their member newsletter which was a thirty-thousand-circulation newsletter that came out about sixteen times a year. And my job was to do most of the writing, editing, photography, design, production coordination—essentially putting out the newsletter. I'd been doing that for two years and, as I say, I was getting a little burned out and stale in that job, so the progression to books from journalism was not a leap.

I think the most important skill I was able to bring to the job was my editorial skills, and that's still, I believe, my essential skill, the thing that I actually do. I couldn't do any of the other things I do in publishing if I couldn't do that one thing.

Now your press publishes poetry and drama—

We don't do poetry at this stage, although it's interesting to look at the genesis or, really, the development of the press's editorial focus. The press started out as a publisher of experimental writing, including poetry and prose and stuff that was not quite either.

That's as New Star Books?

Well, that was even before New Star. The name change to New Star marked an important juncture in the history of the press because the people who were working on the press at the time, even as literary writers, were highly politicized. Essentially a decision was made in the early '70s that certain kinds of nonfiction books about politics, about political issues and social issues, were more important than, you know, bourgeois pastimes like poetry and "litrachah, you know." And the name change to New Star Books apparently was a reflection of that sharpening of emphasis. The name New Star did evoke, was meant to evoke, the image of China which in certain parts of the Left was very much a model of how socialism might actually work. Of course, we know a lot better now. Interestingly also, in the last five or six years there've been many discussions about the name of the press, and there are people, friends and associates of the press, who think the press's

461

name should be changed to something a little less clunky and a little more, shall we say, sleek and Anglo-Saxon, to make things easier to sell.

Such as?
Well, McClellan and Stewart is a big Canadian publishing company. Douglas & MacIntyre. You know, these kinds of double-barreled Anglo names. I guess they're not all Anglo. Simon and Schuster are not Anglo names. But that kind of inoffensive stuffy name. But we have decided to keep the name of the press because we think it is really important to be aware of the press's historical roots, and the fact that it came out of a certain time and place in history, and that time and place was the Left in British Columbia in the late '60s, early '70s. I think it's important to maintain that identity, that very direct link with the past.

Right. You haven't done poetry, then, since the early '70s?
We haven't done poetry since the early '70s, that's correct. A lot of the poets, a lot of the writers that we did do at the time have gone on to become quite distinguished poets in the very small world of Canadian and international poetry. But we haven't done any poetry since then. Again, I think it's part of the general thing that's happened on the Left in the last few years as a result of a whole range of incidents, including what's happening in Eastern Europe. There's been a real reexamination by people on the Left of some of our most basic beliefs and precepts, and what we think society should be like and how should we get there. And one of the ways that's been reflected at New Star is by a real examination of the kinds of books we do, what the role of those books is, and what different kinds of books might have a similar kind of role to play in the world. So in the last couple of years we have done a number of fiction and experimental prose books that are not quite fiction, not quite nonfiction.

I read one of them. Taxi! *by Helen Potrebenko. That's how I discovered New Star Books.*

462

Oh yeah. Yeah. Actually, that is one of the very few fiction books from the mid-'70s that the press did. But that's a good example of the kind of—it certainly isn't escapist fiction. It is fiction but it brings you very up-close, it brings you very face-to-face with realities of life for a very high proportion of people in not just Canada, but in North America—women who work for a living.

Another book that I think is typical of the new, broader approach we're taking is a book we did a couple of years ago called *Buddies* by Stan Persky, which I still find very difficult to describe. You have to read it. I personally think it's a wonderful book. It's unfortunately become a little bit ghettoized as a gay book. I think it's much broader than that. It's a book about the nature of sexual desire in general and how that sexual desire is very much a part of everybody, no matter how quote political unquote they might be.

But, yeah, we are trying to broaden it out and in the context of those discussions about the editorial focus of the press we've also been talking again about the notion of publishing poetry. I think we're still a few years away from moving back into that area, but eventually I believe we will do that.

Aside from political sympathies, is there a particular emphasis about what form you publish? Do you publish more fiction than nonfiction, or—?

Three-quarters, at least, of what we publish is still nonfiction. The reason for that is if you're talking about social issues in a direct way, that is the most direct and simple and easy way to deal with it. We'll always be preponderantly nonfiction.

What are your hopes or intentions for New Star? You speak as though you have a mission. What do you want for New Star in the future?

Well, starting with the simple, mechanical, day-to-day operation of the press, one of our main goals is to create a situation where the press has got enough financial stability so that we're not really worried about our day-to-day existence. Even now we're not really worried

463

about that, but I think we do need to find a way to cut ourselves a little bit more slack. I think that is important because it's only when you have a little bit of slack that you can really approach what you're doing with any kind of imagination.

See, one of the really big questions for anybody in the book trade right now, I think, has to do with the nature of books and the role they play in our society. Now, a century ago books were very important and influential. They were, for the nineteenth century, essentially what motion pictures are now, or television is now, in terms of impact and scope. They were the big-budget medium of the day. Now, in those terms, they're relatively trivial.

To me, as somebody in the book business, it's clear that the role books play in our society is undergoing quite a profound change. And I think that it is very important that a press be in a position to be aware of what is happening in the world, and be very conscious of how the press might have to change in view of the changes that are going on around us. As far as the political hopes that I have for the press, or that the press has, or both of us at the press have, we continue to believe that books do make a difference. I don't think that—I do think of books essentially as propaganda. That is to say, I do not think books can force people to think or do one thing or another. I don't think any medium can really do that. I'm very suspicious of people who say that violence in cartoons makes kids violent or, you know, violent pornography makes men go out and rape. I think individuals are responsible for their own actions and I'm suspicious of anybody who thinks they can fob it off on books or cartoons or something like that.

However, books do have a role, and the role is that they put points of view, they put ideas, on the agenda for discussion. For example, one book that we're working on right now is the book that's coming out on NAFTA, the North American Free Trade Agreement which is now being pursued by all three of our governments [Canada, the United States and Mexico], although it's unpopular in all three countries. We believe—we come from a part of the community that believes very strongly that this deal is bad for a majority of not only Canadians but for a majority of Americans and a majority of Mexicans.

464

We think that this is a debate that has to be held and has to be a serious debate, not one of these bullshit, election-year, pseudo-debates that, you know, I don't know about Mexico so much but certainly the United States and Canada seem to specialize in now.

So we're putting out a book that essentially is anti-Free Trade. Now we do not think the book itself is going to make a big difference. For instance, people are not going to read it or see it on shelves and decide that they're against Free Trade. But what this book will do is it will be one of the things that force this issue onto the public agenda. It will make it something that people are going to be forced to deal with in one way or another.

So, in an indirect way, we believe that if there is a really serious debate on this issue—the anti-Free Trade—and if people really feel that this is a debate they have anything to say about and that they're part of, we believe that that proposal will go down in flames. The biggest danger is that the deal will slip past because people don't really know what's going on; they're not really being kept all that aware by the media. I think that is the almost overt supposition of the people who are promoting the deal. By putting out a book like this we make it harder for people to get away with that. We make it obvious that there is another point of view to be had. And the role of the book essentially is to present the con arguments in a fashion that is rational, credible, and can't be just dismissed out of hand as the work of a bunch of kooks.

So I think a book like that—it's called *Crossing the Line*, incidentally—a book like that is an example of the kind of work that New Star thinks is important to do. The book itself, as I say, is not going to change the world, but it might contribute to a debate involving a large number of people, particularly in Canada but also in the United States and Mexico.

When the book is published and you give it to Inland and Bookslinger, both of whom sympathize with the Left but who are essentially literary distributors, how does this book get to people who have the position to influence decisions?

Ah hah! Well, I'll answer that question by backing through it.

The people who influence those decisions—I think it's interesting to hear you say that because one of the ideas that Canadians have about the United States is that America is a country filled with people who basically feel that they have no real influence over decisions that are made about their lives. In Canada we're getting more that way, especially since we've had a series of small-c conservative governments throughout the last twenty years who essentially don't want to involve most Canadians in important decisions that affect their lives. However, there is in our country, as in the United States, a strong tradition of grass roots influence on large political decisions. So as far as getting this book into the hands of people who make these decisions, that's everybody, as far as I'm concerned.

The other thing that your question suggests is one of these little dichotomies that, because there is such a thing as fiction on the one hand—capital L, Literature; capital A, Art—and on the other hand you have nonfiction, serious books about nonfiction topics, there is a belief that people who read one kind of book are not the same as people who read another kind of book. In fact, there's no truth to that at all. Every bit of research you might do will find that people who read fiction also read nonfiction, people who read nonfiction also read fiction. Now there are some people who don't read one or the other, but essentially, as groups of people, as audiences, they are the same kind of people, the same social class, background, same kind of educational backgrounds. They're really the same people, so you might even have a household where there's a couple where one person reads more fiction and the other person reads more nonfiction, but essentially they're both the kind of people we're trying to reach. There's no essential difference, I don't think. They're not different audiences.

That may be so. In fact, I agree that those who read serious fiction, which is the kind I publish, would probably read some of your books as well, and vice versa. But we don't really sell to the reader. We sell to the bookstore. Or to the distributor.

Yes. That's an important point you bring up. In fact, when I was talking earlier about one of the challenges that is facing book publishers over the next decade or so, that has to do with the question of reaching book readers rather than booksellers. It is a fact, and I think an unfortunate fact, that as publishers most of our efforts are actually devoted to selling our books to booksellers, not to book readers. And I think it's one of the main structural problems in the whole book-publishing world.

Our own press is very interested in using direct mail as a way of reaching readers. I'll give you some basic facts that will put this into perspective. For the last ten years or so, ever since I've been in the business, the big buzz word, or big buzz phrase, has been that the weak link in book publishing is distribution, that there's a problem getting the book from the publisher's warehouse to the bookseller. This is not true. If you go into any bookstore you will find a four- or six-volume book called *Books in Print* or you'll see a little CD-Rom version of it. In Canada the number of books that are in print and theoretically available to readers is somewhere around three-quarters of a million. The number is not quite as high in the United States because the Canadian book market represents an overlap of the British and the American and the Canadian book markets. But even in the United States the number would be well over half a million titles that are in print.

If the book is listed in *Books in Print* any bookseller in North America can get a copy of that book. If you, as a book reader, want a copy of a book, you can go into a bookseller's and, assuming the bookseller is not on hold with the distributor who has the book, that book is available anywhere within three days to three weeks, which is quick, right? Basically, anything that is available within three weeks is available.

The problem is the way books are bought. Most books are not bought by people going into a bookstore, looking for a particular book. They're looking for something to read, something to stimulate their mind, or maybe they have a list of books in their head that they'd like to read and if they see one or two of them they will pick them up and take them home and eventually read them. All the research shows books are what you call "impulse buys." You walk into a bookstore, you walk out of the bookstore with at least one book that you had no intention of buying when you walked in that day. You might have gone in wanting to buy, oh, something by Gore Vidal or Margaret Atwood, and you might buy that book or they might not have that book in the store that day, so you might buy another book by that person. But the key is the book has to be in the store for you to make an impulse purchase.

Now, I told you about that figure of a half million to three-quarters of a million books in print. How many books do you think are available in your local bookstore? Well, I'm not going to ask you; you're a publisher. But most people out there do not realize that a typical bookstore has somewhere between three and seven or eight thousand titles at any given time. A very good bookstore is going to have somewhere around fifty thousand titles. Elliott Bay is probably in the fifty-sixty thousand range.

I think they're closer to a hundred, actually.

They might be closer to a hundred. So if they're a hundred, that means they have at any given time twenty percent of all the books that are theoretically available to readers. So, as far as I'm concerned, the real bottleneck in getting books from the publisher to the reader is not the distribution system. It is the system of selling books through booksellers. And, along with a lot of other publishers, I look at that and say, "Well, how do we deal with this thing?" To me, right now, the answer is direct mail. In a few years it might be electronic communications, but right now the actual means is direct mail. And that, I think, for smaller, specialized presses, is the way to go, because booksellers are also facing certain kinds of pressures. With them, the pressure is on to get books that do not appeal to specialized markets, but books that appeal to the broadest possible audience, and the more specialized you are as a publisher, the more difficult it is now to get into bookstores.

So when you talk about direct mail, you're talking about very specialized mailing lists.

Yes. Over the years we have not ever pursued direct mail in a big way, but we get a lot of people writing in, people who have managed

468

to find our book in a bookstore, and, you know, they send a post card, "Please add me to your mailing list," that kind of stuff. We have got a mailing list of about three thousand names that way. And whenever we can, we try to do a complete mail-out to everybody on that list. We tend to get a relatively low response rate, but—

What is your response rate?
Between one and a half and two percent.

That's fairly typical.
It is fairly typical, but it's not bad. I'd like to see it around two to three percent. If we could do mailings of ten thousand and get two to three percent response, then it would be worth doing three, four, five times a year, maybe monthly. Right now, at the scale it's at, it's not worth it. But I do believe that essentially—

Booksellers, by the way, hate it when you do direct mail. We did a direct mail-out to six thousand people before Christmas and inevitably two or three people on the list were booksellers. And we heard about it. They believe that this is a threat to them. I personally don't think it is at all. None of the research, none of the evidence, suggests that direct mail is any kind of threat at all to booksellers. In fact, all you have to do is look at the history of the Book of the Month Club. If a book is chosen by the Book of the Month Club it is sure to become a bestseller in bookstores as well. Nonetheless, many booksellers feel threatened by this and we've been told a number of times that if we do this, if we continue to do this, they will just not carry our books anymore.

I was forced to make a choice between bookselling to bookstores and direct-mail selling. Although in the immediate term bookstores are much more important to us, in the longer term direct mail is a lot more promising. And I think it is the way to go for small presses.

I just finished reading John Tebbel's history of book publishing in the United States. He talks about that happening in the US, but that was in the nineteenth century. Booksellers still may resent it, buy they're not threatening anybody anymore. Not that I've heard about.

469

Well, they're not in a position really to threaten the Book of the Month Club. But they really do discourage us from doing it. There's no doubt about that. Some of them have their own direct mail efforts and I applaud them for doing that, but still, they're only selling the books that they're carrying in their stores.

How do you define your primary market? Is it libraries, or university classes, or—?

It's to readers. Our primary market is to people who read books for enjoyment or self-improvement, their own education, their own curiosity. That's who we're interested in.

I find myself responding to the notion that books are dead. I think that is utterly laughable. Ten years ago we were reading a lot about the death of books and in the last few months there's been another spate of articles talking about the death of the book and the electronic book and stuff like that. Believe me, as a technological device for storing, for encoding and disseminating certain kinds of information, the book is one of the most fantastic inventions ever. I think it will be many, many, many centuries before books are obsolete. To me, the real source of excitement in bookselling right now is dealing with the question of how the role of books is going to be changing from this generation to the next. In spite of the fact that I'm tired from working six-day weeks and long hours at no pay, I'm really galvanized and excited by the prospect of being a part of publishing in an era when it's really changing dramatically.

Brian Lam
Arsenal Pulp Press

"And that second group drifted away, but there was not a group to take its place. There wasn't that sense anymore of publishing as this great romantic adventure. A lot of them said, 'Well, I'm getting older now and I want to start making some money....'"

I interviewed Brian Lam, co-owner and copublisher, with Stephen Osborne, of Arsenal Pulp Press, at the press's offices in Vancouver, British Columbia on a sunny morning in the first week of September 1992. Born and raised in Victoria, British Columbia, Lam at the time of this interview was thirty years old. He came to Pulp Press from the University of Victoria where he earned a degree in creative writing. As a student he was in a co-op work program that enabled him to work half of each academic year at Pulp and continue his studies for the other half. Upon graduation he was hired full time. That was in 1984. "I've been really fortunate to be able to get my foot in the door in that way. Particularly given the lack of opportunities for publishing on the West Coast. 'Cause most of the people in my position would have to go to Toronto if they want to stay in Canada and if they want to get an actual job in publishing. They certainly wouldn't be able to get a job in the kind of publishing house that Pulp Press is because most of the publishing houses in Toronto are Canadian branch plants. The Penguins and the Random Houses and that sort of thing." In 1991 Lam became a partner in the business.

The press currently employs two full-time people and one part-time person. Seventy-five percent of what it publishes is imaginative literature, the remainder nonfiction, including Native Studies and regional history. In addition, Pulp Press publishes a series of tiny anthologies of quotations on various issues and personalities.

Lam is also on the board of directors of Geist, *a magazine run*

471

by Steve Osborne. Osborne, who was one of the founders of Arsenal Pulp Press, founded Geist *in 1990. He intends it to be the Canadian version of* Harper's Magazine.

That's what's interesting, comparing what's across the border. It's just a physical border, but there seems to be quite a lot of difference in operations. One good thing about being in Canada is that we get a lot more funding than what I hear is available in the US.

Is it difficult to get?
It's fairly difficult. You have to have a certain number of books in print, and some of the programs require certain levels of annual sales in order to qualify. But I think if one is serious about publishing in Canada, then it's fairly good access into these programs. The main rationale for the programs is [based on] the fact that the population of Canada is only twenty-eight million people. Hence, given the scenario of books being published only on supply and demand, a lot of books that should be in print that deal with Canadian issues, Canadian personalities, wouldn't be published because the demand just isn't there. Hence the existence of various grant programs allows that as part of the promotion of Canadian culture.

The way the Canada Council works is that they have what's known as a block grant program. You have to have sixteen titles in print in order to qualify. You submit all the titles that you published that year and then they make an assessment based on the sheer number of titles you published that qualify. Also, they make a judgment in terms of the kinds of things you're doing, where you're going, and that sort of thing.

When you say sixteen titles in print, does that include your backlist?
That's right.

So you can do two titles this year, but if you've got fourteen from previous years, then you'll qualify.

472

That's right. Yeah. Once you qualify for the block grant program, you're basically in. For a lot of presses, especially the younger ones, getting to that point, getting sixteen books in print, is awfully difficult. 'Cause you're asked to go it alone for those first titles. It's almost like a trial by fire, I think. If you can make it to that point, then you're rewarded.

When I was in academia I applied for grants and I found that the people who distributed the money—I'm not talking about individual philanthropists, but government and university clerks—are really contemptuous of people trying to get that money. Do you find that attitude when you apply for a grant?

Um. Well, the grants that are set up in Canada are made specifically for book publishing, so we don't really run into that. We do run into it in the community at times. Especially those who are not convinced of the viability of having these grants for publishers, and feel that the market should be the ultimate factor in getting books published. And there are a lot of people who feel that if the market isn't there to justify its publication, then it isn't worthy of being published, regardless of its content. That kind of rationale I don't agree with. I think there's a lot of valuable material—

There's an implicit reference to time there. If the market isn't there within what period of time?

That's right. And that's ultimately what makes a book profitable or not profitable, is the time factor. And given the kinds of books that we're interested in, in terms of their being literary books and regional books, they aren't going to be instant best sellers, no matter how good they are. That doesn't mean they shouldn't be published.

How many do you print on a first run?

For literary books, it's about fifteen hundred copies. For our nonfiction titles, we do two, three, four thousand.

How long does it take you to sell fifteen hundred copies?

473

Two years. Two to three years. It's the general life span of a first print run for a literary title.

I find the same thing. If it's going to be reprinted it'll come—well, I can't tell. I have one novel that needed reprinting after four months. Another took four years. [Both laugh.] Yeah. And some don't get reprinted at all. Yeah. But I think that's one thing we have in common. You have to look at the long run. The two-week or two-month frame of reference for Dell, for example—they'll print fifty thousand copies of a paperback, expecting to destroy half of them, those that aren't sold within two or three weeks.

Yeah. The racks here at the supermarkets and the drugstores, they're all from that frame of mind. It's like if it doesn't go within two weeks, we'll just get rid of it.

Well, those books are designed to be sold at those places. The fact that they may be sold in bookstores is incidental. They're for the impulse buyer at a supermarket.

They're really more commodities than they are books.

Do you publish chapbooks?

We used to, in the 1970s. Pulp Press has an interesting history in and of itself. It was begun as a cooperative made up of disaffected UBC dropouts, including Steve. Basically, they started Pulp Press as a reaction to the kind of academic traditions of literary presses in Canada, in the sense of publishing the same kinds of writers and the same kinds of books over and over again.

When would this have been?

Pulp Press began in 1971. They financed it with a small printing operation that they started. They bought a second-hand printing press and set up a shop in a little warehouse and just printed poetry books on their own. And started the printing business on their own to finance the books. And with those poetry books they published chapbooks and posters and that sort of thing. It came out of the hippie movement of the late '60s and had a lot of anarchist roots as well. In fact, Pulp Press's most notorious moment was in the mid-'70s when it published a pamphlet called *The Application of Fire to Public Buildings*, which was a satire instructing people on how to go about guerrilla warfare.

[Laughing.] *That's a great title.*
Yeah. It's a satire, of course, but someone in Ottawa got hold of one and was shocked to find out it was a publisher which had just begun receiving Canada Council money. It was actually debated in the House of Commons. Steve has pictures of, you know, the national news when someone stood up in the House of Commons and said, you know, this is where public money is going. So it's quite notorious.

[Laughing.] *That's great. Who wrote it? Is it in your catalogue?*
No. It's gone now. It's out of print. But those are the kinds of materials that they were interested in. It was just—I think it was like a combination of people sitting down and putting this thing together and just writing out posters and taking them to these little stores and selling them. But those are the kinds of things they were interested in at that time. Very subversive, anti-academic kinds of books. And in the 1970s they also started up a typesetting operation. So they had the printing and the typesetting which helped to subsidize the publishing.

It's interesting that they started the business so they could start another business.
Yeah. Well, at that time the Canada Council was just gearing up and there really wasn't a whole lot of money there. There were some grants, but certainly not enough to keep it going on its own. You'll notice a lot of the presses started up in the late '60s and the early '70s— Talon and New Star and so on—and the chief reason for them starting up was the Canada Council.

Your degree is in creative writing. Do you publish through Pulp Press, or through Geist?
Oh, no. Actually, I don't publish. All of my energies have gone

into editing and running the press. I think at some point I do want to get into writing. I'll probably take a leave or something and do it seriously. But right now I feel fulfilled just working on other people's projects. I mean I just don't know if I could handle it psychically.

A lot of writers who go into publishing find that they get absorbed in publishing and don't do their own writing. And then a crisis point is reached and they have to make up their mind what they want to do.

It hasn't happened to Steve, because he's actually doing a lot of writing in addition to running the magazine and helping out at Pulp.

Does he publish his own stuff through Pulp Press?

Yeah, actually. He published one book with us. He's got another one coming out this fall.

But obviously that wasn't why the press was started.

No. Steve didn't start writing until 1985. So a full fourteen years.... But a lot of the people who were there in the beginning, a lot of the members of the cooperative, did write and were published by Pulp Press. Quite a number of the poets and fiction writers who were around at the time.

How did they decide on "Pulp Press" as the name for the press?

It was basically a satirical name. It's a take on the idea of pulps being disposable kinds of literature. They were meant to be read casually, but at the same time they were responding to a different kind of politics than your normal pulp kind of books which are just trashy romance novels, whatever. And the word "Arsenal" in Arabic means "house of skill"—

Oh. I was thinking in terms of a weapons arsenal.

Yeah. That, too. I mean words like weapons are connoted. The reason we called ourselves Arsenal Pulp Press is because legally we couldn't call ourselves just Pulp Press because it's considered a generic

476

name. So Arsenal is our way of describing Pulp Press. Hence the awkwardness of saying Arsenal Pulp Press.

Let's get back to your background for a moment. What kind of work did your parents do?

Totally unrelated to book publishing. My mother worked as a secretary. My father worked with a fruit wholesaler. My own experience, I guess, just came out of a real interest in books and the language and that sort of thing. I'm second generation Oriental, and so my experience has always been a Canadian one as opposed to a Chinese one. My parents were born here as well. And so, I.... Like I don't even speak Chinese. The disadvantage in that, of course, is that I feel removed from my Chinese heritage because I don't know the language. It's as foreign to me as it is to other Canadians. But I think the advantage, in terms of where it's led me, is that I grew to want to know more about books and the English language. It's given me a lot more skills than if I had been raised in a more traditional Chinese family.

I've always grappled with the issue of "Who am I?". Given my heritage and given my experience. Particularly in being a visible minority, you get people's reactions—I mean their first take on me quite often is "You're Chinese, so obviously you must speak the language and you must know this, you must know that." So you're always identified as being part of something that you may not necessarily be a part of. I don't find it so much offensive as just really interesting that people make assumptions about—I'm always interested in issues of identity and whether it's cultural, sexual or—and that sort of led me to what we're trying to accomplish at Pulp Press, which is getting involved with projects that challenge the status quo. My background has led me to that desire, I think.

Was Pulp doing that anyhow, and so you felt comfortable here, or did you make a change in Pulp when you came here?

We made the shift in the last six years. During the '70s and the early '80s they were strictly a literary press. I would say eighty percent poetry. And not necessarily books that have a particular point of view.

They were just collections by poets and writers that the editorial board felt were good in their own way. The last six years we've been making attempts to try to identify those issues that we would like to be involved with in terms of the kinds of books that come in our office, not only for our writers and potential writers and our customers, but for ourselves. To know where we're going, what we're doing.

We still describe ourselves as a literary publisher even though we're increasing the number of avenues that we're going down, in terms of the kinds of things we're interested in. Whether it's fiction or a book on native history or even our little books which deal with provocative issues, they all come from the same political point of view.

Which is?

Which is books that challenge the status quo. Like our little books, which most people assume we publish for commercial reasons because we do sell quite a few of them. At the same time, they do satirize certain social elements that we're interested in in terms of racism and right-wing politics and that sort of thing. We're not ashamed to say we're left of center.

You said "little books". Is that an imprint?

It's an imprint called Little Red Books. Which is based on the Mao book. Our first little red book was called *Quotations From Chairman Zalm* which was quotations from our then premier, Bill Vander Zalm. He was a very right-wing, fundamentalist premier.

When was this?

In the late '80s. He was best known for owning—you might have seen it on the highway—it's called Fantasy Gardens. It's like a Christian Disneyland, south of Vancouver. It's not as big as Disneyland, of course, but it's a very.... I mean that basically was his frame of reference, was this idea of being king of Fantasy Gardens. And the things he would say—he offended everyone from teachers to minority groups to...everyone. And what we wanted to do was a satire on him. It was Steve's idea to collect a book of his quotations over the years and

478

to mimic the Chairman Mao book. We published those as *Quotations From Chairman Zalm*. We printed three thousand copies, not knowing what would happen, and we sold those in a couple of weeks. It just exploded. We sold about thirty thousand copies. That was the first one that hit the mark. It was kind of a freak. We were publishing it for political reasons, not necessarily for commercial reasons. It was a lot of fun. And the news media had a field day with it. Since then we've broadened the Little Red Books to include issues as well as personalities.

By "hitting the mark", you mean success in sales?
Success in sales. Yeah. We had nothing even close to that before.

How many books a year do you do now?
Last year we did twelve. We've increased our publications from about seven or eight a year in the last few years to twelve to fifteen now. Last year we made a big move by hiring our second full-time person. That made a lot of difference. We felt like we were at a point where we could handle it financially. And it's given us a lot more time to develop our editorial program and also to increase our sales to pay for an extra person. So, in the long run, it's helped enormously. It's broadened our publishing program too.

How do you divide up the work?
Well, we are pretty loosely organized in terms of each of us doing a little bit of everything. We do have loosely defined areas of expertise. Our other full-time assistant, Wendy, is in charge of promotion, fulfillment, customer service, that sort of thing. My territory is more administrative and editorial. Also I develop promotion programs. But at the same time, if there's some books to pack, then I'll pack them.

Do all of you carry equal weight in editorial conferences?
Actually, the editorial decisions are made between myself, Steve, and we have another free-lance editor that we use, Linda Field.

479

She's the one who fields most of the unsolicited manuscripts. She weeds out the obviously bad ones from the potential ones. When she does come across manuscripts that are worth a second look, she'll pass them on to either me or Steve.

Do both you and Steve have to agree on what you're going to do?

Actually, Steve lets me make most of the decisions. I think he feels more comfortable in being a referee in terms of if we can't make a decision, if we have a split decision—

If you and Linda—

Yeah. He's going to come in at that point. He's a good resource person. But he feels confident enough to let us handle that.

So it's an issue of personalities. It's how your personalities work together.

Yeah. We've been really lucky in that way, because we all have the same point of view in terms of the kinds of things that we should be doing. There's no conflict there at all.

Many people see the small press movement as something that's social or political or economic or however they want to look at it. Do you see yourself as part of a movement, or—?

Yeah. Very much so. BC has a really vibrant writing and publishing community. I think that comes from the fact that we are so far removed from the rest of the country. Physically, Canada is such an enormous, spread-out country. I think there's the sense that the Rocky Mountains which divide BC from the rest of Canada are a real physical border that separates us and makes us different. There are quite a number of publishers that have made a success of just servicing and publishing for the community here in British Columbia. Are you familiar with *BC Bookworld*? It's made a huge impact on publishing in BC. It started in '88 or so. It has a really populist perspective and treats books as news.

480

Do the daily newspapers review your books?

The Vancouver Sun is great. They have a weekly arts supplement called *The Saturday Review* which is very supportive of local publishing, although I think there's also a sense that if it's local it's not as good as if someone more international comes to town.

Right.

Because we do get our books reviewed in the *Sun*, but at the same time we have to fight really hard to get interviews and that sort of thing, because we're just not as international.

That's interesting. In Seattle we can't get our books reviewed, but they're interested in doing features on us.

Oh. Well, that's interesting. Features on the press, or features on—?

Personalities involved with the press. That doesn't sell books, I don't think.

People aren't interested in the press but they're interested in things that you're doing. That's what sells your books.

We have a press in Seattle which is quite good. Good taste, beautiful covers. They've won a number of awards for writing. They've been in existence for only a few years but they put out a lot of titles every year. And there was a feature done on them in the business section of the Seattle Times. *[Both men laugh.]*

Yeah. That's an ongoing struggle. I mean we get reviews but we don't get the kind of support that I think we should be getting.

You mentioned Bookworld. *How does it differ?*

Bookworld is a quarterly publication in tabloid format. It prints fifty thousand copies, I think, and is distributed free at bookstores, libraries, that sort of thing.

Who publishes it?

Allen Twigg. He's a local guy. He's a really interesting person to talk to because he has a lot of contacts with the small presses. In fact, the last issue was a special on small presses of BC. Just flipping through it, I'm constantly amazed at the number of small presses there are that are just springing up. Not necessarily literary presses, but, you know, very specialized presses dealing with certain regions and certain aspects of the problems. It's just an incredible variety.

Another thing, in terms of local support for the kinds of presses we are, is the fact that in the last few years there have been quite a few alternative local publications, like Gordon Murray's *Noise Magazine* and also *The Vancouver Review,* in addition to *Geist Magazine.* I think a lot of that has to do with a reaction to the conservative nature of the newspapers here. *The Province* is a tabloid that doesn't do any kind of— all the reviews are off the wire. It's not really considered a serious venue for book publishers. There's another magazine called *Step,* which is a glossy magazine covering Vancouver's cultural scene. I think all those publications are responding to the dearth of arts coverage in the city. So even though there are certain aspects that are conservative and difficult to deal with, there are alternatives. There is an audience that justifies their existence.

Bookworld *again. If it's a freebie, how can—?*
Advertising. I think he does get a small grant, but it's basically advertising-driven. It's really given the BC publishing community a high profile. It's reaching people, in a very non-elitist way, who aren't necessarily looking at book reviews and aren't particularly interested in the arts. Nonetheless, we're getting the information to them. I think it's having a positive effect.

Do you know, you're the youngest publisher I've talked with so far?
Is that right?

Yeah. In fact, Karl Siegler told me that it was a real fear of his—now Karl is in his early to mid-forties—he said it was a real fear

482

of his that nobody would continue what he started. What his genera-
tion started. He didn't see any young people getting involved. And I
brought up that idea with a couple of people on COSMEP's board of
directors—they're an international organization of small presses and
magazines—just in conversation, and asked if they were aware of
any young people, younger than middle age, coming into the small
press movement. They couldn't think of any. So you're the first one.

I'm an anomaly.

Well, how old is Steve?

He's actually in his mid-forties. See, what's interesting is that
because a lot of these presses began in the early '70s, late '60s, those
people were all young, they were all in their early twenties when they
started, and there's been a very stagnant period ever since then. Not a
whole lot of new presses have begun since the early '70s, in terms of the
stature of someone like Talon or New Star. And those people who
started them are still there.

Well, Rolf [Maurer of New Star Books] *is pretty young too.*
He's thirty-seven.

That's right.

And you know each other.

Oh, yeah. That's another great thing about the community here,
is that we're very open if we have information. Exchanging, meeting,
doing a lot of cooperative things. Because, though we're all book
publishers, we do have different interests. New Star is specifically
political books. Talon is more specifically literary books, in terms of
experimental literature and that sort of thing. We're all good friends.

I don't think that's true in Seattle.
Is that right? Interesting.

There's not a lot of communication. It isn't that we dislike each
other. We tend to like each other.

Is there an association of Washington publishers?

Something like that. But it's not very strong, and it keeps threatening to fall apart. I'm not in it because nobody else in it does fiction. Fiction is such a strange creature compared to nonfiction. In any event, they meet once a month or once every other month, and that's about it. Oregon, I think, is different. I think there's a strong sense of community and mutual support. In fact, I've asked them about this and they say that's true. The writers and the publishers are all in it together. But not in Washington.

We have a really strong association here.

A formal association?

Yeah. And we have two employees. The association meets regularly and they have strong subcommittees, too. Like one specializes in publicity. There's a publicity group so that all the people who are in charge of publicity for all the presses get together and talk about who's doing this and who's doing that, and there's a real exchange of information. There's all kinds of activities, like seminars on production that the large presses will give to the smaller presses and show them how to do this more efficiently, and that sort of thing.

I found that my eyes just started opening up as soon as I started talking to people in other publishing companies. Just to find out how they operate and what their expectations were, which were totally different from mine in terms of being more ambitious. There are certain things I assumed were impossible, in terms of sales and how many books you could publish in a year and this and that. I found it just incredibly eye-opening to start talking meaningfully to other publishers.

What did you find, for example?

When I first started here our sales were like thirty thousand a year, which is all I thought small literary presses from Canada could do. We're also members of the Association of Canadian Publishers, which is the national organization of publishers.

484

What's the name of your association here in Vancouver?

It's the ABPBC, which is the Association of Book Publishers of BC. And talking to similar-size presses, having similar kinds of lists, and hearing that they were selling at two hundred thousand dollars a year opened my eyes, and I thought, Well, can we do that too? And now we're up to almost two hundred thousand a year.

What did it take to go from thirty thousand to two hundred thousand?

It just took a more concerted effort in developing our lists and opening up new markets and developing direct mail, trying to do more advertising, sending an author out on tour if you could afford to do that. We found that those kinds of investments actually do pay off in terms of getting the word out and producing sales. Those are the kinds of things we didn't think were possible. We didn't bother trying because we didn't think we could afford to do that. But we found that it did pay for itself.

And you started this when you came in?

Yeah. Probably a couple of years after I started here. Probably about '87. That was also the period when there was a sort of team built up of people involved in the press. There was a turning point which I think was a function of the age of the press, because at the time there were a lot of people who were getting older. These were the people who were there at the beginning and kept in with Pulp all those years and then decided they wanted to go back to teaching, or they had other interests. The personnel around the press were evolving so we had to redefine ourselves.

Could we talk a bit about the transition of the press? Pulp began by publishing poetry chapbooks. Many or all of the first ones were by the people who began the press. And that was in 1971.

Right.

And at that time it was a cooperative?

485

It was partially subsidized by the printing and typesetting operation. Actually, what happened was in 1981 Pulp Press had a distributor named Beatty and Church. It was based in Toronto. And they went bankrupt, holding, I think, thirty thousand dollars worth of receivables. And Pulp Press could not handle that financial impact. And so that first company actually went bankrupt. And the new company started up in 1982.

Pulp went bankrupt in '81 and started up again in '82?
Yeah. Started up in '82, brand new. And at that time a lot of the people from the old press didn't return. So that was sort of like the second coming. And at that time a whole bunch of people came to be involved with the press. Some were involved in just the typesetting aspects of the company but they were also interested in book publishing. So the people had changed.

The original contingent came from UBC, was it?
Yeah.

Now the second contingent—
It came from all over. A lot of them were working with the typesetting operation at the time. The method of operation for the press was the same in that it was still a cooperative, and publishing decisions were made cooperatively. I think there were about ten people on the board. From what I understand, it was a real cumbersome process because it led to all these conflicts. Because of personalities and interests and that sort of thing. And so it went along until about '86. And that second group drifted away, but there was not a group to take its place. There wasn't that sense anymore of publishing as this great romantic adventure. A lot of them said, "Well, I'm getting older now and I want to start making some money, and I could do teaching." Which is understandable because at the time most of the people at the press weren't drawing salaries. It was all volunteering. They had families to raise and that sort of thing.

So we had a meeting back in '85 or '86, I think, with the group

486

that was remaining. We had to make the decision as to whether to continue or not. I think Steve and myself were the only two that wanted to make a go of it still. So we were basically left on our own at that time.

When did Steve come into it?

He's been the one who's been consistent from the beginning. He and his brother, Tom Osborne, were two of the founders. And so, back in '86 was another turning point in the press, which we formalized last year by buying the company. Steve and myself. So that's how it's evolved over the years, in terms of the personalities involved.

An observation, having talked so far with only three Canadian publishers. With all three of you, your university life has been important to you. At least compared to the United States where people get their degrees and never think about it anymore. It has nothing to do with publishing. It has nothing to do with anything that they're doing now. It isn't necessarily that publishing in British Columbia follows naturally from university life, although it has for you because of the co-op program you were enrolled in. Or do you feel that your university experience led directly to publishing?

Well, personally, I feel it was a really important thing for me. I think without it I probably wouldn't have the kind of knowledge and direction that I think is necessary to be in publishing. So it's made an impact. I think Canadians do tend to feel that university is an important stepping stone to what they're going to be doing the rest of their lives.

I think Americans do too. But then it just doesn't seem to happen. I think they go to the university with that expectation, but it just doesn't work that way. At least not directly. There may be connections of a social or economic nature that they pick up.

Right.

But I can't think of anybody who did anything at the university that led them to publishing. They may have done other things that led to publishing, but they had nothing to do with the university. Karl, of

487

*course, was in opposition. But that in itself is a kind of relationship.
And then he's doing things with Talon now that he probably would have
liked to have done as a university professor.*

Mm hmm.

*And all three of you have started at universities or started with
other people who were at universities when they started the press. That
didn't happen in the States either.*

Uh huh. Well, how old are most of the presses in the States?

*They tend to be newer. They tend to have arisen, for the most
part, in the '80s.*

'Cause all of us started at the same time.

*Now a number of presses in the US started when you did, but
have not survived. My study is limited to the Pacific Northwest. The only
press I'm aware of in the Northwest that goes back prior to the '80s is
John Bennett's Vagabond Press, which no longer exists.* [Seal Press,
Madrona Publishers, Calyx, Copper Canyon Press, Strawberry Hill
Press, and Mountain Press Publishing all came into existence in the '60s
and '70s. Their publishers are interviewed in this book.] *He had it for
seventeen years, I believe. The last few years he published only himself.
Which is fine. He's a good writer. But aside from that one, I don't think
there are any in the Northwest, though there are a few scattered in other
parts of the country. But that would be different, too. I mean, you've got
this little cluster in Vancouver.*

Right. I think a lot of the reason we're all still around is because
of the grants that are available. There's no way we could be where we
all are today without them. We certainly wouldn't be able to have such
a big publishing program.

488

Karl Siegler
Talonbooks

"Canada is a third-world country.... It's everyone's favorite hinterland, right? We are hewers of wood and drawers of water. Culture? What culture? What legitimacy? Independence? What independence? National identity? What national identity?"

Talonbooks is the premier publisher of Canadian drama. It also publishes poetry, fiction and a nonfiction list focusing on ethnography and social criticism. I interviewed Karl Siegler, president and publisher of Talonbooks, in his office in the old warehouse section of Vancouver, British Columbia on April 28, 1992. At the beginning of the interview he was reserved, perhaps suspicious. But soon, when the questions enabled him to delve into his intellectual biography, distance gave way to gregariousness. He smoked continuously. On the tape his sentences are punctuated with an intake of breath; here he is dragging on his cigarette. His speech is both thoughtful and fluid, as though he has already been through much of this in his mind. Probably he has, for there have been crises in his life that he must have had to work to integrate into a personal history that would rationalize the decisions he has made.

He was born in Hanover, Germany in 1947—

I came to Canada with my parents in 1952. I was totally educated here except that I went back to Germany and took grade eleven in Hanover because, at the time, my ambition was to work in nuclear physics. My parents were very careful about maintaining all of our German-speaking skills but my vocabulary was essentially domestic and current-affairs oriented, and I thought it important to take a year of schooling in Germany to sort of boost my skills in that language in the physical sciences. Because, of course, most of the original texts were written in that language.

So in '63 I went to Germany for grade eleven, came back, graduated in '65, went from there to Simon Fraser University where I was one of many charter students. That was the year the university opened. It was one of the government's showcases at the time, designed by Arthur Erickson, referred to as the instant university. It was completely built and opened within eighteen months. It's one of the places that established Arthur Erickson's reputation.

Now the interesting thing, intellectually, about Simon Fraser University was that it was clean. It wasn't set up as a cooperative venture or with a hell of a lot of input from the University of British Columbia, right? The government appointed a board of directors and the whole university, in terms of its planning and construction and hiring of staff, was all done independently, and it produced a very interesting result.

Because, of course, the great cultural revolution in the so-called developed world began—actually can be dated to approximately 1963 and so was well under way by 1965—so when the people who put together Simon Fraser University hired the professors, they hired on the basis of resumé and reputation. It was early enough in the cultural revolution for the conservatives—small "c" conservatives—who were involved in that university from its origin not to be too sensitive yet to the question of political orientation of the people they were hiring. So, in effect, what happened is in every single department they hired what appeared to be, from the resumés and the letters of recommendation they were getting, the brightest young scholars that were available throughout the world. A lot of them came from the UK and the US, of course.

What the conservative government and the conservative board of directors got, much to their surprise, was the biggest collection of exciting, articulate, committed radicals that you could not have assembled if you'd gone out of your way to do it. Totally unbeknownst to them. So for someone like myself, this was a very, very, very exciting place to be because my own politics by that time were, um, distinctly unconversative.

490

And one of the most shocking things that happened to me when I entered Simon Fraser University with the ambition of becoming a nuclear physicist was that I made a basic realization about myself. Coming from a middle-class background as I did, I had always labored under the misconception that the "real world," in quotation marks, is divided between real work and your job and your obligations. In other words, you go and work as a wage slave or as a corporate citizen for someone else, doing something you don't necessarily like as a career, and then you make as much money as you can to finance your leisure time, during which you become who you really are. Right? That distinction is something that I inherited socioeconomically from my class. And, I must admit, my family.

As long as I could remember, I had always read literature voraciously. But always in my spare time. Like I'd go to school, I'd do my homework, as a kid I'd do my chores, sort of champing at the bit to lock myself in my room and get out my books and read till three or four a.m., right? One of the most shocking discoveries I made in my first year at university was that, in fact, culture, the arts, which means literature, belles lettres, social criticism, all that kind of stuff, could actually be the foundation of real work. Of course, it was stupid of me not to have thought of it before. It was basically a classist prejudice. Because I should have realized that since these books were around and they were commercial products and their authors obviously spent most of their time writing them—I just never made the connection that there were people actually working in culture, right?

So within the first semester at Simon Fraser in 1965 I made the decision that brought me to where I am today. Because I suddenly realized that there was such a thing as a cultural worker. And that the division of your life into working for somebody else and completing someone else's agenda, whether you liked it or not, but for which you got paid as much money as possible to finance your own life in your leisure time, was in fact an artificial, middle-class distinction. I was taught that right away because of the kinds of people that they hired and because of the discourse that was going on in the college because of the age—it was the '60s, right? It just connected.

491

And what I did is, I did a hundred-and-eighty-degree flip. I decided to change from science to the arts, to liberal arts, focusing on literature. And the other reading I did became, and still is, the physical sciences. I belong to scientific book clubs, I subscribe to *Scientific American,* I follow what's going on in nuclear physics fanatically. So I now read when I finish my work the same way I did before I got to university, but the other way around.

So '65 for me was the year of The Great Enlightenment where I suddenly discovered that you didn't necessarily have to divide your life into those two categories, that you could be the same person and pursue the same interests at the same time, that you didn't have to live with this artificial middle-class distinction between labor and leisure time. You didn't have to exist in the world as basically a schizophrenic. You could take destiny into your own hands and shape your own future within the ecology of the evolving commonweal. That's a stunning realization. And, of course, one of the other things that happened was I got very deeply involved in left-wing politics.

So there we were, a bunch of radical revolutionaries, rediscovering and reinventing the world. And it was part of a world-wide movement, the student radicals and so on. And Simon Fraser was very much a part of that because of the way the people had been hired, because of who they got and what their focus was, because they were all young radicals who had just finished their MAs and were still working on their Ph.D.s, or had finished their Ph.D.s and just done their first books. They were all left-wing or anarchists, right? So I got all caught up in that. I had my own great personal enlightenment and I got deeply involved.

I completed my BA in '69, reregistered immediately, worked on my MA, got a job as a teaching assistant—my career ambition, of course, was to become a literary scholar and a writer and translator. I began to translate German authors like Novalis and Rilke, both of which [translations] ended up being published later on. In fact, my MA thesis was an annotated translation of Rilke's *Sonnets to Orpheus*. Got a teaching job and intended to have a literary career.

Unfortunately, because of my involvement in university poli-

492

tics, and being on the wrong side when the Stalinist purge finally came, by the time I had finished my MA and had requested that my contract be renewed so that I could teach for a couple of years and then go on and pursue Ph.D. studies, my contract was not renewed. I applied at almost every university and college in North America that I could think of to get a job and enter the Ph.D. program, and despite the fact that I had an honors BA and a first-class MA I didn't receive a single response. What had happened in the meantime was that the political science department had been purged. A hundred and fourteen people were fired. This happened in the period '69 through '71. The Stalinist purge.

And I got caught on the wrong side of the political fence. They didn't have to fire me, fortunately for them. Because my contract had expired all they had to do was not renew it. As I said, I applied everywhere. I didn't get a single response from anywhere. It became very clear to me that my name was on a list of people not to hire no matter what their academic credentials were. And, as I say, mine were impeccable.

I don't know how it happened. Maybe there was a blanket decision in North America not to hire people from Simon Fraser, although I don't believe that because, of course, many of my colleagues who had other reasons for leaving didn't have any trouble finding placement in other universities and colleges.

I don't know how it happened, I don't really care how it happened, I know it did happen. Because the usual procedure when you get a legitimate job application is at least an acknowledgment, even if it's accompanied by the statement that there are no positions available right now. You know, usually what people say is "Thanks for applying. We'll keep your application on file. We don't have anything now. Don't call us, we'll call you." You know, it's a polite kind of acknowledgment letter. I didn't get a single one of those. Just dead silence. And that told me everything. I have no idea how it happened. And I have no interest, at this point, in pursuing it. These are just the historical facts pertinent to my personal situation, right? And, of course, having gone through that tremendous disappointment....

It was a terrible crisis. And, of course, since I had now become enamored of left-wing politics, I decided I should put my money and my life where my mouth was and go and join the working class, which I did. And I went off and I built logging trucks for a year.

Because, well, one of the skills that I had acquired in my younger days—I've always built custom cars and motorcycles, you know. All those real-men things, right? So one of the skills that I'd acquired was that kind of skill. You know, I had welding certificates and stuff like that. So, yeah, I joined Hayes Trucks which is one of the oldest logging-truck-manufacturing companies in the world. They are based here in Vancouver. They built, as I say, some of the earliest logging trucks. By that I mean like solid steel wheels, and then going on from there to steel wheels with solid rubber tires, and then pneumatic tires, and so on. So Hayes Trucks and the logging industry are kind of bound up. Truck logging and Hayes Trucks are synonymous. And it was there that I encountered the other political things that needed to happen to me to bring me here.

I discovered at Hayes Trucks that of all the classes of person that I have ever been associated with, no one was more bigoted, racist, avaricious, petit-bourgeois in our society than the working class. I was appalled. Of course I joined the union, I went to all the union meetings, I had coworkers. It was a very large plant: I was introduced to the working class in a very big way.

And I had another of those great enlightenments. That experience at Hayes Trucks totally disaffected me with left-wing politics. Because if this was going to be the answer to capitalism, if these jerks ever got into power, I didn't want to have any part of it. I was disgusted by [their espousal of] what they considered to be self-evident truths. Well, it was really one of those great personal crises. It was of the same magnitude as my introduction to Simon Fraser and the stuff they taught me earlier.

I injured myself on the job late in the year. I was too much, I guess, a bourgeois individual and too macho to go through proper channels and do all the whining and crying that's required, and filling out the bureaucratic forms, and registering with Workers Compensation, and so on. And the combination of severe pain, which I thought

494

was temporary, and my absolute disgust with the working class caused me to quit. I just quit. I walked out one day. Said, "Fuck this. I'm not coming back." Right? "I've had it. I've seen everything I want to see of the working class. Goodby."

The pain didn't go away for three weeks or a month. I finally went to the doctor and discovered that I had crushed three discs in my back. I hadn't reported the accident I had on the job because I was a tough guy, right? You don't whine and moan about pulling a muscle, right? You know, you grin and bear it. And it became clear to me after seeing the doctor and finding out about this, and recognizing that there was no way that I could now apply for compensation, that what I had done to myself was preclude physical labor as an option for the rest of my life.

So there I was. I was not a nuclear physicist. I was blacklisted in the academic community vis-à-vis my literary career. I was totally disaffected with the working class. And, over and above that, I had made it physically impossible for myself ever to join the working class again. And I felt—I mean that's the low point in my life. I had lost my politics, I had lost my career opportunities, I had screwed myself physically, and I spent about a year in just utter, total, personal despair. I didn't know what to do.

I was on unemployment insurance for that year. It was running out. And I needed to find something to do. I wanted a literary career. And I heard about this place called Talonbooks which was a very small, mostly poetry, publisher which had done a few plays. And they were looking for a business manager. And I thought, Hell, I've tried everything else. The middle class, the working class. I've abandoned my left-wing politics. And so, why in the hell not try that? I don't know anything about business.

So I came here on January the first, 1974 and the offer I made to the company was that I would work for four months for free, given the fact that I knew absolutely nothing about business. I was very open about why I was here. I explained my situation. I said I still wanted a literary career. This is about as close as I'm going to get, as far as I can tell, and I want a shot at it. I'll work for four months for free. I admit I know nothing about business. I have no formal training in it. I'll work for four months for free and if you think I'm doing a good job at the end of that time, hire me. If not, tell me to take a hike.

So I enrolled immediately in a course called "Accounting for the Manager" at British Columbia Institute of Technology, which is what it was called at the time. An evening course. Started here January one, and by the end of April I had a job. By the end of the year I had doubled sales, put into place bookkeeping systems, invoicing systems, hired sales reps across Canada, created cost-accounting systems, did all the business things and installed all the business systems and made all the business decisions and hired all the right people and signed all the right contracts to make this place work like a real business.

The first year I worked here I made thirty-five hundred bucks. Gross. Period. The company didn't make much more. By the end of that first year sales had doubled. They'd been growing at a rate of, say, between ten and twenty percent since 1967 when the company was founded. By the end of the first year that I was here sales had doubled and systems were in place. People were so impressed that I not only had the job, I was made a full partner at the end of 1974. For one dollar.

That's my personal history, and that's how I got here. There is a parallel history at Talonbooks that, curiously, starts in '63 as well. Which is quite interesting.

Speaking of 1963, you said that the world-wide cultural revolution could be dated to 1963. How is that? Why 1963?

I mean a lot of things happened that year. It's around that time that the Beatles were playing the Star Club in Hamburg. They just broke—in fact, the day I arrived back from my one year in Germany, in August '64, the day I arrived the Beatles were playing Empire Stadium. While I was in Germany I didn't get to Hamburg, but that's where they were playing, the Star Club in Hamburg, and their reputation was just breaking. Um, it's the year that the Rolling Stones appeared on Ed Sullivan, I believe. I'm not sure about that. Kennedy was assassinated in November '63. And, of course, that whole movement which I date to that year—you should also know that I'm an ex-musician, a rock-and-roller, and so on—um, so I date it personally to that year. That's the year I went to Europe, that's the year Kennedy was assassinated, that's the year the Beatles broke out of the Star Club ghetto in Hamburg, and Liverpool—

So it's sort of a confluence of forces. There's no particular date in that year—

Yeah, a confluence. A whole bunch of things came together. Now, of course, the background to all that stuff that came together started really in the Beat movement of the '50s, right? I mean you had Ginsberg, you had the birth of rock and roll, Gene Vincent, Elvis Presley, and so on. So the precursors of all of that you can find in the '50s.

The reason '63 is key to me is 1963 is when that underground stuff, that counterculture stuff that began in the '50s—the Beat movement, rock and roll, all the rest of it—that's the year it broke. The big wave broke and it became, increasingly, the cultural choice for young people throughout the world. It moved from the dingy espresso houses in the bad parts of town, and the underground blues bars and all the rest of that in Chicago, to these honkies from Britain who were playing this great blues music. Like Eric Clapton and the Yardbirds, right? Look at all the early Beatles hits. They're covers of '50s tunes. And so '63 to me is the year where something that had sort of been brewing burst out through the surface and became the big wave, the big popular wave. Right? Just dragged everybody with it. It's a huge tidal wave. That's what I mean about the significance of that year.

Um, this company was started as a high school poetry magazine, which was very unusual, in 1963. Not a high school newspaper—an exclusive high school literary-slash-poetry magazine. I believe it was McGee [High School]. I'm not sure. And—oh God, this is so complicated.

At that time in Canada, if you wanted to be published, you got published in Toronto. There were no publishers outside of central Canada doing anything. And the corollary of that was that the authors outside of central Canada basically were ignored. Part of the great revolution was that it could happen anywhere, right? And there was this tremendous push all over the region to abandon the heartland-hinterland model of culture and create it where you are. And *Talon Magazine*, in '63, at that high school, was part of those beginnings, right? Of people really taking their fate into their own hands and doing things themselves. And it lasted from '63 to '65.

In '65 that magazine went to UBC [University of British Columbia] and became a magazine coming out of UBC. The students took it with them. And one of these students who went from that high school to UBC was a guy called David Robinson. Now David Robinson was not in on the founding of *Talon Magazine* but he joined it in its high school period. So he became one of the high school students who took that magazine to UBC, and between '65 and '67 it came out of UBC.

By 1967 *Talon Magazine* had published early work by young authors who had enough stuff together and were ready to do their first books. Because they'd been writing for four years, right? Poetry. At first nobody was interested in them. Certainly Toronto wasn't interested in them. I mean, who the hell was this, right? The US wasn't interested in them, although there was a heavy connection between UBC and the whole Charles Olson-Black Mountain movement in the US, and also the New American Poetry stuff coming out of San Francisco. Creeley, Duncan, Blaser, you know. Allen, all the rest of them.

See, UBC had a big poetry conference, also in '63, that brought all those people up here. It was a huge, huge poetry conference. That conference drew together all the young writers in Vancouver, particularly poets. Here was this huge conference, here were all these great hot poets all in one place at one time. Creeley, Duncan, Dorn, Blaser, Olson, you know? It went on and on and on. All the young poets in town were there and that particular conference, in that seminal year, gave a lot of these people a focus, and a lot of things started up. *Tish Magazine* started up, a great poetry magazine of the time. It's supposed to be a joke, right? It's shit spelled backwards, phonetically.

You know, a lot of really exciting, seminal things came out of

498

there. A lot of the big Canadian established poets now, people like George Bowering, Fred Wah, Frank Davey—they were all there. And it galvanized the whole local community. I have no doubt, although I know very little about the very early history of Talon, but the students who founded *Tish Magazine* in '63, a lot of them must have been at that conference as well. So that's kind of how things got started.

Anyway, between '65 and '67 *Talon Magazine* came out of UBC. By this time a lot of the early contributors were ready to have their first books published. No one was interested in them, so *Talon Magazine* evolved into Talonbooks and began to publish the first volumes of poetry that had come out of the writers who had been supplying the magazine with material. The whole prospect of doing books became so exciting and time consuming, of course, that *Talon Magazine* just faded away very quickly. There was a period of less than a year when there was an overlap. Talonbooks started very quickly. I mean there was lots of stuff to do. A lot of those contributors had a lot of books ready. So the decision was simply made to—boom! You know? Let's do the books! Let's start something!

It must have been organized something like a collective or a cooperative.

It was. I mean that's the way people did things at the time. It was the '60s. It became increasingly less of a collective, and ownership was established, and so on. We were incorporated in 1975. Just like a key year, you know? That's when the revolution was over. That was the end of the collective, right? So we were right on target. Nineteen seventy-five. There we were, incorporated, November twelfth. I'm now in the process of buying out my last partner. And then I'll be it.

It was a very loose collective. bill bissett did some joint ventures with us. He later started his own press called *Blewointment*. It was sold, I guess five, six years ago, and has been totally transformed into something else, renamed, and now does other stuff. Children's books, if you can believe it. So, yeah, *Blewointment* was a big force at the time.

Talonbooks started, was a very loose collective, did mostly poetry books in its early years, and then in 1969 came the first Simon

Fraser connection. Up until then it had been very much a UBC phenom-enon, right? And UBC was the old, conservative university and Simon Fraser was the new, radical university. And the students and the profs and everything else—it was quite a different ecology, right? And so we didn't have much to do with each other. We thought that those guys over there were the conservatives and they thought we were the lunatic radicals, and that's kind of the way it broke down.

In '69—one of the people that Simon Fraser had hired in '65 to teach drama was a guy called Peter Hay. Peter Hay is the son of Hungary's probably—well, definitely—Hungary's most famous play-wright of the twentieth century, a guy called Julius Hay. I hate to use comparisons. Ed Dorn says comparisons are odious, and I agree, but think of this guy as Hungary's version of Berthold Brecht. He's a cult hero. He enjoyed a status—imprisoned by the Nazis, imprisoned by the Commies, imprisoned by everybody. Julius Hay's voice was the last voice speaking on Radio Free Hungary during the Russian intervention in '56.

Julius had sent his son Peter to London to study at Oxford where he did very well. And then he joined one of the top drama agencies in London and worked there for a while as a drama agent, had been hired from there by Simon Fraser on the basis of his academic credentials and drama work and so on. He came to Canada and he tried to teach drama in Canada the way you teach drama in any other civilized country to first-year students. Because, of course, it's a new university, everybody's a first-year student, right? Well, the vast majority of them were. I mean there were people who came from other places to start their MA there, but they were really a minority. It's a brand new university, right? So the vast majority of the students who signed up were first-year, right? And so the vast majority of courses being taught were, in fact, introductory survey courses.

And Peter—this is one of Peter's favorite stories, and it's a beautiful story, actually, because the way drama is taught, as I say, in every other civilized country in the world in an introductory course to the citizens of the country is you base your course around your own playwrights. So if you're in Hungary the list includes Julius Hay. In

500

Germany an opening survey course includes Berthold Brecht. And here he is in Canada. And he figures, Okay, I'm going to teach a survey course, but where's the Canadian drama? Where are the Canadian dramatists that I can base this around? There's got to be like a connection to, you know, what is known locally. Right? The local culture. The voice of the local culture.

Couldn't find a damn thing. Drama was not a genre that was in print in this country. And he was just appalled by that. He couldn't believe it. So what he did—there were some dramatists around who were part of that '60s counter-culture movement who were getting their plays produced in, you know, off-off—whatever. Little theaters. And he knew about them. So he got himself a mimeograph machine and in his basement produced mimeographed versions of the theater scripts so that he could have some Canadian drama to teach in his survey course, "Introduction to Drama."

And he thought that there was something fundamentally wrong about this. Of course, what is fundamentally wrong about it—and this relates to my view that Canada is a third-world country—is that Canada culturally, until the '60s, suffered from a colonial mentality. Which began, of course, with Britain and France. During and after the Second World War, the colonial groveling was transferred to New York and Washington from Britain. But many Canadians nowadays still see themselves as also-rans in the Anglophone world, right? If it's from New York or London or whatever, Los Angeles, it's better, you know? And if it's from Canada it's somehow second-rate. You can't make it in Canada as a cultural worker unless you go to—you know, if you really want a career, at some point you have to leave your country and go to the imperial center. You go to London, you go to New York, you go to LA. And we had a very second-class view about what we do here. Culture was always somewhere else. These were the rough-hewn colonies. Nothing that came from here could possibly be of cultural interest. That was the basic attitude.

And the manifestation of attitudes such as that was that Canada had no dramatic literature in print. And so in '69 Peter came to Talonbooks, who till that time had basically done poetry books, and proposed—"Look, guys, Canada needs a drama list. I know what you're trying to do with Canadian authors and poetry and so on. Think about expanding to drama, get a drama list together." And he proposed a drama list and said, "I'll edit it for you. I got three books for you to start with." And the three dramatic works that he wanted the company to start with were Beverly Simons' *Crabdance*, followed by George Ryga's *The Ecstasy of Rita Joe*, which is Canada's most famous play, and a play by James Reaney called *Colours in the Dark*. Beverly Simons was here at the time, in Vancouver, George Ryga was in Summerland, which is British Columbia, and James Reaney was in Ontario.

So right from the beginnings of the earliest poetry contributions to the magazine, the earliest books published, in every genre the authors have been basically Canadian, ninety-nine percent Canadian, with a very heavy local emphasis, of course. Right now about half of our titles—I think fifty-one percent of our titles are by BC authors.

Fifty-one percent. That sounds like a policy.
It's an accident. It's an historical accident. Talon has never thought of itself as a regional press. Talon has always thought of itself, right from the beginning in '63, as making a contribution to Canadian culture, and beyond that, to world discourse, world cultural discourse. We've all been nationalists here. There's a very heavy nationalist streak running through here because, of course, our beginnings come from not having a literature. Right? We created companies like this, and there are a number of correlatives in Canada—House of Anansi in Toronto, Coach House Press in Toronto, Oberon in Ottawa—who all started at the same time.

We all started around '63 to '67. Doing the same thing. And we were all thinking of ourselves as creating a Canadian literature in print with the intent of legitimizing our voice in the international discourse. Creating a Canadian culture which was not secondary to or derivative of our old colonial masters, the UK and France, or our new colonial master, the US, but was our own voice, an image of our own culture, our own people, our own ambitions, our own imagination.

So, yeah, Talon has never thought of itself as a regional press in

502

the sense that you have a policy that you only do local authors. It's kind of a myopic view. We saw it the other way around. Sure, we were in a region. Sure, most of the authors we dealt with were around us in our literary community. But the push was always outward. The focus was outward, not inward. And that's remained to this day.

So that's what started our drama list. *The Ecstasy of Rita Joe* ended up—all three of those books are still in print—*The Ecstasy of Rita Joe* ended up as Canada's most famous play. It's been translated into five languages and has been transformed into an opera, a ballet and a television movie. It had its most recent production down here a couple of weeks ago at the Firehall Theater, and I just reprinted that book last year in its eighteenth printing.

So, clearly, because we were in drama, because there was nothing in print with the exception of a few historical pieces that really belonged to the older generation—the University of Toronto Press had a couple of plays in print, but those plays were from older-generation authors. They weren't part of this new cultural revolution, right? We were the ones who were doing the hot Canadian drama. Those three books came out in '69, '70.

From 1970 to 1974 we were publishing drama titles from all across Canada, including, in '74 for the first time, from Quebec, in translation, work from Michel Tremblay. We started with *Les Belles Soeurs*, which is Canada's second most famous play, certainly Anglophone Canada's second most famous play, Francophone Canada's most famous play. *Les Belles Soeurs* is the first instance of commercial success in Quebec of a play that used Joual, which is the Francophone Canadian term for their dialect—the kind of French that is spoken in Quebec and which the Parisian French like to poke so much fun at, right? It's sort of like the upper class. If you have a Windsor accent, you went to all the right schools; a cockney accent will offend you, right?

Les Belles Soeurs is the first successful—it's called the first play that used Joual. I'm not prepared to say that, because I'm sure there were earlier experiments which just didn't come to anybody's attention. But it's the first play that broke the barrier in Quebec in terms of using your own language. Up until that time, literary artists in Quebec slavishly parroted Parisian French which over the colonial years had drifted further and further and further away from what people in Quebec were really speaking. Joual had become an identifiable dialect. It contained a hell of a lot of English-language words. It paid no attention whatsoever to the French Academy's purity-of-language laws. It contained different pronunciations, it contained native words, Anglophone words, all kinds of stuff. That's the French of Quebec and it is distinctly different, profoundly different, from Parisian French.

Now, again, this is part of that '60s cultural revolution. Up until Michel Tremblay and *Les Belles Soeurs*, literature in Quebec was colonial literature. It was written in a language that was increasingly divorced from the language of the people of the community. It was, in fact, becoming like Latin in the Middle Ages. And so Michel Tremblay, in a way, was like the Chaucer of Francophone Canada. And we signed up that play in '74.

So by '74 we were publishing dramatists all across the country, including from Quebec in translation. We were publishing poets from all across the country. And, of course, '74 was the year that I joined the company. So from '67 to '73 it was basically poetry, drama starting in '69. In '73 we published our first fiction titles. Both were by feminist authors. You see, again here are people who are coming out of this counter-culture; the '60s was also the birth of feminism as an -ism that one pays attention to, if one is worried about correct thought. So there we were with Jane Rule and Audrey Thomas published in '73, the year before I came here.

By the time I got here in '74, Talon had established itself as a poetry publisher, a Canadian poetry publisher, *the* Canadian drama publisher—because, of course, if there isn't anything and you start something, the moment you've got somebody from every region in the country you are the drama publisher. So by 1974 we were known around the world, not just in this country, as the publisher of Canadian drama, which is a reputation that we have maintained ever since, because of course we were the first in there, we've got all the original hot properties and nobody can touch us, right?

Later on Penguin, a colonial competitor in this country, a branch

504

plant, Penguin Canada, tried to do a drama anthology, and of course they phoned us, trying to get the rights from us. And I told the rights manager at Penguin, I advised her not to do this, that I considered this my market and if and when Canada was ready for a drama anthology I was going to do it, and I was not interested in a scenario in which I had established through this company the genre for the nation so that by the time the branch plants were interested in creaming the crop I could just turn over the rights to them. I got quite hot about it. I said, "I would advise you to abandon this idea. I'm not selling you a right to a single one of our plays. I'm warning you to abandon this, and if you try it I'm going to do my own drama anthology and I'm going to blow you out of the water." They went ahead and did it. I said okay. We did ours. We blew them out of the water.

The standard Canadian drama anthology is called *Modern Canadian Plays*. It has twelve plays in it. A good many of them are ours. Some of them aren't; we didn't catch everything. And it's the one that's used in university drama courses across the country now. If you want to study Canadian drama you use the Talon anthology supplemented by one or more of our plays, right? It was a disaster for Penguin.

So anyway, by '74 we had established ourselves as a leading, serious publisher of fiction, poetry, drama—the national leader in drama. By 1979 we diversified into nonfiction, beginning with ethnography titles. The nonfiction that we have done traditionally has all been either ethnography or social issues. We did a couple books on the Japanese-Canadian internment during the Second World War. We've done books on native health care. So by 1979 we had basically diversified into all the genres that we wanted to be active in. Poetry, drama, fiction and, finally, serious nonfiction of a specific belles lettres or social criticism variety, right? Social conscience variety. And that's where we've been ever since.

What proportion of your list yearly is nonfiction?
We don't have any rules about that. We publish the best stuff that's available annually. We are of a size and cash flow now where we

505

can manage fifteen new titles a year on average. But we are also doing ten or fifteen reprints a year now. The basis of our market has become the college course adoption market. Sixty percent of our sales come from college course adoptions in the fields of literature, anthropology, women's studies and so on.

Do you send out samples to faculty?

No, we don't send out samples. We send catalogues. If they ask for samples our standard response is "Stanley Tools does not supply every carpenter in the world. Books are the tools of your trade. If you want to see 'em, buy 'em." They like that. They must like that because they sure as hell use our books.

The stability of this company is the backlist. We have a hundred and seventy-eight titles in print now, which is approximately half of everything we've published since 1967. And the reason it's still in print is because it's in its sixth or its twelfth or its eighteenth printing. It isn't because it hasn't sold. We remainder the stuff we don't sell. So that gives you some sense of the—I suppose you may interpret this as pride, I don't know. I think it's justified pride. That tells you that the publishing decisions we made when it came to quality literature and social issues that matter did actually matter and the literature was, in fact, of some quality. Because it's used in universities all over the world. In Canada and in this growing phenomenon around the world called Canadian Studies.

Let me get back now to the Third World problem. When Simon Fraser started—this is the problem that Peter Hay confronted, and every student confronted this—when Simon Fraser started, in the field of literature they had three introductory courses: Introduction to Drama, Introduction to Poetry, Introduction to Fiction. English 101, 102 and 103, respectively. In the first year that I was there—and I took all three of those courses in my first year—there was not a single Canadian author studied in any one of those three introductory courses. Every single author in the fiction survey, drama survey and poetry survey was either from Great Britain or the United States. It wasn't until two years later that the English Department of Simon Fraser University intro-

506

duced a course, owing to a lot of pressure from the students and faculty, called Canadian Studies. It was a fourth-year course. It was the only course in which, and had the only reading list from which, one could get some kind of overview of Canadian writing.

Now here we were in the—1967, incidentally, is Canada's first centennial, right? So Canada is by now a hundred years old as an independent country, right? We're celebrating our first centennial. And in the English Department of a brand new university with progressive instructors and students we have the emergence of something called Canadian Studies. Like here we are with a literature faculty of a Canadian university in the year of the country's first centennial where we are studying the literature of our own country as if it were someone else's. You know what I mean? You know the signal that's giving, right?

The assumption is that English literature, which is what is being taught, is British and American. And there are a few, maybe, of our own authors writing in English that you might want to be aware of while you study the real body of English literature, which is British and American. So in your entire baccalaureate program we will give you one course, right at the end, that makes a concession to the fact that there are some Canadian literary authors around. Right?

Now, again, that's what I mean by saying Canada is a third-world country, in everything but lifestyle. It's everyone's favorite hinterland, right? We are hewers of wood and drawers of water. Culture? What culture? What legitimacy? Independence? What independence? National identity? What national identity?

The recent opposition to the Free Trade Agreement and the Cultural Industries Exemption that we fought for and won in this country over George Bush's dead body, according to his most recent speech on the subject, is our doing. I was president of the Association of Canadian Publishers in 1983, and I organized the Canadian resistance to having culture included in the Free Trade Agreement, which ultimately resulted in the Cultural Industries Exemption which has been a sore point for Carla Hills and, I understand, the man himself ever since. We ain't gonna give up, right?

The reason Canada doesn't look like a third-world country, of course, is that Canada is geographically the second largest country in the world, it has the population of Holland and has every known natural resource in the world in abundance. So we can afford to be exploited by our colonial betters. The only reason we don't enjoy a lifestyle that is analogous to those of small West African countries is because we got so much to give away that if we charge only a penny a ton, the volume is so gigantic that we can afford to drive cars and have refrigerators. For now.

You know, the depth of the current Canadian recession is due, in some analysts' view, and I share this view, due entirely to the fact—where is the recession deepest? It's in the province of Ontario. Ontario is the only province in the country that ever had the critical mass of population to viably build secondary industry. It's the Free Trade Agreement in particular that threatens whatever fledging efforts Canada has made to construct a secondary industry. That's where all the jobs are being lost in Canada now: in secondary industry, in the manufacturing center, in the value-added sector. That's why Ontario, of all the provinces, is just decimated. They are rapidly approaching the unemployment level of Newfoundland, a rock in the middle of the Atlantic.

So as you can tell by my rather hostile remarks—part of the job of those presses like Talonbooks has always been, against impossible odds, against structural odds built into our own educational systems that keep telling us that we are a second-rate colonial culture and will never amount to anything in terms of being an international competitor, economically, culturally or on any other basis—part of the ideology of these Canadian publishing companies which all started at the same time in the '60s, part of our job in the larger picture of the cultural and political life of this country is to insist that we do not retreat after the tremendous gains we've made since the mid-'60s, we do not retreat to the old colonial mentality. Canadian literary expression, Canadian cultural expression in literary form, would not exist without my generation and what we did and the conclusions we came to, the great life-changes that we experienced as part of that whole world-wide revolution in consciousness in the '60s. I still consider it part of my job, part of what I do as a publisher, part of what motivates me, part of what keeps me here.

Because, of course, we don't make any money, right? I still don't own a house. I make a pathetic salary. I'm a very highly qualified individual. If you go back to the old middle-class premise that I started with, this isn't a real job. My family keeps asking me still when I'm gonna get a real job. 'Cause this ain't it.

In one of Steinbeck's essays he says that Americans don't think you're working if you enjoy it.

Exactly! Exactly! That's part of where I come from, right? And that was one of the things I learned that was not necessarily true, right? I have just come back from Toronto, actually, having been elected for the second time as president of the Association of Canadian Publishers. One of the most important things we do, particularly with our current government which is so enamored of opening the borders to everything and pursuing the Free Trade Initiative at the North American level, one of our most important jobs is to keep reminding this government that it has a responsibility for maintaining its own culture if, at the end of the day, it wants to maintain its own sovereignty. Because public discourse and culture is the basis on which sovereignty is built. It's the basis on which difference is built. And I mean difference in the current, post-modern, critical sense. Culture defines The Other. That's our most basic definition of The Other. And that's a job that I've been engaged in as long as I've been here. Since '74. It's a job that I've played a leadership role in at some very crucial points in Canadian history.

I mean, this is a battle that's being fought all over the world. Look what just happened to the Soviet Union. Look what's happening in the Balkans. There are two major forces at work in the world today in the big socioeconomic picture. And those are the forces of the global village who want to homogenize everything and open a Disneyland outside of Paris, and the forces of indigenous cultural preservation. Right? Opposition to the global village. Opposition to homogenization. Insistence on the maintenance of cultural difference.

That's the current struggle. George Bush is a man who represents the forces of homogenization and globalization. So that's the conflict. Now that the Cold War is over, that's the big issue. Now that the Cold War is over—these forces have been brewing all along. Right?

They've never gone away.

No, it's never gone away. But now that we're rid of the imminent threat of the apocalypse—what I referred to as the tremendous distraction of the Cold War, right?—this stuff has resurfaced. It's always been there. And the essence of the conflict in the twentieth century is empire versus autonomy.

What was Stalin trying to do? What was Hitler trying to do? What was Mussolini doing in Abyssinia, for Christ's sake. Right? And so on and so forth. And what are the counterforces to all those movements? I mean that's the history of the twentieth century. Are we going to have a global village? Are we going to have the millennium? Are we going to have the Third Reich? Or are we going to have autonomy and independence and multiculturalism? That's the battle. And it's a battle that, as I say, this press has been involved in since its beginning.

Now the reason I say that this may be a one-generation phenomenon, at least in the Western world, is that one of my biggest problems, both as a publisher seeking authors and worrying about the industry per se—you know, being president of the Association of Canadian Publishers, looking around for the bright new presses that are starting, right?—is that there is a real absence of bright, agressive young writers working in the literary genres, and bright young people starting or joining small presses, medium-size presses. There's no one pushing me who is younger. I mean, the exception proves the rule, right? You can point to this person, that person, this press, that press, but the point is that it's increasingly difficult to find young cultural writers.

It's a good point. I've noticed in my other interviews that we're all middle-aged. Almost all of us. Even the people who are coming into it brand new are already middle-aged.

Exactly. The reason I fear this is a one-generation phenomenon is that I fear that the generation that followed ours—we were all the young radicals, right?—we all know, we don't have to go into the details, that from the mid-'70s on, and certainly in the '80s—we all know about the '80s, the "me generation," the yuppies and so on—my big fear is that the conservative backlash that happened from about '75, '76 on and really took off in the '80s has created a younger generation that has, in fact, embraced the global-village model and not the independent-autonomy model, the multicultural model. The rise of anti-Semitism, the rise of racism, you name it. You can point to it all over the world. In the younger generation, you see. I mean that's what's fascinating.

Those issues were never resolved before the advent of twentieth-century imperialism.

No. No. And they haven't been resolved yet. But my big fear is, you see, that there aren't the innovative radicals. I see the generation younger than mine. My students, when I taught in university, have turned out to be what I was when I first entered university.

I agree. But my daughter is a freshman in college. She reminds me very much of my own youth. The person, for better or worse, rebelling against middle-class values.

Right. You see, we live in hope, right? All I'm saying to you is that so far I don't see the inheritors of this dream that we all had lining up, pushing me. Right? Which would be a very healthy thing. I mean, Jesus, I'd be delighted if I had some real competition from a bunch of young Turks who were trying to raid my office. Uh uh. It ain't happening. So, you know, I worry about that. I worry about losing the struggle.

Let's go back to our real context. I'm worried about losing the struggle to create a Canadian culture and identity that is different from America's. I'm worried about the triumph of Free Trade, at the end of the day losing the Cultural Industries Exemption and being swamped by Los Angeles and New York again, just like it was before the '60s in this country. I fear that by the next century there's a real danger, if there are not those people on my tail willing to carry on the good fight, that we will have done it, it will have been a product of that generation, of that cultural revolution. And without that backup, without the inheritors, without the competitors, it'll die with us.

Of course, I'm just telling you that that's my fear. If I was convinced that that was the way it was going to be, if I had given up all hope—we live in hope, right?—if I had given up all hope that this would outlast our generation, [if I believed] that the global village would triumph, right? I'd quit today. I'm not a big fan of losing battles and I think the martyr complex is a dangerous psychological syndrome. So, you know, one continues to struggle but it's a fear I have. I mean I recognize the same things you recognize with your daughter. Just now there are a bunch of new—I'm very interested in the new ecology movement. So perhaps that kind of social conscience will reemerge.

Of course, it's never the same. Thank God, the next generation will have their own version of it. I am actually heartened by the fact that this struggle has finally reemerged publicly. You see it happening all over. You turn on the television news—that's the struggle. Are we going to have empire or are we going to have multiculturalism? Are we going to have homogeny or are we going to have difference? That's the struggle all over the world. And there are lots and lots of signs—my oldest kid is eighteen, you know, he's going to graduate this year— there are lots of signs coming from them that things will go on. And like I say, if I didn't have that certainty that it's okay, there will be some historical point to this—I mean, fuck it, I'd quit. So, yeah, I look forward to the future with some confidence. But that is my fear. It is a real possibility that it will all come to naught.

We're not the first generation to be caught in that—
No. No. No. Enough said. But, yeah, that is Talonbooks. That's the history of Talonbooks. This is our twenty-fifth anniversary. We've just produced a gorgeous catalogue which has all our titles in it. They're all illustrated. We're proud of what we've done and we're anxious to continue.

512

John Rimel
Mountain Press Publishing

"You've probably heard the old joke about the way you make a small fortune in book publishing is to start with a large one."

Mountain Press Publishing of Missoula, Montana was founded as a print shop by Dave Flaccus shortly after the end of the Second World War. Around 1960 the company published its first book, one on how to identify flowering plants. In the decade that followed it published a series of six medical textbooks and manuals. This series was sold in the early '70s to a larger company. Currently, Mountain Press's list focuses on natural history and Western history.

I interviewed John Rimel, Mountain Press's publisher, in mid-September 1993. Rimel was born in Missoula and raised on a ranch just outside of town. He went to the University of Montana for two years, then transferred to the University of Oregon. At the University of Montana he had dabbled in business administration, but at Oregon he majored in English literature.

I had a feeling I was going to be coming back and going to work for Mountain Press. By my sophomore year I was at the point where I decided I should decide what the hell I should do with the rest of my life. And after a great deal of thought, decided that I liked books more than anything else that came to mind.

There was only one person that I knew of who was involved in publishing at that time, and I went and knocked on his door, told him I was interested in book publishing, and asked if he had any work. (In fact, one of my early exposures to Mountain Press was some of the first books that Mountain Press did. My mother would proofread galleys with Dave's wife in the living room of their house. I had known Dave,

513

growing up. My sister had gone to high school with his kids. They're all, for the most part, five to ten years older than I am. So one of my early recollections of the publishing business is Harriet Flaccus and my mother sitting in the living room of the Flaccus house, pouring over these long sheets of galleys that hadn't been pasted up yet, and marking them up.) And he said, "Let me think about it for a while," and he called me back in a week, or I went back in to see him in a week, and he said, "How about if we give you a car and ten percent of anything you can sell in the bookstores, and you can hit the roads and call on bookstores in Montana?" So that's what I did the summer of 1977. It was a great introduction to book publishing.

Were you able to make a living that way?

Barely. I didn't have much of an expense account. I was sleeping on the floors of friends' houses and camping out. I discovered fairly early on that some days you made what I considered at that time a decent day's wage, sometimes you made it by ten o'clock in the morning and, yeah, you felt like you could probably take the rest of the day off and go fishing. But on the other hand, the next two or three days you might not sell a nickel's worth. So you had to keep going.

Do you have your own sales reps now?

We use commission reps, not in-house reps. For a long time we kept Montana for ourselves, and either Dave or I would get around to most of the bookstores in the state two or three times a year. That's something that's sort of gone by the wayside the last few years. We leave it more up to other people to make those calls now.

Is Dave still active in the company?

No, he's not. He retired about two years ago. He's in a retirement home—a nursing home situation in Bend, Oregon near where his daughter lives.

You got your bachelor's degree at the University of Oregon. Did you go on to graduate school?

514

No. I came back to Missoula. Got married right after I graduated and came back to Missoula. That was in '81—I'd taken a year off between—well, I took '79 off and came back to Missoula and worked up at the ranch some and then worked some for Mountain Press. When I came back in '81 Mountain Press was pretty much in the depths of what I think is generally acknowledged now as a nationwide, book-industry recession. 'Eighty-one was an awfully bad year for the book industry. They were just barely holding on. In fact, I think they were operating out of the basement of Dave's house at that point. Rob Williams, who is our financial officer, accountant and business manager, I think spent most of the year working gratis and doing other work on the side. He and Dave pretty much kept the thing afloat, but just barely. It wasn't until about '83 that Mountain Press started to pick back up and expanded beyond a two- to three-person shop.

Did you grow up with books? Where did your love for books come from, have you any idea?

My mother had been trained as an English teacher, although she never—well, she taught for a very short time, and always loved books. My father died when I was two years old so I never really got to know him. And my sister, who is ten years older than I, wound up leaving in '65 as soon as she got out of college but would send me books from Oberlin. She sent me, when I was a kid, the entire Narnia series. And I grew up reading a lot, I guess. Like any kid, I devoured the regulatory amount of comic books, but also got into reading a lot of other things. I went through a phase in high school where I was polishing off a Western paperback—the Zane Grey-Louis L'Amour type of book—I would read about one of those per evening. We didn't have a TV a lot of the time I was growing up, and I think that helped immensely because I wasn't sucked into that. But one entire wall in our living room was always dedicated to a library, and there were always books on the shelf. My mother had a deep, abiding love for literature and I think she managed to instill that in both of her children.

My sister went on to become a librarian and was a librarian until—she was living in California when Proposition 13 went through and she found herself all of a sudden—instead of being a branch librarian and the head of this little branch library, she found herself suddenly with no employees and shelving books. And she decided that that wasn't what she had gone to college for five years to do. So she went back and went to law school and became a lawyer. Kind of a scary thought, hey? But she has this love of books and I have this love of books and I think it most likely came from my mother or my grandmother. My grandmother was real instrumental in my upbringing. I was read to a lot when I was a kid and just have always had this love of books.

When I was still in school here, I took a class that was being offered by—actually, I don't think it was a class for credit at the university. It was outside the university system. It might have been what they called a "Center course" which was taught through the UC [University Center]. I think it was called "The Art of the Book." It was taught by a fine-press printer who had a shop here in town. The press was called Blackstone Press. The man who ran it was Peter Koch, who has since gone on to become a pretty well known typographer in the Bay Area. I got an awful lot out of that class in just the appreciation of the fine-press book.

I remained friends with Peter and would go in and see some of the work he was doing and try to put it together in my own mind with the work that I was doing for Mountain Press. Where he was producing art work, using a press and doing chapbooks and just barely making it— I mean it was a real struggle for him to survive financially—I was doing or involved in the selling of something that was much more commercial. I had to sort of put the two together and make some compromises in my own mind as to the sort of publishing I wanted to be involved in. And I guess I realized fairly early on that the sort of work that Peter was doing was meant for a very few. I think that what Peter himself discovered in moving the press to San Francisco was that, yeah, I can't make a living doing this in Missoula, Montana. You can't have a fine art/craft press in Missoula, Montana. In the Bay Area there's a whole community of fine-press printers and a history and a tradition of fine-press printers. And that tradition has probably influenced commercial

516

publishers.

Do you write? Or did you write?

I did when I was in high school and in college quite a bit. Except for correspondence now, I don't much.

You never had the obsession to do it?

Well, I think I had the obsession to do it, but when you're in college a career in book publishing is dismal enough to contemplate, as far as the economic realities of it go, and the sorts of things you hear about writers are—it's just downright discouraging. There are very few people who really are encouraged to write. And everything you hear is what a struggle it is—the years of rejection notices before someone finally accepts your piece.

When we talked before [in arranging for the interview] *you alluded a little bit to how Mountain Press got started, how Dave Flaccus started it during World War Two, was it, or right after?*

Right. Yeah. He'd graduated from Haverford. He was from a Quaker family. And he was a conscientious objector during World War Two and he came out here to do his alternative duty, which was with the Forest Service. And they set up a camp for conscientious objectors out at the Nine Mile Remount Station just outside of Missoula. And they trained these kids to be smoke jumpers and fire fighters. The smoke-jump program was very much in its infancy then. It was a very new program and he worked as a fire fighter and smoke jumper for a couple of years during the war. Of course, that was a time when all the able-bodied men in the country, except for conscientious objectors, were out fighting the war. So they really needed people to keep the home fires from burning the forest down. And that's what he did.

As it turned out, he met a woman here whom he married, who was also a Quaker, and they started the first offset printing company in Missoula. It was right after the war, I think. 'Forty-eight, maybe. Somewhere in there. It was when things had wound down enough that he was no longer employed by the Forest Service or had served his time, one or the other.

And they started an offset printing company on Front Street, in a building that's about to be demolished, actually. And ran it as an offset printing company until, oh, I think the printing part of the business was sold in the early '70s. He had had a heart attack and by that point he had also gotten more intrigued by book publishing than he was by printing. I think he'd been doing printing long enough to feel like it was time to move on.

He also, during that time, during the '60s and early '70s, was one of several people instrumental in founding the local ski area, Snowbowl. I think that was a very frustrating experience for him because while they took it from bare hillside to skiable mountain, and sort of grew with what was at that time very much an industry in its infancy—the chairlift they installed is still operating today—it was never financially profitable. And he wound up selling Snowbowl and taking a loss on it and, you know, having to move on. He'd put his heart and soul into the ski area as well as into the publishing company. So at that point he turned his resources away from skiing and away from printing and focused on publishing, initially on medical texts.

We did several—the early books that Mountain Press published are very...oh, there's no way to quantify them into a class. Now we're very much into niche publishing and trying to focus on bringing out series or categories of books. Back then it was whatever looked good and was available.

What became the life's blood of the company after the medical textbook business subsided was pretty much the Roadside Geology series. If we're known for anything now, it's probably as the publisher of Roadside Geology books. It's been incredibly popular, far beyond anybody's expectations. The first one came out in 1972. It was *The Roadside Geology of the Northern Rockies*, which is now out of print after selling—I think it went through a dozen printings and sold sixty or seventy thousand copies in its lifetime, maybe more.

You do some natural histories and some general histories, too.
Yeah. We also do a lot of Western history, a lot of outdoor

518

books.

Are these mostly pictorials?

No. Most of our books rely heavily on the written word to convey information. We think of ourselves as an informational publisher. If there's one way to describe what we do, it's probably by using the Roadside Geology series as a model, where we take something that is generally complex and not very well understood by the general public and make it accessible.

If you think about a field like geology, or if you've ever tried to read anything written by a professional geologist, it's akin to reading a foreign language. It's English but it isn't any more understandable than the insurance binder on your house. It's all done in a language that pretty much requires a degree from a major institution, a four-year degree in geology, before you can understand what's being talked about. And even then, if they get outside your area and specialty, you're probably not going to understand what's going on. So we take these books— they're all written by professional geologists—and we put them through fairly rigorous editorial workings in an effort to make them understandable.

Do you have in-house editors or do you contract out?

The Roadside Geology series is edited by the two original authors of the first couple of books. And they are under contract with Mountain Press to be the series' editors, although they both work outside of our offices. They are both professors at the University of Montana. Dave Alt and Don Hyndman. They're also both partners in Mountain Press.

Is their partnership a result of their editing the series?

Yeah. It grew out of that. It grew out of the popularity of the series and their contribution to the company.

When you were describing your books a moment ago, you sounded as though you have it very clearly in mind what your press is about. Do you have a written mission statement?

We have one, I guess, consciously in mind. We're in the process of developing a written document. That was one of the things that occurred as the press grew. It was always, as I think a lot of entrepreneurial publishing operations are—they start out relatively small and they start out with one person doing everything and having it all in the back of his head. And when that one person is gone all of a sudden, you may have an established company that has been in existence for years and an established sort of bureaucratic way that things happen, but you don't have much written down. And one thing we discovered when Dave left and I took over was that Mountain Press didn't have in place a lot of the fundamental things that are done in most start-up companies now. They just didn't have that foundation.

So that's one of the things we've been developing. Unfortunately, because of the necessity of keeping everything else moving forward at the same time, sometimes those things like developing a mission statement take a back seat to some of the other tasks—sending the mail out every day, trying to keep books on schedule, you know, day-to-day things.

This idea of succession: a lot of the publishers I've talked with are concerned with it because...well, they're all middle-aged or older and they're concerned about who's going to get their company and is there going to be something left to get.

Right. It's a very real concern. And they should be concerned about it and they probably ought to make the time to do a lot of planning, and also set up a realistic plan for succession. It's awfully difficult to do and it's particularly dependent on how the company is structured. In this case Mountain Press is set up so that the majority ownership continues to be held by the family of the founder. And yet none of the three children—they all have their own lives and their own careers and don't really have a desire to come back and take over their father's legacy. And that is a continuing question on the plate at Mountain Press—what are they going to want?

The other thing is that Mountain Press has been able to grow

520

because all the profits from the company, when there were profits, have been plowed back into the company. It's very hard to start a publishing company. There is very little capital available for book publishers. I mean the SBA [Small Business Administration], the source of a lot of small business loans in the country, specifically excludes publishers from the application process, by federal regulation. And of course banks don't really—very few people really understand the publishing business. I mean when you tell people that you're a book publisher, they go "Oh, you're a printer?" "No, not really."

And then, if you do explain publishing, how do you explain that even bookstores really have your books on consignment?
Yeah. The whole system is arcane enough that most people don't understand why anyone would want to choose it as a livelihood. You've probably heard the old joke about the way you make a small fortune in book publishing is to start with a large one. But nobody's going to loan you money, or very few people are going to loan you money, to get books out. The banks won't touch you even if you have healthy inventory. I think they're scared to death at the thought of having a warehouse full of books that may or may not be salable. I don't think there's a very high level of understanding or trust, and so far our efforts to educate them haven't been very successful.

Is Mountain Press still growing?
Yeah. We're actually going through quite a growth phase right now. This year, so far, I think our sales are up about twenty-six percent over last year. Which is getting into the realm of being frightening. I would be more comfortable with somewhere around twelve or fifteen percent. You get up over the twenties and it starts to create problems in and of itself.

How do you explain the increase in sales?
We're doing some different things. A year ago we started to distribute other publishers' titles. In a very select fashion, if you will. We started to distribute *Western Horseman Magazine*'s book line last

521

June. And that's been a very good experience for us and, I think, a very good experience for them. Before that they were being distributed by Gulf Western, and they were a very small part of a very large company. And Gulf was not identifying them as Western Horseman books; they just had them lumped under a page with some other horse books.

They started out with about a dozen titles. The magazine is the largest equine publication probably in the world, and one of the oldest, and is very well thought of and respected. Not to build on that, I think, was a very bad mistake for Gulf.

I'd like to go back a little bit to problems of succession. I haven't really been able to talk with anybody who's had to deal with it. I guess one question would be: What specific problems did you run into when Dave Flaccus was pulling himself out of the company, if that's what he did?

Well, it was probably more difficult for him, and for us, in that, because of his increasing medical problems, he was really unable to run the company and yet also hadn't really turned loose of it. So we spent from six to twelve months, I suppose, sort of betwixt and between, where we weren't really sure what was going to happen.

I was, at that time, primarily responsible for marketing, although I was also doing a lot of the production coordination. And about that time I handed the production coordination off entirely to somebody here at the office and began to focus more and more on management and less and less on marketing. We still, to date, have not gone back in and hired someone in-house who does just marketing. We do have a part-time marketing-and-sales person who is essentially a freelancer who works for us. That has been a very good stopgap and we're able to benefit from his experience without having the expense of hiring someone full-time. Which has been a big plus for us.

But, essentially, I moved from being the marketing person to being management, and Rob and I took up more and more of the slack as Dave was less and less active. And then it finally became official. And then about six months after that, after I took over as general manager, he had what was referred to as a subdural hematoma, or bleeding on the brain. And that pretty much...well, he has not returned to Missoula since then. That occurred when he was in Bend, Oregon and he was hospitalized for quite a while and then has stayed in Bend and really been unable to return.

That was probably one of the most difficult situations to deal with, was having someone who may never have been a very strong manager, was always considered to be a nice guy, but was probably too involved in book publishing himself to want to give up too much control to anyone else. So instead of really becoming a manager as the company grew, he would continue to just sort of go around and take on various tasks.

He knew a lot about the printing trade, being a printer, but it also meant that he thought like a printer. And some of the early books that Mountain Press did probably didn't get the editorial attention that they really should have. Essentially a manuscript came in, he would read it, mark it up a little, and it would be typeset. Back in those days there weren't a lot of publishers around, so the books had very high production values and were very good books, but sometimes a few of them were pushed a little too quickly and were not the books they could have been.

I think that was one of the more difficult things to deal with. He wasn't a particularly strong management type, but he was very much a mentor to me. And his presence was definitely still there after he had left the office. And it was somewhat of a challenge to come in and realize there were some things that weren't really being done the way they should be done, and try to correct those and move the whole beast forward in a progressive way and bring some change to it, but without completely rebuilding it from scratch.

Companies tend to be very difficult things to change. You read about these very large companies that lay off five thousand employees. The toll on human lives that are dispensed with in those sorts of restructurings must be tremendous. With a small company you want to be a little bit more judicious and try to work things around in a way that doesn't bring that sort of pain and suffering to all the people involved. But corporations have a life of their own and they are very difficult to bring change to.

One of the difficult things to convince Dave of in his later years was the need for thorough editorial review of every book we did. Because he was a printer, and because he thought like a printer, there was a tendency to—you know, the manuscript's here, the book can be done in six months or three months or less. I mean what else is needed? Let's do it.

Granted, we've slowed the whole process down, but it also means that each manuscript gets a lot more individual attention than it did before, and I think the end result is a better book. I think Mountain Press, and all publishers probably, could get away with a little looser approach a decade or so ago when there wasn't the increased competition from a lot of small presses who are taking the desktop tools that have been provided by the rise of the personal computer and looking at some of the products that are out there and going, "Oh, I can do something like this, except I can do it better," and then coming out with a similar product that is sometimes more thoroughly thought out.

When I first went to work for Mountain Press they were setting type on a Mergenthaler VIP and Dave knew that machine inside and out. He could tell from the way it kachunked along whether something was wrong. It was a very noisy machine, too. It was a real beast. It was purchased in 1972 for thirty-six thousand dollars. That's a princely sum. It was a great phototypesetter. It was a real beast, this sort of bizarre marriage between mechanics and computer technology. It had a lot of moving parts. It had a lot of computerized components. It ran on an 8K program. We upgraded it, Dave and I did, shortly before we took it out of service, to a 32K program. First to a 16K, then to a 32K program. We thought it was really a speed demon back then, with a 32K program. It would do hyphenation and justification.

When they first started using it, they had a keyboard that had a screen that you could see only one line of type on at a time. And it saved everything on punch tape. Then they upgraded and had one that had a screen that you could see maybe a paragraph, paragraph and a half at a time, and it still saved it on punch tape. To make corrections after you played it out, you had to go back and find that spot and fix it and then replay that correction. It was an incredible process compared to what we have today where you have programs that can go through your manuscript, go through the file, check it for errors in spelling, check it for errors in grammar, though not very accurately, and, as all of us in the business know, you can't trust spell-checkers either.

There was a great line in a locally published self-help book that I caught when I was glancing through it at the bookstore. It obviously had been done on an early desktop system. They were talking about self-image and how, if you lost weight, your self-image would improve. And at one point they referred to shedding "ponds of flesh." The image that created in my mind. It was obvious that the spell-checker had gone over that and said, "Yup. No problem." And it sort of worked, you know? Ponds of flesh. I could just see these shimmering ponds of fat out there that people had lost, but I'm sure that isn't what the author intended.

But Dave never was completely comfortable with the—he knew the Mergenthaler inside and out, he knew the punchtape machine inside and out. Fortunately, we were able to keep the Mergenthaler alive. He taught me a tremendous amount about the Mergenthaler, and through that I learned a great deal about the setting of type and about typography. We were able to keep that alive until the Macintosh got to the point where it was capable of doing professional typesetting. We switched to Macintoshes when the first Mac II hit the market. At that point it had gotten to where it was better than what we had and we embraced the technology.

The technology has come so far and we can do so much more now, so much quicker, but it's upped the ante of everything. Even with all the tools we have, I think it's increasingly difficult to produce a really good product. Because there's still an urgency. What a few years ago would have been acceptable to have take two weeks, now, with the advent of fax machines and everything else—hell, if you can't get it done in an afternoon, you're just not trying hard enough. So there's this rush-rush about it that I think a lot of publishers don't like, and those of us who are trying to craft something, well, we find it frustrating.

The problem of succession is a tricky one and I don't feel as though I addressed it very well, but then each company has to come to grips with it in its own fashion. I think each generation looks at things differently. I think Dave was probably a little frustrated toward the end of his career in publishing in that the technology had come so far since he had started that he was no longer completely comfortable with it, and he no longer had control of it.

Catherine Hillenbrand
The Real Comet Press

"But, you know, the other thing about publishing is even though it's very isolated, you're part of it. It's a community. It's like this world-wide community, and that part of it I really like. Being part of this funny community."

When Cathy Hillenbrand's father was sixteen he entered Cornell to major in engineering. In those days, engineering students took classes pertaining only to engineering. But he wanted to take classes from other disciplines as well and he went to his dean and made his case and the dean allowed him to take other classes too. He has since taken credit for the introduction of liberal arts classes into the engineering curriculum at Cornell.

After the divorce of her parents, Cathy's father moved to Venezuela to make his career and Cathy and her mother moved in with her grandmother in Birmingham, Alabama. Although Cathy's mother was twenty-eight when Cathy was born, she "was always kind of like an older sister or something. I was really raised by my grandma. My mother painted, and she danced, and she did all these things. She'd go from thing to thing, and she's very, you know, cultured in certain ways. My grandmother was kind of a civic leader and a philanthropist in Birmingham. A very forceful person. She did a lot of good works, you know.

"A big issue for me now is missing home. I feel like a fish out of water. I really miss the South. There are things about it I miss terribly. The way people are with each other, I really miss. And then to think that I'm married to, you know, a Yankee. You know, it feels very bizarre. I mean I don't know if Joseph sees the humor in it, but it's kind of funny. My grandma always said the worst thing on earth was what she called the Midwest Yankee. Which is, of course, who I married.

"So there's a lot of regional chauvinism, and racism, in my family. In a way I was inculcated with certain values, which of course led me to thinking that was antithetical to their thinking. But there were the sorts of things like noblesse oblige. *You know, if you have a certain class position, it is your obligation to do certain things. I mean that's probably one of the things that drove me—of course it drove me into completely different politics from my family's, but I was sort of raised to be the that person I am.*

"Seattle's a real funny city that way. It's not very giving. It does have an established upper class, but they're just not that—the younger ones—I don't know, it's interesting that people just don't give."

I interviewed Cathy Hillenbrand at her house near Volunteer Park on Seattle's Capital Hill on the last day of winter, 1992. It was a sunny day and, like every other day of the previous week, unusually mild and pleasing. We talked in the attic which was currently being used as an office and warehouse. The detritus of years of publishing cluttered every plane of the room. "Stuff" was stacked on the floor so that we moved between it along a narrow aisle leading from the door to where we would sit. At the table where I set my cassette recorder there was room for one stool. Cathy took a seat in the only other convenient space near the table, on the other side of a partial wall, and we talked to each at an angle around the wall.

The flow of her speech alternates from slow, with rephrasing and long pauses between words as she pushes her thought forward, to torrential, where the words tumble from her like boulders carried along in a flooding current.

I had a bar. Well, see, I was a lawyer a couple of years and then I bought The Comet Tavern in 1977. Seven-seven-seven-seven was the day we got our license. I mean, to take it over. It was an institution. I had that till '82 and I started the press in '80. Well, I sort of officially started the press in '81. I published the first book I ever published in 1980, a book called *Propagandist's Lament*. It was the text of a performance by a woman named Annie Grosshans. She used to have Art In Form. I don't know if you know her. She's a writer and a performance artist.

And so she did this piece and I put up the money to publish this little book that we did like a hundred copies of. It was a chapbook, yeah. It was stitched. It was a really wonderful little book, and it had lots of voices. It looked like a bible or, like, there's a wonderful artist's book that was done many years ago in New England that's divided up like a bible, so it's got all these different voices happening. I don't think Annie consciously copied it. She just took, you know, the characters and the chorus and stuff. Her book was on vellum and parchment and it was neat. It was beautiful. We sold maybe five copies of it. But that was the first book I ever published and that was before I officially started The Real Comet Press.

See, I would actually call that book an artist's book. You could call it a chapbook but it's really more in the tradition of artists' books, which is a little bit different tradition from chapbooks'. It's sort of like artists' books are chapbooks by writers and poets. In the mid-'70s there was this explosion of artists' books, which was what got me interested in all of this anyway. It was part of like, I think it came out of conceptual art and was probably related to like concrete poetry and new music and that stuff, all those kinds of currents. So there was this big explosion of artists' books in the mid-'70s, although there'd been artists' books over the years and there's like the French, the *livres d'artistes*, which are, say, writing with prints. But artists' books were kind of more merging of text with image. A lot of them were very self-exploratory things and they were—I was just so bowled over when I discovered artists' books. This was actually before I bought The Comet. I considered opening with some friends, we were going to open a bookstore and sell art books and artists' books, and then that kind of blew up, and then we— my then boyfriend and I bought The Comet instead. And I was just fascinated with these little treasures of—little jewels, you know?

I hung out at And/Or. And I was just real involved. I was always interested in art and whatever. I had gotten out of law school, I was practicing law, I got divorced, and I just kind of wanted to get hooked into art. And then I had this boyfriend who was a painter, and so he kind of pulled me into all that. I don't know how I discovered—I think I was just, like, you'd go to talks and things at And/Or and I discovered, I just found these books and, um, there was a bookstore in New York that started around that time—Printed Matter, which still exists. And they are like the biggest distributor and seller of artists' books, books made by artists.

And then there was a place called Franklin Furnace which is an archive for artists' books, and they also do a lot of performance art and stuff now, and they've gotten a lot of—I don't know if you've read about it, but they've had a lot of trouble over the last few years because of sex content in their performances, and the NEA's [National Endowment for the Arts] been really down on the Franklin Furnace and so....

So I kind of bumped into all this stuff. I really love conceptual art, and I just liked that idea and I started buying art also. Like in '75, I think, I bought my first—I'd bought like a couple of lithographs or something, but I bought my first piece of art, you know, three-dimensional art, and I kind of got into buying art 'cause I just loved it, and I met a lot of artists and got real involved in that and a lot of the ideas and stuff. So when I had the bar, I was just kind of burned out on the bar and then finally I thought, "Oh, here's a great idea. I should publish these things. This is like better than buying art and having your house—" It's like why not publish this stuff and disseminate—the whole notion of disseminating ideas through books, I mean, which is why anybody publishes a book, and, um....

But that's why I published books. And also because I, um...um...because I was like looking for my voice. I was burned out and I didn't know what I wanted. I didn't want the tavern anymore, I was burned out, and I didn't know what I wanted to do.

But all of these years I was looking for my voice, which was why I went to law school, because I had gone to college and I graduated a year early. I was really young when I got out of college and I graduated a year early to get married. The reason I majored in psychology was because it had the least requirements of any major there. I went to Duke. And it had the least requirements. Because I had like a million things I wanted to know about. But I knew I was never going to go to graduate school

530

'cause I knew I didn't want to be a professor and I didn't have it in me to write a dissertation. That just seemed impossible. But I also knew that I had to do something else before I could find whatever work I was going to do, but I didn't know what it would be.

You know, like I got out of college and I had a bachelor's degree in psychology and I was like I just turned twenty when I moved here and I just knew that, you know, what kind of job was I going to get? You know—nothing. So I figured, at some point I'd have to get some other training, but I didn't know what it—I was just kind of—and I wanted to be a social—I was always fascinated by social work. And I used to go to the bookstore and go down to the textbook section and get social work books. I was interested in politics, community organizing and all that stuff. But I'm not really—I can't really do those things. So I got the application for social work school, and you write this big essay about why you wanted to do it and then you had to talk about what in your life made you qualified. And I looked at that thing and I thought, "God. They'll find out I'm crazy if I go to social work—"

And then we had this like really crazy friend who was going to go to law school in Montana. The University of Montana. He got flunked out of there. He had a horrible year. They treated him like he was crazy. He was kind of crazy but they also treated him pretty weird and he flunked out of there the end of that first year. He's not the only person I know—I mean many, many people have had weird experiences at the University of Montana. But he was starting to go to law school and I thought, "Ah ha! I could help the world, but it's more intellectual. It's not like this emotional stuff." And so it's, you know, I don't have to deal with whatever crazy I am, I can go help the world. Be a lawyer. And I thought if I went to law school they'd teach me how to stand up and say the truth in twenty-five words or less. I really imagined this. And I had no idea how hard it was. I just went and took the LSAT and I got in. I applied to the U. [University of Washington] and I got there and I found out that it was this horrible thing, you know? People flipped out over it and it was like going to medical school, everybody was crazed and, you know, it was very bizarre.

I remember about halfway through my first year in law school

I sat down and I thought, "I am going to die, I hate this so much." I didn't know what to do. And then I thought, "Well, if I drop out I really don't know what I'll do," so I figured out I wouldn't have to be a lawyer my whole life if I finished, and then it was okay to finish. I hated it. I spent a lot of time in the—they had—well, before they built the new law school, in the old building they had—like women's bathrooms always had to be bigger and had day beds in them. This is in the old days. Women's bathrooms always had to have a place where you could lie down. And so my law school class had, like, the biggest...it was like twenty-five percent women, and it was like the first year there'd been like this huge group of women. And we spent a lot of time in that bathroom. You know, sitting on the tables and lying on the couch and just shmoozing. And then I got in a women's group that year. So that was kind of the great part about law school. But I hated law school. And I didn't practice law very long either.

So anyway, I was trying to find—and I forgot about things like when I was in college I couldn't stand up and give a class presentation because I couldn't talk in front of a group of people. And then you had to do this moot court stuff, and...I actually got through all this. My moot court was terrible. I got through all this and when I was a lawyer for a couple of years I actually loved going to court. Somehow I had the ability to do it when I had to do it. It really shocked me. But I didn't find my voice, being a lawyer, and the legal profession and my personality did not work out. Law school didn't teach me how to say the truth in twenty-five words or less and it didn't give me my voice.

And so then the tavern thing just kind of happened. And I actually really enjoyed that, 'cause I was kind of the center of this whirlwind and that was really fun. But it's pretty draining, hanging around with drunks all the time and realizing you're kind of, you know, drinking a lot yourself, and you're feeding all these people and they come in at noon and drink all day and it's not very—it doesn't feed you after a while. It didn't feed me.

And so I just kind of—I don't know why I decided I would publish books but I just decided that I would. And I thought, "Well, I can just let other people say what I can't say. This will be nice. This will be fun." My idea was so vague. It was like I believed in artists' books and I thought, "Well, I'll publish some books that will make money and they'll support these artists' books."

And so my friends Annie Grosshans and Laura Millin had this bookstore called Art In Form which they started at the same time I started The Real Comet. We really started at the same time. And I remember Laura said, "Well, you know, why don't you publish a book of Lynda Barry's stuff, 'cause she's got enough work to make a book." And Lynda had already actually done some self-made books and stuff. I thought, "Well, that's a good idea. I'll do this." It was that simple and that dumb. And I thought, "Well, Seattle is like this special place and there's all this wonderful art that happens here and it's not like local art and stuff from outside that happens because of the public art program. There's just something that happens here around art. So that'll be the idea of my press." I mean it was that undefined.

And so when I first started everything kind of had to have some relationship to Seattle somehow. And that was, really—I didn't know you were supposed to—I mean, to really be in business—I was interested in, like, becoming a big publisher. Not a big publisher, but being a publisher and selling books all over the world and...being a legitimate publisher, yeah. But I didn't think, "Well, maybe I should go get a job in publishing and figure it out." I just thought, "Well, I can make beautiful books. I know people who know how to make books. I'll do this."

And I called up Peter Miller. He used to have Montana—he has the architecture bookstore [Peter Miller Architecture and Design Books] and he had Montana Books in Wallingford with Ray Mungo years and years and years ago. They actually, I think, might have published a book or two back then. But I called up Peter. So he says, "Cathy, when you get this book printed, how are you going to distribute it?" And I just remember thinking, "How can you ask me that? I don't even know what you mean." Now I don't know how I thought I was going to get this book in the bookstores. I mean I'd never thought about that. I just thought about making the book. So that's what I knew, which was nothing. Otherwise I never would have done it. I'm not real good at researching stuff beforehand.

I keep thinking, "Well, if I'd only spent a year figuring some of this out, maybe I'd still be in business." But the other thing I figured out, kind of painfully, was that The Real Comet Press was really an extension of me. And that was something that got in the way of it ever really being a full-fledged business that functioned and survived financially. Because I just wanted to do these things that I wanted to do and I didn't want to compromise. And my understanding of compromise and marketing and stuff evolved over time to where I think I could have done things differently and survived, which in the long run is maybe the better thing to have done. I lost like—I don't know how much and I wouldn't say anyway. But I lost a lot of money doing this. Although I'm proud of what I put out.

But, personally, it's a failure. I view it as a failure. That's kind of a hard thing to come—because my idea of what I wanted to happen failed. I didn't succeed. By the time I figured out some things about distancing myself and letting other people have room to grow in the business and all that kind of stuff, I just couldn't—I had a kid and I wanted to have another kid—I just couldn't do that.

I'm not really a businesswoman. I'm kind of a—I don't know what I am. An entrepreneur maybe. The tavern was so different from that 'cause it was like this ongoing business and people came in, they put their money on the bar, they bought their beer and that was it. It was really straightforward.

I made money with the tavern when I sold it. I made money running it and I made money when I sold it. That was, you know, pretty simple. Other people give me more credit for that place than I give myself, because it was kind of an institution when I bought it and I always viewed myself as the caretaker of it. But I did things there, too, and, you know, it was a great place and I was in *The Seattle Sun*, they named me one of fifty people who make Seattle wonderful. You know, when I was there. So that was okay. And there was money that came out of that that went into The Real Comet Press. That disappeared along the way.

I kept thinking I had to do things—I tried to do things big

instead of sort of the boot-strap way, because I thought, "You just gotta—well, you gotta do it, follow the rules and do the stuff and maybe this will work." I don't know, maybe if I'd done it in a better way it would have—I mean I still try to figure out....

You know, there's a point at which you have like a critical mass. And it's real hard if you want it to be a business and you want to earn a living off of it or even pay somebody to work there. It's like there is a system out there, especially if you're in trade book publishing. I mean trade book publishing is a certain kind of business and if you don't really do—it's hard not to do it by the rules. I mean Thatcher's [Thatcher Bailey, former publisher of Bay Press] done it not by the rules. Now InBook [a major distributor] distributes him but, you know, when he did that first book of his that really made it big, *The Anti-Aesthetic*, the book on post-modernism....

And originally, you know, he did some stuff about Port Townsend, and then it took him a little while to find exactly what he was doing, and now he's doing this very specific, heavy-duty, art-critical-theory-cultural-critique stuff. But it's much more narrowly defined than what Real Comet Press did. He knows exactly what his niche is. And so he's done really quite well.

And *The Anti-Aesthetic*—that book came out and he never had a review in *Publishers*—he never sent books to *Publishers Weekly*. I mean he didn't know to do it, he never subscribed to *Publishers Weekly*. And that book got this big review in the *Village Voice*. It was like the first anthology on post-modernist literary theory. And that book just hit, you know? And, like, everybody in the country had to have that book. It's like one of those books that, you know, there's probably many unread copies around. It sold in Europe and, I don't know, I think he sold like forty thousand of them, or whatever—but it was just like one of those you-have-to-have-it things. And that kind of catapulted him forward.

And then, through a childhood friend who runs a thing called the Dia Foundation in New York—do you know it? The Dia Art Foundation? They do a lot of—it's like a big Texas oil family and they funded a lot. Like they'll buy an artist, sort of. Like they'll buy a mountain for an artist who wants to build an earthwork on it, and stuff like that. They kind of come and go. But they have a lot of funding and they run this thing called The Dia Art Foundation and a friend of Thatcher's is the administrator of it. And so Thatcher, over the years, has put out this series of anthologies based on symposiums that the Dia Art Foundation's held, and he's the publisher for those. Like there's one on Andy Warhol and there's one on AIDS. There's another one on homelessness. And then he just did a book, *How Do I Look? Queer Film and Video.* It's an anthology of writing on gay cinema. You know, it's just right there. Stuff everybody wants and has to have. It's good. They're really good books.

Not for Seattle. He's, like, for New York. I mean there are certain bookstores in the country where they sell really well. People in Seattle don't read books like that. I mean, here's Thatcher, Bay Press, he's a hometown boy. And they sell better in, you know, St. Mark's in New York sells them but nobody [in Seattle] buys them but in Elliott Bay [Book Company].

This is like a big book city, but...oh, I don't know. I think it's anti-intellectual here, myself. Although I wouldn't say all my books were intellectual. I mean, my books were so varied, and some of them just didn't sell anywhere, so it didn't matter what the market was. But there is a certain kind of anti-intellectualism, I think, here.

Oh, I don't know. I mean, it's like you look back and you realize you're who you were, whether you wanted to be it or not. So I've done the thing I was raised to do, even though I thought I wasn't doing it. Like having to be the gentleman publisher. I don't know. I mean there's also a funny thing about that because it's not like a business. That probably has something to do with why I didn't succeed as a businessperson in publishing.

Like I hired designers because I don't think of myself as being able to do anything. So, yeah, I had designers. Let's say *War Against War!* Now *War Against War!* in Germany is like a little mass market paperback which had sold—not the original book, but the contemporary book—and that book came out like nineteen eighty-whatever and it sold like one hundred eighty thousand copies. Now that's

Germany. It's not the United States.

But I made a conscious choice to make that book a nice book. Now if I'd done it as a mass market book it wouldn't have cost me nearly as much money and maybe it would have sold better. But I had this concept of book-making; I really wanted the books to be as nice as they could be and very individual. None of this, like, well, we'll do the five-and-a-half-by-eight-and-a-half format and we'll just plug all our books into it and the page design will all be the same and blah blah blah. I mean these books are all like art. They're all individual. And, of course, that's very costly.

Unwinding The Vietnam War didn't do well. That's that anthology we did. It didn't do horribly but it didn't do all that well, either. I was going to try to get it to therapy-type people, but we never figured out how to get it to those people. I mean some people hated it. But I thought it was pretty good. It was okay. It was an interesting book. It's touchy stuff, you know. I mean the whole thing of who's saying what about the Vietnam experience, and where are you coming from, and, I don't know, who's got the authority to say who's in here and, you know, who was omitted, who was included, so.... We just never hit it. We remaindered a lot of it.

It was actually done by an institution, Washington Project for the Arts. They basically sold us the publication. I mean we were sort of like the commercial publisher for the book. It's sort of like doing book publishing for a museum. It got reviewed. That was an interesting thing, because we sent it out for review and it got some good reviews, but then it was part of—it was an element of a big show. And so when the people sent the show around, promoting it, they didn't understand about promoting the book as a book. That show that it was a part of, which had a different name—it was called like "War and Memory"—got a lot of press. But *Unwinding the Vietnam War* just got like little mentions. So it missed a lot of its audience because...just trying to work with an institution that didn't understand books.

We always said we do not publish poetry, although *Unwinding the Vietnam War* had poetry in it. We didn't really publish fiction or poetry, but then we published Lynda's first novel. So it's like, you know....

We had gift reps—sales reps to the gift trade—and about five markets around them. Like we had Chicago, Washington, New York. It's interesting, we did pretty well with those gift reps. I don't know if we ever did well enough to cover the cost of using them for dealing with the stores. Because when you have the gift reps you're still individually holding the accounts. It's not like having a distributor who has reps and pays you. So you're managing all those accounts, doing the collections and the invoicing and all that, so that's expensive. But we had quite a few books that did nicely in the gift trade.

And what's interesting is like the books of Lynda's that Harper published never were in the same places as ours. So we had *Girls and Boys* which is like ten years—it's twelve years old now—now it's not in print because we ran out and Harper has the right to reprint it and I don't know if they'll even bring it out. Who knows. But we kept that book in print for ten years. We sold thirty thousand copies of it. It was like you walk into any store and find it. And you could walk into all kinds of funny, funky stores in New York City and there that book would be. They'd have that book and they'd have our second one and they wouldn't have any of the Harper books. Lynda's manager would say to me, you know, "I get calls all the time for Lynda's books and they can find yours but they can't find the new ones." 'Cause we had those reps and we got those books out. I mean it's just an interesting thing.... I had this like real funny blend of very serious books and sort of silly books. Not silly books—

What I finally realized was I was trying to be a general trade— I would never call myself a general trade publisher, but the effect of having all those really different kinds of books was to be a general trade publisher. Although there was stuff I didn't do. There were directions I didn't go. I suppose if I'd stayed in—I mean I think it could have been turned into something that worked better. I mean made money. But it just required effort and focus and stuff I didn't have. Maybe I could have hired a manager.

But at the point I figured all this out I didn't have enough money left to do that. And hiring somebody to do it for me would have meant

538

that I would have had to give up the editorial stuff, which is why I did it in the first place. I wanted to do something that I wanted to do. I mean you could say that's a good tenet for being in business. But you do have to understand—you have to have a vision that fits with the reality. Like I have this book, *The Female Gays*. I'm reprinting that. And that actually was a British reprint of feminist essays, mostly on American popular culture about the whole—there's this whole issue and theory about the gays, and the male gays, female gays, blah blah blah. And it was like one of the first books out on the subject. And so that book is just selling like hotcakes. And it's an okay book. It's not a fabulous book. It's not a bad book. It's okay. And it's doing really well. And it's very cheap to print. It's just a little tiny book with a few pictures in the middle and that's it. It's not ambitious. I probably would have done more reprints.

I remember—do you know Thunder's Mouth Press? He's like just going great guns and he's doing stuff—that Mark Lane book, you know? That Kennedy thing he sold a couple hundred thousand copies of, it's on the best-seller list and, you know, he started out doing black stuff. He did all black cultural stuff, and he's really moved away from that. But I remember him saying to me, "Well, look at you. I wish I had the money to do original books." And I did almost all original books. So I guess that's a difference.

And I think I probably would have done more reprints from England. I mean that's a nice way to—if you pick the right books you can make money doing that. If it just had more of a blend of—instead of being like really ambitious things that required all this design and all this putting-together and these weird sizes....

Probably all of them were grossly underpriced. I mean Harper now, they made the size of the Lynda Barry books a little bit bigger but they're nine bucks. I think we finally went up to six-ninety-five after a while. We started out four-ninety-five, five-ninety-five, six-ninety-five. They raised the trim by just a hair and they charged nine bucks.

I don't know. I don't know. You know, it's a hard thing to give up. It's hard. It's the most identified I've been with anything I ever did.

But you know, the other thing about publishing is even though it's very isolated, you're part of it. It's a community. It's like this world-wide community, and that part of it I really like. Being part of this funny community. I went to the ABA [American Booksellers Association conference]. I went to the Stanford publishing course one summer. I went to Frankfurt [the Frankfurt Book Fair] a couple of times, which was really fun. And there's just all these people. I mean no matter how off-the-wall you are, there's at least one other person doing similar things to what you're doing. That's really amazing. And there's even like normal quote unquote mainstream people who get what you're doing. When somebody comes up and they really love—I mean it's really great to have somebody come up and really kind of get it. You know? I like that. I just liked being part of that. I mean it's an interesting world to have entered. Much more interesting than being a lawyer.

Dan Levant
Madrona Publishers

"...ideally, I would have applied for a job as a senior editor and eventually become editor-in-chief of a major national trade publishing house based in Seattle. But since there wasn't one, all I could do was try to start one myself."

I interviewed Dan Levant on a Wednesday evening at the end of January 1992 at his home on Seattle's Portage Bay. With Bill James, he founded Madrona Publishers in the early 1970s. That story is told below. In 1989 he helped start the literary agency Levant & Wales, for which he is now a consultant. He is also a consultant and a member of the board of directors of Epicenter Press. Levant is an enthusiastic raconteur, his manner of speaking at times resembling stream of consciousness, at other times reflecting a slow thoughtfulness that holds the listener, perhaps for several seconds, until the next word.

Born in Boston, raised in Boston and its suburbs—"mostly Newton"—he graduated from Babson College in 1952 with a degree in business. Drafted into the Army, he was sent to Germany where he met Sara, whom he would marry. Returning to the United States, he enrolled at Columbia University where he took an MFA in theater arts. Until 1959 he worked at a reservations desk in New York for United Airlines and wrote television plays in his off time. In 1959 "we went to Spain"— Ibiza—"so I could have that year to write whatever great work I was going to write. It was going to be a novel originally, but I had to write a play to satisfy a thesis requirement. I wrote one good play, won some awards, got produced in a couple of places."

The play was The Third Watch. *It won a Western States Arts Federation award, among others, and was performed in Seattle and Colorado Springs. "But that was all. I had only one play in me. I wasn't a writer. But it always made it easy for me to have compassion for writers. Because they had to do it, not me."*

The year he had allowed himself lengthened to more than four. His and Sara's children were born in Spain. For two years he ran, with another man, a restaurant and bar located on an old cargo schooner. His partner took off at the onset of a nervous breakdown, leaving Levant to operate the business alone, then finally returned. "I was sort of running the place five, six months a year. I was writing but I stopped writing very much. I went back, tried to reenter America." He spent a few months working at temporary jobs. Then—

I needed a job. We were in New York, it was 1964, I was thirty-four years old, and I had no idea where I was going to get one. I tried the Columbia graduate placement office—I got my master's degree at Columbia—and they told me there was a job opening at Doubleday for a college traveler. They also told me that Doubleday wouldn't hire me for that job because I was a married man with kids and the job had too much travel—and in those simpler times it was okay to discriminate—but I could use the opportunity to get in there for an interview.

What do you mean, "it was okay to discriminate"?

Well, I don't think it was illegal. A college traveler is a salesman for textbooks who goes around calling on faculty to get them to adopt books, and you're on the road most of the time. Most publishers wouldn't hire women for the job in those days. But I went in for the interview all psyched up and said, "I'm here for the job as a college traveler but I don't want it and do you have anything open in the editorial line?" We had a nice interview.

At that time I had a temporary job working for a book packager. He was an elderly gentleman who'd come in every day on the same train from Westchester County at about eleven o'clock and go home on the same train about three-thirty or four in the afternoon.

It was a real Dickensian scene up in this garret office right across from Grand Central Station. There were three or four of us unemployed artistic types. I was alphabetizing entries on index cards for a paperback

542

biographical dictionary. It was a good place to job hunt from because you knew the boss would never turn up before eleven o'clock and would leave at the same time every afternoon. The pay—I remember the pay—he offered me ninety-five dollars a week and I said that it was hard-going with a family with two kids, could he make it a hundred? And he very graciously, reluctantly, made it a hundred dollars a week—reluctantly because he had hoped to give me a raise to a hundred after a month or two to reward my good work. I think I got the idea then that I was never going to make a lot of money in book publishing.

It was a temporary job, a survival job. It wasn't going to last, but I was working. I'd had a very nice interview at Doubleday and about two or three weeks later I got a telephone call from the woman who'd interviewed me, telling me there was a job opening in subsidiary rights and asking me if I was interested. I can honestly remember this, my saying "Yes, I certainly am. What's subsidiary rights?" And I got the job.

I started at Doubleday with the title of assistant manager of the syndicate department, a piece of the subsidiary rights department. My responsibility was handling serial rights: magazines and newspapers, first and second serial, and what was then the most active syndicate selling book serializations to newspapers. I also handled motion-picture rights for authors who didn't have agents, which was really just getting taken to lunch at places like Sardi's by motion-picture-studio story editors, because all the stuff that had real possibilities was agented. It was a wonderful, wonderful starting job. I mean, I just walked in through the personnel department into something like middle management, had a couple of people working for me, a British secretary with a great accent—high status at the time—and sixty-five hundred a year. Terrible pay compared to real business, but otherwise a wonderful place to work. Those were near the end of the great days of book publishing as a gentleman's profession.

This was the mid—'60s then?
Mid—'60s. I started in '64. My job was mostly having lunch. Literally. Long lunches almost every day, mostly with magazine edi-

tors, but also some newspaper people. And you didn't start talking business until you got to the coffee.

When did those days end? I have the impression it ended right around 1970.
Yeah, that's about it, I think.

What ended it? Were you still in New York then?
Business. No, I left New York in '67. I think the economic pressures got too great. Book publishing is a capital-intensive business, but there's never enough capital. I think it was in the '60s that the first serious overtures came from other businesses offering cash to a cash-starved industry.

Other companies being acquiring companies?
Acquiring companies, yes. So the cost of the capital was to become more industrial, more businesslike. It wasn't nearly as much fun. Doubleday was an interesting place. It had a short, fat, pyramid shape. They hired a lot of people they saw as raw talent, and fed the industry with people they didn't have room for. It seemed in those days that everybody had worked for Doubleday at one time or another. They hired me as raw talent.

Was that typical for the industry?
For Doubleday, but I don't think as much for the rest of the industry. I was very fortunate. You either moved up or you moved out. I was there for two years. My salary was up to ten thousand, but it was nowhere near enough for a middle-class life. I would have liked to become an editor but that didn't really seem likely. And then a job opened up in the literary department of the William Morris Agency. I had a good contact through one of the motion-picture people I'd been dealing with, an old-timer. I became a literary agent with the William Morris Agency. I was there for five months.
It was very glamorous. Archibald MacLeish took me to lunch at the Century Club because he had learned that I was his agent and he

544

thought he ought to meet me. I talked to a lot of famous people. The literary department of the agency was going through a major change at the top and it was my job to talk to the clients, keeping everybody calm and reassuring them. I didn't make a lot of deals.

And after five months—I think it was having lived for four and a half years on an island in the Mediterranean that made me unfit for that life—I quit. The stress was much too much. Late in the morning until very late at night, and too much pressure, and too much that I found distasteful. So I resigned and started looking for another job.

I actually remember the moment when I was being interviewed for a job opening at NAL [New American Library], looking out the window *down* at the smog and realizing that my mind was wandering. I didn't want the job.

Then there was some foolishness about almost going into the wig business with my brother-in-law in Boston. You see, I wasn't wedded to book publishing. I got into it because I needed a job. I enjoyed the time I spent at Doubleday. It seemed like an appropriate place for me to be. I got into the big time at the William Morris Agency, on a very fast track, and that wasn't the place for me to be. So now it was a matter of getting out of New York. We—Sara and I—decided what the hell. We picked Seattle off the map. Sent our furniture ahead—there wasn't much—with no address, figuring it would go into storage. This was the great romance of my life.

Even more than going to Ibiza?

Oh yes. Oh yes. Going to Spain was easy. We were young and free. But now we had two kids, six and seven years old. We had just enough money saved to buy a car. We were pioneers going west, westering, day after day into the sun. Sara and I slept in a fifteen-dollar Boy Scout pup tent, and the kids slept in the back of our VW Squareback. We camped at state parks most of the way with a few nights in Jackson Hole. We made the whole trip for a hundred and fifty dollars, including gas and oil. One oil change. One meal in a restaurant. That was breakfast in Jackson Hole while the oil was being changed. And one night in a motel in Boise because we had a flat tire out in the desert and got in late and the camp ground was gravel and it had cooled down to ninety-five degrees. So we sprang for a cheap motel room. It was on that trip that I became an American.

What do you mean?
I grew up in a very closed, recently Americanized Jewish community around Boston. Newton, Massachusetts, where we moved when I was ten years old, was, I think, the first place labeled as a "golden ghetto." My grandparents were the ones who came to America. My father was born here and my mother was born in England where her family stopped for a few years. She came here as an infant.

When did your grandparents come over?
Eighteen ninety-six, '97.

That was the first wave.
That was the biggest wave of Jewish immigration from Eastern Europe. My father's family was from Lithuania. *Litvaks.* My mother claimed that her family was from Lithuania, too, until she was in her seventies and it sort of slipped out that they had come from Poland, from Warsaw. Vilna, Lithuania was the intellectual capital of Eastern European Judaism in the last century, so it had higher status. In any case, we had no connection with the world my grandparents had run from, thank God, and we weren't yet rooted in America. Well, whatever it was, I never really felt like an American until we headed west. With my gentile wife, of course.

So you got a sense of the country.
The country, yes. The size of it. I always think of the wonderful scene in *Doctor Zhivago* of traveling across Russia on a train, day after day. It was like that, coming to understand how our country is defined so much by its enormous space, and here we were westering, a one-way trip west for the same reason Americans had been doing it for a couple of hundred years: to get away from the East.

So we arrived in Seattle with five hundred dollars in the bank.

I had no intention of getting back into book publishing, but just to cover myself, I had checked out the one publisher I knew of in Seattle, the University of Washington Press, and I'd told the sales manager at Doubleday that I was going to Seattle and he put in a word for me at the press. But I really didn't want to go back into book publishing. I'd done that.

I got an interview at Safeco where you couldn't smoke, even in '67, and you had to wear a white shirt every day. I checked in at Boeing where I'd heard they hired a lot of technical writers. I wasn't interested in book publishing as a career, but I wasn't interested in anything else as a career, either. All I wanted was a decent American job at a decent American salary. But they didn't have a job for me at Boeing or Safeco. I think they knew better than to hire me. But there was an opening at the University of Washington Press for a new assistant sales manager, so that's where I went. This was '67. John Collins was the sales manager and he left about a year later and opened the Fifth Avenue Music Store. An extraordinarily knowledgeable classical music buff.

So there it is. The only job I could find was in book publishing. My karma. A career in book publishing? I got into it in New York because nobody else would hire me. I got back into it in Seattle because I needed a job and nobody else would hire me. I joined the UW Press as assistant sales manager, a year later I was sales manager and a year or two later marketing manager. And after four or five years I was bored stiff with selling scholarly books. I was courted, or at least approached, for two jobs in other places.

Here in Seattle?

No. Outside, in the scholarly publishing world. But we didn't want to leave Seattle. This was home and that was it, even though it was fun to think about other jobs and places. We wouldn't leave Seattle, so I started.... Madrona published its first book in '74. One day, years later, going through our archives, I discovered our first invoice was from 1971, for letterhead stationery, of course. So the idea of Madrona Publishers goes back at least to '71.

It seems like a big leap to go from a job in publishing to starting your own company.

It is a big leap. I was bored with the job I had. But I was reconciled to being in book publishing by then, you know, for the usual romantic reasons: you're doing something that's real, that's substantive, that has some meaning. And it's been constantly challenging, every book brand new—all those reasons which I haven't tried to articulate in years. It was those other jobs that I was offered or might be offered that pushed me.

By other university presses.

Yeah. One was a very prestigious East Coast press. I was treated to a very nice, elegant dinner by the director, and I waited till dessert—that was my Doubleday training—to tell him that I had already decided I was going to have my own book publishing company. And there was another job that would have had me traveling all over the world, which would have been wonderful if I'd been single, but not for a married man with children. It was selling scholarly books.

I had written a couple of articles on marketing for a journal of scholarly publishing, and I was getting some reputation in this small world. I traveled to meetings all over the country for book exhibits, I knew a lot of the people, was involved in setting up a regional association. I was involved in university press publishing, but I was bored.

Actually, if I had been an editor, I might have stayed there forever, but I was sick of selling books and there didn't seem to be any other opportunity at the UW Press. Seattle was our first real home. For me, it was the first home anywhere. Sure, ideally I would have applied for a job as a senior editor and eventually become editor-in-chief of a major national trade publishing house based in Seattle. But since there wasn't one, all I could do was try to start one myself.

First I talked about this with Bill James—he is long retired, he's now in his late seventies—the production manager at the UW Press. He had been there for many years. And I talked with Bill because I knew practically nothing about the production side. Bill was interested and we started with seventy-five hundred dollars. I put in five thousand and he put in twenty-five hundred. Ownership was two-thirds, one-third. We published two books while I was still at the university press. It wasn't a secret, I didn't hide it.

Well, it was a different marketing niche.

There seemed to be no conflict of interest. And those two books—it was fun. The first one—all we had was seventy-five hundred dollars. My intent was to start a general trade publishing company modeled after the publishing I'd known in New York, a tiny Doubleday. At the time it seemed feasible. I knew the rights field, and rights was the tail wagging the whole dog. I certainly knew the basics of marketing. It just seemed possible.

The first book we did was called *Superspill*, an account of a hypothetical oil spill in Puget Sound. I found a couple of people to write it who were active in the Coalition Against Oil Pollution and were happy to write it as an ideological act. The book was very well received regionally and was given some of the credit for helping to keep oil tankers out of Puget Sound.

This was '71?

No, '74. Yes, it takes a while to get a book done, as you know. I was surprised to find that first invoice from '71, the one for letterhead stationery. That's what everyone does. You start a business, you get stationery and business cards, so it's real. I was aware that with my New York experience, plus the time at the university press, I had far more experience than anybody else in Seattle at that time.

Who else was here?

There was The Mountaineers, Pacific Search, Superior Press. What happened with *Superspill* was that I sent galleys to *Library Journal* and *Publishers Weekly*, but because I was also responsible for promotion at the UW Press, I was concerned about conflict of interest and didn't identify myself. I just sent them in cold, over the transom. A new publisher. And the book got rave reviews in both. In fact, I got the galleys out late for PW's deadline, and in order to justify running the review late, somebody there changed the pub date I'd given them. Boy, was that encouraging. We sold out the first printing of five thousand and went back for another printing. We didn't make much money.

How did you distribute them?

See, I knew the book trade here. Pacific Pipeline [a regional book wholesaler] was just getting started. Vito [Vito Perillo, the owner] was storing books in the basement of the apartment building he was managing on Capital Hill. Pipeline as it is today was just a dream. Books were stored in the furnace room, I think. I knew the buyers and I was able to get the books out through the book trade and through the Coalition Against Oil Pollution, which bought a whole lot of them and was distributing them to the state legislature.

Then there was another book that we published at about the same time that I picked up from a contact I had through the UW Press, a Canadian publisher then called J.J. Douglas, now Douglas and McIntyre—a children's book called *Sea and Cedar*, about Northwest Coast Indians and Northwest Coast Indian art. And this is something I'll never forget: I got a call at home early one morning from an editor at *Booklist*. They wanted to use the cover art from the book as the cover of the magazine. *Booklist*! I don't know how they found me but I remember it was before eight in the morning.

That was enough to spring library sales for *Sea and Cedar*, and there we were, two for two. Hell, we knew this couldn't last, but it was great. I decided then to commit to Madrona. I still kept my day job at the press, but I was committed.

I left the UW Press March 31st, 1975, the last day I could leave and take with me in cash the money I had in my pension fund. That was it. Sara had a part-time job with the Seattle School District, but then in April the school levy failed and she got laid off. So there we are with no money in sight from Madrona and nothing else coming in. It was like setting off across the country again—adventure. First Sara got a job at Metro as a secretary, then later she went to *Alaska Northwest* as an editor. She'd been an editor working for house publications in the past.

550

So Madrona started at one end of our living room. Our problem was getting books to publish, having no money to pay advances. One of our neighbors was one of the first women in the area interested in soccer, and she did a book called *Enjoying Soccer*. Another neighbor had a children's book she'd done. Bob Peterson did a picture book, *Seattle Discovered*, the first kind of upbeat, lifestyle photo book on the city, and that sold ten thousand copies. It was kind of a joke that the first ten books we did, everybody lived in our neighborhood.

And then I took on a part-time person. Then commission sales reps. Then a full-time person. Within three or four years we were over a quarter of a million a year in sales. It was 1977 or '78 when we took a place down by the Market on Western Avenue where the Elliott Bay Bicycle Shop is now. I had the whole thing there. I had a warehouse, I had a staff, I was building a list. We made some money from a book called *Snackers*—health-food type snacks for kids, sold sixty thousand. *The Best Places*, we started that.

And then Sasquatch took it?

We sold it to Sasquatch. Yes. We started it with Brewster [David Brewster, president of Sasquatch Publishing Company] as the editor. Then, after three editions, Sasquatch was up and running and they bought it from us.

We had some very bright, talented young people. Faith Conlon [now copublisher of Seal Press] came to Seattle from Doubleday. Her first job in Seattle was with us. We had a sales manager from Spokane who was a Rhodes Scholar. Later, when things got tough, I had to lay him off and he went into the Foreign Service which had wanted him a few years earlier, and ended up in a bunker and one of the last ones out of Beirut. Later, he was in Jerusalem as a political attaché to the West Bank Palestinians. Really talented. We had really talented people.

I was also involved with some other people in organizing the Pacific Northwest Book Publishers Association, and I was its first president. There were seminars, AAP [Association of American Publishers] stuff. An exciting time.

It was great. It was great fun. It was very exciting. We had a lot of books coming out. Ten, twelve a year was a lot of books. We were up to about three-fifty, three hundred and fifty thousand a year.

And then, when was it, when did Mount St. Helen's go off? 'Eighty. May of 1980. I got the idea of doing a book on St. Helen's with Longview Publishing Company. They won the Pulitzer Prize for newspaper coverage of the eruption. We made a deal and got out a book in less than eight weeks, an instant book. It went national, six weeks on the *New York Times* Bestseller List, sold about three hundred and fifty thousand. And we had our first million-dollar year. Two of them, actually. That was a big jump from about three-fifty to a million dollars. We got the state-of-the-art computer system for fulfillment for small publishers, the Cat's Pajamas. It was developed in-house by Ten Speed Press. That was a big investment.

And then the recession came along in '82. 'Eighty-one, '82. I guess I wasn't paying close enough attention. We had a lot of bank credit and the bank kept pushing more money at us, and then in '82, at one moment, the bank, Seafirst, turned on us and called in our loan. It was having its own problems and beating up on small businesses all over the region. Besides that, sales were down and returns were way up, the subsidiary rights market disappeared and I suddenly woke up to discover we had three hundred and fifty thousand dollars of short-term debt. The bank debt was at prime plus two and prime was twenty-one percent. And the bank wanted its money.

At that point we had about eighty or ninety titles in print. We had commission sales reps covering the country, we had an agent in New York for rights, we had a British company handling our distribution in the United Kingdom. we'd sold translation rights in Germany and Scandinavia and South America, Spain, Japan.

And there it was. It was a model, a little general trade publishing company. And—I love this part; remember, we were pioneers who went west—I think Madrona, for a few years, was the largest independent general book publisher north of Berkeley and west of Chicago. That's a lot of American geography.

How did you decide what to publish?

552

We had an enormous number of submissions coming in from all over the country. We had an internship program and we had interns doing the initial screening—the same way they still decide today in New York. After that it was mostly my picking out what I thought would sell, what seemed to fit in what we were doing, the best of what was available to us. The principal joy of publishing is that arrogant exercise of power in determining who and what will be published. I mean, who shall live and who shall die. It's an awesome power. It is such an arrogant, entrepreneurial business. The great publishing houses of old were not named "Amalgamated Publishing" or "Consolidated Publishing." They had names like Simon and Schuster, and Doubleday, and Harper, and Knopf, and Scribner, and Macmillan. Egos right up front. It requires a kind of temperament, doesn't it? Even in quiet, shy people who publish books. Ego is a large part of it.

Wow. Okay. Now you did fiction for just a short time.

We did a few novels. We managed to lose money on almost every one of them. But if we wanted to be a general trade publishing company, we had to publish fiction. This distinguished Madrona from most of the small independent publishing that was going on then, and still is. Mostly it comes from an interest in a subject, something about which somebody wants to publish. And the subject of the publishing is identifiable. But for me, for Madrona, the subject of our publishing was publishing. It wasn't the individual books I had the investment in. It was the creation of a publishing company.

That's a good point.

It certainly wasn't typical, and it puzzled some people. The word I heard other people use to describe us most often was "interesting." That's because they didn't know what else to say. And it certainly was a real weakness.

A weakness that you didn't have a specialty?

Yes. Even back then it was part of conventional wisdom that you had to specialize, even before the word "niche" had become popular. You have to understand that the '70s were great days for independent publishing. It really began in California in the late '60s. Some people called it "hot-tub" publishing. Lifestyle stuff. Bookpeople [a wholesaler for independent press titles] was getting started. *The Whole Earth Catalog* came out. It was new and innovative and it was West Coast. You know, there'd been only two places for book publishing in America until then: New York—which stretched from Boston to Philadelphia—and every place else. California had Ten Speed, Capra, Black Sparrow, Scrimshaw, Kaufmann, And/Or.... There was a West Coast publishing scene. It was brand new, innovative, exciting. And it was getting national attention. Here was an alternative to New York, a regional style, an escape from homogenization.

Did you get local press then?

Lots of local press. Lots and lots of it. I think it was in 1980 that the *Seattle Times* did a feature on thirty people to watch in '81, and I was one of them because of the publishing. Oh, yes, publicity was easy to get. Emmett Watson had a good column in the P-I [the *Seattle Post-Intelligencer*] and we could get something in there on just about every book. We did publishing parties, a big Christmas party in our warehouse. We really had style.

I remember Larry Rumley [the *Seattle Times* book review editor prior to the current editor] *saying in one of his columns that he had a bias against small presses and that he didn't ordinarily review books from them. Maybe he didn't consider yours a small press.*

Larry was very supportive and very helpful. He took what we were doing very seriously. I took it seriously. I was attempting to publish books to the standards of the national book publishing industry. And I had one great advantage over most of the people who got into publishing. That was Bill James who knew how to design books so they looked like real books, like Random House's books or Simon and Schuster's books.

Bill knew the printers and they knew him. He knew how to get books manufactured, and because they knew him we started off with credit from our suppliers, which was a big help. Our jackets weren't up to standard for quite a while, but I think our books were taken seriously in part because they didn't look amateurish or small press-ish. Some fine books were coming from local publishers like Graywolf and Copper Canyon, but ours looked like commercial books, which is what they were intended to be. And that's because of Bill James.

He's out of it now? Were you partners all through—?

He stayed until the mid-'80s. He was ready to retire and we bought him out. But he taught me what I needed to know about book manufacturing.

So what happened when the roof fell in? When Seafirst called in its loan.

When the roof fell in...we were over-extended; that was the mistake I made, not paying attention to what was happening out in the world, the recession. When the volcano book hit, we finally had the capital. We finally had the working capital to do what I wanted to do, to expand, to really build a list. Up till then every penny had to be worked and worked and worked.

We went right to the brink. 'Eighty-two, '83, we went right to the brink of bankruptcy. I mean right to the very edge. We had a lawyer fighting off the bank. He sat down with Sara and me at dinner one night and explained to us how, if we got divorced, we could double the homestead exemption on our house. Sara and I looked at each other and I said, "Okay, but can we still live together?" He said, "Oh, sure. You just have to get divorced." We thought that would be kind of funny, explaining it to the kids. We were prepared to do what we had to but it never came to divorce.

What we did was arrange a twenty-four-month work-out with the printers, and, to their surprise, made every one of those twenty-four payments on time—apparently that's almost historic, that rarely happens—and we worked out a deal with the bank, never declared Chapter Eleven, and kept the business running. I had to lay off most of the staff, give up our own reps and go to a succession of national distributors (who later went broke, but that's another story), and retreat back to the house where we started. I take a lot of pride in the fact that we opened for business every day and never stopped shipping books.

We were still doing books until '88. Along about '86, '87, we were out of debt, everybody caught up with, author's royalties current, didn't owe anybody a penny past due. But it really wasn't fun anymore. There wasn't any money to grow with. And we were exhausted. And I said, "That's enough."

The last books were on alcoholism, a tactical move to build up a little cluster of books that could be sold as a package. We had done one very successful book on alcoholism, Jim Milam's *Under the Influence*. It sold over fifty thousand for us in hardcover, we sold paperback rights to Bantam which has sold close to a million copies by now. And, after that, another book on nutrition and alcoholism that did very well. This is general publishing: you never really know what you've got until you publish it. Well, we had a little package of books which we sold to Bantam, contracts and all, for enough money to come out alive.

It was a soft landing. Since 1988 we've just sold off inventory, and I do some consulting. Madrona still exists as a corporation. A couple of years ago I did some work as an expert witness on book publishing in a couple of lawsuits. We still have royalties coming in on a few rights contracts. We have an office in the house, a computer and a fax.

Could you have got the same satisfaction from another type of business, do you think?

I doubt it. Possibly something I was doing myself, running myself.

What about the boat bar?

Oh God, the restaurant business is awful! The floating bar and restaurant, oh, that was an awful business. I tried that, thank you. The food goes bad if you don't sell it, though liquor will keep. And books don't spoil in a couple of days. No, book publishing has been a wonderful business for me, a wonderful "accidental profession." You used that expression, "accidental profession" [in conversation before turning on the recorder], and I'm an absolute, pure example of an accidental profession. I will say that I've explored every avenue of frustration and aggravation and dismay in book publishing, but never boredom. Never boredom. I'm just as optimistic as I've ever been about book publishing and the future of the book. My own experience certainly didn't leave me with anything like despair.

Glossary

ABA: American Booksellers Association. Also refers to the ABA's annual conference and trade show.

Book distributor: handles book sales and fulfillment to bookstores and wholesalers. A major distributor represents the publishers with which it contracts exclusively. An important feature distinguishing distributors from wholesalers is that distributors employ sales representatives to present titles to buyers.

Book wholesaler: fulfills orders as they come in. Responds to demand but does not try to create demand. Does not employ sales representatives, or employs very few.

Bumbershoot: Seattle, Washington's annual arts festival, held over Labor Day weekend.

Canada Council: A Canadian federal funding agency.

CLMP: Council of Literary Magazines and Presses.

COSMEP: an international association of independent publishers. The acronym is obsolete.

NEA: National Endowment for the Arts. A United States federal funding agency.

Index

561

566

567